THE BRADLAUGH CASE

THE
BRADLAUGH CASE

Atheism, Sex, and Politics among
the Late Victorians

BY

WALTER L. ARNSTEIN

UNIVERSITY OF MISSOURI PRESS
COLUMBIA, 1983

TO MY MOTHER AND FATHER

Library of Congress Cataloging in Publication Data

Arnstein, Walter L.
   The Bradlaugh case.

   Reprint. Originally published: Oxford: Clarendon
Press, 1965.
   Bibliography: p.
   Includes index.
   1. Bradlaugh, Charles, 1833–1891.   2. Oaths—Great
Britain.   3. Great Britain. Parliament. House of Commons—
Rules and practice.   I. Title.
KD4354.A85   1983   342.41'055'0264   83–6814
ISBN 0−8262−0417−1   paper   344.102550264
ISBN 0−8262−0425−2   cloth

CONTENTS

vi CONTENTS

LIST OF PLATES

ACKNOWLEDGEMENTS

RESEARCH for this book was done in numerous libraries on both sides of the Atlantic. These include Columbia University Library and the main branch of the Public Library in New York City; the Northwestern University Library in Evanston, Illinois; the Newberry Library, Main Public Library, the Roosevelt University and University of Chicago Libraries in Chicago; the British Museum, the Public Record Office, the Institute of Historical Research, the University of London Library, and the Guildhall Library in London; the Central Public Library in Northampton; the City Library of Newcastle upon Tyne; Sheffield University Library; the University Library and the Oratory in Birmingham; the County Record Office in Warwick; and the National Library of Ireland in Dublin. I am grateful to the staffs at all these institutions as well as to the persons named in the Bibliography who permitted me to see manuscript collections still in private custody.

I much appreciate the assistance of Miss W. D. Coates of the National Register of Archives in London; and of Mr. Colin McCall, General Secretary of the National Secular Society, and Mrs. R. Siebert of the same organization. I am grateful to Professor Herman Ausubel of Columbia University for introducing me to this subject; to the late Dame Lillian Penson and Dr. R. W. Greaves of Bedford College (University of London) for their assistance; and to Professor Lacey Baldwin Smith of Northwestern University for his valuable advice and steadfast encouragement. I am indebted to Professor Hermann C. Bowersox of the English Department at Roosevelt University for faithfully combing the typescript for faults of syntax and coherence, and to the advisers of the Clarendon Press for saving me from numerous errors of historical detail. My friend Professor Justin L. Kestenbaum of Michigan State University was kind enough to prepare the photographic prints of the illustrations. My wife deserves immense credit for devotedly typing and improving the manuscript and patiently awaiting its completion. The final handiwork necessarily remains my own. I wish to express my particular gratitude to the American and British authorities whose Fulbright Scholarship made possible the greater part of the research for this book; and to Roosevelt University, whose Faculty Research Fellowship facilitated its completion. Brief portions of the book appeared first in a different form in the *Journal of the History of Ideas*, *Victorian Studies*, and *Irish Historical Studies*, and are incorporated by permission of the editors.

WALTER L. ARNSTEIN

Chicago, June 1964

ABBREVIATIONS

B.M.	British Museum.
Bonner & Robertson, *Bradlaugh*	Hypatia Bradlaugh Bonner, *Charles Bradlaugh: A Record of his Life and Work, with an Account of his Parliamentary Struggle, Politics, and Teaching, by John M. Robertson*, 2 vols. London, 1895.
G.P.	Gladstone Papers.
Hamilton Diary	The Manuscript Diary of Edward Walter Hamilton, one of Gladstone's private secretaries.
N.R.	*The National Reformer*, Bradlaugh's weekly journal.
P.R.O.	Public Record Office.

I

PRELUDE

THREE times in the course of its history—1868, 1880, and 1906—the Liberal party of Britain tasted the joys of overwhelming triumph. Two of the periods of rule which followed these electoral successes have won historical renown: Gladstone's First Ministry (1868–74), with its fundamental political reform programme, and the great Liberal Ministry of 1906–14, which laid the foundations for the welfare state in Britain and permanently trimmed the power of the House of Lords. As an electoral victory the results of 1880 were equally decisive: 347 Liberals, 240 Conservatives, 65 Irish Home Rulers.[1] Since at least a third of the Home Rulers proved to be more sympathetic to Liberalism than to Irish nationalism, the Liberal majority was even greater than these figures indicate. And yet, except for the Reform Bill of 1884, the Second Gladstone Ministry left no significant mark in the annals of British history. 'There has seldom been a more inspiriting victory', writes George Macaulay Trevelyan, 'than that of 1880, and seldom have the fruits of victory, through combined misfortune and mishandling, tasted so like the fruits of defeat. Bradlaugh, Ireland, Transvaal, Egypt—in these four deep bogs the victorious Liberals floundered for four years . . . .'[2] It is with the first of these 'bogs', Charles Bradlaugh, atheist, republican, advocate of birth control, and Member of Parliament, that this book deals.

The election of 1880 had marked the last great contest between those two larger-than-life antagonists, Benjamin Disraeli and William Ewart Gladstone; and their respective reactions to its outcome were characteristic. For Disraeli the defeat marked the sunset of a long career, and he attributed

---

[1] R. H. Gretton, *A Modern History of the English People, 1880–1922* (London, 1930), p. 38. The *Quarterly Review* calculated the major party popular vote totals as: Liberals 1,877,296, Conservatives 1,431,805. Cited in S. Maccoby, *English Radicalism, 1853–1886* (London, 1938), pp. 255 f.

[2] G. M. Trevelyan, *The Life of John Bright* (new ed., London, 1925), p. 478.

it to economic circumstances beyond his control. 'I am the unluckiest of mortals,' he mused; 'six bad harvests in succession, one worse than the former, this has been the cause of my overthrow; like Napoleon I have been beaten by the elements!'[1] His Foreign Secretary, the Marquess of Salisbury, agreed: 'I suppose bad harvests and bad trade have done the most. A sick man who makes no progress is apt to change his doctors, though the doctor may not be in fault.'[2] The victorious Gladstone, on the other hand, was able to see 'the hand of God manifest in what is going on . . .'.[3]

Gladstone found himself, to be sure, in a peculiar position as the electoral returns rolled in. He had officially resigned the leadership of the Liberal party five years earlier. His outrage at the Bulgarian atrocities had, however, drawn him back into politics, and he had gone on to condemn Disraeli's pro-Turkish Near-Eastern policy and the expense and immorality implicit in the Afghan and Zulu wars. Gladstone's indignation had manifested itself in the great Midlothian campaign, a salvo of thunderous speeches to ever greater and more enthusiastic crowds of Britons, in every sense but the professed one a call for the popular mandate which had now been granted him. The only problem was that Gladstone was not the party leader—the Marquess of Hartington and Earl Granville shared that task between them—and it was Hartington whom Queen Victoria called upon to assume the Prime Ministership. 'I never could take Mr. Gladstone . . . as my Minister again,' she had written in 1879, 'for I never COULD have the slightest *particle* of confidence in Mr. Gladstone *after* his violent, mischievous, and dangerous conduct for the last three years.'[4] But Hartington was a realist. He was aware that Gladstone would refuse subordinate office, and he recognized that a Liberal Government without Gladstone in it was an absurdity; Gladstone, after all (in Arthur Balfour's words), '*was* the Opposition'.[5]

[1] Cited by Lord Ronald Gower, *My Reminiscences* (London, 1883), ii. 354–5.
[2] Salisbury to Beaconsfield, 7 Apr. 1880, Beaconsfield MSS.
[3] Gladstone to Bright, 12 Apr. 1880, Bright MSS. 43385, fol. 274 (B.M.).
[4] Cited by Frank Hardie, *The Political Influence of Queen Victoria, 1861–1901* (Oxford, 1935), p. 67.
[5] A. J. Balfour, *Chapters of Autobiography* (London, 1930), p. 131.

Hartington, therefore, turned down Queen Victoria's offer, thus (noted Disraeli) 'abandoning a woman in her hour of need'.[1]

And so Gladstone became Prime Minister again. Radical as such a step may have appeared to the Queen, the resultant Cabinet was a moderate one except for the inclusion of two men, John Bright, the survivor of an older radical tradition, and Joseph Chamberlain, the representative of a newer variety. Middle-of-the-roaders and Whigs predominated, however. As the judicious Granville observed, 'the Government is like bread sauce—made of two substantial elements. The few peppercorns are very obvious, and perhaps give a little flavour, but do not affect the character of the food.'[2]

It was this government which, almost before its organization was complete, was faced with the baffling problem of whether Charles Bradlaugh, the newly-elected Radical from Northampton, might be admitted as a fully fledged member of Parliament. For three weeks the problem posed itself—whether Bradlaugh might substitute an affirmation for the customary Parliamentary oath; but from then on, for more than five long years, the central question was whether an avowed atheist ought to be allowed to take that oath at all, even if he were willing to do so.

The case of Charles Bradlaugh had a dual background. Not only was this the age in which the highest goal of almost any Englishman was to become a Member of Parliament and public interest in Parliamentary affairs was at a zenith, but the age also saw the high-water mark of Victorian middle-class respectability.[3] It is not surprising then that the personality of Charles Bradlaugh, in all his professions so un-Victorian an Englishman, should give both the man and his attempt to storm the citadel of respectability and statesmanship a surpassing notoriety.

The story told here has been told in full only once before, in the pages which John McKinnon Robertson contributed to the two-volume biography Hypatia Bradlaugh Bonner

---

[1] Gower, *Reminiscences*, ii. 355.

[2] Cited in Philip Guedalla, *The Queen and Mr. Gladstone* (London, 1933), ii. 29.

[3] Cf., for example, Viscount (Herbert) Gladstone, *After Thirty Years* (London, 1928), p. 159; J. L. Garvin, *The Life of Joseph Chamberlain*, i (London, 1932), 395.

wrote of her father shortly after his death.[1] This work has both the virtues and the defects of the better multi-volume Victorian biographies. It is, on the one hand, written with great care, so that few if any factual errors may be found in its pages. It is, on the other hand, an apologia, a deliberate attempt posthumously to vindicate, often in overwhelming detail, a beloved father and friend against the slings and arrows of two generations of outraged contemporaries. J. M. Robertson earned in his lifetime a well-deserved reputation as an historian of free thought, but it was as participant as well as historian that he wrote his report on Bradlaugh's parliamentary struggles. Not only did he sometimes fail to appreciate the subtle shadings of opinion among the actors in the drama, but he lacked the materials to give a multi-dimensional portrayal of the impact of the case upon the various political parties and personalities.

This deficiency exists no longer, and the manuscript collections of the Conservative leaders, Disraeli, Northcote, and Salisbury; of the Speaker, Henry Brand; of one of Gladstone's secretaries, Edward Walter Hamilton; and, most important of all, the 750 massive volumes of the Gladstone Papers themselves represent a veritable treasure-house of new insights and forgotten memories. To these must be added more than a dozen other manuscript collections, the pages of *Hansard*, numerous newspaper and periodical files, as well as several bookshelves of printed memoirs and autobiographies, not always reliable in detail but very often providing yet another tiny piece to fit into the vast jigsaw puzzle an historical study embodies. One manuscript collection—the papers of Lord Randolph Churchill—has not been used because it is still unavailable, while another—the Bradlaugh papers—has not been used because it does not exist. Bradlaugh made a practice of destroying most of the letters he received, and the comparative handful that was not destroyed did not apparently survive the ravages of the Second World War. One major compensation for this lack lies in the fact that Bradlaugh was, among other things, an industrious journalist, a man who took few actions and had yet fewer ideas which were not reflected sooner or later,

[1] Bonner & Robertson, *Bradlaugh*.

either directly or between the lines, in the pages of his weekly *National Reformer*.

What emerges from a consideration of these varied sources? Not a new biography of Charles Bradlaugh (except perhaps for half a decade of his life), nor a complete re-interpretation either of Robertson's work or of the many brief summaries of the case to be found in a variety of biographies and general works. This study, though it propounds no single all-inclusive thesis, will yet take issue, at least in part, with a number of traditional opinions concerning the case. Sir Robert Ensor in his volume of *The Oxford History of England*, for example, tends to dismiss the struggle as the result of two 'fumbles' by the Speaker of the House of Commons, Henry Brand.[1] John Morley in his biography of Gladstone and, to a large extent, Sir Winston Churchill in his biography of his father see the struggle as essentially a political manœuvre by a group of 'Young Turk' Conservatives, headed by Lord Randolph Churchill, to embarrass the Second Gladstone Ministry.[2] A popular textbook attitude is that the case was merely the last of a long series of conflicts which relaxed the religious restrictions upon membership of the House of Commons.[3]

All these points of view have some justification. There was no lack of fumbles. There was no dearth of politics. And the case is tied to a lengthy series of parliamentary precedents. But certain other factors have been neglected. Historians such as D. C. Somervell have argued too readily that 'as the century approached its close, ecclesiastical questions became less and less interesting to the general public'.[4] If so, the Bradlaugh case forms a prominent exception. Among political parties, the Irish Nationalists played a much more vital role in the case than has usually been recognized, and Parnell's curious reversal has not thus far been altogether

[1] *England, 1870–1914* (Oxford, 1936), pp. 67–68.

[2] John Morley, *Life of William Ewart Gladstone* (London, 1903), iii; Winston S. Churchill, *Life of Lord Randolph Churchill* (London, 1906), i. Robert Rhodes James, *Lord Randolph Churchill* (London, 1959), gives the same impression.

[3] e.g. J. Salwyn Schapiro, *Modern and Contemporary European History* (new ed., Boston, 1946), pp. 267–8.

[4] D. C. Somervell, *English Thought in the Nineteenth Century* (London, 1929), p. 221.

satisfactorily explained. Among religious bodies, the Roman Catholic Church under Cardinal Manning played a much more significant part than its numerical strength warranted. The role of Gladstone was considerably more complex than is implied by either Morley or Magnus,[1] that of a statesman defending, for the sake of principle, the rights of a man he loathes. It will be maintained, moreover, that the divisions within the Liberal party on the case did not always fall by any means into a neat threefold Radical/Middle-of-the-road/Whig division. Professor Asa Briggs has written of 'the bitter struggles of the 1880's, when Irish nationalism moulded English history and Victorian radicalism overlapped with twentieth-century socialism'.[2] To a considerable degree this study is an elaboration of how these twin developments affected the struggle of Charles Bradlaugh to enter Parliament.

There is perhaps a final justification for recreating the details of that struggle: the fact that the historian, be he part scientist, part psychologist, or part political analyst, ought never altogether to neglect his role as story-teller; and the tale of Charles Bradlaugh is a story worth retelling. Not only does the cast of characters include all the political giants of late Victorian England: Gladstone and Disraeli; Randolph Churchill, Lord Salisbury, and Sir Stafford Northcote; Joseph Chamberlain and Charles Stewart Parnell; Cardinal Manning and Cardinal Newman; John Morley and Frederic Harrison; but it also involves men of a much earlier age, such as John Bright, who had helped bring the repeal of the Corn Laws in 1846, and Lord Shaftesbury, who had sponsored the Ten-Hours Act of 1847; and men of a much later age, such as Herbert Asquith, the future Prime Minister, and George Bernard Shaw, and, on the periphery, even Mohandas Gandhi, all of them essentially twentieth-century personalities. But finally, and not least among them, it includes Charles Bradlaugh himself, a man who did not merely embody a cause—and if an analogy with the Dreyfus affair in France seems far-fetched then an analogy with the case of John Wilkes in eighteenth-century England appears defensible—

[1] Morley, *Gladstone*, iii. 11–21; Philip Magnus, *Gladstone* (London, 1954), *passim*. [2] *Victorian People* (Chicago, 1955), p. 1.

but who also was a dynamic personality in his own right. Technically speaking, his story is a success story, but it is a success story tinged with sorrow, even with tragedy. It is a story that, to apply the precept Herbert J. Muller urges for all history, may be looked back upon both with reverence and with a sense of irony. Yet it remains a story that involves ideas and principles by no means dead, ideas and principles no more irrelevant to the present day than those expounded in John Stuart Mill's *On Liberty*.

II

THE LIVES OF CHARLES BRADLAUGH

FOR a future Member of Parliament in Victorian England, Charles Bradlaugh's beginnings were unpromising. He was born on 26 September 1833 in Hoxton, a village which was in the course of the century to become part of metropolitan London.[1] His father was a poor but conscientious lawyer's clerk, his mother a one-time nursemaid. Charles's formal education ended at the age of eleven, when he was apprenticed first as an office boy in a lawyer's office and then as clerk to a coal merchant. Most of his meagre income went to his family, though occasional extra pennies were spent at a second-hand bookstall. At the age of fourteen he copied out by hand and committed to memory the greater part of Ralph Waldo Emerson's essay on 'Self-Reliance'.[2] Although by this time attracted by the Chartists and temperance advocates who lectured in Bonner's Fields, a mecca for open-air orators, Bradlaugh, who had been baptized in the Church of England and had received some religious training, was also serving as a youthful but apparently promising Sunday School teacher. Puzzled on one occasion by the seeming contradictions between the Four Gospels and the Thirty-Nine Articles of the Anglican Church, he approached his minister with the problem. The Reverend John Graham Packer peremptorily denounced young Bradlaugh as an atheist and suspended him from his Sunday School duties. In due course Mr. Packer denounced Charles to his father as well, and the latter gave his son the alternative of repenting or else being expelled from the parental home and losing his employment in the bargain. Bradlaugh's stubbornness had been aroused; he took the ultimatum literally and left home.

[1] Unless otherwise noted, the information in this chapter is derived from Bonner & Robertson, *Bradlaugh*. Bradlaugh's name is pronounced 'Bradlaw'.
[2] *N.R.*, 7 May 1882, p. 362.

He lived for a time with the widow and family of Richard Carlisle, free-thinker and republican of an earlier generation, made the acquaintance of a number of Chartists, and on one occasion met the elderly Robert Owen. His religious views passed quickly from Christianity to deism to outright atheism, and by 1850 he endeavoured to combine the running of his coal business with Sunday open-air lecturing. He succeeded for a while, but when his chief customer, a baker's wife, discovered that her coal supplier was 'an infidel', she cut off her orders. 'I should be afraid', she explained, 'that my bread would smell of brimstone.'[1]

The burden of a £4. 15s. debt persuaded Bradlaugh to join the army and collect the customary bounty. He was at first the laughing-stock of his fellow soldiers in the 7th Dragoon Guards, for they encountered him attired in a silk hat and with an Arabic dictionary in his luggage. (Bradlaugh was to show a noteworthy facility in learning languages and became fluent in French, read Hebrew well, and had more than a smattering of Arabic, Greek, Italian, and Spanish.) The fact that his company was stationed in Ireland brought Charles face to face with 'the Irish question'. He was often to recall the occasion on which a local landowner had erected a gate across a traditional right-of-way, barring it both to soldiers and to the neighbourhood peasantry. Deciding upon examination that the landowner's action was illegal, Private Bradlaugh led a small group of soldiers to pull down the gate and break it up. No attempt was made to restore the barrier, and Bradlaugh henceforth became something of a hero to his fellow soldiers and to near-by tenant farmers.

These incidents of Bradlaugh's youth are characteristic of the man he was to become. He was very much a man of independent spirit. A decision might be forced upon him by the pressure of accumulated debts, but when called upon to choose between his livelihood and the advocacy of his beliefs, he invariably chose the latter. Some of the key themes of his life—atheism, political reform, and an interest in suppressed nationalities such as the Irish—were already apparent by the early 1850's. Not least significant was the legal training he had received in his earliest years and resumed when he left

[1] Cited by Bonner & Robertson, *Bradlaugh*, i. 18.

the army in 1853. Bradlaugh's mind worked in lawyer-like fashion, and to the earlier English tradition of popular free thought he contributed an emphasis upon legalistic niceties.[1] Critics were often to call Bradlaugh a litigious man who used his self-acquired legal training not only to advance the political causes he favoured but also to institute lawsuits against apparently minor libels and slanders. These libel suits, even when technically victorious, were to prove one of Bradlaugh's heaviest financial liabilities. But 'what am I to do?' he complained on one occasion. 'If when I am libelled I take no notice, the world believes the libel. If I sue I have to pay about one hundred pounds costs for the privilege, and gain the smallest coin the country knows as a recompense.'[2]

His army years over, Bradlaugh began quickly to make a name for himself in London free-thought circles, so that by 1859 he had become President of the London Secular Society and editor of *The Investigator*. He had graduated from the soap-box to the lecture hall and, as 'Iconoclast', was beginning to tour the provinces as well, declaiming on topics such as 'The Existence of God', 'The Divine Revelation of the Bible', and 'Has Man a Soul?' Bradlaugh's policy was to charge an admission price ranging from 2*d.* to 1*s.* for all lectures; he retained whatever surplus remained after the hall rental and other expenses had been paid. During the the early 1860's these surpluses were frequently non-existent, and Bradlaugh was often hard put to it to raise the price of a railway ticket. Even successful lectures were often hampered by local trouble-makers who tried to break them up physically or by local city officials who placed pressure upon lecture-hall owners to cancel rental contracts. As time went on such handicaps became less common and Bradlaugh's audiences grew larger, numbering often in the hundreds and sometimes in the thousands. Occasionally he varied the the routine by engaging clergymen in debates on such subjects as 'Can Miracles be proved Possible?', 'Are the Scriptures the Authentic and Reliable Records of Divine Revelation?', 'Atheism, is it Rational?', and 'Is it reasonable to worship God?' Many of the clergymen were members

---

[1] Chapman Cohen, *Bradlaugh and Ingersoll* (London, 1932), pp. ix, 35.
[2] Cited by Bonner & Robertson, *Bradlaugh*, i. 293.

of the Christian Evidence Society, an evangelical group within the Church of England; but occasionally a Roman Catholic clergyman, a spiritualist, or a fellow secularist such as George Jacob Holyoake was Bradlaugh's sparring partner.

Bradlaugh was called many things in his life: free-thinker, infidel, secularist, materialist, atheist. He admitted to them all, though much preferring the word 'monist' to 'materialist'. Its derogatory connotations notwithstanding, Bradlaugh never hesitated to employ the word 'atheist', a word he defined, in accordance with its Greek origin, not as 'against God' but 'without God'. He did not deny there was 'a God', declared Bradlaugh in 1859, 'because to deny that which was unknown was as absurd as to affirm it. As an atheist he denied the God of the Bible, of the Koran, of the Vedas, but he could not deny that of which he had no knowledge.'[1] Technically then, his definition differed little from that which T. H. Huxley was to give to 'agnostic', a word which carried none of the odious connotations of 'atheist'. For Bradlaugh, however, the agnostic, in failing to oppose the churches actively, was merely evading the consequences of his own convictions. Agnosticism was thus 'a mere society form of Atheism'.[2]

Bradlaugh supported atheism primarily along lines first popularized by Thomas Paine in his *Age of Reason*, on the basis of Biblical self-contradictions. He was not unaware of nineteenth-century higher Biblical criticism nor blind to the religious significance of Darwin's theory of biological evolution. Yet in many respects these studies supplemented

---

[1] Cited ibid. i. 87.

[2] *N.R.*, 15 July 1883, p. 44; Bonner & Robertson, *Bradlaugh*, ii. 115–64. 'The Atheist', wrote Bradlaugh, 'does not say "there is no god", but he says "I know not what you mean by god; I am without idea of god; the word god is to me a sound conveying no clear or distinct affirmation. I do not deny god, because I cannot deny that of which I have no conception and the conception of which by its affirmer is so imperfect that he is unable to define it to me."' (*N.R.*, 25 Nov. 1883, p. 346.) This is not very different from T. H. Huxley's definition of 'agnostic'. 'I invented the word "Agnostic"', wrote Huxley in the *Agnostic Annual* of 1884, 'to denote people who, like myself, confess themselves to be hopelessly ignorant concerning a variety of matters about which metaphysicians and theologians, both orthodox and heterodox, dogmatize with the utmost confidence.' (Cited in *N.R.*, 11 Nov. 1883, p. 316.)

rather than supplied the foundation of his opposition to organized religion. The Darwinian influence, to be sure, is noticeable in some of his later debates on the subject of secularism. 'Between the cabbage and the man', declared Bradlaugh on one occasion, 'I know no break. Between the highest of which I know and the lowest of which I know in the scale of life I know no break. I do not say no difference, but no break.'[1] To some extent Bradlaugh was influenced also by contemporary currents in anthropology, such as the study of comparative religions, and in 1882 he published a pamphlet entitled *Anthropology*.

His audiences were generally working-class, if only because the avowal of unbelief tended to be more obviously harmful—sometimes economically and almost always socially—to middle-class Victorian Englishmen. There was, moreover, a widespread working-class conviction that middle-class church-goers were snobs and parsons hypocrites.[2] Though his audiences lacked formal education, Bradlaugh's arguments were not slipshod. 'There is an impression in some quarters', wrote Bradlaugh's contemporary critic, Professor Flint of the Edinburgh University Theology Department, 'that Atheism is advocated in a weak and unskilful manner by the chiefs of Secularism. It is an impression which I do not share.'[3] Nor did Bradlaugh condescend toward his followers. In reviewing a *History of Ireland* for *The National Reformer*, Bradlaugh comments that the book, an edition of 569 closely printed pages, 'should not only be in every workingmen's library, but should be carefully read by all interested in forming an accurate judgment on the grievances of Ireland, and the possible remedies for such grievances'.[4] Reviewing another book, Bradlaugh remarks: 'If workingmen will read this book, and we advise them to, we can promise them much wholesome mental stimulus.'[5]

Bradlaugh took strong exception to the argument that

[1] Rev. D. L. McCann and Charles Bradlaugh, *Secularism: Unphilosophical, Immoral, and Anti-Social: Verbatim Report of a Three Nights' Debate* (London, 1882), p. 20.

[2] Cf. Maccoby, *English Radicalism, 1853–1886*, p. 141.

[3] *Anti-Theistic Theories*, 4th ed., pp. 518–19, cited by Bonner & Robertson, *Bradlaugh*, ii. 125.

[4] *N.R.*, 12 Feb. 1882, p. 108.   [5] *N.R.*, 9 Nov. 1884, p. 315.

atheists showed great presumption in the face of the supernatural by advocating the power of human reason. As far
as he was concerned, the situation was the reverse. It was
the believer who was presumptuous in claiming to know the
mind and personality of an infinite and eternal power. The
atheist made no such claim. Bradlaugh equally resented the
equation of atheism with immorality. The greatest good of
the greatest number remained for Bradlaugh the final standard of right and wrong. 'Our only wish and purpose is to
make men happy,' he had written in *The Investigator* many
years before, 'and this because in so doing we increase our
own happiness. . . . Man can never be happy until he is free';
and to free him from outmoded intellectual shackles was seen
by Bradlaugh as his immediate task.[1]

Though Bradlaugh's forte lay in oratory and to a lesser
degree in popular pamphleteering, he also revealed excep-
tional talents as an organizer in an area of belief which, by
its very nature, has traditionally been hostile to organization. In 1866 he founded the National Secular Society and
assimilated various local free-thought societies throughout the kingdom. Additional branches were added over the
years, and by 1880 the society claimed some 6,000 members
in over sixty active branch societies. These formed only the
nucleus of Bradlaugh's supporters, for in a city such as
Birmingham with but ninety members Bradlaugh might
attract a lecture audience of 4,000.[2] In some ways, to be sure,
the National Secular Society had become a religious organization in its own right, with Bradlaugh, though subject to
a vote of the membership at each annual congress, its chief
priest. More than one observer, by accident or design, mis-
took Bradlaugh for a clergyman.[3] As *The Northern Echo* put
it in 1880:

Although Mr. BRADLAUGH gives prominence to his disbelief,
it is his belief in many essential elements of Christian morality
which gives him his power. In some respects he reminds us of
a Puritan who has lost his way. The apostolic zeal, the vehement

[1] Cited by Bonner & Robertson, *Bradlaugh*, i. 80.
[2] *N.R.*, 5 Sept. 1880, p. 196.
[3] See Moncure Daniel Conway, *Autobiography* (London, 1904), ii. 361–2;
Eduard Bernstein, *My Years of Exile: Reminiscences of a Socialist*, trans. Bernard
Miall (London, 1921), p. 233.

impatience with false doctrine, the abiding faith in great principles, the assertion of his doctrine in season and out of season,
the eagerness with which he seizes an opportunity to proclaim the
faith that is in him—are all characteristic of the Puritan.[1]

The National Secular Society, in addition to promoting
propaganda activities and political agitation on behalf of
secular education and the removal of legal disabilities from
religious minorities, sponsored a benevolent fund to aid
aged and ill free-thinkers. It was Bradlaugh's ideal that each
branch sponsor circulating libraries, weekly musical evenings
(wives and daughters would be invited and non-alcoholic
beverages served), and political and literary discussions, and
that it make provision for draughts, chess, and other games,
with gambling strictly prohibited.[2] During the 1860's London secularists had issued a *Secularists' Manual of Songs and
Ceremonies*, and many secularists wanted Bradlaugh publicly
to 'name' their children as well as to conduct marriage
and funeral services. Bradlaugh did his best to discourage
this type of ritualism, but he obviously did not oppose it
altogether.[3]

The physical centre of the National Secular Society was
the Hall of Science in Old Street in the City of London. If
one approached the building during its hey-day on a Sunday
in the 1870's one would first have to evade evangelists passing out Christian tracts outside the near-by Golden Lane
Mission, which featured the words 'God is Love' outlined in
gas jets above the door. The big lecture of the week took
place on Sunday evening, and the large auditorium—it seated
1,200 people—filled quickly. Seats cost either 2*d.* or 4*d.* apiece.
Men invariably outnumbered women. While men of 'the
tradesman and artisan class' predominated, an occasional
naval officer, white-collar worker, or even unskilled labourer
was also present. Then, with the hall crowded to suffocation,
a roar of cheering burst forth when, on the very minute
announced for the lecture, a tall, commanding figure passed
swiftly up the hall to the platform. Bradlaugh was a vigorous,

[1] *The Northern Echo*, 26 May 1880.
[2] *N.R.*, 4 Feb. 1883, p. 65.
[3] Bonner & Robertson, *Bradlaugh* i. 311. See also John Edwin McGee,
A History of the British Secular Movement (Girard, Kansas, 1948), p. 51, and the
Rev. Charles Maurice Davies, *Heterodox London* (London, 1874), ii. 120, 171.

powerful-looking man, with a clean-shaven face, a massive
jaw, and a full head of hair brushed straight back from his
high forehead. He began his lecture quietly and simply,
and as he went from point to point his voice grew in force and
resonance, till it rang round the hall like a trumpet. . . . Eloquence,
fire, sarcasm, pathos, passion, all in turn were bent against
Christian superstition, till the great audience, carried away by
the torrent of the orator's force, hung silent, breathing soft, as he
went on, till the silence that followed a magnificent peroration
broke the spell and a hurricane of cheers relieved the tension.[1]

During the 1870's, Bradlaugh made two significant 'converts': Mrs. Annie Besant, who had been separated from her
clergyman husband and who during the 1870's and 1880's
contributed her facile pen and tongue to the atheist cause,
and Dr. Edward J. Aveling, a Professor of Comparative
Anatomy at the London Hospital, who gave new emphasis
to scientific aspects of the movement. Under his direction
classes in chemistry, biology, botany, and other subjects were
introduced to the Hall of Science. Both Mrs. Besant and
Dr. Aveling were active on the lecture platform, and they,
together with Bradlaugh, became 'the trinity' for older free-
thinkers, some of whom considered the pace of their advance
within the movement too rapid.[2] All three were regular
contributors to *The National Reformer*, a journal which Bradlaugh founded in 1861 and of which he became chief editor
in 1866. It was subtitled: 'Radical Advocate and Freethought
Journal', and it became, Bradlaugh's daughter recalled, 'not
merely a weekly journal, . . . [but] my father's voice, my
father's sword, my father's shield'.[3] Each issue displayed
a motto like the one used during the second half of 1879:
'Infallible authority in religion, and free inquiry in science,
can never be reconciled.'

A representative issue of the winter of 1879–80 includes a
front-page article by Bradlaugh attacking Disraeli's imperialistic policies and a hostile review by another contributor

[1] Annie Besant, *An Autobiography* (London, 1893), pp. 134–6. See also
Davies, *Heterodox London*, pp. 117, 120, 146, 189; and Gertrude M. Williams,
The Passionate Pilgrim: A Life of Annie Besant (London, 1932), p. 57.
[2] Williams, *Passionate Pilgrim*, p. 118.
[3] Cited by Arthur Bonner and Charles Bradlaugh Bonner, *Hypatia Bradlaugh Bonner: The Story of Her Life* (London, 1942), p. 63.

of a recently published volume of sermons. There follows the seventh in a series of excerpts from Darwin's works, and other articles dealing with Biblical Negroes and 'the fable of Exodus'. The obituary of a recently deceased free-thinker contains the customary phrase: 'Death had no terror for her.' A letter from Paris reports on the political situation in France. This is followed by a report on Brad-laugh's Election Fund and by an article dealing with the recent *National Reformer* concert and ball at which the Ladies' Choral Union of the London Secular Society had performed. The journal also provides a weekly summary of the news compiled by Bradlaugh's daughters, advertises National Secular Society lectures throughout the country, and answers correspondents. The issue concludes with a series of book reviews and advertisements for books, herb medicines, and Turkish baths.[1] *The National Reformer* laboured under a number of handicaps, not the least of which were Govern-ment prosecution in the late 1860's and the persistent refusal of W. H. Smith & Son, the largest newspaper distributor in the country, to handle the paper. But during the 1870's it was obviously a flourishing concern.

During the 1850's and 1860's Bradlaugh had combined his anti-religious activities with a succession of private business ventures in the 'city', none of which had proved altogether successful. In 1855 he married Susannah Lamb Hooper, the daughter of an ex-Chartist and free-thinker, Abraham Hooper, who remained Bradlaugh's steadfast sup-porter in all his activities and outlived him by five months. The marriage was happy at first and produced three children, Alice (1856), Hypatia (1858), and Charles (1859). In the course of time Bradlaugh's wife became addicted both to alcohol and to a style of financial extravagance Bradlaugh could ill afford. Economic and personal reasons prompted Bradlaugh in 1870 to give up his private business and London home to concentrate upon free thought. His wife and children moved to the home of their maternal grandfather in a Sussex village. Here Bradlaugh's son, Charles, the apple of his father's eye, died of scarlet fever that same year; his wife died of heart disease in 1877. Although the later years of

<hr />

[1] *N.R.*, 28 Dec. 1879, pp. 833–48.

marriage were for Bradlaugh a most painful episode, his daughters remained devoted to both their parents and after their mother's death joined their father in a small London apartment above a music shop. Bradlaugh never became a rich man, and his one luxury, if one may call it that, was his library, which at his death numbered over seven thousand volumes.

Atheism represented for Bradlaugh not an end itself but a means which would promote desirable and political objectives. Thus he took an intense interest in the nationalistic movements which affected much of Europe during the 1850's, 60's, and 70's. At the time of the Italian struggle for national unification in 1860, Bradlaugh made a number of speeches to raise money for Garibaldi and on one occasion carried secret dispatches from the Kingdom of the Two Sicilies to London.[1] At the time of the Polish rising against Russia in 1863, Bradlaugh became an advocate of Polish nationalism. He was also well acquainted with a number of revolutionary Russian exiles such as Alexander Herzen. Consistency bade him support Irish nationalism as well. 'Englishmen have long been eloquent', declared Bradlaugh during the 1860's, 'on the wrongs of Poland and other down-trodden nations, insisting on their right to govern themselves; but they have been singularly unmindful of their Irish brethren. Advocacy of the claims of Poland showed a love of liberty and freedom. Advocacy for Ireland spelled treason'.[2]

Bradlaugh aided the Fenian movement of 1867–9 and apparently wrote the first draft of a proclamation of 8 March 1867, listing Irish grievances and announcing the establishment of an independent Irish republic. He also defended the 'Manchester Martyrs', a group of men tried—and afterwards hanged—for using violence to aid two of the Fenian leaders to escape from jail. In March 1868 he spoke in Dublin under the auspices of an Irish Reform League.

The country Bradlaugh loved best, however, apart from his own, was France, though his hopes for it were frequently disappointed. He was strongly opposed to Napoleon III and contributed to the Orsini Defence Fund in 1859. At the start

---

[1] Bonner & Robertson, *Bradlaugh*, i. 152–7.
[2] Cited ibid.

of the Franco-Prussian War he favoured neither side, since Napoleon was 'one of the greatest modern scoundrels' and Bismarck merely 'a crafty diplomatist striving to make a great German Empire under Prussia'. Once Napoleon had abdicated, however, Bradlaugh began to lecture throughout England in favour of aid to the French Republic and against German annexation of Alsace-Lorraine. The Provisional Government of Gambetta thanked him profusely; and when new French elections were held in February 1871, Bradlaugh was nominated by the city of Paris as a candidate for the National Assembly. The situation in France was soon confounded, however, by the civil conflict between the French Government under Thiers and the Paris Commune. On one occasion Bradlaugh attempted to act as intermediary between the Commune and Thiers, but by that time Thiers had become too suspicious of Bradlaugh's friendliness towards certain Commune leaders as well as his rather paradoxical friendship with Prince Jérome Napoléon, a fellow free-thinker, to permit him to enter France.

In 1873 Bradlaugh undertook a journey to Spain to extend the best wishes of the English republican clubs to Emilio Castelar, the dominant figure of the short-lived Spanish republic. Later that same year Bradlaugh paid his first visit to the largest republic of them all, the United States. His professed purpose was to earn money by means of lectures (on political rather than theological subjects), and he visited New York City, Boston, Cincinnati, St. Louis, and Kansas City. His visit to Boston impressed Bradlaugh most, because it gave him the opportunity to meet a number of men he had long admired—Charles Sumner, William Lloyd Garrison, the venerable Ralph Waldo Emerson, and Henry Wilson, Vice-President of the United States. He received a most cordial welcome from Wendell Phillips, who greeted him as an English Samuel Adams. His American journey was interrupted by an injury to his hand—the result of a fall on the ice in Kansas City—and it was cut short by the call for parliamentary elections early in 1874. Bradlaugh returned to the United States for a second visit later that year and for a third in 1875. This last was marred by an attack of pleurisy and typhoid, and Bradlaugh lay seriously ill for several weeks in a New York hospital before returning to England. Although he frequently considered a further visit, he never crossed the Atlantic again. Curiously enough, Bradlaugh never met his most obvious American counterpart in the free-thought arena, Colonel Robert Ingersoll.[1]

It is not surprising that the advocate of a republican form of government for France, Germany, Italy, and Spain should have wished his own country to advance in the same direction. In this he was but following the footsteps of Paine and Richard Carlile; and Crane Brinton observes justly that 'Bradlaugh's republic was not in conception very different from the republic of Robespierre. Bradlaugh belongs to that now old-fashioned school of politics stemming from the revolutions of the eighteenth century.'[2] Bradlaugh had been active in London politics as early as 1859, when *The Times* of London referred to him as 'a youthful orator who seemed a great favourite with the noisier Democrats'.[3] He had taken part in a great many Hyde Park meetings, particularly at the time of the Reform Bill agitation of 1866–7. During the early 1870's, when the private life of the Prince of Wales and Queen Victoria's failure to fulfil even her ceremonial role in government were encouraging a widespread, if temporary, republican movement, Bradlaugh took the lead.

His *Impeachment of the House of Brunswick* is a vitriolic review of the careers of the Hanoverian monarchs, emphasizing their private vices and their failure to contribute anything useful to public life in return for the expense they entailed. The monarchy can be abolished by Act of Parliament, contends Bradlaugh, and his hope is that Parliament will take such a step at the end of Victoria's reign. The book disdainfully dismisses George I and his successors as useless foreigners whom Englishmen paid to 'perpetuate a pauper prince race'.[4] Outspoken as he was on the question, Bradlaugh did not apparently at any time consider the use of violence. 'Our republic will, I trust,' he declared in 1873, 'come nursed

[1] *N.R.*, 8 June 1884, p. 398.
[2] *English Political Thought in the Nineteenth Century* (2nd ed., London, 1949), p. 245.
[3] Cited by Bonner & Robertson, *Bradlaugh*, i. 82.
[4] Charles Bradlaugh, *The Impeachment of the House of Brunswick* (8th ed., London, 1881), p. 99 and *passim*.

by the school, the brain, the pen, and the tongue and not heralded by the cannon's roar or carved by the sword.'[1] Bradlaugh never gave up his republican sentiments altogether, but as the popularity of the movement ebbed in Britain he came to the conclusion that agitation on behalf of an ideal government was less likely to prove fruitful than agitation against particular abuses, especially the remnants of class privilege.

Perhaps the most notorious of the causes Charles Bradlaugh served in late Victorian England was neither atheism nor republicanism but birth control or (in contemporary usage) neo-Malthusianism. Malthus's original writings had hardly been in keeping with the optimistic radicalism of the era of the French Revolution, but as early as the 1820's Englishmen like Francis Place had reached the conclusion that political radicalism was not merely reconcilable with a programme of limiting the size of families but indeed required it. Only thus could the curse of poverty be laid low. Bradlaugh himself began to advocate neo-Malthusianism as early as 1861 with the publication of his essay, *Jesus, Shelley and Malthus*. 'Liberty, equality, fraternity', he observed, 'are words used very often about the Republican institutions of the world; but you can never have liberty, equality, and fraternity as long as there is poverty dividing one class from another.' Birth control was the most important step which might be taken to eliminate poverty.[2] Such a doctrine was all the more appropriate at a time when child-labour laws, more complex machinery, and the growth of universal primary education were making children less of an economic asset than they had been either in a primarily agricultural economy or in the industrial system of the early nineteenth century.

Most critics identified the espousal of birth control with the advocacy of 'free love'; and Bradlaugh laid himself open to that charge by his praise for George Drysdale's *Elements of Social Science*. This book, first published in 1854 and often reprinted, not only supported birth control but provided a radical treatise on sex education and a critique of the institu-

[1] Cited by A. Headingly, *The Biography of Charles Bradlaugh* (London, 1880), p. 144.
[2] Cited by Bonner & Robertson, *Bradlaugh*, ii. 172.

tion of marriage.[1] Though disagreeing with the book in part, Bradlaugh noted that it was written 'with honest and pure intent and purpose'. This praise, notes Mrs. Besant, 'was the origin of his worst difficulties . . . '.[2] Though he approved of the legality of divorce, Bradlaugh was, as a matter of fact, rather conventional in his treatment of sex and marriage. He once observed, for example, that even though divorce might be desirable in certain instances, he would not regard remarriage as appropriate while a divorced wife was yet alive.[3]

Bradlaugh's connexion with neo-Malthusianism came to the fore most notably in 1876 and 1877 when the Government decided to prosecute the English publisher of a book on birth control, *The Fruits of Philosophy*, written more than forty years earlier by Charles Knowlton, an American physician. When the English publisher pleaded guilty, Bradlaugh and Annie Besant decided to make a test case of the matter. 'I deny', declared Bradlaugh, 'the right of any one to interfere with the full and free discussion of social questions affecting the happiness of the nation. The struggle for a free press has been one of the marks of the Freethought party throughout its history, and as long as the Party permits me to hold its flag, I will never voluntarily lower it.'[4] As soon as Bradlaugh's and Mrs. Besant's newly organized Freethought Publishing Company had produced a new edition of the book, the two were arrested and prosecution was instituted against them. The result was one of the most significant trials in late Victorian English history.

Upon Bradlaugh's motion, the trial was transferred from the Old Bailey to the Court of the Queen's Bench before the Lord Chief Justice, Alexander Cockburn. Bradlaugh defended himself essentially on the basis that the doctrine of family limitation and comparable physiological descriptions were to be found in other works, sold at popular prices, that had not been prosecuted. The jury's verdict was a paradoxical one: 'We are unanimously of opinion that the book in question

[1] Norman Himes, *Medical History of Contraception* (London, 1936), p. 233.
[2] Besant, *Autobiography*, p. 197.
[3] Cited in *N.R.*, 26 June 1881, p. 22.
[4] Cited by Bonner & Robertson, *Bradlaugh*, ii. 17.

is calculated to deprave public morals, but at the same time we entirely exonerate the defendants from any corrupt motives in publishing it.'[1] The defendants were sentenced to six months in prison and fines of £200 each. Before the sentences could be carried out, the Court of Appeal had quashed the indictments on the technical ground that they had been improperly prepared. It was for Bradlaugh an impressive if not altogether clear-cut legal triumph. The trial had also given the subject of contraception greater publicity than it had ever received in England before. An immediate result of the trial was to divide the free-thought movement— Bradlaugh's secularist critics dubbed his organization the 'Erotic School of Freethought'[2]—and to create a popular impression that in England atheism necessarily implied the doctrine of 'free love'. Bradlaugh was legitimately fearful that his hopes of establishing himself as a candidate for a seat in Parliament had been irrevocably damaged.[3]

The long-run effects of the trial were more significant. A Malthusian League was established under Dr. Charles Drysdale, with Bradlaugh as Vice-President, and in 1879 Annie Besant herself replaced *The Fruits of Philosophy*, of which some 185,000 copies had been printed, with a more up-to-date volume entitled *The Law of Population*. 'It is clearly useless', argued the first woman to advocate contraception publicly, 'to preach the limitation of the family, and to conceal the means whereby such limitation may be effected. If the limitation be a duty, it cannot be wrong to afford such information as shall enable people to discharge it.'[4] Within six years 200,000 copies of Mrs. Besant's book had been sold in Britain and the United States, and it had been translated into Italian, Swedish, Dutch, German, and French.[5] The trial thus did much to make legal the general distribution of contraceptive knowledge within England, a development which contributed to a steady drop in the English birth-rate from the 1870's on. During the mid-1870's the birth-rate was still 35 per 1,000

[1] Cited by Bonner & Robertson, *Bradlaugh*, ii. 24.

[2] Charles R. Mackay, *A Biography of Charles Bradlaugh, M.P.* (London, 1888), p. 29.

[3] Williams, *Passionate Pilgrim*, pp. 85–87.

[4] Annie Besant, *The Law of Population* (London, 1879), p. 31.

[5] *N.R.*, 24 June 1883, p. 459; 18 Jan. 1885, p. 39.

(a figure comparable to that of the average for the eighteenth century); by 1931 it had dropped to 16 per 1,000.[1]

It was a man's duty, believed Bradlaugh, not merely to express ideas but to act upon them. This axiom had served as the theme of his life before 1880 and was to continue to do so thereafter.

[1] Himes, *History of Contraception*, pp. 243–4.

III

AN ELECTION IN NORTHAMPTON

Charles Bradlaugh first visited Northampton in 1855 and lectured there from time to time during the early 1860's as 'Iconoclast'. During the great Reform Bill campaign of 1865–7, in which he enthusiastically participated, he spoke there again, and having by this time acquired a small circle of loyal friends in the town, he chose Northampton in 1868 for his first attempt to gain a seat in Parliament.[1]

It was a logical choice. Northampton had a tradition of widespread public interest in politics. Before 1832, indeed, the franchise there had been so wide that the Reform Bill of that year had actually reduced the number of voters. In contrast to other boroughs, elections there were always contested, yet in fifty years there had been not a single unseating for bribery.[2] Northampton was the capital of the boot-and-shoe industry of England and, for that matter, of much of the British Empire. Its residents, numbering 54,080 in 1871 and 57,544 in 1881, included a sizeable population of skilled and comparatively highly-paid workers. Such workers were the traditional backbone of nineteenth-century British radicalism. As very little mechanization had taken place in the shoemaking industry, large groups of men working together had therefore ample opportunity for talking politics.[3] And in Northampton, as Henry Labouchere observed in 1880, 'every one is more or less a politician'.[4] These, then, were the men who received the vote in 1867. The Reform Bill more than doubled the total number

---

[1] Bonner & Robertson, *Bradlaugh*, i. 228–9, 263–4. Bradlaugh's first recorded appearance in Northampton, according to Mrs. Bonner, was in 1859, but in an article in *N.R.* (2 Sept. 1883, p. 145) Bradlaugh places his first visit in 1855. [2] *N.R.*, 11 Feb. 1883, p. 81.

[3] Partly based on conversations in February and April 1957 with Victor A. Hatley, Reference Librarian of the Northampton Central Library and prospective author of a book on Northampton in the nineteenth century.

[4] *Truth*, 8 Apr. 1880, p. 468.

of voters, who now totalled 5,729 in a two-member constituency.

In 1868 Bradlaugh was, of course, contesting Northampton not as atheist propagandist but as radical politician. Indeed, from the time he decided to stand for Parliament, Bradlaugh was never again to preach atheism in Northampton. Not until 1884 was a National Secular Society branch started there. Radicalism meant for Bradlaugh a number of things, such as a system of compulsory national education and a change in the land laws abolishing primogeniture and entail and giving greater security to tenant farmers. Although Bradlaugh's land-reform proposals never went as far as land nationalization, they were described by a Whiggish Liberal even in 1881 as 'revolutionary doctrines'.[1] Bradlaugh also advocated a less generous attitude on the part of the Government toward 'destitute members of so-called noble families', a reform of the House of Lords, equality of labour and capital before the law, the complete separation of Church and State, and, not least important, 'the abolition of all disabilities and disqualifications consequent upon the holding or rejection of any particular speculative opinion'. At this time, also, he favoured a plan of proportional representation, an idea he was later to discard.[2] The other proposals were to prove recurrent themes in his political career.

Both members standing for re-election in Northampton in 1868 were Liberals, Charles Gilpin and Lord Henley. Bradlaugh hoped to defeat Henley, whom he regarded as a Whig and thus on the right of the Liberal spectrum. It proved to be a long and tumultuous campaign, which attracted considerably more national attention than particular local campaigns usually do. Bradlaugh had some trade-union support, but his most prominent supporter by far was John Stuart Mill, who sent a £10 donation and thereby forfeited his own re-election for Westminster.[3] This assistance was counteracted by letters from both Gladstone

[1] Earl of Dunraven, 'The Revolutionary Party', *Nineteenth Century*, Aug. 1881, p. 189.
[2] His first election programme is reprinted in Bonner & Robertson, *Bradlaugh*, i. 264–5.
[3] John Stuart Mill, *Autobiography* (New York, 1924), pp. 219–20.

and John Bright in favour of Gilpin and Henley. Since Bradlaugh had little newspaper or financial backing and since his anti-religious opinions were given full publicity by his opponents, it is not surprising that he came in a rather poor fifth with 1,086 votes as opposed to 2,632 for Gilpin and 2,105 for Henley—who were thus re-elected—and 1,625 and 1,378 for each of the two Conservatives. A sixth candidate, a temperance advocate, received 485 votes.[1]

When the general election of 1874—the first to be held after the Secret Ballot Act—was announced, Bradlaugh was on his first lecture tour of the United States. Despite his absence and a Conservative trend, he increased his total vote to 1,635. Of these, 1,060 were cast by 'plumpers', who did not vote for a second candidate. As a result, Henley was defeated, and Gilpin and Pickering Phipps, a Tory brewer, were elected. When Gilpin's death later that same year neces-sitated a by-election, it was a three-way contest between Merewether the Conservative, Bradlaugh the Radical, and William Fowler the Moderate Liberal. Fowler bitterly attacked both Bradlaugh's morals and lack of religion, and Bradlaugh responded by calling Fowler 'a liar and a coward'. The election results were predictable: Merewether won with 2,171 votes, while Fowler and Bradlaugh received 1,836 and 1,766, respectively. Bradlaugh's supporters gave vent to their frustration by injuring a number of Fowler's adherents and wrecking the printing plant of the hostile Northampton *Mercury*. The riot had broken out after Brad-laugh's departure from the city, but the resultant memo-ries of violence were often to be revived by Bradlaugh's opponents in later years.[2]

It had now become obvious that only by uniting could the radical and moderate factions of the Liberal party in North-ampton regain the two seats lost to the Conservatives. Some co-operation did take place in the local elections of 1875 and 1876, but the notoriety gained by Bradlaugh as a result of the prosecution of *The Fruits of Philosophy* in 1877 and 1878 divided the two factions anew. While Bradlaugh announced his candidacy for the next general election as early as 1878, three other Liberals were also in the running for the two seats.

[1] Bonner & Robertson, *Bradlaugh*, i. 277.   [2] Ibid., pp. 392–400.

Bradlaugh was to be aided, however, by a most important institution, the Freehold Land Society. This was one of many similar local organizations founded in the late 1840's under the inspiration of Richard Cobden with the purpose of enabling workers to build their own homes by regularly contributing small sums, usually a shilling a week. During the late 1870's this society was reinvigorated by two of Bradlaugh's most faithful lieutenants in Northampton, Joseph Gurney and Thomas Adams, with the result that by the mid-1880's Northampton could proudly boast that it had more workers who owned their own homes than any other English town. Such work had the added result of bringing at least 1,000 new voters within the scope of the franchise law between 1874 and 1880. A majority of these were Bradlaugh supporters.[1]

When a general election became imminent early in 1880, the Liberal split had not yet been healed. The victory of five Radicals in the Northampton School Board election in January seemed a good omen for Bradlaugh's influence, but in February he was forced to admit that 'no real progress has been made towards union with the moderate Liberals'.[2] The Radical Association then issued a manifesto pledging its support to whomever the Moderate Liberals would put up for one of the two seats, provided that they would support the Radical candidate for the other seat. The Moderate Liberals retorted with a counter-manifesto which freely admitted the right of the Radicals to nominate a candidate for one of the two seats, provided that he was anyone but Bradlaugh. According to the Moderates, the sole cause of Liberal disunity in Northampton had been 'the persistent endeavour by a section of the Radicals to foist upon the Constituency a Candidate who is insuperably objectionable to the majority of the Liberals of this Borough', and the only solution would be the withdrawal of Bradlaugh.[3]

Since this possibility was out of the question for the

[1] Northampton Town and County Benefit Building Society, *A Century of Service* (Northampton, 1948), *passim*. Also *N.R.*, 21 Mar. 1880, p. 177, and conversations with Victor A. Hatley and with Alderman Percy Adams (a grandson of Thomas Adams) in Northampton in February 1957.

[2] *N.R.*, 18 Jan. 1880, p. 41; 15 Feb. 1880, p. 106.

[3] Papers in Northampton Central Library collection of election clippings.

Bradlaugh supporters, the deadlock would, in all probability, have led to another Liberal defeat, had it not been for two accidents. A. S. Ayrton, the most prominent prospective Liberal candidate, was thrown from a horse and severely injured only three weeks before the poll; he was forced to withdraw. A second Liberal was also struck down by illness, whereupon the name of Henry Labouchere was suggested to the local party leaders by the central Liberal organization. Labouchere had served in Parliament briefly before, but he had no previous acquaintance with either Northampton or Bradlaugh.

Labouchere, although the candidate of the Moderate Liberals, soon discovered that 'this was mere nomenclature, and that the mildest Liberal in Northampton would be termed a Radical elsewhere'.[1] He observed also that Bradlaugh was one of the most effective electioneering speakers he had ever come across: 'After calmly replying in detail to some of the trash that forms the staple of Conservative oratory, he raises his voice until the very walls re-echo with it, and winds up with a fierce appeal to the electors to do their duty.'[2] Labouchere was quick to note that Bradlaugh had a well-organized and powerful political machine consisting of volunteers who loyally did his bidding. It was the first constituency he had encountered in which the candidate was not regarded as 'a pigeon who is to be plucked'. Since Labouchere felt that the Radicals were entitled to one of the two seats and that continued Liberal disunity would result in another Tory victory, he immediately brought all his influence to bear in order to unite the two factions, and he and Bradlaugh held a joint election meeting on 22 March. Another Liberal candidate, Thomas Wright, was still in the running, however, and it was not until 26 March, a week before election day, that Wright—influenced in part by the

---

[1] *Truth*, 1 Apr. 1880, p. 435.
[2] Ibid. Bradlaugh's vocal prowess is a legend in Northampton. When speaking in the Market Square, it is said that he could be heard at least a quarter of a mile away. He also possessed a remarkable ability to hold the attention of an audience. Conversation with Mrs. A. Ball, who heard Bradlaugh speak in 1886. (June 1957.) Cf. the recollections of W. W. Hadley, a one-time Northampton *Mercury* reporter, in *Northamptonshire Past and Present*, 1959, p. 273.

advice of W. P. Adam, the Liberal campaign manager in London—decided to retire from the contest. Adam gave a mild national organization blessing to the new alliance, and a complete Liberal triumph in Northampton at last seemed probable.[1] As one of the campaign songs put it,

Unity at last has come to this good old Liberal town,
  Now, as brothers, we will work hand in hand,
For the grievance of the past shall be banished from our mind,
  And our victory shall echo through the land.[2]

It was a strange partnership, that of Bradlaugh and Labouchere. The differences between the two men, the first large and powerful in appearance, the second rather slight and wiry, were reflected in the journals each of them edited. Bradlaugh's *National Reformer*, addressed to the most literate section of the working class, was steadfastly serious and didactic, devoted to its editor's vision of a better society. Bradlaugh's closest approach to humour was a rather heavy-handed irony. Labouchere's *Truth*, on the other hand, was essentially a light-hearted magazine intended for an upper-class clientele. Several pages of each issue were filled with society gossip, Labouchere himself contributing a weekly financial column under the pseudonym 'Mammon', in which he exposed humbugs and swindles. *Truth* could comment with a straight face: 'The general election has played havoc in hunting quarters.'[3]

Labouchere himself came from an old French Huguenot family and had been educated at Eton and Cambridge. He had served in minor diplomatic posts in both hemispheres, had inherited a fortune from an uncle in the banking business, and had gained a deserved reputation as one of the most entertaining of English wits and raconteurs. His comment on Gladstone—'I do not mind Mr. Gladstone having an ace up his sleeve, but I do object to his always saying that Providence put it there'—has been often quoted.[4] Labouchere's

---

[1] *N.R.*, 28 Mar. 1880, p. 193; 4 Apr. 1880, p. 209. The local Liberal organization did not endorse Bradlaugh outright. See Northampton *Mercury*, 27 Mar. 1880, p. 5.
[2] Northampton Library collection of election clippings.
[3] 25 Mar. 1880, p. 387.
[4] Algar Labouchere Thorold, *The Life of Henry Labouchere* (New York, 1913), p. xii.

attitude toward Parliament was one of semi-cynical equanimity—'If one is out, one feels that one would like to be in; if one is in, one feels very frequently that, on the whole, one would rather be out'; for Bradlaugh, on the contrary, a seat in the House of Commons, 'a Parliament in which any man may well be proud to sit, if only for the memory of the gallant things it has often done for liberty', was the summit of a lifelong ambition.[1]

It is not surprising that Bradlaugh at first distrusted Labouchere, but the latter's political loyalty soon altered this attitude. While Labouchere's radicalism may have been dictated by reason and Bradlaugh's by a type of idealistic humanitarianism, the two men were agreed on almost every point in their political creed. Bradlaugh's election programme in 1880 emphasized a reform of the land laws, 'resistance to our present scandalously extravagant National Expenditure', the separation of Church and State, and the reform of the House of Lords; it also demanded county suffrage and shorter Parliaments. Only on the question of women's suffrage did the two disagree—Bradlaugh favoured it and Labouchere opposed it—but this was hardly a pressing issue at the time. The Liberal campaigners that year concentrated their fire upon Lord Beaconsfield's foreign policy. Labouchere satirized 'the swagger abroad and inaction at home' of 'our Grand Vizier' and was to hail his defeat as 'the Sedan of Emperor Jingo'; while Bradlaugh waxed eloquent about the expense and immorality implicit in wars against the Zulus.[2] Both could agree with Gladstone on the continued relevance of 'Peace, Retrenchment, and Reform'. Although Labouchere was nominally a member of the Church of England—he was later to refer to himself as 'the Christian Member for Northampton'—he was completely non-religious in outlook. Unlike Bradlaugh, however, he willingly conceded the utility of religious belief in others and perhaps even in society as a whole. He had never read any of Bradlaugh's works; and he had too little faith in human nature to support Bradlaugh's overt attacks upon

[1] *Truth*, 1 Apr. 1880, p. 435; *N.R.*, 9 May 1880, p. 287.
[2] Northampton Library collection of election clippings; *Truth*, 18 Mar. 1880, p. 365; 8 Apr. 1880, p. 460.

1. Bradlaugh and Labouchere (in the early 1880s)

IV

THE CLAIM TO AFFIRM

THE new Parliament assembled on 29 April 1880, but was to accomplish little for several weeks. Under a law dating back to the reign of Queen Anne and not to be repealed until 1918, the new Cabinet members, having 'assumed an office of profit under the Crown', were obliged to return to their constituencies to seek a second election. In the meantime the swearing-in of members was the chief Parliamentary activity. Most observers agree that this was generally an informal and even undignified affair. 'The members stood up in rows, and were sworn in battalions and admitted in platoons'; and the entire procedure took place 'amid jokes and good-humoured merriment'.[1]

It was on the third of May that Charles Bradlaugh marched up the aisle to the Table of the House for a similar purpose. Considerable curiosity had been expressed as to what course the huge, determined-looking representative from Northampton would take. He asked the Clerk to be permitted to take an affirmation instead of an oath. (In an affirmation, the words 'I swear' are replaced with 'I solemnly, sincerely, and truly declare and affirm' and the words 'So help me God' are omitted.) The Parliamentary Oaths Act of 1866 had granted the right of affirmation only to Quakers, Moravians, and Separatists. Asked therefore by Sir Erskine May on what basis he wished to affirm, Bradlaugh cited the Evidence Amendment Acts of 1869 and 1870—whose passage he had been influential in securing—and under whose provisions he had been affirming in courts of law ever since. The Speaker was undecided about the validity of this reasoning and so left the matter to the House. Lord Frederick Cavendish, the Financial Secretary of the Treasury, who led the Liberals in the absence of the senior Cabinet members, suggested that

[1] T. P. O'Connor, *Gladstone's House of Commons* (London, 1885), p. 1; *Hansard*, ccliii (1880), 1315.

a Select Committee be appointed to decide upon the question. Sir Stafford Northcote, the leader of the Conservative opposition, supported the motion, which, despite the grumbling of several Conservative back-benchers, was adopted without a division. When several days later, on 11 May, Lord Richard Grosvenor, another junior member of the Government, moved the complementary motion that the Committee consist of nineteen members, Sir Henry Drummond Wolff, a Conservative, objected on the technical ground that such business ought not precede the Queen's Speech and was therefore 'if not an infringement, an evasion of the Royal prerogative'. This was disputed by the Liberals on the ground that the swearing-in of members necessarily came first, and Grosvenor's motion was adopted by a vote of 171–74.[1] As a matter of fact, the events of 3 May and the choosing of a Select Committee merely made public several decisions that had been reached beforehand. The only thing that did not go according to plan, indeed, was that on 11 May seventy members of the Conservative Party—in voting to oppose a Select Committee—failed to follow the advice of their supposed leader, a decision with portentous consequences.

Bradlaugh had on 29 April written identical letters to the Speaker, Sir Henry Brand, and to the Clerk, Sir Erskine May, in which he explained that he desired to affirm. 'Should my letter be an impertinence', Bradlaugh had concluded, 'I must beg you to excuse it, as my only object in writing it is to avoid giving trouble in the House.'[2] Brand's and May's immediate reactions were unfavourable; but Brand requested S. K. Richards, a veteran clerk, to prepare a report on the subject. The report must have been finished within a few hours because the very same day Brand sent copies of it both to Gladstone and to Sir Richard Cross, the former Conservative Home Secretary, who in turn passed the information on to Northcote. Richards briefly outlined the relevant statutes. The Oaths Act of 1866 gave the option of affirmation to

[1] *Hansard*, cclii (1880), 20–63. The title of 'Lord' in the case of Lord Frederick Cavendish, as in that of other 'Lords' in the House of Commons, is an honorary one. It indicates that he is the younger son of a peer (in the case of Cavendish the Duke of Devonshire).

[2] Hampden MSS.

Quakers, Moravians, Separatists, 'and every other person for the time being permitted by law to make a solemn affirmation or declaration'. Bradlaugh had pointed out that the Evidence Acts of 1869 and 1870, by giving him the right to affirm in the law courts, had brought him within the scope of the earlier act. Richards concluded, however, that the later acts had not had the effect of amending the Oaths Act, since the Evidence Acts related to judicial oaths and the Oaths Act to promissory oaths. 'In strict law, therefore, I consider that Mr. Bradlaugh's contention cannot be sustained.' He added the opinion that it might be desirable to amend the law.

The Speaker found himself in agreement with Richards's report, though he duly noted that the last comment raised a question of policy irrelevant to the issue in dispute. It was obvious to the Speaker—if not to all subsequent historians— 'that the question is one for the judgment of the House, & that I must await instructions from the House'. He suggested to Gladstone that the appointment of a Select Committee might be the solution, a procedure adopted in 1833 when Joseph Pease, a Quaker, had asked to affirm.[1] The Speaker then sent for Bradlaugh, informed him that the House of Commons would have to be consulted on the propriety of an affirmation, and asked him to defer presenting himself until 3 May. Bradlaugh respectfully replied that he was sorry to cause trouble, but that he felt bound to assert his claim to affirm.[2]

Thus the drama began to unfold. Cross mentioned the matter not merely to Northcote but also to Sir John Holker, the ex-Attorney-General, and Sir Hardinge Giffard, the ex-Solicitor-General. In the meantime Gladstone, before returning to Midlothian to run for re-election, had consulted his Law Officers, Sir Henry James (the new Attorney-General) and Sir Farrer Herschell (the new Solicitor-General). Both men agreed that Bradlaugh's reasoning was

[1] Hampden Diary, 29 Apr. 1880; G.P. (B.M.), 44194, fols. 190–1; Iddesleigh MSS. (B.M.) 50041, fols. 11–12, includes a copy of Richards's report. As early as the summer of 1880, John Bright observed to the Speaker: 'It would have saved us a great deal of trouble, Sir, if you had decided it for yourself.' *Hansard*, ccliii (1880), 497.

[2] Hampden Diary, 30 Apr. 1880; *N.R.*, 9 May 1880, pp. 289–90.

valid and that he was fully entitled to affirm. James, indeed, went so far as to suggest that a Select Committee was therefore quite unnecessary but that it might be best not to oppose the appointment of one, should the Opposition contest Bradlaugh's claim.[1]

With such conflicting advice before him, Gladstone decided in favour of a Committee. He therefore asked Lord Frederick Cavendish to propose a Select Committee to the Commons and to take charge of any debate.[2] Gladstone probably did not devote much thought to the matter before departing for the North. He was, however, fully informed, and it is doubtful whether, as has been asserted,[3] matters would have taken a different turn had the obsolete re-election law not existed. Cavendish had the feeling, to be sure, that 'trouble' was likely to result, and he specifically asked Sir Charles Dilke, the new Under-Secretary for Foreign Affairs, to be in the House on 3 May.[4]

The question arises, why did Bradlaugh wish to affirm, when, as he himself conceded, he was 'raising an entirely new parliamentary question'?[5] He felt in part that it would be more 'decorous' for an avowed atheist not to take an oath. But he also acted out of pride. Had he not paved the way in winning the right for atheists to dispense with oaths in law courts? What a fine omen for his Parliamentary career, to begin it by establishing the same precedent in the House of Commons. To the atheist of the time, it must be remembered, the affirmation was more than a legal technicality; it was a veritable badge of respectability. Not that Bradlaugh either wished for, or expected, a prolonged struggle. A careful study of law books had convinced him that he already had the right; and before he took the fateful step he had been informed that the new Law Officers of the Crown shared his view. Under such circumstances—when a choice seemed so clearly open to him—his decision was the obvious one. In any case, what would his followers have said if Bradlaugh,

---

[1] James to Gladstone, 1 May 1880, G.P. (B.M.), 44219, fol. 30.

[2] (Copy) Gladstone to Cavendish, 2 May 1880, G.P. (B.M.), 44544, fol. 2.

[3] e.g. Viscount (Herbert) Gladstone, *After Thirty Years* (London, 1928), p. 162, and W. W. Hadley, 'Bradlaugh and Labouchere', *Northamptonshire Past and Present*, 1959, p. 276.

[4] Dilke MSS. (B.M.), 43934, 168.   [5] *N.R.*, 9 May 1880, p. 290.

'being assured that he had free choice between oath and
affirmation, had deliberately preferred to call upon the name
of God, which to him is a meaningless expression'?[1] The
suggestion was made later that Bradlaugh should merely
have affirmed quietly, without asking permission.[2] Such
a course would have gone both against Bradlaugh's ingrained sense of courtesy and his sense of legality, and it
might well have provoked objections.

The Select Committee held only one brief meeting. It
selected a Conservative, H. Spencer Walpole, as its chairman,
and spent one afternoon behind closed doors discussing the
legal issue involved. Bradlaugh was permitted to attend, but
he was not formally a witness. He was pleasantly surprised,
none the less, to find himself among a tribunal of English
gentlemen, 'none of whom agreed with me in my heresy',
yet all of whom were willing to listen patiently to his case.[3]
When it came time for a decision, however, the vote was
8 to 8. The chairman's vote was thus decisive, and he ruled
that Bradlaugh's claim to affirm was invalid. The Attorney-
General, the Solicitor-General, and John Bright were among
those in the minority.[4] All the Conservatives on the Committee had voted against Bradlaugh's claim and all the
Liberals but one had favoured it; Charles Henry Hopwood,
the single exception, was later convinced that his vote 'did
Mr. Bradlaugh an injustice',[5] and he was to become one of
Bradlaugh's stoutest Parliamentary champions. Bradlaugh
was apparently prepared for the worst. 'That the decision
was against me is only natural', he conceded almost too
readily; 'the wonder is that the majority was so minute.'[6]

There was considerable speculation within the Government as to Bradlaugh's next move. Would Bradlaugh
'swallow the oath', wondered Hamilton, Gladstone's secretary, or would he ask the Government for a change in the
law?[7] Speaker Brand, who was relieved to have the Select

[1] N.R., 19 Feb. 1882, p. 132.
[2] George Jacob Holyoake, *Life of Bradlaugh* (London, 1891), p. 13.
[3] N.R., 23 May 1880, p. 321.
[4] Great Britain, *Parliamentary Papers*, 1880, vol. xii, 'Report from the
[First] Select Committee on the Parliamentary Oath'.
[5] *Hansard*, ccliii (1880), 480.   [6] N.R., 23 May 1880, p. 321.
[7] Hamilton Diary (B.M.), 48630, p. 23.

Committee confirm his judgement, confided to Gladstone that Bradlaugh would probably take the usual oath; 'at least such was his frame of mind before he presented himself at the table to make an affirmation'.[1] This comment should dispose completely of one of the persistent myths about the Bradlaugh case, that Bradlaugh at any time refused to take the oath, a myth which continues to be repeated by otherwise reputable historians.[2] Bradlaugh did not leave the issue in doubt for long; he notified both the Speaker and Sir Henry James on 13 May that he would take the usual oath as soon as the Committee's report had been published. Gladstone in turn assured Queen Victoria, who had taken an early interest in the matter, that it would soon be satisfactorily settled.[3]

[1] Brand to Gladstone, 13 May 1880, G.P. (B.M.), 44194, fol. 196.

[2] e.g. Erich Eyck, *Gladstone* (London, 1938), p. 292: 'He [Bradlaugh] informed the Speaker that his convictions forbade him to take an oath.' Philip Guedalla, *The Queen and Mr. Gladstone* (London, 1933), ii. 29: 'Bradlaugh . . . declined to take the oath.' G. D. H. Cole, *British Working Class Politics, 1832–1914* (London, 1941), p. 263: 'Bradlaugh was unseated on refusing to take the oath.' L. E. Elliott-Binns, *Religion in the Victorian Era* (2nd ed., Greenwich, Conn., 1946), p. 211: 'Bradlaugh himself became notorious for his refusal to take the oath . . . .' Eric Taylor, *The House of Commons at Work* (4th ed., Harmondsworth, Middx., 1961), writes on p. 42 of Bradlaugh's 'initial refusal to take the Oath . . .'. See also comments by J. P. Gilmour (ed.), *Champion of Liberty: Charles Bradlaugh* (London, 1933), pp. 176–7.

[3] Bradlaugh to Brand, 13 May 1880, Hampden MSS.; G.P. (B.M.), 44219, fol. 33; Guedalla, *Queen and Gladstone*, ii. 95.

V

THE LETTER AND THE CONSEQUENCES

On 21 May 1880, the day on which Bradlaugh planned to take the oath, he decided to explain his position more fully in an open letter to *The Times* and several other newspapers. He began by pointing out that so long as he believed he had the legal right to affirm,

it was then clearly my moral duty to make the affirmation. The oath, although to me including words of idle and meaningless character, was and is regarded by a large number of my fellow countrymen as an appeal to deity to take cognizance of their swearing. It would have been an act of hypocrisy to voluntarily take this form if any other had been open to me, or to take it without protest, as though it meant in my mouth any such appeal.

Two courses were open to him, Bradlaugh continued, either to appeal to the House against the Committee's decision or to comply with the ceremony and at some later date deal with a form which other M.P.s considered 'as objectionable as I do, but which habit and the fear of exciting prejudice has induced them to submit to'. To appeal to the House to overrule the Committee would delay public business and might cause the Liberal party to be unfairly burdened with his anti-theological views, even though the party had never given him any electoral help. He was sure that he would have been elected even if the Radical and Liberal forces in Northampton had failed to unite.[1]

He would therefore follow the second course.

My duty to my constituents is to fulfil the mandate they have given me, and if to do this I have to submit to a form less solemn to me than the affirmation I would have reverently made, so much the worse for those who force me to repeat words which I have scores of times declared are to me sounds conveying no clear and definite meaning. I am sorry for the earnest believers who see

[1] It is only fair to observe that Bradlaugh, with good reason, had been much less confident on this score in March 1880.

words sacred to them used as a meaningless addendum to a promise, but I cannot permit their less sincere co-religionists to use an idle form in order to prevent me from doing my duty to those who have chosen me to speak for them in Parliament. I shall, taking the oath, regard myself as bound not by the letter of its words, but by the spirit which the affirmation would have conveyed had I been permitted to use it. . . . I comply with the forms of the House.[1]

The letter created a sensation. Whatever Bradlaugh's fellow free-thinkers may have thought of it—and it was, in a sense, addressed to them—the Members of the House of Commons regarded it as a direct provocation. It was *the* topic of conversation in the House of Commons lobbies, and the Whips notified Gladstone that should any objection be raised to Bradlaugh's right to swear, the Liberal majority could not be relied upon to defeat it outright. So Gladstone, after a hasty meeting with the Speaker and the Law Officers, had to content himself with the plan to propose another Select Committee, should such an objection arise.[2] As he unhappily reported to Queen Victoria in his daily letter, 'the case of Mr. Bradlaugh has this day become the occasion of considerable difficulty, partly in consequence of a letter from him in the papers of this morning . . .'.[3] Gladstone's daughter was more succinct: 'The fat is in the fire about the . . . Bradlaugh mess', she wrote in her diary.[4]

As Bradlaugh, amidst cries of horror from the Conservative benches, advanced toward the Table to take the oath—'I, Charles Bradlaugh, do swear that I will be faithful and bear true allegiance to Her Majesty Queen Victoria, her heirs and successors according to law, so help me God'—Sir Henry

[1] *The Times*, 21 May 1880, p. 4.
[2] Hampden Diary, 21 May 1880.
[3] Philip Guedalla, *The Queen and Mr. Gladstone* (London, 1933), ii. 96. The practice of a daily personal report by the Prime Minister to the monarch was instituted by Lord North, reached its high point under Disraeli, and was given up only in the twentieth century. The function is continued by a lesser member of the Government, usually the Party Whip. See J. P. Trevin and E. M. King, *Printer to the House* (London, 1952), p. 238. Gladstone's reports, according to his secretary, 'are a very masterly summary of the proceedings of the House; and, written on his knee as they are in the House while debates go on, they are a marvel of correctness & tidiness'. Hamilton Diary (B.M.), 48635, p. 107.
[4] Mary Gladstone Diary, 21 May 1880 (B.M.), 46259.

Drummond Wolff, the Conservative M.P. for Portsmouth, sprang from his front bench seat, apparently ready to block Bradlaugh's passage by physical force if necessary. 'I object, Sir, to the Oath being administered to the hon. Member for Northampton. . . . I protest against the hon. Gentleman being sworn.' The Speaker asked Bradlaugh to withdraw for a moment, and in reply to a Liberal member who asked as a 'Point of Order' whether such interference with oath-taking was permissible, the Speaker conceded that he knew of no precedent. Yet, the Speaker went on, if Wolff had any observations to make, he did not feel it his duty to interpose.[1]

Sir Henry Drummond Wolff had a number of observations to make, among them the blunt remark that 'the hon. Member is a professed Atheist—and by the Common Law of England an Atheist is not entitled to take an oath'. Wolff ended his speech by moving a resolution to the effect that Bradlaugh ought not to be allowed to take the oath because he had previously claimed to make the affirmation under an act which provided that the potential affirmer had first to satisfy the presiding judge that an oath 'had no binding effect' on his conscience. Since Bradlaugh had by his own admission repeatedly affirmed under that act, an oath was therefore necessarily not binding on his conscience.

The intent of that particular provision of the Evidence Amendment Acts of 1869 and 1870—inserted, incidentally, by the House of Lords—had been to prevent persons who looked upon oaths as sacred promises from dodging them. The actual effect had been to stigmatize unbelievers as necessarily untrustworthy, and not all judges sought such assurances from those who wished to affirm.[2] Yet Bradlaugh, it now seemed clear for the first time, had fallen into a constitutional trap. In the very act of choosing to affirm rather than to swear he had technically cut himself off from the alternative possibility.

Wolff, it should be noted, had not been personally influenced in his course by Bradlaugh's public letter. He had begun to ponder such an objection soon after Bradlaugh

---

[1] *Hansard*, cclii (1880), 187–90; Henry W. Lucy, *A Diary of Two Parliaments* (London, 1886), ii. 11.

[2] e.g. Bonner & Robertson, *Bradlaugh*, ii. 214; *N.R.*, 9 Sept. 1883, p. 171.

first appeared at the House on 3 May, and he had consulted several colleagues. He had publicly announced his intention and had discussed the matter with the Speaker two days before[1]. Speaker Brand's decision to permit the interruption —his second fumble, according to Ensor—was therefore a premeditated one, although Brand, generally regarded as able though slow-witted, is unlikely to have foreseen all the consequences of his action.

Gladstone interposed with the hastily prepared counter-proposal that a second Select Committee be appointed to decide whether interference with any member taking the oath be permissible, and a long debate ensued. According to *Punch*,

> In this great battle Tories take the field,
> Echo the cry of 'Wolff', and scorn to yield![2]

The debate was adjourned over the weekend, and when it was resumed on Monday, 24 May, the House was packed with more members than had been present on any single occasion for several years. Lord Randolph Churchill, descending from the back benches to the front row below the gangway, was the first speaker. He was happy that enough time had elapsed to permit the gravity of the question to be appreciated not merely by the House 'but by the public out-of-doors'. This was not a question for a committee, but a question of principle, one to be decided by the 'unerring instinct of the House of Commons'. To allow Bradlaugh to take the oath was to acquiesce in his opinions; but the Liberal party had not been given a huge majority 'in order that the House of Commons might become a place where the solemn forms and practices of the Christian religion might be safely derided, and the existence of God publicly and with scorn denied'. Speaking with a half-restrained passion which commanded attention and evoked repeated cheers from the Conservative benches, Churchill began to read excerpts from Bradlaugh's *Impeachment of the House of Brunswick:* 'I loathe these small German breast-bestarred wanderers, whose only merit is their loving hatred of one another. In their own

[1] Henry Drummond Wolff, *Rambling Recollections* (London, 1908), ii. 254–5; *N.R.*, 16 May 1880, p. 305; Winston S. Churchill, *Lord Randolph Churchill* (London, 1906), i. 125–6.   [2] 22 May 1880, p. 232.

land they vegetate and wither unnoticed. Here we pay them highly to marry and perpetuate a pauper prince race. If they do nothing, they are good; if they do ill, loyalty gilds the vice till it looks like virtue.'

At this point Lord Randolph flung the offending paper to the floor and crushed it with his foot. Such passages showed, he went on indignantly, that Bradlaugh's ideas of loyalty were akin to his ideas of religion. If Bradlaugh took the oath, it would become 'an absolute impossibility that either loyalty or religion could occupy in the minds of Members of Parliament or of the English people the same lofty, unshaken, and unassailable position which they had occupied without interruption down to the present day'. Churchill felt sure that an overwhelming majority of the English people shared his views. In a dramatic conclusion he observed that no one in the House could regard Bradlaugh's opinions with greater aversion than the Prime Minister himself, the leader of a tremendous majority. 'Do not', he appealed to Gladstone, 'let it be in our power to say that the first use you made of that powerful weapon was to mark it with an indelible stain, and that the first time you led the Liberal Party through the Lobby in this new Parliament was for the purpose of placing on those benches opposite an avowed Atheist and a professedly disloyal person.'[1] The House went wild.

In years to come Churchill was to be credited with beginning the anti-Bradlaugh crusade, though he himself was quite willing to share the plaudits with Wolff. And in the summer of 1880, a Conservative journal like *The Saturday Review* was still able to note dispassionately that 'if Sir Drummond Wolff had been accidentally detained on his way to the House, no moral, religious or constitutional issue would have been raised'.[2]

Churchill's speech had another effect, however. It marked the beginning of the 'Fourth Party', a group of four dynamic Conservatives who considered the leadership of Sir Stafford Northcote unsuitable for the assault upon Gladstone's huge majority. The Irish Home-Rulers had already dubbed them-

---

[1] *Hansard*, cclii (1880), 334-9; Churchill, *Churchill*, i. 129; Harold E. Gorst, *The Fourth Party* (London, 1906), pp. 56-57.
[2] 26 June 1880, p. 807.

selves a third party, and it was an Irish M.P., Philip Callan, who in mock-seriousness first bestowed the title of Fourth Party upon the quartet of Lord Randolph Churchill, Sir Henry Drummond Wolff, Sir John Gorst, and Arthur James Balfour. All four sat on the front Opposition bench below the gangway, Lord Randolph occupying the corner seat traditionally associated with the most unsparing of Government critics.[1] In proportion to its numbers the Fourth Party was to prove—according to Sir Winston Churchill—'the most formidable and effective force for the purposes of Opposition in the history of the House of Commons'. By 1885 it was to catapult the little-known Lord Randolph into the position of being 'far and away the most popular Conservative in the House of Commons'.[2]

This was hardly the case at the beginning of 1880. Lord Randolph Churchill, born in 1849, was the third son of the seventh Duke of Marlborough and, after an uninspiring stay at Oxford, had in 1874 been elected M.P. for Woodstock. His election occasioned no surprise since, despite the Reform Acts of 1832 and 1867, Woodstock remained the pocket borough of the Duke of Marlborough. Churchill had participated little in the Parliament of 1874. Indeed, having in 1876 quarrelled violently with the Prince of Wales (the future King Edward VII) and having been consequently ostracized by London society, he was exiled by his father to Ireland, where the Duke was himself serving as Lord-Lieutenant and where Churchill became acquainted with Irish politics. As a reconciliation with the Prince of Wales did not take place until 1883, the snubs of high society may well have served to steer his interests toward politics.[3] Upon returning to London in 1880, Lord Randolph seemed, much like the

---

[1] Gorst, *Fourth Party*, p. 131; Churchill, *Churchill*, i. 131; T. P. O'Connor, *Memoirs of An Old Parliamentarian* (London, 1929), i. 62.

[2] Churchill, *Churchill*, i. 132; (Copy) Sir Michael Hicks-Beach to Salisbury, 10 June 1885, St. Aldwyn MSS., PCC/30.

[3] The cause was Churchill's public flaunting of letters linking Edward non-platonically with the Countess of Aylesford. Dilke MSS. (B.M.), 43925, fol. 52. This adds irony to Lord Randolph's defence of the royal family against Bradlaugh. When Queen Victoria received anonymous threats against her life by 'persons of rank' in 1881, she confided to the Home Secretary that she did not see who could be meant 'unless it was Lord Randolph Churchill'. Dilke MSS (B.M.), 43935, fol. 101.

young Disraeli, to be a clever young dandy with a contempt for incapacity, a turn for sarcasm, and a penchant for recklessness.[1]

Wolff, fifteen years older than Lord Randolph, was an experienced world traveller, minor diplomat, and inveterate story-teller. He, too, had first entered Parliament in 1874. 'Shrewd, suave, witty, and imperturbable' is Sir Winston Churchill's verdict.[2]

John Eldon Gorst, like Wolff in his middle forties, was an established lawyer and a Member of Parliament since 1866. He was more serious than either Churchill or Wolff and as aide to Disraeli had helped organize the successful Conservative electoral campaign of 1874. He felt himself ill-rewarded for these services and harboured a sense of grievance against the party leadership.[3]

The fourth member of the Fourth Party was A. J. Balfour, the nephew of Lord Salisbury and himself a future Prime Minister. He was a likeable but rather languid young man, reminiscent more of Melbourne than Disraeli. Although he sat with the other three, he exerted himself less energetically, and in the Bradlaugh Case he participated not at all. Apparently amused by it all, he looked upon the dispute more as a tempest in a teapot than as a major political issue.[4] The year before, he had published *A Defence of Philosophical Doubt*, which, though essentially a criticism of the philosophy of science rather than an attack on theology, nevertheless contained passages such as this: 'Should criticism succeed . . . in demonstrating an essential inconsistency between religious and scientific belief—then . . . Religion would at once be relegated to the class at present occupied by delusions and detected superstitions.'[5] The original title of the essay had been 'A Defence of Philosophic Scepticism', but Balfour had altered 'Scepticism' to 'Doubt' upon his uncle's advice, since

[1] See, for example, Lucy, *Two Parliaments*, ii. 47; T. P. O'Connor, *Memoirs*, i. 59, 64–65. Churchill was highly strung and a chain-smoker of cigarettes, a distinction he shared in that Parliament only with Labouchere.

[2] Churchill, *Churchill*, i. 132–3.

[3] Ibid., pp. 133–4; Gorst, *Fourth Party*, p. 22 and *passim*; Robert Rhodes James, *Lord Randolph Churchill* (London, 1959), p. 81.

[4] Churchill, *Churchill*, i. 134; Gorst, *Fourth Party*, p. 62.

[5] Arthur James Balfour, *A Defence of Philosophic Doubt* (London, 1879), 301.

the former word had a definite anti-religious connotation. 'It was well to be on the safe side', Balfour agreed, and as a result of his failure to take part in the Bradlaugh debates, few Liberals in later years found it worth while to counter-attack by bracketing Balfour's doubts with Bradlaugh's disbeliefs.[1]

Apart from a tendency toward 'Tory Democracy', the Fourth Party had no distinctive creed except that of criticizing the Liberal Government whenever possible. Each of the four supported his colleagues whenever they were attacked in debate. The Party could, indeed, never have achieved the publicity it did, had it not been for the positions occupied by William Ewart Gladstone and Sir Stafford Northcote. Gladstone completely dominated his Ministry and was by far the greatest parliamentarian of his age. He had one recurring weakness, however—he tended to treat the most trifling question or debating point by an Opposition speaker as a question of State, to be answered seriously, even solemnly, and in a high moral key. The Fourth Party took full advantage of this characteristic.

As for Sir Stafford Northcote, he had by 1880 a lengthy political career behind him. He had been co-author of the influential Northcote–Trevelyan Report of 1853, which provided the blueprint for the competitive civil service system; he had served as President of the Board of Trade, Secretary of State for India, and for six years as Chancellor of the Exchequer. Since 1876—when Disraeli moved to the House of Lords—Northcote had led the Conservative Party in the Commons. Northcote, though an able departmental head and a likeable man, was an uninspiring political leader. His manner of speaking was one of quiet exposition, and he invariably credited other men with having motives as sincere as his own. He rarely took a decision without first consulting his two front-bench colleagues, Sir Richard Cross and W. H. Smith, and when it came to a Parliamentary fight, he was, in A. J. Balfour's words, 'no more a match for Mr. Gladstone than a wooden three-decker would be for a Dreadnought'.[2]

---

[1] Arthur James Balfour, *Chapters of Autobiography*, ed. Mrs. Edgar Dugdale (London, 1930), pp. 63–64.

[2] Cited in Gorst, *Fourth Party*, p. 141. Disraeli is reported as confiding that he would never have retired from the Commons had he not regarded Gladstone's resignation of 1875 as final. Ibid., p. 4.

Northcote had been Gladstone's Private Secretary in the 1840's, and he always retained the almost reverent respect he had then formed for Gladstone's abilities. What was worse from a party point of view, Northcote's own political orthodoxy was suspect. Left to himself, suggested one observer in April 1880, Northcote 'would have governed England on principles not very different from those of moderate Liberalism'.[1] It is not surprising, therefore, that Bradlaugh's entry upon the scene failed to stir Northcote with indignation. 'Would it not be better', he reflected in his diary, 'to do away with the members' oath altogether and make the affirmation general?'[2]

Conservatives like Wolff had frequently been exasperated with Northcote in the days when the Conservatives were in the majority. Angered by the electoral defeat of April 1880, they found his calm willingness to agree to the first Select Committee on the Bradlaugh case—without attempting to make party capital on the issue—as merely a new sign of 'lamentable weakness'. There is evidence, indeed, that their opposition to the appointment of the first Committee was directed as much against Northcote as against Bradlaugh. 'It would teach Northcote not to be always jumping up and agreeing with the other side', opined Wolff.[3] Northcote met the problem in what was to be his usual manner; he did not deny having agreed to a Select Committee, but he failed to back it with his vote. He simply walked out of the House.[4]

When the issue arose whether Bradlaugh ought to be excluded altogether or whether a second Select Committee ought to be appointed, Northcote privately expressed his belief that the Conservatives could not refuse reference to a committee altogether. 'I think we must take care that we do not overshoot the mark', he wrote to Lord Beaconsfield, but he finally gave way to the more radical spirits in his party.

[1] J. Guinness Rogers, 'A Non-Conformist's View of the Election', *Nineteenth Century*, April 1880, p. 630.

[2] Andrew Lang, *Life, Letters, and Diaries of Sir Stafford Northcote* (Edinburgh and London, 1890), ii. 154.

[3] Wolff to Salisbury, 12 May 1880, Salisbury MSS.

[4] Lucy, *Two Parliaments*, pp. 8–9. Robert Rhodes James erroneously implies that Northcote voted against Wolff's motion. See James, *Churchill*, p. 77.

On at least two occasions, though, he repeated his practice of walking out of the House before a division, amidst 'ironical cheering' from the Liberal benches.[1]

Three other Conservatives were to play leading roles in the anti-Bradlaugh campaign: Sir Hardinge Giffard, who as Solicitor-General (1874–80) had battled against Bradlaugh in the law courts on the occasion of the appeal in the *Fruits of Philosophy* case; Edward Gibson, the representative of the University of Dublin (Trinity College) and ex-Attorney-General for Ireland; and Charles Newdigate Newdegate, a thin, tall man, invariably dressed completely in black, who ever since his arrival in Parliament in 1843 had led a one-man crusade against religious minorities: Jews, Catholics, and now Bradlaugh.[2]

What was Gladstone's reaction to all this? There is little doubt that, as a long-standing champion of religion, he found the defence of Bradlaugh's rights a most distasteful undertaking and that he detested Bradlaugh's opinions. Whether he detested the man himself, as Gladstone's most recent biographer asserts, is more debatable.[3] Perhaps he did in the summer of 1880, but not thereafter. What is certain is that he was surprised by the virulence of the Opposition. 'I confess', he wrote to the Speaker on 24 May 1880, 'that I had no idea before the discussion on Friday to what an extent there would be a disposition in the House to make capital out of Bradlaugh's loathsome & revolting opinions by a deviation from judicial impartiality.'[4] There lay the rub. At the very time that the Opposition speakers were buying up Bradlaugh pamphlets for use as debate ammunition and a few Liberals such as Bright were defending him as a martyr gone wrong, Gladstone was moving further and further above the battle. The very man who had less than a year before roused a nation by his intensive attacks upon a Conservative

---

[1] Northcote to Beaconsfield, 22 May 1880, Iddesleigh MSS. (B.M.), 50018, fol. 189. Lucy, *Two Parliaments*, p. 17.

[2] *Dictionary of National Biography*. For Giffard, see also A. Wilson Fox, *The Earl of Halsbury: Lord High Chancellor (1823–1921)* (London, 1929), pp. 109–10, inaccurate in detail; for Newdegate, see T. P. O'Connor, *Memoirs*, i. 70.

[3] Morley, *Gladstone* iii. 11; Magnus, *Gladstone*, p. 278.

[4] Gladstone to Brand, 24 May 1880, Hampden MSS.

Ministry on grounds of morality now claimed to stand above the battle as the advocate of 'the driest light of reason'. Gladstone fastidiously avoided any reference whatsoever to Bradlaugh's character or writings. 'I have felt it my duty on every occasion', he recalled two years later, 'to exclude, not only from my discourse, but from my mind, all reference to them, for fear I should be biased by one single hair's breadth from the strict path of justice.' It was no more his duty to denounce Bradlaugh's doctrines, he argued, than it would be the duty of a counsel defending an atheist for murder to stir up animosity by referring to his client's beliefs.[1]

Gladstone's underlying assumption was that the House of Commons had no jurisdiction over the matter. At the time that he first countered Wolff's motion by proposing the second Committee, Gladstone did indeed privately admit to Brand that it was 'difficult to deny very broadly the competence of the House'. A week later, however, having studied the relevant statutes and regulations, he came to the conclusion that it was indeed Bradlaugh's statutory duty to take the oath and that no one legally 'administered' it. The House of Commons, he concluded, lacked jurisdiction. No one could be a greater 'stickler' for legal distinctions than Gladstone, especially when they involved religious questions which Gladstone had over the years come to see as increasingly inappropriate for parliamentary discussion.[2]

An attitude of judicial impartiality, however reasonable, was difficult to dramatize, especially when the pressures upon Gladstone are considered. There was, for example, the Queen, writing almost daily to the Prime Minister, 'rejoicing in the feeling of indignation exhibited ag[ain]st such a man's sitting in the House', and warning Gladstone not to let it be supposed that the Government sympathized in any way with Bradlaugh's opinions.[3] This was still an age, it must be recalled, when according to the Liberal *Westminster Review*, 'no

---

[1] *Hansard*, ccliii (1880), 567; cclxvi (1882), 1321–2.

[2] Hampden MSS.; E. W. Hamilton to Ponsonby, 7 Dec. 1880; Ponsonby MSS. (B.M.), 45725, fol. 4. Gladstone's attitude to the Public Worship Bill of 1874 had been similar. *Hansard*, ccxx (1874), 1374–8.

[3] Guedalla, *Queen and Gladstone*, ii. 96–97. To say, as Guedalla does on p. 29, that the Queen and Gladstone were 'of one mind' on the matter is at best an oversimplification.

practical politician denies that the Sovereign has and ought to have considerable influence on the course of public affairs'.[1] Liberal back-benchers like Hussey Vivian, on the other hand, sought immediate legislation permitting Bradlaugh to affirm.

The Cabinet, to be sure, was at one with Gladstone on his course. It might have been wiser simply to oppose Wolff's resolution—rather than to suggest a counter-proposal—but once the Whips reported that the Government would lose such a vote, it is difficult to blame Gladstone for seeking to avoid defeat and taking what appeared the easier way out, the appointment of another committee. Garvin reports, to be sure, that Joseph Chamberlain urged the Cabinet in vain 'to wield its parliamentary majority', but he fails to specify the occasion. Indeed there is no evidence in the Chamberlain papers that he disagreed with his colleagues at the time.[2]

Despite the objections of Churchill and of one Conservative M.P., who cited Disraeli's opinion that 'a Committee of the House of Commons is an elaborate machinery to find out something which everybody knows', Gladstone managed by a vote of 289 to 214 to defeat Wolff's motion to bar Bradlaugh. A second Committee was approved instead, but only after its terms of reference had been broadened to include the fact that Bradlaugh had previously asked to affirm. The Committee was to inquire generally into the facts and circumstances under which Bradlaugh claimed to take the oath, to define the law applicable to such cases, and to advise the House as to its jurisdiction over the oath.[3]

The second Committee was to consist of twenty-three members—including all nineteen of the first Committee. Northcote, disliking further controversy on the issue, privately asked Gladstone whether they could 'not come to some

---

[1] April 1880, p. 492.

[2] J. L. Garvin, *The Life of Joseph Chamberlain*, i (London, 1932), 316; Joseph Chamberlain, *A Political Memoir, 1880–92*, ed. C. H. D. Howard (London, 1953), p. 5. In a letter to Gladstone on 25 June 1880, Chamberlain wrote: 'At present the government stands well in the matter.' G.P. (B.M.), 44125, fol. 33.

[3] *Hansard*, cclii (1880), 393, 416, 421; 'Second Committee Report', *Parliamentary Papers*, 1880, vol. xii, p. ii.

agreement outside the House, instead of fighting the names'.[1]
Lord Randolph Churchill had other ideas, however, and
publicly criticized the list. Thirteen of the twenty-three were
lawyers, he complained. Apparently, retorted Gladstone,
'the noble Lord thinks the lawyers are less likely to go right
on this question than other men'.[2] Churchill complained
further that there were but two Nonconformists on the Committee and only one Catholic. 'The Roman Catholic population and clergy of Ireland', he reported, 'have the strongest
possible feeling on this question.' Churchill's attempt to
enlarge the Committee by four men of his own choosing
was, however, decisively rejected.[3]

The Committee, which comprised eleven Liberals, eleven
Conservatives, and one Irish Nationalist (and thus failed to
reflect the Liberal majority in the House),[4] contained a large
number of distinguished men. Among the Conservatives
were three members of the outgoing Ministry, Holker, Cross,
and Gibson, and among the Liberals, two Cabinet members,
Bright and Childers (the Secretary for War), as well as three
other members of the Ministry, Sir Henry James, Sir Farrer
Herschell, and George Otto Trevelyan.

If his early weeks in Parliament had brought unexpected
difficulties for Bradlaugh, then he could solace himself with
the realization that no other newly-elected member had
become front-page news so soon.

[1] Northcote to Gladstone, G.P. (B.M.), 44217, fol. 187. The letter is
misdated in G.P. as 26 Apr. 1881. The probable date is 26 May 1880.

[2] *Hansard*, cclii (1880), 653.

[3] Ibid., cols. 648, 876.

[4] Gladstone's Cabinet Minutes of the time indicate that, as a result of the
First Committee's decision, he had become dubious about the tradition that
the majority party had a mere majority of one on Select Committees, no
matter what its actual majority in the House of Commons. If the Committee
membership reflected that of the House, he calculated, 'Liberals and Home
Rulers should outnumber Tories by at least 9 to 6'. G.P. (B.M.), 44642,
fol. 20. The matter was discussed at the Cabinet of 20 May 1880, but no
immediate changes resulted.

VI

BRADLAUGH AS VILLAIN

In order to appreciate fully the impact of the Bradlaugh case upon the House of Commons and the public at large in the spring of 1880, we must first look at the prevailing picture of the man and the issue. For most M.P.s the key issue involved not constitutional technicalities but Bradlaugh's character. A composite portrait assembled from the attacks of his parliamentary critics will make this evident.

First of all there was Bradlaugh the atheist. The essential question for many of Bradlaugh's opponents was simply this: was an acknowledged atheist to be admitted into Parliament? 'No one has ever yet attempted to come into the House as a professed Atheist',[1] observed one Conservative, William Grantham, and he was doubtless correct. Bradlaugh might well retort that he was not entering the House in a religious (or non-religious) capacity, and that any official notice which the House had of his theological beliefs had been the result, not of his professions, but of conclusions drawn from answers to questions asked him by the Clerk of the House. Such an explanation no more satisfied his critics, however, than did the admission by Arthur O'Connor, an Irish Home-Ruler, that a House whose membership rolls had included David Hume and John Stuart Mill had nothing to fear from Bradlaugh.[2] Neither Hume nor Mill, after all, had derived their fame from their unbelief as had Bradlaugh.

Not only was Bradlaugh an atheist; he was a man who deliberately 'intends to take God's name in vain'.[3] Hence Earl Percy derided as hypocrisy all of Bradlaugh's assurances that he would regard the oath as a most solemn promise. Bradlaugh, Edward Gibson was sure, had 'deliberately

---

[1] *Hansard*, ccliii (1880), 490. For purposes of clarity and consistency, quoted selections from certain speeches reported by *Hansard* in the past tense have been restored to the present tense.

[2] Ibid. col. 482. [3] Ibid. cclii (1880), 208.

elected to obtrude himself on the House and the country'. He had done so, according to J. G. Hubbard, 'out of simple vanity, and for the purpose of advertising himself and his detestable doctrines'.[1]

Moreover, there were 'the honour . . . and the moral sense of Parliament to be considered', for Bradlaugh was propagating infidelity not on an East End street corner but in the House of Commons itself. To admit an avowed atheist on terms of equality with the other members would lead the English people to doubt if their representatives believed in a deity at all.[2] Any comparisons made between Bradlaugh's case and that of religious minorities previously admitted to the fellowship were deemed insulting to Catholics, Jews, and Nonconformists alike. 'All those sects', noted Sir Henry Drummond Wolff, 'have a common standard of morality, a conscience, and a general belief in some divinity or other.'[3] It was consequently appropriate, maintained a fellow Conservative, that the question be dealt with 'by the religious instinct which Jew and Christian alike possess'.[4] Many an opponent of Bradlaugh thus emphasized that the vital distinction was one of theism, and that Bradlaugh did not meet that test. No M.P. was more insistent on this point than Dr. Robert Dyer Lyons, an Irish Liberal, who concluded a lengthy address with these stirring phrases:

This country has been great under Plantagenet and Catholic sovereigns, it has been great under Protestant Sovereigns, from the days of the Imperial Elizabeth, and it is great under the milder sway of Victoria when every religious denomination is recognized; but woe betide the day when the ship of State should be left to go on the waste of waters with her bulwarks of religion and morality stove in, and left a prey to all the immoralities and godlessness which will be sure to prevail among a community represented by men who have no belief in God.[5]

Radicalism in religion was easily equated with radicalism in politics. 'Admit the Atheist, and you will have, in course of time, Atheistical legislation', warned P. J. Smyth. 'Thus

---

[1] *Hansard*, cclii (1880), 197–8, 373.   [2] Ibid. ccliii (1880), 479, 561.
[3] Ibid. cclii (1880), 191.   [4] Ibid., col. 374.
[5] Ibid., col. 364.

came the excesses of the French Revolution, the seeds of which were sown . . . by the speculations of English philosophers.'[1] Atheism, according to Charles Newdegate, was 'no passive principle'. It had swept Louis-Philippe from the throne of France in 1848 and had brought on the Paris Commune in 1871. Did law-abiding Englishmen wish to follow such examples?[2] The question was not one of mere atheism but of 'Atheism in its most revolting form. . . . Nowhere can there be found a more offensive representation of Atheism than Mr. Bradlaugh.' He was 'the Cerberus of Atheism, treason, and filth'.[3]

Here we move on to the second aspect of Bradlaugh's villainy, his republicanism. It was not stressed as much as his atheism, though Churchill's use of *The Impeachment of the House of Brunswick* has been noted above, and at least one other critic made much of the idea that Bradlaugh 'would be willing to overthrow the Throne and the Constitution . . .'.[4] Queen Victoria herself was most upset by this facet of Bradlaugh's personality, and she pictured the man as 'the most heavy desperate sort of character'. Earlier that year she had, after all, expressed her strong opposition to Cabinet office for Sir Charles Dilke, the most respected of the leaders of the republican movement of the late 1860's and early 1870's. Yet, invective aside, all that Bradlaugh had stated in his republican pamphlets, observed one Liberal, George Otto Trevelyan, was that Parliament had the power to alter the succession to the Throne, and that had long been an accepted constitutional principle.[5]

Bradlaugh's views on the subject of birth control were more abhorrent than his republican leanings, and probably caused more genuine outrage than did his theological unbelief. It was, to be sure, difficult to make Bradlaugh's Neo-Malthusianism seem relevant to the question of the oath, but once the subject had been raised, there were few limits to the venom of Bradlaugh's critics. Bradlaugh was termed a 'moral monster'. If Liberals would but read *The Fruits of Philosophy*, warned Sir Henry Tyler, their cheers

[1] Ibid. ccliii (1880), 1289.   [2] Ibid., col. 559.
[3] Ibid., col. 1318; cclii (1880), 365.   [4] Ibid. ccliii (1880), 300.
[5] Guedalla, *Queen and Gladstone*, ii. 105; *Hansard*, cclii (1880), 381.

would turn into 'shudders of abhorrence'. Bradlaugh was a man, added Tyler, 'whose livelihood, whose profession for a series of years, has been to disseminate cheap and pernicious literature among the mass of the people'. He 'had poisoned and was poisoning the souls of millions of his fellow creatures'.[1] Indeed, concurred Dr. Lyons, the doctrines advanced by Bradlaugh injured not merely those now living, 'but on the authority of physiologists, they are likely to lead to a deteriorated population . . . a diseased population'.[2] It was charges such as this which caused one Conservative to urge privately that Bradlaugh ought to be flogged in Trafalgar Square.[3]

The charge of corrupting public morals was one that even the most courageous Liberal hesitated to answer on Bradlaugh's behalf. Yet Bradlaugh did have some defenders. Despite the fear of guilt by association—or, as the *Westminster Review* put it, despite the fact that 'throughout the debates on this question there has been a want of clearness in distinguishing between complicity with a man's views and maintenance of his rights'[4]—there were some Liberals who dared say a good word for Bradlaugh's character as well as for his rights. Ordinarily they prefaced their comments with an expression of regret for Bradlaugh's beliefs. As the Attorney-General put it, 'to every educated man, there can be no spectacle more painful than to see a person of undoubted talents at war with society, and rendered less useful by the avowal of opinions which are altogether out of harmony with those of the majority of his countrymen'.[5]

Of the leading Liberals only John Bright forthrightly commended Bradlaugh's character. These were Indian summer days for the hero of 1846 and 1867, whose post as Chancellor of the Duchy of Lancaster held little practical significance. But Bright's support was important, because, as Gladstone's secretary observed in another connexion, his name was 'a household word among numbers of electors who hardly know Lords Granville & Hartington, and in whom

[1] *Hansard*, ccliii (1880), 592; cclii (1880), 367–9.
[2] Ibid. cclii (1880), 362.
[3] Lord Norton, cited by Bradlaugh in *N.R.*, 4 July 1880, p. 45.
[4] *Westminster Review*, October 1880, p. 337.
[5] *Hansard*, cclii (1880), 372.

these statesmen at any rate fail to elicit enthusiasm'.[1] Bright was specific: 'I pretend to have no conscience or no honour superior to the conscience and honour of Mr. Bradlaugh.'[2] Bright was joined by a few Liberal back-benchers such as Charles Henry Hopwood, who, still regretful that his vote on the first Select Committee had been so injurious to Bradlaugh's cause, assured his fellow members 'I cannot conceive that he might be otherwise than an ornament to the House'.[3] Such tributes remained rare, however, and if, as a leading Nonconformist layman estimated, at least fifty M.P.s shared Bradlaugh's views on the existence of God, they all kept discreetly silent on the matter.[4]

It is small wonder that in the pages of Bradlaugh's *National Reformer* John Bright was virtually idolized during May and June of 1880.[5] It was in the *National Reformer*, too, that Bradlaugh was able to allay some of the frustration built up by hearing his character assailed day after day without chance of reply. Thus Lord Randolph Churchill was characterized as 'the rowdy and drunken nobleman, whose adventures led him to the Oxford Police Court' in 1870, a reference to Lord Randolph's undergraduate days. F. H. O'Donnell was described as an adventurer who had changed his name from Francis MacDonald in order to acquire an historic coat of arms and impress his Irish constituents.[6]

Bradlaugh was most vindictive when assailing Jews who opposed his admission to the House of Commons. He noted, for example, that Sir Henry Drummond Wolff's father had been a German Jew who joined the Anglican Church; 'comparing his birth and his conduct, he appears to be a hybrid rather than highbred'. Bradlaugh was yet more derisive about Baron de Worms, a Jewish Conservative. 'Go to your Ghetto, Baron H. de Worms', he advised. 'The dust of the great ones of your grand old Hebrew race would almost be indignantly stirred in their graves by the bigot-breath of your maiden House of Commons speech, Baron H. de

---

[1] Hamilton Diary (B.M.), 48632, p. 181.

[2] *Hansard*, ccliii (1880), 500.   [3] Ibid., col. 481.

[4] The estimate, made by Samuel Morley, is cited by T. Gasquoine, *In Memoriam: Charles Bradlaugh* (*A Sermon*) (Northampton, 1891), p. 7.

[5] e.g. 20 May 1880, p. 343.

[6] *N.R.*, 4 July 1880, p. 43; 6 June 1880, p. 371.

Worms; your place is not in a free assembly of true Britons.'[1] Bradlaugh could be a match for his opponents in invective as well as in legal learning.

Bradlaugh became not only the most notorious Member of Parliament in the spring of 1880 but also the major topic of conversation—in the streets and in the homes, in private clubs and in public houses. 'The home and foreign policy of the Government, the rendering of justice to Ireland, and solution of the Eastern question,' commented one journal, 'all seem to fade into insignificance at present in front of the problem whether or not Mr. Bradlaugh is to be admitted . . . in[to] the House.'[2] Early in May there had been, to be sure, another controversial issue mingling religion with politics, Gladstone's appointment of a Catholic, Lord Ripon, as Viceroy of India. The *Glasgow News*, the Scottish Reformation Society, and other journals and organizations had protested vigorously to the Prime Minister, citing his own writings of less than a decade before, which had cast doubt upon the political loyalty of Catholics; but Gladstone stood fast and by the end of the month the grumbling had died down.[3]

With Bradlaugh, the situation was the reverse. The more the matter was discussed the greater was the protest. The case broke upon a reading public already accustomed to magazine articles dealing with the threat of unbelief. Scarcely an issue of the *Nineteenth Century*, for example, went by without one article touching that subject.[4] A majority of such articles dealt with agnosticism, but Bradlaugh was a self-confessed atheist. And atheism, as the Conservative *Saturday Review* discovered—almost to its surprise—seemed to excite a feeling of horror which agnosticism did not, even though 'in nine cases out of ten Agnosticism is but old Atheism "writ large"'.[5] For most people atheism connoted not mere

[1] *N.R.*, 6 June 1880, pp. 378, 374.

[2] *Freeman's Journal*, (Dublin), 23 May 1880, p. 6.

[3] The *Glasgow News*, 25 May 1880, asserted that Ripon would 'rule India as the Pope's rather than as the Queen's Viceroy'. Even Bradlaugh was deemed preferable to Ripon. See also G.P. (B.M.), 44464, fol. 109 and fol. 3, a letter of praise by a Catholic layman. Cf. *Tablet*, 22 May 1880, p. 641.

[4] See, for example, Bertha Lathbury, 'Agnosticism and Women', April 1880, and W. H. Mallock [a prolific religious propagandist], 'Atheism and the Rights of Man', May 1880.   [5] 26 June 1880, p. 817.

unbelief but immorality as well. And for most people, the Bradlaugh case was not 'a legal puzzle to be solved by the ingenuity of lawyers',[1] but the problem of whether or not a man with Bradlaugh's views should be tolerated in the House of Commons.

Among religious bodies one can discern almost from the beginning the positions which were to be taken up more formally during the years that followed. The Church of England and the Roman Catholics were to be predominantly opposed to Bradlaugh's admission. The Methodists (or Wesleyans) and Scottish Presbyterians were to be seriously split, though tending to oppose Bradlaugh's acceptance. The Baptists and Congregationalists, together with such numerically minor groups as the Quakers, Unitarians, and Jews, were predominantly to favour Bradlaugh's admission. A few exceptions can be cited, however, for every group mentioned.

A typical Church of England reaction may be found in a long letter to Gladstone by an Anglican vicar. 'I am one of hundreds of Clergy, who, with feelings of deepest admiration and gratitude, follow you as their trusted leader in political matters, and look up to you as a model example of a pure and noble life. I have never made any secret of this with my Congregation.' And yet, he went on, he was deeply distressed by Gladstone's role in the Bradlaugh case. Why could not Gladstone publicly proclaim the detestation he must feel for Bradlaugh's views, for 'is it not preeminently first a religious question and then second a legal one'? He personally would far sooner see Parliament transgress against human law than give any support whatsoever to a man who held the Saviour to be an impostor. To ask God's blessing upon a Parliament containing such a man bordered on profanity.[2]

Though such a reaction was far from unique, the Churches took no formal notice of the matter at this time, except for one Methodist petition against Bradlaugh's swearing the 'awful name' of God. However, speeches and sermons dealing with Bradlaugh and with excerpts from his writing became commonplace. It was frequently observed that Christianity was still 'part and parcel of the law of England'.

[1] *Tablet*, 26 June 1880, p. 806.   [2] G.P. (B.M.), 44465, fols. 73–77.

(One Lord Chancellor, the *Westminster Review* recalled, had observed that while this might well be true, he for one did not know how to frame an indictment against a man for not loving his neighbour as himself.[1]) There were the beginnings of petition campaigns, but the particular issue changed so rapidly that spring that only some 318 petitions with 41,689 signatures hostile to Bradlaugh were sent to Parliament.[2] One open letter calling for 'The Disfranchisement of Northampton, a National and Just Duty!' was sent to every M.P., and thousands of little cards were distributed gratis in the streets with these immortal lines imprinted:

> Who dares uphold an Atheist!
>   In our good Christian land?
> Shall he who says 'there is no God'
>   Be shaken by the hand
> In our Senate and our homes
>   And be treated as a friend?
> Woe to the Christian nation!
>   Woe to our Kith and Kin!
> Woe to a Christian Government!
>   Woe to a Christian Queen!
> Woe to a Christian Parliament
>   Which 'an Atheist' sits in!
> Scorn such—shun such—friend Working Man,
>   He brings no joy to thee—
> No love, no peace, no happiness—
>   His Gift is Misery![3]

Throughout the battle Bradlaugh was to retain the allegiance—not to his principles, to be sure, but to his right to sit in Parliament—of the great majority of Nonconformist bodies. His initial decision to affirm had been hailed by Liberal Nonconformists as an issue of conscience. The Northampton *Mercury*, a moderate Liberal paper which had steadfastly opposed Bradlaugh until his election-eve alliance with Labouchere, praised him warmly for taking a step

[1] 'The Parliamentary Oath Question: Mr. Bradlaugh's Case', *Westminster Review*, October 1880, p. 346.

[2] *Report of Select Committee on Public Petitions*, 1880. 522 petitions with 45,356 signatures were sent supporting Bradlaugh's admission.

[3] Cited in *N.R.*, 20 June 1880, p. 427. The author is one Tracy Turnerelli who proclaimed himself 'Founder and Organising Secretary of the National Anti-Atheist Association' (*N.R.*, 5 Nov. 1882, p. 308).

'which will, in the long run, commend itself to the judgment and conscience of religious men'. It was 'a real service to religion . . .'.[1]

Once the first Committee had decided he could not affirm, Bradlaugh seriously compromised his position with the Nonconformists by announcing he would take the oath. Many a Liberal Nonconformist echoed *The Times* in deploring his 'want of consistency'. If Bradlaugh had no objection to taking the oath, why had he raised the question in the first place?[2] Why could he not have acted as did the atheist 'hedging for eternity' once referred to by Cardinal Newman: 'Oh, God, if there be a God, save my soul, if I have a soul.'[3] Bradlaugh's reversal, pontificated the Roman Catholic *Tablet*, surely did not 'speak well for the ethics of Atheism'.[4] Perhaps the blow which hurt Bradlaugh most was the public opposition of George Jacob Holyoake, a man whose reputation was second only to Bradlaugh's among the English Secularists at the time. 'I should like to assure you', he wrote to Gladstone, 'that I & a considerable number I represent on the side of Secular thought would not, if we were in Mr. Bradlaugh's place, have proposed to take the oath, nor have assumed that the House of Commons could sanction that.'[5] In vain did Bradlaugh argue that he was not in the place of O'Connell, or Pease, or Rothschild; he did not have religious scruples against particular words or phrases. For him it had first been a matter of preference and then a matter of not letting mere words stand in the way of service in Parliament. Somehow this position, though not as illogical as some of his friendly critics made out, did not seem to represent a single clear-cut dramatic principle. Nonconformists could easily agree that it might be desirable to eliminate oaths altogether, but to launch a drive to give an atheist the right to swear was a less appealing prospect.

In his own National Secular Society, to be sure, Bradlaugh had an effective political force which had no doubts whatsoever about its leader's consistency. A League for the Defence

---

[1] Northampton *Mercury*, 8 May 1880, p. 5.
[2] Rev. Charles Williams cited in *N.R.*, 27 June 1880, p. 10; *The Times*, 22 May 1880, p. 12.
[3] Cited in *Westminster Review*, October 1880, p. 340.
[4] 29 May 1880, p. 678.   [5] 30 June 1880, G.P. (B.M.), 44465, fol. 40.

of Constitutional Rights was organized to begin a petition campaign. Bradlaugh held a large meeting in Trafalgar Square and smaller ones elsewhere, and started a 'Fund to Fight the Bigots'.[1] Some of his supporters indeed did not limit themselves to sending the 'temperate' petitions he urged but mailed threatening letters to Opposition M.P.s![2] His Northampton supporters seemed loyal as well:

> Shall victory for which you've fought
> And which twelve years' hard work have brought
> Be wrung from you and set at nought?
> We look to you, Northampton!

Most Northamptonites took the tumult occasioned by their new M.P. in their stride.[3]

[1] N.R., 4 July 1880, pp. 49–50.   [2] Freeman's Journal, 26 May 1880, p. 5.
[3] N.R., 11 July 1880, p. 62.

VII

THE PAST AS A GUIDE

W HILE most M.P.s and the public at large saw Bradlaugh's beliefs and character as the crux of 'the Bradlaugh Case', the second Select Committee on the Parliamentary Oath had been specifically appointed to decide the legal issue. Unlike the first Committee, it held lengthy hearings and explored in detail the historical background of the Parliamentary Oath. This oath, though analogous to medieval oaths of fealty, was essentially a product of the English Reformation. No specific oath for Members of Parliament had been required before 1563, when under Queen Elizabeth I a revised Oath of Supremacy was extended to include not merely ecclesiastical and secular officials but all persons in Holy Orders, all university graduates, lawyers, and school-masters, and all future members of the House of Commons. This act, like the original Oath of Supremacy instituted by Henry VIII in 1534, was essentially a political weapon against Roman Catholics. The House of Lords was at the time—and, indeed, until 1678—exempt since, according to the statute, 'the Queen's Majesty is otherwise sufficiently assured of their faith and loyalty'.[1]

As a result of the Gunpowder Plot of 1605, each prospective member of the House of Commons was required to take an additional Oath of Allegiance and Abjuration by which he swore not merely that he recognized the reigning monarch as supreme political and spiritual governor of the realm but that he specifically abjured the authority of the Pope, 'upon the true faith of a Christian', and that he did from his heart 'abhor, detest, and abjure, as impious and heretical, the damnable doctrine and position that princes which may be excommunicated or deprived by the Pope may be deposed

---

[1] J. E. Neale, *Elizabeth I and Her Parliaments, 1559–1581* (London, 1953), pp. 116–17. Also, E. and A. G. Porritt, *The Unreformed House of Commons* (Cambridge, 1903), i. 128–9.

or murdered by their subjects, or any other whatsoever'. Both oaths had to be taken twice, once outside the House before the Lord Steward (the representative of the monarch) and then inside the House at the Speaker's Table. An additional religious test—which hampered though never effectively barred Dissenters from sitting in the House of Commons—was the requirement instituted in 1614 according to which each new member had to take communion at an Anglican church. This requirement was to be enforced with varying degrees of severity throughout the century.[1] As a by-product of the Titus Oates affair, a third oath was added in 1678 in which the prospective member specifically rejected the doctrine of transubstantiation, invocation of saints, and the sacrifice of the mass; all three oaths, moreover, were extended to the House of Lords. No Roman Catholic sat in either House between 1678 and 1829, though the Catholic Dukes of Norfolk continued to exert considerable electoral influence.[2]

The first simplification in this increasingly complicated ritual came with the Revolution of 1689, when the old oaths of Supremacy and Allegiance were considerably shortened. As a result, however, of the ostentatious recognition of the Stuart Pretender by Louis XIV in 1701, a fourth oath was added abjuring the Pretender's title. This was indeed the longest oath of all. Finally, an act of 1714 provided a penalty of £500 per vote for anyone voting in Parliament without having taken the proper oaths; anyone found guilty was also prohibited from suing in court, receiving a legacy, holding office, or voting in Parliamentary elections.[3]

As a result of this accumulation of oaths—each directed against a specific political danger rather than against speculative theological opinions—Quakers, Roman Catholics, and Jews found themselves at the beginning of the nineteenth century effectively barred from seats in Parliament.

Quakers, whose religious tenets forbade them from swearing, had indeed been given the right to substitute affirmations

[1] Porritt, i. 130–4. See also 'The Evolution of the Parliamentary Oath', in Michael MacDonagh, *Parliament: Its Romance, Its Comedy, Its Pathos* (London, 1902), pp. 180–4.   [2] MacDonagh, pp. 185–8; Porritt, pp. 138–9.
[3] Ibid.; see also 'The Oath of Allegiance', in Frederick Pollock, *Essays in Jurisprudence and Ethics* (London, 1882), p. 193.

for most required oaths by an act of 1696 which was periodically renewed and finally made permanent during the reign of George II, at which time a similar privilege was extended to Moravians. The provisions of the act were not, however, applied to the Parliamentary oath, and John Archdale, a Quaker elected to the House of Commons of 1699, was consequently unable to take his seat, since he was denied the affirmation and refused to take the oath. Not until 1833 did another Quaker, Joseph Pease, claim to affirm. A Select Committee was then appointed to explore the issue and it decided that the relevant acts applied to the House of Commons after all; the House accepted the decision and Pease took his seat.[1]

The return of Roman Catholics to Parliament came in 1829, when after thirty years of agitation a Catholic Relief Bill was enacted. Daniel O'Connell had led the movement in its later years, and the statute was the indirect outcome of his election for an Irish constituency in 1828. The new oath continued the abjuration of the civil authority of the Pope but dispensed with the declarations against all other Catholic practices. O'Connell was not, however, the first Catholic to benefit from its provisions; the Earl of Surrey (son of the Duke of Norfolk) had that distinction. Despite a dramatic speech by 'the great Liberator' at the bar of the House of Commons, the House refused to grant O'Connell the right to make use of the new measure because he had been elected before its enactment. He was therefore asked to take the usual three oaths, including the Oath of Supremacy. Declaring that the oath 'contained one proposition which he knew to be false, and another proposition which he believed to be untrue', O'Connell refused. Ultimately the dispute over O'Connell proved to be no more than a 'minor piece of spite', since O'Connell was re-elected and the House then permitted him to take the new oath without further ado.[2]

The Oath of Allegiance of 1610, which had introduced the

---

[1] Porritt, i. 136–7. See also Appendix to Report of Second Select Committee, *Parl. Papers*, xii (1880), 27, 30.

[2] Report of Second Select Committee, p. 29; Porritt, i. 138–40. See also E. L. Woodward, *The Age of Reform, 1815–1870* (Oxford, 1938), p. 329.

words 'on the true faith of a Christian', had thus excluded Jews from Parliament. This was, to be sure, a wholly incidental result, since Jews were in any case banned from England at the time. During the century after Cromwell permitted them to return, their naturalization was legally impossible, and popular hostility forced Parliament to repeal the Jewish Relief act of 1753 within a year of its enactment. Even that Act had carried the proviso that the naturalization certificate of every Jew was to have written across its face the statement that the holder was ineligible to be a member of Parliament.

Although by 1830 numerous Englishmen had come to question the justice of excluding Jews from Parliament, the matter came to a head only in 1847 with the election of Baron Lionel Nathan de Rothschild, who claimed to take the oath on the Old Testament rather than the New—the form he declared to be 'most binding on his conscience'—and to omit the words 'on the true faith of a Christian'. The House permitted the first but refused the second; a Jewish Relief Bill introduced soon thereafter by Lord John Russell was repeatedly passed by the House of Commons and blocked in the House of Lords. Baron Rothschild was content to wait, year after year, sitting in the Chamber in a section technically outside it and without the right to speak or vote. Alderman David Salomons, elected in 1851, was less disposed to be patient, and on one occasion, having taken the oath without the words 'on the true faith of a Christian', he insisted on sitting within the House. The Speaker finally forced him to withdraw, and a resolution was passed excluding him from the House until the complete oath had been taken. Salomons was sued for having sat without taking the appropriate oaths, and in the case of *Miller* v. *Salomons* he tried to prove that the offending phrase was not a material part of the oath. The judicial decision, with one dissenting voice, went against him. He retired from Parliament for the time being and was chosen Lord Mayor of London in 1855.

In 1858 the House of Lords at long last consented to a compromise by which either House might by sessional order dispense with the words 'on the true faith of a Christian' for persons professing the Jewish religion, and both

THE PAST AS A GUIDE

Rothschild and Salomons were admitted. The sessional order was made a standing order in 1860.[1]

Finally, all previous oaths were swept away by an act of 1866 introduced by Sir George Gray and replaced by a single oath applicable to all members which—as amended two years later—read: 'I, A. B., do swear that I will be faithful and bear true allegiance to Her Majesty Queen Victoria, her heirs and successors according to law. So help me God.' This is the oath which, with the name of the reigning monarch necessarily substituted, is still taken today.[2] The act of 1866 also provided for the substitution of affirmations by Quakers, Moravians, Separatists, 'and every other person for the time being by law permitted to make a solemn affirmation or declaration'—a phrase which, as we have seen, had proved tantalizingly imprecise. Sir George Gray, it is true, believed that he had solved the oath question for all time to come, since in his introductory speech he had declared: 'Let no man be asked any question as to his religion, but let him take his seat in the House, if qualified to sit there, on taking the Oath of Allegiance as a loyal subject of the Crown.'[3]

The incidents mentioned above were not the only possible precedents for the question the Committee had to answer. Sir Erskine May had made a thorough search in the Commons Journals for every occasion on which a member had been mentioned because of a refusal or inability to take the appropriate oaths. Bradlaugh, to be sure, discovered at least one incident which even May had overlooked, that involving Attorney-General Sir Francis Bacon, whose oath in 1607 to the effect that he was duly qualified to sit had been questioned on the basis of a medieval law barring practising barristers as Knights of the Shire. On that occasion the House decided: 'Their Oath their own conscience to look into, not we to examine it.' Bradlaugh also—and not for the last time—pointed to the relevance of the case of John Wilkes, the only member ever to have been excluded specifically for his opinions. 'The House has solemnly decided', recalled

---

[1] Report of Second Select Committee, pp. 30–33; Porritt, i. 140–4; MacDonagh, pp. 197–201; Pollock, pp. 193–5.

[2] Pollock observes that the brief oath of 1868 was remarkably similar to many medieval oaths of fealty, both in form and in length.

[3] Cited in the report of Second Select Committee, p. xiii.

Bradlaugh, 'that it did wrong there, and I submit that it ought not do it again.'[1]

The Committee came to the inevitable conclusion that no precise precedent for the Bradlaugh case existed. There were three types of precedents: (1) members who refused to take an oath, (2) claims to make an affirmation instead of taking an oath, and (3) claims to omit a portion of the oath. Bradlaugh did not seem to fall into any of the three categories.

Committee Room Number 13 was crowded as the hearings went on, and not only Sir Erskine May but Bradlaugh himself was questioned at length. The spectator area was packed to overflowing, and the space reserved for other M.P.s who wished to look on was always filled. On one occasion, indeed, an official whose duty it was to be inside the room found it literally impossible to open the door.[2]

Bradlaugh, speaking deferentially but forthrightly, explained his position at length. He assured the Committee repeatedly that 'the essential part of the oath is in the fullest and most complete degree binding upon my honour and conscience, and the repeating of the words of asseveration [i.e. 'So help me God'] does not in the slightest degree weaken the binding effect of the Oath of Allegiance upon me. . . . I would go through no form, I would take no oath, unless I meant it to be so binding.'[3] It was only when the Committee members asked him to distinguish between oaths and mere promises that Bradlaugh became reticent:

[Question Number] 115. Then what greater weight do you attach to a promise made under statutory obligation than to an ordinary promise?—I would prefer not to make any promise that I did not intend to keep; but the law has attached a weight to statutory promises, and a penalty and disgrace on the breaking of them.

116. That is a consequence resulting from human action; you do not attribute any other weight to such a promise beyond what results from such penalties?—I object to that question. . . .

179. In taking such an oath, do you consider yourself as appealing to some Supreme Being as a witness [that] you are speaking the truth?—I submit that having said that I regard the oath as

---

[1] Report of Second Select Committee, pp. 34, 11.
[2] N.R., 6 June 1880, p. 399; *Freeman's Journal* (Dublin), 3 June 1880, p. 5.
[3] Report of Second Select Committee, pp. 9–10.

binding upon my conscience, this Committee has neither the right nor the duty to further interrogate my conscience.[1]

Bradlaugh objected also to the introduction of the letter of 20 May, but once the Committee had formally deemed its inclusion desirable, he did not protest further. He merely requested that the letter be read as a whole, and he reminded the Committee that, according to at least one legal decision, the words 'So help me God' did not form an 'essential' part of the oath.

The impression Bradlaugh made upon the Committee was on the whole a favourable one. A man who had scores of legal decisions at his finger tips could hardly be dismissed as a mere street-corner demagogue. John Bright, for one, concluded that Bradlaugh 'showed much knowledge of the question and great skill in conducting his case'.[2]

The Committee came to the justifiable conclusion that while there was 'no precedent of any member coming to the Table to take and subscribe the Oath, who has not been allowed to do so', neither—it added by a vote of 11 to 10— was there a precedent 'of any Member coming to the Table and intimating expressly, or by necessary implication, that an oath would not, as an oath, be binding on his conscience'. The report was discussed and voted on paragraph by paragraph, and a good deal of party line crossing went on. It was Holker, Disraeli's former Attorney-General, who advocated Gladstone's thesis that the House lacked jurisdiction, but he was supported in this contention by only three Liberals and Major Nolan, the Home Ruler; sixteen members disagreed. Sir Henry James readily conceded the jurisdiction of the House and its right to pass a resolution stopping Bradlaugh from swearing; yet he did not wish the Committee to suggest such a course. By another vote of 11 to 10, the Committee decided, however, to recommend specifically that Bradlaugh be prohibited from going through the form of taking the oath.

Aware that such a step would bar Bradlaugh altogether from taking his seat, the Liberals on the Committee suggested that Bradlaugh be permitted to affirm after all, subject to any

[1] Ibid., pp. 16, 20.
[2] *The Diaries of John Bright*, ed. R. A. J. Walling (New York, 1931), p. 442.

penalties according to statute. The proposal was carried
12–9 along straight party lines, Nolan again voting with the
Liberals.[1] The second Committee, whose report was published on 16 June, had thus, in effect, reversed the decision
of the first Committee, and the situation was left in a greater
muddle than ever.

> Says one committee
> To affirm he is free:
> Says the other, He *must* take the oath,
> One says *non*, one says *oui*,
> Which is right, O B. P.?
> Is it either—or neither—or both?[2]

---

[1] Report of the Second Select Committee, pp. 10, iii–xviii.
[2] *Referee*, 20 June 1880. B. P. stands for 'British Parliament'.

VIII

THE ROAD TO THE CLOCK TOWER

EVEN before the second Committee had formally presented its report to the House of Commons, Henry Labouchere announced his intention to introduce a resolution that Bradlaugh 'be admitted to make an Affirmation or Declaration, instead of the Oath required by Law'.[1] Gladstone was personally inclined to oppose such a step. His preference was for Bradlaugh to write a respectful public letter to the Speaker announcing his determination to affirm on the basis of the Committee's report. Should any Conservative then interpose as Wolff had done, the Liberals would simply attempt to defeat his motion—successfully, Gladstone hoped—and 'the House would then be committed to no doctrine and no novelty whatsoever on the subject'. Sir Erskine May disagreed, however. Even if such a hostile motion were voted down, he wrote to Gladstone, nothing definite would have been decided. If Bradlaugh then appeared on the scene and Wolff interrupted the proceedings again, the Speaker would still lack specific authority or instructions from the House, the very same difficulty he had faced before. If, on the other hand, Labouchere's motion were carried, the subject could not be reopened.[2] Gladstone acceded to May's view, and the Cabinet, after discussing the matter on 19 June, threw its support behind Labouchere's motion.[3]

Labouchere opened the debate on 21 June with a review of the case thus far. He rested his argument on Bradlaugh's original contention: that the Act of 1866 had granted the right to affirm to 'every person of the persuasion of the people called Quakers and every other person for the time being by law permitted to make a solemn Affirmation', and that since subsequent legislation had given Bradlaugh the

[1] *Hansard*, ccliii (1880), 443.
[2] G.P. (B.M.), 44154, fols. 66–70.
[3] G.P. (B.M.) (Cabinet Minutes), 44642, fol. 38.

right to affirm in courts of law, this provision necessarily applied to him.

Labouchere went on to add some remarkably prescient observations:

> As practical men we ought to look at the consequences of not allowing Mr. Bradlaugh to affirm. I do not myself precisely know what he is to do. But I will suppose that, not being allowed to affirm, he goes to that Table and asks to be allowed to take the Oath. He is ordered to retire. If he does not retire, I presume he would be taken into custody. He would, I presume, be put in confinement. We will assume that he would be at some time let out. He would then come again to the Table. I think it possible the House would get tired of this, and would then say—'We can declare the election void.' Mr. Bradlaugh would go down to Northampton. He would be re-elected. . . . He would again tender himself to take the Oath. The same scene would be gone over again. Mr. Bradlaugh would again go back and would again be re-elected. You would then, if you still declined to allow him to enter the House, create a species of martyr. The consequence of your not allowing him to affirm would be that in the end Mr. Bradlaugh would come to that Table and repeat the words which we regard as sacred and he does not.[1]

That Labouchere was sincere can hardly be doubted. None the less, he laboured under the disadvantage of a reputation as satirist rather than as espouser of libertarian principles. Nor was the House in a mood to listen. Sir Hardinge Giffard answered Labouchere's motion with a nullifying amendment —that 'Mr. Bradlaugh be not permitted to take the Oath or make the Affirmation'. Both avenues were to be barred. Labouchere's appraisal of the Act of 1866 was fallacious, contended Giffard, since it applied only to men with 'religious scruples' about oaths. Bradlaugh had no such scruples; he had no religious beliefs whatsoever.[2] Edward Gibson, the Conservative member for the University of Dublin (Trinity College), was even more specific. 'We say that under the existing laws, as they stand, it is impossible, without their alteration or amendment, that Mr. Bradlaugh can take his seat.'[3] The only solution was a new law. However, not many

---

[1] *Hansard*, ccliii (1880), 450. [2] Ibid., cols. 455–61.
[3] Ibid., col. 602.

Conservatives or hostile Home Rulers confined themselves to the legal issue. There were more appetizing matters to discuss, such as the 'perverse mental conformation of Mr. Bradlaugh', owing to which, contended Beresford Hope, 'he tries to make his admission to this House as difficult as possible'.[1]

Both Gladstone and John Bright supported Labouchere's resolution with speeches. The matter 'ought to be viewed in the driest light of reason', urged Gladstone; new legislation was neither necessary nor desirable, since it would merely add fuel to the controversy. 'Nobody can say', urged Bright, 'that Mr. Bradlaugh was not legally entitled to offer himself as a candidate, or that the electors of Northampton were not legally entitled to elect him.'[2]

Gladstone was not happy about the way the debate was progressing. 'With the renewal of the discussion', he informed the Queen, 'the temper of the House does not improve. . . .'[3] Nor had it improved by the night of 22 June. Yet the Government still expected to be able to defeat Giffard's amendment.

The House divided amidst great excitement, and when the result was announced, pandemonium broke loose. Giffard's amendment had been adopted by a vote of 275 to 230. Bradlaugh was to be kept out of Parliament, and the triumphant victor of Midlothian had been defeated on this 'first great division of the new Parliament'.[4] 'There was shouting, cheering, clapping of hands, and other demonstrations', recalled Sir Stafford Northcote, the Conservative leader, 'both louder and longer than any I have heard in my parliamentary life.' Gladstone too reported an ecstatic 'transport of excitement' which exceeded any parliamentary demonstration in his memory.[5] Members of the unexpectedly victorious side vehemently waved their hats, jumped on seats, leapt into the air, and engaged in comradely embraces.[6]

[1] Ibid., col. 476. [2] Ibid., cols. 567, 496.
[3] Cited in Morley, *Gladstone*, iii. 15.
[4] Churchill, *Churchill* i. 130.
[5] Lang, *Life of Northcote* ii. 168. *The Letters of Queen Victoria*, Second Series, ed. G. E. Buckle (New York, 1928), iii. 116.
[6] *Punch*, 3 July 1880, p. 305; Lucy, *Diary of Two Parliaments* ii. 35; *N.R.*, 4 July 1880, p. 34.

Of the 230 members who had stood steadfast for Brad-laugh's admission, 2 were Conservatives, 10 were Home Rulers, and 218 were Liberals. The 275 who had opposed him included 210 Conservatives, 31 Home Rulers, and 34 Liberals.[1] Who was responsible for the defeat—the Tories, the opposing or abstaining Liberals (88 Liberals had either abstained deliberately or were absent for other reasons), or the Irish Home Rulers? All three groups were at one time or another to be held responsible. But Gladstone may have been at fault as well; he had failed to make the vote a Government question, and while he had given faithful personal support to Labouchere's motion, he had let the party Whips be lax in lining up support while the opposition had done its utmost. At least one Liberal who voted for Giffard's amendment afterwards defended himself on the ground that 'it was distinctly understood that it was not a party question'.[2] Gladstone may have felt the question inappropriate for the imposition of party discipline; he had, in any event, attempted to fight the battle with one hand tied behind his back. He had courted unpopularity without receiving the reward which would have justified such action.

Few Members of Parliament expected Bradlaugh to accept his defeat without protest. The next day (24 June) the approaches to the Houses of Parliament were crowded with Bradlaugh supporters, and the House of Commons itself was packed when the day's proceedings began. Promptly Brad-laugh marched down the aisle to the Speaker's Table, asking to be sworn. When the Speaker, as a consequence of the previous night's vote, denied him that privilege, Bradlaugh asked to be heard. He was granted permission, though only with the proviso—based on the precedent of O'Connell's case in 1829—that he speak from the bar, the brass pole which was ceremoniously drawn across the aisle from the sockets in which it customarily reposed, a quarter of the way from the entrance door to the Speaker's Table. The bar signified

---

[1] The statistics as to party affiliation in this instance, as in all others to be cited, are derived from a comparison of voting statistics in *Hansard* or the relevant volume of *Division Lists* (issued annually) with party affiliations as indicated in Dod's *Parliamentary Companion*, 1880–6.

[2] Cited in *N.R.*, 31 Dec. 1882, p. 488. See Lord John Manners to Beacons-field, 23 June 1880, Beaconsfield MSS.

"KICKED OUT." (?)

3. "Kicked Out?" (*Punch*, 3 July 1880)

4. "The Arrest of Charles Bradlaugh" (*Illustrated London News*, 3 July 1880)

that Bradlaugh, although literally within the chamber, was technically outside it. At the same time, his location gave the orator the unintended advantage of being able to face the entire assembly at once.[1]

It was an extraordinary occasion for a maiden speech, and Bradlaugh made the most of it. Standing erect—at attention like a soldier, according to one observer[2]—he spoke, without reference to notes, for twenty minutes, often rising to heights of impassioned eloquence. He had no desire, he declared, to impose either himself or his opinions upon the House. Not that he was ashamed of those opinions.

I am no more ashamed of my own opinions—which I did not choose— . . . opinions into which I have grown, than any member of this House is ashamed of his; and much as I value the right to a seat in this House, much as I believe the justice of this House will accord it me before the struggle ceases, I would rather relinquish it for ever than it should be thought, that upon any shadow of hypocrisy, I had tried to gain a feigned entrance here by pretending to be what I am not.

But the nub of the issue was one of law, insisted Brad-laugh, and, last night's resolution notwithstanding, law was on his side when he claimed to take the oath. 'I beg you, not in any sort of menace, not in any sort of boast, but as one man against six hundred, to give me that justice which on the other side of this Hall the Judges would give me were I pleading before them.'[3]

Cheers broke out on the Liberal benches. Gladstone considered Bradlaugh's address 'that of a consummate speaker',[4] and even one staunchly hostile Conservative, who described Bradlaugh to Disraeli as a man 'with ugly features and a bad expression', conceded that 'he spoke with vigour and a certain dramatic power'.[5] Yet the speech had been delivered too

[1] Lucy, *Two Parliaments*, pp. 37 ff.
[2] Wolff, *Rambling Recollections*, ii. 262.
[3] *Hansard*, ccliii (1880), 634–8.
[4] Gladstone to the Queen, cited by Morley, *Gladstone*, iii. 16.
[5] Lord John Manners to Beaconsfield, June 23, 1880, Beaconsfield MSS. 'The maiden speech . . . was a success the brilliancy of which even the outcast member's bitterest opponent admitted.' H. W. Lucy, *A Diary of the Salisbury Parliament, 1886–1892* (London, 1892), p. 340.

late to influence the all important vote of the previous night. Although Bradlaugh's loyal Northampton colleague, Labouchere, immediately offered a motion to rescind the resolution adopted the night before, Gladstone pointed out sensibly enough that the House could hardly be expected to reverse its decision at such short notice, any more—one might add— than Bradlaugh could be expected to submit to a resolution he had just, with due politeness, proclaimed invalid.

Labouchere accordingly withdrew his motion, but when the Speaker officially called upon Bradlaugh to withdraw, the latter again insisted on his rights as a duly elected Member of Parliament: 'I respectfully refuse to withdraw.' When Bradlaugh repeated this refusal, the Speaker appealed to the House for instructions, since without specific authority he did not consider himself empowered to use force.[1] Cries of 'Gladstone' echoed through the House, but the Liberal Party leader made no move. He had warned the assembly against defeating Labouchere's resolution. He did not feel it his duty to save the Opposition from the consequences of their action. And so, attired in his grey-cream summer coat with gloves and walking-stick rather than in his customary black frock-coat—a symbolic indication of his temporary abdication from his official position—Gladstone kept silent.[2] It was Northcote who then, albeit reluctantly, officially moved (in accordance with the precedent of Alderman Salomons in 1851) 'that the Honourable Member now withdraw'. Bradlaugh continued to stand impassively at the foot of the Speaker's Table while the rest of the assembly departed through the Division Lobby doors. The motion was approved by a top-heavy vote of 326 to 38, since there was little inclination among the Liberals to challenge a motion sustaining the legal authority of the House of Commons.

When the Speaker announced the result of the vote, Bradlaugh reiterated that the order was against the law, 'and I positively refuse to obey it'. The Speaker ordered the Sergeant-at-Arms to remove Bradlaugh below the bar.

[1] *Hansard*, ccliii (1880), cols. 647–8. Also, Brand to Gladstone, 23 June 1880, G.P. (B.M.), 44194, fol. 208, in which Brand cites the precedent of the case of Alderman Salomons on 21 July 1851 for this course.
[2] Lucy, *Two Parliaments*, ii. 36; T. P. O'Connor, *Memoirs*, i. 73.

Elderly Captain Gossett accordingly tapped Bradlaugh on the shoulder, and the latter followed him for a few yards, only to return to the Table a moment later, shouting above the uproar: 'I admit the right of the House to imprison me; but I admit no right on the part of the House to exclude me, and I refuse to be excluded.' Gladstone again made no move, whereupon Northcote supported his earlier motion with one to the effect that Bradlaugh, having disobeyed the orders of the House and resisted its authority, be for this offence 'taken into the custody of the Sergeant-at-Arms'. This motion was adopted by a vote of 274 to 7, and Bradlaugh, offering no further resistance, accompanied the Sergeant-at-Arms from the battle arena.[1]

Bradlaugh was not dissatisfied with the outcome of the day's proceedings. His claims to public sympathy were more likely to be heeded as a prisoner in the Clock Tower than as a free man. His quarters, in any case, were pleasant enough, and he was permitted to entertain his two daughters, Mrs. Besant, and three other guests at dinner that evening. 'I don't like being in prison', Bradlaugh contemplatively observed to an interviewer of the Central News Agency, but the Sergeant-at-Arms was an excellent custodian, much better than the French Commissaire of Police with whom he had once had dealings. This, he said, surveying his room, 'is Paradise compared with that. I hope', he added quickly with a quiet laugh, 'the House won't think that profane.'[2]

While Bradlaugh was preparing himself for a long imprisonment, Annie Besant, in a broadside entitled 'Law Makers and Law Breakers', appealed to the English people against 'the motley herd of renegade Nonconformists, Roman Catholics, Jews, and Protestants' who had helped make the majority which had deprived Bradlaugh of his liberty. Her appeal concluded with a flourish: 'Let the masses speak!'[3] Under the circumstances, no one was more surprised the next afternoon than Bradlaugh himself to hear that he had been released. After a comfortable night,

---

[1] *Hansard*, ccliii (1880), cols. 649–60.
[2] Interview is printed in *Freeman's Journal* (Dublin), 24 June 1880, p. 5.
[3] *N.R.*, 4 July 1880, pp. 42–43; Besant, *Autobiography*, pp. 259–60.

interrupted only by the thunderous gongs of Big Ben immediately above his chamber, he was engaged in opening telegrams from dozens of well-wishers when the news
came.[1]

The cause of this dramatic reversal would appear to have
been the advice of Disraeli (then Earl of Beaconsfield).
Northcote, immediately upon having taken the lead from
Gladstone, and thus acting 'as if I were sitting in my old
place', had asked Beaconsfield what step he should take next.
Northcote had now assumed formal leadership of the 'Fourth
Party's' anti-Bradlaugh hobby-horse, but he took only sub-
dued pride in the fact that 'we are making history'. He was
not the man to make a major decision without consulting
his party leader. 'The immediate question is,' he advised
Beaconsfield, 'Are we to take any further step with regard
to Bradlaugh or not?' Fearful that Bradlaugh as prisoner
would appear a martyr and successfully enlist public sympathy and embarrass the Conservatives 'by a passive resistance', Northcote favoured his speedy release.[2] He met
Beaconsfield and other Conservative leaders the next morning, and the party chieftain's feelings were apparently decisively in favour of Bradlaugh's release. Beaconsfield, while
showing no particular sympathy toward the iconoclast, had
no desire to make a martyr of the man, and saw the matter
as a tempest in a teapot rather than an issue of political importance. 'Bradlaugh makes the most noise,' he observed
to one of his correspondents, 'but the Irish Eviction Bill is
much the most serious thing.'[3]

And so the very next afternoon, amidst laughter on the
Ministerial benches, Northcote proposed that Bradlaugh,
having expiated his offence against the House, be discharged
from custody. The step caught the House by surprise,
and Labouchere immediately warned that the prisoner was

[1] N.R., 4 July 1880, p. 33. Speaker Brand was similarly surprised. Hampden
Diary.
[2] (Copy) Northcote to Beaconsfield, 23 June 1880, Iddesleigh MSS.
(B.M.), 50018, fols. 201–4. See also Northcote to Salisbury, 24 June 1880,
Salisbury MSS.
[3] *The Letters of Disraeli to Lady Bradford and Lady Chesterfield*, ed. the
Marquis of Zetland (London, 1929), ii. 279. For Disraeli's attitude see also
Chamberlain to Gladstone, 25 June 1880, G.P. (B.M.), 44125, fol. 33.

unrepentant; but no opposition to Northcote's motion developed. Bradlaugh had been the first Member of Parliament to be jailed in the Clock Tower in thirty-five years—though several other men had served brief periods of custody there within that thirty-five year period—and no one has been imprisoned in the Tower since.[1]

During the summer of 1880 Gladstone and others in the Liberal Government felt at times that the problem of what to do with the controversial M.P. for Northampton was a 'scrape' into which the Conservatives had plunged the House. Joseph Chamberlain, for example, in a letter to Gladstone, writes of 'the mess' into which the Opposition had landed itself.[2] Other Liberals, however, had begun to be aware that 'the mess' was more likely to redound to the benefit of the Opposition, and Edward Hamilton, one of Gladstone's private secretaries, began to refer in his diary to the 'wretched Bradlaugh business', a phrase he was to echo many a time during the next five years.[3] Gladstone, in any event, came to the conclusion after the Clock Tower episode that he would have to take personal charge of the case. On the one hand he did not wish Bradlaugh to come down to the House repeatedly to disturb its proceedings, and on the other hand he disliked being put under pressure to support police measures against the man. On the day after Bradlaugh's release, Gladstone assured him—through Labouchere—that the Government would do something soon, though exactly what was to be done was still undecided.

One faction of Liberal back-benchers who had voted against Labouchere's resolution, headed by Hussey Vivian and privately supported by the Speaker, strongly urged legislation to abolish both the oath and the affirmation (or at least the former) 'upon the broad and traditional lines of Liberalism, viz. that no religious test should be permitted to intervene between any man and his rights as a Citizen'. Vivian did not think it would take long to pass such a bill,

[1] *Hansard*, ccliii (1880), 720; Lucy, *Two Parliaments*, ii. 42. The last M.P. to be imprisoned in the Clock Tower had been Smith O'Brien in 1845. He had refused to serve on a Parliamentary committee to which he had been legally appointed. *Freeman's Journal*, 24 June 1880, p. 5.

[2] 25 June 1880, G.P. (B.M.), 44125, fol. 34.

[3] Hamilton Diary (B.M.), 48630, p. 42.

nor did he believe that the Conservatives would offer serious opposition to the proposal, at least no more than they were likely to offer any 'temporising proposal' such as Labouchere's resolution. Gladstone was much more dubious about the prospects of an Oaths Abolition Bill, nor was he sure that Bradlaugh would wait patiently for its passage.[1]

Gladstone was still inclined to avoid legislative innovation. Consequently he at first suggested to his colleagues a simple motion to rescind Giffard's resolution. Both the Whig wing of his cabinet represented by Lord Hartington and the Radical wing represented by Chamberlain concurred, although with varying degrees of enthusiasm.[2] The Cabinet ultimately agreed to a motion to rescind phrased in such a fashion as to eliminate all personal reference to Bradlaugh. The Cabinet also concluded that Gladstone himself, rather than a private member, should introduce the resolution. This was in line with the Speaker's strongly worded hint in a letter to Gladstone: 'I presume that the matter will not be left with Labouchere, but placed in stronger hands.'[3]

The net result was a resolution to the effect

that every person returned as a Member of this House, who may claim to be 'a person for the time being by Law permitted to make a solemn Affirmation or Declaration, instead of taking an Oath', shall henceforth (notwithstanding so much of the Resolution adopted by this House on the 22nd day of June last as relates to Affirmations) be permitted without question to make and subscribe a solemn Affirmation . . . subject to any liability by statute; and secondly that this Resolution be a Standing Order of this House.[4]

Gladstone's resolution differed from Labouchere's in two ways: it was phrased in general terms rather than applying to a particular person, and it specified (what Labouchere's resolution had at most implied) that Bradlaugh was still subject to possible penalties in the law courts should the judges find him guilty of having violated the statute concerning oaths and affirmations.

[1] G.P. (B.M.), 44464, fols. 26–28, 35–36; 44544, fols. 27–28.
[2] Ibid., 44125, fol. 34; 44145, fols. 67–69.
[3] G.P. (B.M.) (Cabinet Minutes), 44642, fol. 41; Brand to Gladstone, 27 June 1880, G.P. (B.M.) 44194, fol. 212.
[4] Hansard, ccliii (1880), 972.

Northcote's immediate reaction was to propose a substitute motion to the effect that any changes in the interpretation of the statutes relating to oaths and affirmations should be made by means of a law rather than a resolution. He soon thought better of it, however, since such a substitute motion might be interpreted as a pledge on the part of the Conservative Party to support such legislation, and he therefore confined himself to opposing Gladstone on the ground that the House should not rescind one week what it had enacted the previous week.[1] The Speaker ruled, however, that there were 'essential' differences between the new resolution and the old. The Opposition then went on to argue disingenuously that if, as a consequence of the resolution, Bradlaugh affirmed and thereby incurred a fine, 'the House would be bound in common fairness to give him an indemnity'.[2] The Liberal retort was that the resolution did not 'invite' Bradlaugh; it merely applied to him if he chose to make use of it.

Gladstone argued forcefully in favour of his proposal, placing stress on one aspect of the case which some Liberals found distasteful, that his resolution would spare the House a repetition of 'committals and releases' every time Bradlaugh came forward to take the oath.[3] As influential as Gladstone's personal intervention was the widespread rumour that the Government had made the question one of confidence and that, if defeated, it would resign. One influential lay religious leader wrote a worried note to Chamberlain deploring a general election on the Bradlaugh case. Chamberlain assured him that the resolution had not been made 'a Cabinet question', though admitting that defeat 'would involve a serious blow to the prestige of the Government and some personal humiliation to Mr. Gladstone'.[4]

The House of Commons was packed to suffocation on the night of 1 July, when after another lengthy debate the decisive vote came. It went 303 to 249 in favour of Gladstone's

---

[1] Northcote to Beaconsfield, 28 June 1880, Iddesleigh MSS. (B.M.), 50018, fols. 205–6.
[2] *Hansard*, ccliii (1880), 1302. [3] Ibid., col. 1269.
[4] R. W. Dale to Chamberlain, 28 June 1880; Chamberlain to Dale, 29 June 1880. Chamberlain MSS., JC 5/20/3; JC 5/20/34a. An 'urgent' Whip was issued to round up Liberal M.P.s. *Freeman's Journal* (Dublin), 1 July 1880, p. 6; 2 July 1880, p. 5.

resolution. The majority comprised 287 Liberals, 15 Home Rulers, and one Conservative; the minority included 3 Liberals, 22 Home Rulers, and 224 Conservatives. An attempt by A. M. Sullivan, an Irish Nationalist, to amend the resolution so that it would apply only to future eventualities (and thus not to Bradlaugh) was defeated by a vote of 274 to 238.

And so, on the following day, amidst 'utter quietude', Bradlaugh—as he had first intended in early May—'made and subscribed a solemn Affirmation', shook hands with the Speaker in the customary manner, and took his seat in the House of Commons.[1] The battle seemed to be over, but in truth it had only begun. Northcote, characteristically, was not altogether unhappy about Gladstone's triumph, since at heart he was a little afraid that, should the vote have gone against the Government, Gladstone would have resigned and appealed to the country on the issue of religious liberty. Northcote did not think any legal question about Bradlaugh's right to his seat would be raised, though he felt sure that with the iconoclast a member of the House 'grumbling . . . will increase, rather than diminish'.[2] Northcote proved to be mistaken on both counts. There was little grumbling within the House for the time being, but a writ served on Bradlaugh on the very afternoon of his affirmation, charging him with sitting in the House illegally, was in due course to have momentous consequences.

The Liberal reaction to the passage of Gladstone's resolution was one of quiet satisfaction. The Whiggish *Edinburgh Review* publicly commended the House for having reversed its decision within a week. 'Inconsistency! Long life to it! There is a vast deal of inconsistency in politics which may not only safely be condoned but received with approbation and gratitude.' Indeed, concluded the journal aptly enough, 'without the grace of inconsistency, our Prime Minister might still be a hot Tory and a bigoted Churchman . . .'.[3]

[1] O'Connor, *Gladstone's House of Commons*, p. 40.
[2] Northcote to Beaconsfield, 2 July 1880, Iddesleigh MSS. (B.M.), 50018, fols. 208–9.
[3] 'The New Parliament in Session', July 1880, p. 282.

IX

A RADICAL IN PARLIAMENT

On 2 July 1880 Bradlaugh became a member of the House of Commons. It is true that his right to sit was immediately challenged by a legal writ, but while the case meandered through the law courts—and this, as it turned out, meant until the end of March 1881—Bradlaugh was in every sense a fully fledged Member of Parliament. A bill 'to incapacitate from sitting in Parliament any person who has by deliberate public speaking, or by published writing, systematically avowed his disbelief in the existence of a Supreme Being' was introduced by three Conservatives on 14 July, but the proposal was never seriously considered.[1]

The controversy occasioned by Bradlaugh's admission was rekindled by Conservative candidates during several by-election campaigns; and Cardinal Manning, the head of the Roman Catholic hierarchy, publicly entered the controversy in the August issue of the *Nineteenth Century*. The decision to admit Bradlaugh, he declared, had undermined the theism of the British Empire and the stability of all civil society. The purity of Parliament depended upon the probity of its members, a quality tested by the oath of allegiance whereby the M.P. bound himself by 'a sanction higher than that of mere human authority to be faithful to the Commonwealth'. Bradlaugh had been let in, but there was yet time to expel him. 'The moral sense of this great people has not yet been asked.' The article was significantly entitled 'An Englishman's Protest'.

Although the Catholic *Tablet* was sure that Manning had appropriately expressed 'the sentiments of a vast majority of his fellow countrymen',[2] the protests of no Englishman appeared to be of any avail for the moment. As a sympathetic Liberal M.P. observed a few months later, 'I am told that there are some legal proceedings still pending, but no one

[1] *Hansard*, ccliv (1880), 463.　　[2] 14 Aug. 1880, p. 198.

expects that they will have any result.'[1] Liberal M.P.s generally looked upon Bradlaugh as just another colleague, and the Government consulted him on appointments in his constituency in the customary manner.[2]

Bradlaugh carefully avoided making any reference to religion during these months in Parliament and never entered the chamber until after the opening prayers. As he himself explained this decision a few years later, 'men who in political or social meetings unnecessarily thrust upon others, whom they knew to differ from them in thought, things which must be offensive to them, were simply guilty of impertinence, for which they deserved rebuke'.[3] There was in any case little occasion to refer to religion, even had Bradlaugh wished to do so. One exception was the debate on the Burials Bill, in the course of which Bradlaugh pleaded unsuccessfully that working-class Nonconformists, whom the bill entitled to burial in Church-of-England graveyards (provided the latter were the only ones available), might be allowed to hold funeral services on Sundays.[4]

Bradlaugh wished both to be and to seem respectable; it would never even have occurred to him—as it did to Keir Hardie a decade later—to enter Parliament wearing a cloth cap instead of the customary top hat. He was positively scandalized to see an obviously drunk Irish M.P. arise to address the House one evening.[5] It was equally 'monstrous' that during debates on the Employer's Liability Bill Lord Randolph Churchill's 'Fourth Party' could waste 'hour after hour of the public time and yet escape public and severe rebuke'. At the same time Bradlaugh acknowledged that 'in the present dearth of Conservative statesmen' Lord Randolph might go far.[6]

Bradlaugh's new parliamentary duties necessarily increased the volume of his mail—as many as a thousand letters a week—and limited his other activities without adding to

[1] Cited in N.R., 28 Nov. 1880, p. 392.
[2] See, for example, letter from Lord Richard Grosvenor to Bradlaugh asking the latter to nominate a 'Keeper of Post Office', 21 Mar. 1881. Thomas Adams MSS.
[3] N.R., 28 May 1882, p. 411.   [4] Hansard, cclvi (1880), 930.
[5] N.R., 12 Sept. 1880, p. 207; Lucy, A Diary of Two Parliaments, ii. 96.
[6] N.R., 15 Aug. 1880, p. 145; 25 July 1880, p. 97.

his income. Thus he had to forgo the International Conference of Free-thinkers in Brussels, and once the Parliamentary session of 1880 was over in September, he had to devote himself to his lecturing and pamphleteering with renewed vigour.[1] Bradlaugh took considerable interest in imperial affairs, which he generally viewed as a confirmed 'Little Englander'. He was chairman at one discussion of 'British Misgovernment of India'; he made a personal appeal to Gladstone on behalf of some imprisoned Maoris in New Zealand; and his National Secular Society went on record as opposed to the annexation of the Transvaal.[2]

It was in domestic affairs, however, that his Victorian Radicalism was most evident. He protested against Richmond Park being used as a private game preserve by the Duke of Cambridge. He favoured the opening of museums on Sundays. He urged the Home Secretary to end the use of plank beds in prisons. He was influential in exempting the poorer farm labourers from paying duty on beer brewed for their own use. He was one of fifteen members supporting a resolution, prompted by the rejection of the Irish Relief Bill in the House of Lords, stating 'that it is no longer just or expedient that all measures for the improvement of the condition of the people of England, Ireland, and Scotland shall be at the mercy of a body of legislators hereditary and irresponsible'.[3] Naturally, he vigorously opposed the return to protective tariffs implied by the incipient 'fair trade' agitation of the early 1880's.[4]

The biggest question facing Parliament during Bradlaugh's nine months was, of course, Ireland. Although disappointed by the hostility shown toward him by a majority of the Irish M.P.s earlier in the summer, he appealed to the Government, in his very first speech in the House, 'not to be generous with half a hand' in its 'Compensation for Disturbance' Bill, which was intended to indemnify victims of

[1] N.R., 5 Sept. 1880, pp. 185–6; 19 Sept. 1880, p. 225. 'Life has its bread and cheese demands . . .', wrote Bradlaugh.
[2] G.P. (B.M.), 44111, fol. 83; N.R., 7 Nov. 1880, p. 346; 6 Mar. 1881, p. 147.
[3] N.R., 18 July 1880, p. 81; 8 Aug. 1880, p. 129; 22 Aug. 1880, p. 161; 5 Sept. 1880, p. 200.
[4] See, for example, Annie Besant, Free Trade v. 'Fair Trade' (London, 1881).

eviction proceedings.[1] The rejection of this bill by the House of Lords brought to an end the preponderantly constitutional course the Home-Rule Party had been following during the spring and summer of 1880 and initiated the 'land war' of the following autumn and winter.[2]

'To think', observed Bradlaugh with surprise in August, 'that towards the close of the nineteenth century Irishmen in the House of Commons should speak with as much hatred against Englishmen and English rule as, a few years ago, Italians spoke against Austria and Austrian rule.'[3] As the year wore on his sympathy with Irish ends diverged with increasing sharpness from his hostility toward Irish means. Bradlaugh genuinely wished for co-operation between English and Irish land-law reformers. But, as Annie Besant noted by the end of October, 'at present Mr. Parnell and his friends are losing the respect and good wishes of English Radicals. . . . Mr. Parnell is wrong-headed, violent, abusive.'[4] Bradlaugh and his associates might be Radicals, but they were also Englishmen, and they resented the virtual damnation of everything English. Irish agitation also helped kill for the time being the land law reform movement in England which Bradlaugh had helped launch only a few months earlier, as he cautioned his followers against attending meetings in England at which Irish Land Leaguers might advocate violence.[5] At the same time he deplored the Government's prosecution of Parnell and others on charges of conspiring to prevent the payment of rent, and he contributed to Parnell's legal defence fund.[6] Not until early in 1881 did Bradlaugh begin to be unsure whether the Irish really were appealing for the aid of English Radicals. In retrospect, it seems clear that this was not their primary objective at the time. Reliance on Liberal generosity was, after all, one of the criticisms the Parnellites had made of Isaac Butt's policy. Their own policy, while less revolutionary in actuality than it seemed to be on the surface, did not go out of its way to appease the English Radicals, except for a small group

[1] *Hansard*, ccliii (1880), 1472.
[2] Conor Cruise O'Brien, *Parnell and His Party, 1880–1890* (Oxford, 1957), p. 49.   [3] *N.R.*, 29 Aug. 1880, p. 177.
[4] *N.R.*, 31 Oct. 1880, p. 332.   [5] *N.R.*, 13 Feb. 1881, p. 106.
[6] *N.R.*, 7 Nov. 1880, p. 337; 21 Nov. 1880, p. 379.

of English socialists led by H. M. Hyndman, whom Brad-laugh then regarded as an unimportant competitor for the allegiance of the working classes.[1]

Bradlaugh saw his own duty plainly, however. It was 'to work honestly for the redress of Irish grievances, although even every Irishman should be personally unjust to us'. Bradlaugh was one of eight English Radicals who in January 1881 supported Parnell's amendment to the Address in reply to the Queen's Speech. Parnell's move was defeated, 435 to 57.[2] And when the Protection of Persons and Property (Ireland) Bill was introduced, Bradlaugh argued cogently that the Government had not provided enough information to warrant legislation giving it extraordinary powers to suspend traditional legal guarantees, and that in any case legislation to redress rather than to punish was what was needed. Justin McCarthy, then assistant chairman of the Home-Rule Party, called this 'a powerful and impressive argument'.[3] It was Bradlaugh, with but six other Liberals, who—in the absence of Parnell—led the Irish contingent into the division lobby in opposition to the second reading of the bill.

At the same time, Bradlaugh failed utterly to understand or to sympathize with the deliberate Irish obstruction which wearied the House night after night and which finally led to the famous forty-one hour sitting, the net result of which was to end the right of unlimited debate in Parliament. However much he opposed the measure the Government had seen fit to propose—and Bradlaugh continued steadfastly to side with the Parnellites as each amendment was discussed in committee—he was still more against what he deemed 'the destruction of Parliamentary government and true liberty of speech'.[4] And so, 'with a heavy heart', he voted against the various purely obstructive amendments and ultimately for the temporary suspension of the great mass of the Irish members. Though he might sympathize with the grievances of Ireland, his respect for Parliament came first. And, indeed,

[1] N.R., 2 Jan 1881, p. 10; O'Brien, Parnell and His Party, pp. 62–63.
[2] N.R., 28 Nov. 1880, p. 393; Hansard, cclvii (1881), 803.
[3] Hansard, cclvii (1881), 1260–5.
[4] Ibid., col. 1909.

as far as he could see, 'the foolish obstruction . . . in no fashion advantaged poor Ireland'.[1]

Although he also voted in favour of the Arms Act, because he 'opposed placing arms in the hands of starving men', Bradlaugh was, with the possible exceptions of Joseph Cowen and Henry Labouchere, the most effective English opponent of Irish coercion in the winter of 1880–1.[2] The Roman Catholic *Tablet* was one of several journals which noted 'Mr. Bradlaugh's ostentatious defence of Irish interests in Parliament'.[3]

The issue which Bradlaugh made peculiarly his own during his nine months in the House of Commons was that of 'Perpetual Pensions'. The English Crown had at various times in the previous three centuries rewarded its servants— most often its military heroes—by pensions which were in turn inherited by their descendants. In the 1880's over £30,000 of each year's budget was devoted to paying such annuities. It was a type of reward which struck a considerable number of late Victorian Englishmen as anachronistic; and Bradlaugh's doubts reflected an earlier Radical tradition, Joseph Hume having led an unsuccessful drive against the practice in 1837.[4]

Edward Hamilton might deplore the fact that 'the cry for economy is a thing of the past. The want of it is the worst characteristic in the Modern Liberal & Radical.'[5] Financial retrenchment was still, however, a basic ingredient of Bradlaugh's Radicalism, and retrenchment could hardly be sweeter than at the expense of the idle rich. The three greatest beneficiaries of these pensions in 1880 were Earl Nelson, who received £5,000 a year, and the descendants of William Penn and the Duke of Marlborough, each of whom received £4,000 a year.

---

[1] *N.R.*, 30 Jan. 1881, p. 66; 13 Feb. 1881, p. 97; 27 Feb. 1881, p. 129.

[2] *Division Lists*, 1881, pp. 358–60. See, e.g., Frank Hugh O'Donnell, *A History of the Irish Parliamentary Party* (London, 1910), ii. 15. Cf. Humanitas [William Platt Ball], *Charles Bradlaugh, M.P., and the Irish Nation* (London, 1885), p. 11. The only issue on which Bradlaugh's Radicalism might be challenged was in regard to the Arms Bill, which had been proposed by the Government over the opposition of Gladstone, Bright, and Chamberlain. Dilke MSS. (B.M.), 43935, fol. 39. [3] *Tablet*, 26 Feb. 1881, p. 328.

[4] *N.R.*, 29 Aug. 1880, p. 184; 19 Dec. 1880, p. 433.

[5] Hamilton Diary (B.M.), 48632, p. 54.

His interest in the matter gave Bradlaugh an opportunity to do some historical research into the original grant of each of these pensions. It is hardly surprising that the pension which intrigued him most was that of the Duke of Marlborough. For not only did he conclude that the first Duke 'was scarcely a great man, unless exceeding baseness may stand for greatness', but he was fully aware that Lord Randolph Churchill, his clever opponent of the previous spring, was personally interested. As Bradlaugh caustically observed, 'His Lordship has already some of the characteristics of his illustrious predecessor'.[1] And when Lord Randolph made what Bradlaugh considered an extremely unfair attack upon him in a speech at Portsmouth in November 1880 Bradlaugh consoled himself with the thought that, while he might not be able to appeal to Churchill's honour, 'I shall next Session direct my arguments to his sensitive part. I shall menace his pocket.'[2]

For the moment, however, Bradlaugh did not take a particularly drastic course. He merely gave notice in August 1880 that he would during the coming session move for the appointment of a Select Committee to inquire as to what extent perpetual pensions ought to be continued, 'having due regard to any just claims of the several recipients and to economy in the public expenditure'.[3] With this in mind, he launched a drive for petitions advocating the creation of such a Committee and by the time the new session opened in January 1881 Bradlaugh had succeeded in arousing considerable interest in his project. By 22 March favourable petitions bearing over 264,000 signatures had been submitted, the Government had proved co-operative in supplying Bradlaugh with information, and some one hundred Liberal M.P.s had—Bradlaugh announced—pledged themselves to support his resolution.[4] Gladstone himself had

[1] N.R., 5 Dec. 1880, p. 406.
[2] Ibid., 401. Interestingly enough, neither Sir Winston Churchill nor Robert Rhodes James, in their respective biographies of Lord Randolph, refer to the 'perpetual pension' issue.
[3] N.R., 19 Dec. 1880, p. 433.
[4] N.R., 17 Apr. 1881, p. 294; 6 Feb. 1881, p. 82; 20 Jan. 1881, p. 74. The final total of signatures for the year was 278,787 on 1,019 petitions (N.R., 23 Oct. 1881, p. 343).

taken no official stand, but his son Herbert had promised his enthusiastic support.[1]

The proposed inquiry had drawn the support of such diverse journals as the *Catholic Times* and the South Wales *Daily News*. The latter reported that Bradlaugh had 'succeeded in kindling public interest to an extent which those who do not agree with his sentiments will hardly credit'.[2] The Conservative *Saturday Review* had become sufficiently aroused to speculate that the attack upon perpetual pensions might 'form part of a general movement against all property which has not been gained by the owner's labour'. If so, 'the general sense of insecurity will be very great'. The *Saturday Review* conceded, to be sure, that some kinds of property were more easily comprehended than others, and perpetual pensions admittedly fell into 'the less intelligible class'.[3]

As it turned out, Bradlaugh's motion was several times subjected to delay—the accidental by-product of Irish obstruction—and when an opportunity for a vote came, Bradlaugh was no longer an active Member of Parliament. The issue of perpetual pensions was to hang fire for several years.

Bradlaugh had proved himself during his months in Parliament a conscientious and able Radical politician, even if he was not, as one sympathetic editor claimed on his behalf, 'a century in advance of the rest of the Liberal Party'.[4] As a matter of fact, Bradlaugh's respectability during these months was attested to by the Prime Minister, who observed that he had shown himself 'a man of great ability, integrity, honour, and public spirit . . .'.[5] 'Nothing', acknowledged Samuel Morley, one of Bradlaugh's opponents among the Liberals, 'could exceed the propriety of his conduct.' Similar testimony may be found in several independent newspapers such as *The Times*, which observed that 'many, whom the choice of Northampton naturally did not content, have been conciliated by Mr. Bradlaugh's manly

[1] *N.R.*, 23 Jan. 1881, p. 58.
[2] Cited in *N.R.*, 13 Feb. 1881, p. 106; 30 Jan. 1881, p. 74.
[3] 22 Jan. 1881, p. 102.
[4] *N.R.*, 3 Oct. 1880, p. 266. The paper cited was the Nottingham *Journal*. Bradlaugh was absent only once. *N.R.*, 10 Apr. 1881, p. 277.
[5] *Hansard*, cclx (1881), 1216.

and moderate attitude'.[1] Under the circumstances, it is, at first glance, difficult to understand how completely this interlude in Bradlaugh's career was to be forgotten in the years that followed. Bradlaugh's enemies soon discovered, however, that there was little in his Parliamentary record to warrant their attacks, while Bradlaugh's supporters proved to be more interested in advocating a principle than in defending the man who embodied it. Both sides therefore tended later on to ignore these months.

[1] *N.R.*, 26 Nov. 1882, p. 369. *The Times* of 1 Apr. 1881, cited in *N.R.*, 10 Apr. 1881, p. 285. Sir Henry Drummond Wolff, in his *Rambling Recollections*, ii, entirely overlooks Bradlaugh's Parliamentary interlude.

X

CLARKE VERSUS BRADLAUGH

ON the very day that Bradlaugh had taken his seat in the House of Commons, 2 July 1880, he had been handed a writ issued at the behest of Henry Clarke, a private citizen, charging Bradlaugh with having sat and voted in Parliament without having taken the required oath and claiming the £500 indemnity which the Parliamentary Oaths Act of 1866 prescribed for each such unlawful vote. During the session of 1880, Bradlaugh had voted on ninety additional occasions and was therefore presumably liable to £45,500 if found guilty as charged. But the case of *Clarke* v. *Bradlaugh* revolved only about the very first vote.[1]

The case did not come up for immediate hearing, and though Bradlaugh submitted a written précis of his defence in November 1880 it was not until 7 March 1881 that the case was heard in the High Court of Justice, Queen's Bench Division, with Mr. Justice Mathew presiding. Bradlaugh's defence rested on the same legal points he had cited during the opening days of Parliament in support of his claim to affirm: that since he was a person who, according to the Evidence Acts of 1869 and 1870, might affirm in courts of law, he belonged to the class of persons who, together with the Quakers, Moravians, and Separatists, might substitute an affirmation for an oath in Parliament; and that on 2 July 1880 he had made just such an affirmation. Bradlaugh went on to observe that in accordance with a resolution of the House of Commons, the Clerk had permitted him so to affirm; and he cited in detail the minutes and report of the second Select Committee, which had favoured his right to affirm.

While Bradlaugh argued his own case, the plaintiff was represented by the able and experienced barrister and M.P.,

[1] *Parliamentary Papers*, 1881, vol. lxxvi, '*Clarke* v. *Bradlaugh*', *passim. N.R.*, 24 Oct. 1880, p. 314.

Sir Hardinge Giffard, who in demurrer contended that Brad-laugh's case was 'bad in law'. Giffard placed special emphasis on the preamble to the Evidence Act of 1869: 'Whereas the discovery of truth in courts of justice has been signally promoted by the removal of restrictions on the admissibility of witnesses, and it is expedient to amend the law of evidence with the object of still further promoting such discovery. . . .' The act applied only to the affirmations of witnesses, main-tained Giffard, and therefore had no connexion with the promissory affirmation Bradlaugh made as a Member of Parliament. Indeed, Giffard went on, the Parliamentary Oaths Act of 1866 'must be construed as if it contained a proviso that none but persons with religious belief' (such as Quakers) were entitled to affirm. Furthermore, he added, the Parliamentary Oaths Act of 1866 applied only to England and Ireland—Scotland's legal system being different—making it even more unlikely that the framers of the Evidence Act should have intended then to amend the Oaths Act.

Bradlaugh took issue with each of these arguments. The Evidence Acts of 1869 and 1870 defined the words 'court of justice' and 'presiding judge' as including any person or persons 'having by law authority to administer an oath for the taking of evidence'. The House of Commons was, Brad-laugh maintained, such a court, and its Clerk had the power to administer such oaths. Bradlaugh conceded that the Evi-dence Acts of 1869 and 1870 did not expressly amend the Parliamentary Oaths Act of 1866, but that act had granted the right to affirm to several specifically named religious groups 'and every other person for the time being by law permitted to make a solemn affirmation . . .'. Bradlaugh claimed to fall into that last category; and, he added point-edly, 'I contend that all enabling clauses in statutes must be interpreted liberally, not restrictively, in favour of the person claiming the benefit, and not harshly against him.' There lay the crux of the matter. If the judge reasoned in accordance with the expressed intention of the legislators, Bradlaugh's case was lost, since it rested essentially upon an implication. As for the distinction Giffard had drawn between the earlier act applying to the entire kingdom and the latter excluding

Scotland, Bradlaugh's reply was a simple one: 'I cannot and ought not to be defeated here, by showing that some other person, under different circumstances, does not come within the enabling words.'[1]

Mr. Justice Mathew decided against Bradlaugh. He reviewed both sets of arguments in detail and came to the conclusion that the Evidence Acts of 1869 and 1870 should be interpreted strictly rather than liberally. The acts did not specify, he observed, that their purpose was to amend the Parliamentary Oaths Act of 1866, 'and it seems difficult to understand, if the Legislature intended to make a change in the law in an important matter which affected both Houses of Parliament, that this intention should not be expressed in clear and decisive language'. Mr. Justice Mathew disagreed, it is true, with Giffard's contention that the Oaths Act of 1866 must necessarily be construed as permitting only persons with religious beliefs to affirm, but this *obiter dictum* was not relevant to the decision. The only grain of comfort for the defendant was the judge's comment that Bradlaugh's arguments 'in vigour and clearness left nothing to be desired'.[2]

Mr. Justice Mathew's decision was announced on 11 March 1881 and before the day was over John Gorst, one of the members of the 'Fourth Party', had given notice of a motion vacating Bradlaugh's seat in Parliament and ordering a writ to be issued for a new election in what, in his haste, Gorst called 'the borough of Nottingham'.[3] The Attorney-General, in a memorandum to Gladstone, noted that Bradlaugh had promised to appeal against the decision immediately, and that 'it would produce very inconvenient results if, Mr. Gorst's motion being accepted, the Court of Appeal should in a few weeks reverse the present judgment and hold that the seat had never been vacated'.[4] The Cabinet decided therefore to oppose Gorst's motion for the time being, and Northcote, once the Attorney-General had explained to him that an appeal was under way, was also willing to wait.[5]

---

[1] '*Clarke* v. *Bradlaugh*.' Also *N.R.*, 27 Feb. 1881, p. 132; 13 Mar. 1881, pp. 177–9; 3 Apr. 1881, p. 246.   [2] '*Clarke* v. *Bradlaugh*.'
[3] *Hansard*, cclix (1881), 802.   [4] G.P. (B.M.), 44219, fol. 45.
[5] G.P. (B.M.), 44642, fol. 158; Northampton *Weekly Reporter*, 4 Apr. 1881.

Gorst's motion consequently was not brought to a vote, but Lord Randolph Churchill expressed his own fear a few days later that Bradlaugh might wait a year before even initiating his appeal. Bradlaugh quickly rose to point out that he was legally required to prosecute his appeal within twenty-one days 'as the noble Lord would have discovered on reference to any ordinary law book'.[1]

This by-play mattered little. Bradlaugh had grave doubts whether his appeal would be upheld, and the Government was similarly dubious. 'There is simply no end to their persistent bad luck', noted Gladstone's secretary in his diary.[2] Speaker Brand himself received the decision with mixed feelings. On the one hand, he was pleased that Mr. Justice Mathews 'able and clear judgment' had vindicated him in his own original doubts about Bradlaugh's interpretation of the law. On the other hand, he feared 'a renewal of Bradlaugh incidents'.[3]

The hearings of 30 March 1881 before a Court of Appeal consisting of Justices Lush and Bramwell went over the same ground that the lower court had gone over before. Once again Bradlaugh sought to prove that, whatever the intentions of the framers of the Evidence Act of 1869, the act had in effect created a new class of persons who necessarily had the right to affirm under Section Four of the Parliamentary Oaths Act. For the first time, Bradlaugh advanced an additional argument: that Henry Clarke's claim as 'a common informer' was archaic and that the suit was thus doubly invalid.

Justices Bramwell and Lush ruled against Bradlaugh on both counts. The Act of 1869 had not created a new class of persons who might affirm—since they were allowed to affirm only in the role of witness and not for the purpose of making promissory affirmations—and a common informer *could* sue. Justice Bramwell, indeed, considered this 'as plain a case as can possibly be'. In Justice Lush's decision one can detect a note of hesitancy. He was also most complimentary to Bradlaugh: 'If you will allow me to say so, you have

---

[1] *Hansard*, cclix (1881), 898–900.
[2] *N.R.*, 20 Mar. 1881, p. 196; Hamilton Diary (B.M.), 48631, p. 3.
[3] Hampden Diary, entries for 11 and 31 Mar. 1881.

argued the case with great propriety as well as great force.'[1] But compliments were not sufficient to keep Bradlaugh in Parliament. His seat was immediately vacated and a new election was called for in the Borough of Northampton.

By-elections in late-nineteenth-century England were held promptly, so that the new election was scheduled for 7 April 1881, scarcely a week after the writ had been issued. The political campaign was consequently a short but intense one. Although there were rumours that Northampton's moderate Liberals would put up a third candidate of their own,[2] Bradlaugh was re-nominated with Conservative opposition only. Northampton Liberals who had supported him in 1880 saw little reason to oppose him in 1881, and there was in any case a tradition that a local party organization which had made its selection at the previous General Election would continue to support its choice.

National attention was necessarily concentrated much more closely upon this election than upon Bradlaugh's role in the General Election of the previous year, and there was a widespread expectation that Bradlaugh would be defeated. Labouchere's assurance to the contrary in the House of Commons the previous June had, after all, been greeted with 'incredulous laughter'.[3] The consensus was that Bradlaugh would be weaker without Labouchere. Yet there seems to have been little eagerness among Conservative candidates to tackle the Northampton electorate, and the chief qualification of Edward Corbett, the young man chosen for the task, was that both his father and grandfather had served as Members of Parliament.

Corbett's positive programme was deliberately kept vague in order to attract the largest number of moderate Liberals. Corbett himself went so far as to argue that Bradlaugh's defeat would not injure the Liberal Government. He criticized Bradlaugh for having sided so often with the Home-Rule Party in the Coercion Bill debates of the previous winter. The Northampton *Mercury*, the chief voice of the Moderate

---

[1] '*Clarke* v. *Bradlaugh*', also *N.R.*, 3 Apr. 1881, pp. 243–51; 10 Apr. 1881, pp. 258–63, 265–7.

[2] Cf. *Freeman's Journal* (Dublin), 2 Apr. 1881, p. 5.

[3] Lucy, *A Diary of Two Parliaments*, ii. 30.

Liberals, similarly suggested that Bradlaugh 'would have acted more wisely by giving firm support in this matter to the Government'.[1]

It was not his actions in the House of Commons, however, which were brought under greatest attack by the Conservatives, but Bradlaugh's moral and religious views. To help in this attack, there appeared, just in time for the election, a pamphlet by one Henry Varley, *An Address to the Electors in the Borough of Northampton*. It began with a ringing preamble: 'I sound a clarion blast against Charles Bradlaugh, the champion advocate of iniquity and lawlessness.' Future editions were to be addressed not merely to the Electors of the Borough of Northampton, but also to the Members of the British House of Commons and 'to the Men of England Generally FOR THEIR PRIVATE READING ONLY'. That last phrase obviously did not hurt sales, for in little over a year nine editions had been printed and over 70,000 copies distributed.

Varley's pamphlet was essentially a compendium of what seemed to be the most damaging quotations that could be culled from Bradlaugh's debates and other writings over thirty years. Varley alternated between Bradlaugh's anti-religious views and his views on birth control. He cited the original legal indictment of *The Fruits of Philosophy*, which had damned the book as 'lewd, filthy, and obscene'. He identified Bradlaugh as the author of the notorious *Elements of Social Science*, an encyclopedic work which had cast doubt, among other things, upon the desirability of monogamous marriage. (As mentioned above, Bradlaugh's closest connexion with the work had been a partly favourable review he had written in the *National Reformer* many years before.) Finally Varley quoted an 'English Marseillaise' written some years earlier by Annie Besant:

> We are sworn to put tyranny down,
> We strike at the Throne and the Crown,
> To arms Republicans!
> Strike now for liberty.

'Our objection to Mr. Bradlaugh', Varley summed up, 'is

---

[1] *N.R.*, 10 Apr. 1881, p. 282; Northampton *Mercury*, 9 Apr. 1881, p. 5.

that he is socially lawless, devoid of moral sense, untruthful, morally unclean, a coarse blasphemer, and an avowed atheist.'[1]

There is little doubt that Varley's pamphlet injured Bradlaugh. It was by far the most effective of many anti-Bradlaugh pamphlets to be issued during the 1880's. A copy was not only sent to every Northampton elector and distributed in every Northampton workshop but was also mailed to every Member of Parliament.[2] Bradlaugh found Varley's pamphlet difficult to combat because it was a mixture of accurate quotation, misquotation, and half-truth. Among other things, Bradlaugh had, after all, at one time called Christianity 'an accursed creed'. Bradlaugh asked Varley to submit the pamphlet to an independent arbitrator to be appointed by a judge and have that arbitrator judge its truth or falsity. Varley refused and dared Bradlaugh to sue him for libel. This Bradlaugh hesitated to do, partly because it would have involved a great deal of time and also—one suspects— because Bradlaugh felt unsure whether he could present the issue in a fashion sufficiently clear-cut to win the case. Thus all that Bradlaugh or Annie Besant could do was to pinpoint Varley's errors in the columns of the *National Reformer*. The pamphlet continued to be sold, however, and in April 1883 Bradlaugh once again publicly voiced his exasperation: 'The trade of slanderer seems an easy one in England when "noblemen" and "gentlemen" lend willing ears to the cowardly calumnies of a reptile like Henry Varley.'[3]

One final campaign tactic of the Northampton Conservatives was based upon the legal liability which the Parliamentary Oaths Act of 1866 provided for those who sat and voted without taking the appropriate oath. The Member's seat was to be vacated 'as if he were dead'. Consequently, election posters signed by Corbett's election agent warned all Northampton voters the day before the election that 'the said Charles Bradlaugh is therefore ineligible for Election to fill the Vacancy thus created and that all votes given for the

---

[1] Henry Varley, *An Address to the Electors in the Borough of Northampton* (London, 1881), *passim*. Also, ibid. (9th ed., London, 1882), *passim*.

[2] *N.R.*, 17 Apr. 1881, p. 289.

[3] *N.R.*, 12 Feb. 1882, p. 97; 26 June 1881, pp. 3–5; 17 June 1883, p. 442.

said Charles Bradlaugh at this election will be thrown away'. To underscore the point, the word 'Dead' was boldly printed across Bradlaugh's own election posters the same night.[1]

Bradlaugh, who had been campaigning night and day, stoutly defended his record in the House of Commons, his occasional independence—'You did not send me to the House of Commons to be a lickspittle'—and his success in obtaining petitions for an inquiry into the subject of perpetual pensions. 'There is no other independent member of Parliament', he boasted, 'who for 25 years has ever received as much support for any measure advocated by himself alone.'[2] His key argument was that his re-election was necessary to vindicate the right of a constituency to select its own candidate and to insist upon that candidate, when duly elected, sitting without hindrance in the House of Commons.[3] Bradlaugh's claim to represent the cause of religious freedom was hampered by his express intention to take the oath if necessary. The Northampton *Mercury* could not understand why Bradlaugh should not follow the precedent set him by Baron Rothschild (of waiting patiently for eleven years until Parliament changed the law), and the *Daily News* regarded it not inconsistent of 'those who voted for Mr. Bradlaugh by way of protest against the oath' to decline 'to vote for him in order that he may take it'.[4] Yet neither the oath nor the affirmation had been an issue during the previous election, and there is no reason to believe that any of Bradlaugh's supporters in April 1880 had regarded their vote as a protest against the Parliamentary oath.

Bradlaugh's most loyal backer in the campaign was his colleague Henry Labouchere, who upon arrival in Northampton described in moving terms—and with considerable poetic licence—his leave-taking of Gladstone in London. 'And men of Northampton, that grand old man said to me, as he patted me on the shoulder, "Henry, my boy, bring him

[1] Great Britain, *Statutes at Large*, 29 and 30 Vict. c. 19, 'Parliamentary Oaths Act'. Northampton Central Library collection of election clippings.

[2] Northampton *Weekly Reporter*, 18 Mar. 1881.

[3] *N.R.*, 10 Apr. 1881, p. 274.

[4] Northampton *Mercury*, 9 Apr. 1881, p. 5; London *Daily News* cited in Northampton *Mercury*, 16 Apr. 1881, p. 5.

back, bring him back." [1] Bradlaugh's supporters did not hesitate to link the names of Gladstone and Bright with that of their hero.

> Although fanatics madly rave,
> And hypocrites may scheme,
> True men indeed of ev'ry creed
> His cause the just one deem.
> When Gladstone and Bright declare it right
> In the Senate he should be,
> The canting train may howl in vain
> But Bradlaugh there they'll see. [2]

When the votes were counted, Bradlaugh was found to have won with 3,437 votes to Corbett's 3,305. His margin of more than 600 votes at the General Election had been cut to fewer than 150, but he had been re-elected. The decline in the size of his majority can be attributed largely to the abstention of Moderate Liberals who had half-heartedly favoured Bradlaugh on the previous occasion because it was a General Election and Gladstone seemed to need every adherent he could get. The Conservative press alternated between rejoicing in the diminished majority and criticizing the Central Conservative Committee for not presenting a stronger

[1] The nickname Gladstone bore in his later years, 'Grand Old Man' (often shortened to G.O.M.) is widely—but apparently inaccurately—attributed to Labouchere and to that incident. Algar Labouchere Thorold, *The Life of Henry Labouchere* (London, 1913), pp. 143–4. Edward Hamilton (Hamilton Diary, entry of 25 June 1882 (B.M.), 48632, p. 141), also attributes the phrase to Labouchere. Bradlaugh himself, however, had used the phrase two weeks earlier in the *National Reformer* of 27 Mar. 1881 (p. 210), in which he speaks 'with firmer admiration than ever of the grand old man who is England's Premier'. Robert Rhodes James, *Lord Randolph Churchill* (London, 1959), p. 117, erroneously calls it Northcote's phrase. According to Lucy, *A Diary of the Salisbury Parliament, 1886–1892*), p. 229, the phrase was first used by Sir William Harcourt in an address to his constituents shortly after the election of April 1880. By August 1882 it had, according to Hamilton, become a cliché, affectionate if 'irreverent'. Hamilton Diary (B.M.), 48632, fols. 141, 221. The following advertisement began to appear in the *N.R.* soon thereafter: 'The "GRAND OLD MAN" CIGARS are so named because, like the "Grand Old Man" himself, they are unequalled. All Liberal and Radical clubs should try them.' As for Gladstone himself, he had confided to to his wife on his seventieth birthday in 1879: 'Do what I will, I *cannot* feel myself to be an old man.' Lord Kilbracken, *Reminiscences* (London, 1931), p. 108.

[2] Northampton Library collection of election clippings.

candidate.[1] As one Northampton clergyman was reported to have put it: 'God had not answered their prayers in rejecting Mr. Bradlaugh, but he rejoiced that He had done something towards it in reducing his majority.'[2]

[1] See, for example, Northampton *Mercury*, 16 Apr. 1881, p. 5, and *Whitehall Review*, 14 Apr. 1881, p. 483; *N.R.*, 24 Apr. 1881, p. 314.
[2] Cited in *N.R.*, 24 Apr. 1881, p. 309.

XI

THE QUESTION OF THE OATH

A SIGNIFICANT aspect of any historical incident is the tendency for both the newspaper-reading audience and the very actors themselves to forget the details of Act One by the time Act Two is well under way. And so it was in the spring of 1881 with Charles Bradlaugh's attitude toward the oath. His announced intention upon re-election to enter Parliament by means of the regular oath was greeted by newspapers otherwise friendly to his cause as a step both patently blasphemous and utterly novel. True, he had entered the House the previous July on the basis of an affirmation now judged illegal; but in the notorious letter of 20 May 1880 he had explained his intention to take the oath should the option of affirmation be closed to him. He had been imprisoned in the Clock Tower for insisting on the oath. Yet he now found his decision one that had to be explained all over again.

Gloated the staunchly Anglican *Rock*:

> Northampton's elected is ready to swear
> If only his seat he may hold;
> His much-vaunted scruple's thus thrown to the air,
> And consistency's out in the cold.[1]

The opinion of the *Rock* alone would not have troubled Bradlaugh. But that the otherwise sympathetic *Daily Telegraph* should accuse him of marring his cause 'by want of directness and straight-forward dealing'[2] and that the leading Liberal organ, the *Daily News*, should term his willingness to swear gross expediency—'It is not by personal accommodations of this sort that victories of principle are won'[3]—such charges did wound Bradlaugh. Perhaps most of all he was hurt by the attitude of the Radical *Pall Mall Gazette*, a daily

---

[1] 22 Apr. 1881, p. 273.
[2] Cited in *N.R.*, 8 May 1881, p. 371.
[3] Cited in Northampton *Daily Reporter*, 4 Apr. 1881.

edited by John Morley, an avowed agnostic, and the only evening paper Gladstone read regularly.

The effect [wrote the *Pall Mall Gazette*] on ordinary men, whatever their creed, of Mr. Bradlaugh's taking the oath is certain. Their moral sensibility will experience a shock. . . . The moral position of every Secularist, of every Freethinker, of every man who protests against Theological exclusiveness, will be lowered. . . . Why in the name of honesty should a Freethinker show less respect for his own conscientious feelings than has been shown by Catholics and Jews?[1]

In vain did Bradlaugh retort that he was not being inconsistent. Until 1869, it had been illegal for secularists to affirm in the courts; if they wanted to appear as witnesses they had to swear an oath. Should they have cut themselves off from resort to courts of law for that reason? Bradlaugh had not done so nor had other free-thinkers. The same problem had now arisen in Parliament. Should he now exclude himself from Parliament for an indefinite number of years until legal relief should come? He was not nearly so sure as his friendly critics that his own patience would speed the course of an Affirmation Bill; the Quakers, after all, had been forced to wait 135 years. It was, in any case, not the form but the underlying reality which mattered, and it had surely been wrong of Bradlaugh to tender himself for re-election if he had not meant to abide by the formalities necessary for taking his seat. Bradlaugh had, after all, done his best to soft-pedal his religious views in Northampton. He had been elected there not as an atheist, but in spite of the fact that he was an atheist. Was it consistent of him now to claim otherwise? Would it be fair to his constituents to deprive them for this reason of their representation in the House of Commons?[2]

Both the *Daily News* and the *Pall Mall Gazette*, whatever their opinion of the propriety of Bradlaugh's swearing, conceded that legally the right was his. In a lengthy review of the matter, the *Pall Mall Gazette* went so far, indeed, as to suggest 'that the Speaker, not now taken by surprise, will

---

[1] Cited in Northampton *Weekly Reporter*, 22 Apr. 1881.
[2] Northampton *Daily Reporter*, 2 May 1881, p. 3; *N.R.*, 24 Apr. 1881, p. 305.

not suffer this right to be questioned . . .'.¹ It was this article, wrote Gladstone to the Speaker on 18 April 1881, which had roused his 'flagging and wearied attention' once again to the Bradlaugh case. He agreed, the Prime Minister continued, that while Bradlaugh would be wrong in taking the oath, it was not the business of the House of Commons to prevent him from doing so.² The Speaker, in acknowledging Gladstone's letter, concurred that Bradlaugh would be better advised 'to stand aloof under protest' until Parliament had passed an Affirmation Bill; but since he had announced his intention to do otherwise, the Speaker saw no way 'although the proceeding may shock the moral sense of mankind . . . that the House can, according to law, do otherwise than admit him'.³

Gladstone found convincing the *Pall Mall Gazette*'s suggestion that the Speaker consider any attempt to interfere with Bradlaugh's oath out of order. Brand, however, had already made up his mind that, considering all that had passed the previous year, he could not justifiably oppose such an interruption. His hope was that such a decision would not be forced upon him, and in order to bring about a behind-the-scenes settlement, he privately urged Northcote 'that the House would do well & wisely, according to the Constitution, to admit him without question'. If the House did not do so 'I apprehend . . . it will be going beyond the Law & the Constitution'.⁴

Bradlaugh's re-election had coincided with the beginning of the Parliamentary Easter recess, so that Northcote had had several weeks to think over his course of action. As so often, Northcote was hesitant. He was inclined to think that the Conservative minority 'could not decently sit still' if Bradlaugh chose to take the oath, but he was not sure. What is clear is that in 1881 no more than in 1880 did Northcote look upon the case as an occasion for gaining political advantage.

---

¹ Cited in Northampton *Weekly Reporter*, 22 Apr. 1881. As has been noted in Chapter V, the Speaker had *not* been caught by surprise the previous year.
² Hampden MSS.
³ Brand to Gladstone, 20 Apr. 1881, G.P. (B.M.), 44195, fol. 37.
⁴ (Copy) Brand to Sir George Grey, 18 Apr. 1881, Hampden MSS.; Brand to Northcote, 20 Apr. 1881, Iddesleigh MSS. (B.M.), 50021, fols. 208–10.

He would genuinely have preferred either the Speaker or Gladstone to relieve him of the necessity of doing anything.[1] Besides he stood in too much awe of Bradlaugh himself. 'We have a terribly clever fellow to deal with', he once confided to Giffard.[2] And so Northcote, after some delay, replied to Speaker Brand's letter of 20 April with an extended explanation as to why he could not accede to the Speaker's request. The events of the previous year could not be ignored; the new election had not wiped the slate clean; and thus the Conservative party could not acquiesce in Bradlaugh's taking the oath 'without any explanation on his part which would remove the difficulty which we feel'.[3]

The Speaker's attempt to have Northcote silence his followers had failed. What kind of explanation did Northcote require of Bradlaugh, expostulated Brand privately to Gladstone; 'he cannot expect him to recite the first Article of the Creed'. In his diary the Speaker noted what he considered the real reason for Northcote's reaction: he had been forced on, against his better judgement, 'by his more ardent supporters, who control him constantly'.[4]

Only two leading Conservatives had taken what might be considered pro-Bradlaugh stands—Sir John Holker, the ex-Attorney-General, and Lord Derby, a one-time member of Disraeli's Cabinet and the son of the late Prime Minister. But by the spring of 1881 Holker was a sick man far from the inner circles of his party, and Derby was on the road to fully fledged Gladstonian Liberalism and a place, by 1883, in Gladstone's Cabinet.[5] On Northcote's other side stood the Musketeers of the Fourth Party, and their actions in asking for a new writ immediately after Mr. Justice Mathew's decision had indicated to Northcote that in a revived Bradlaugh case they once more scented political meat. The Fourth Party, after Bradlaugh's admission to Parliament, had occupied itself with other things, such as Gladstone's Employer's

[1] Northcote to Salisbury, 6 Apr. 1881, Salisbury MSS.; Northcote to Gladstone, 21 and 26 Apr. 1881, G.P. (B.M.), 44217, fols. 180, 183.
[2] Halsbury MSS.   [3] Northcote to Brand, 25 Apr. 1881, Hampden MSS.
[4] Brand to Gladstone, 26 Apr. 1881, G.P. (B.M.), 44195, fol. 42; Hampden Diary, entry for 25 Apr. 1881.
[5] For Derby's views see N.R., 15 Jan. 1882, p. 33. Holker died in May 1882, shortly after being appointed to a judgeship by Gladstone.

Liability Bill, which they criticized not on the conventional basis that it implied too much governmental interference with the activities of manufacturers but on the basis that the bill did not go far enough.[1] The four men met two or three times a week at little dinners at which they discussed future plans. When Northcote in September 1880 politely requested its members to return to their proper place within the Conservative ranks—'I am inclined to think the "Fourth Party" has done enough for its fame'—his plea went unheeded.[2] Balfour's and Wolff's success in persuading Lord Salisbury to be the guest speaker at a dinner in Lord Randolph Churchill's honour in Woodstock that November had been widely interpreted by the Liberal press as public recognition of the power of the Fourth Party.[3]

During the winter of 1881, however, the foursome virtually dissolved. They disagreed on tactics in dealing with the Irish Coercion Bill; Churchill, who had lived in Ireland for several years and was well acquainted with many Irish politicians, was inclined to show more sympathy to the Irish than did his colleagues. The reopening of the Bradlaugh case restored unity to the Fourth Party. Its members were at once prepared to revive the *jeu d'esprit* of the year before and to plot strategy in a manner such that 'the uninitiated might have thought the subject was a game of chess'.[4] Churchill's interest may have been given a special spur by Bradlaugh's proposed inquiry into the Marlborough pension, but quite sufficient for all four was the underlying conviction that there continued to exist among the British electorate a widespread revulsion against Bradlaugh and his proposed 'blasphemy'. 'There is one fundamental truth in politics', wrote Wolff to Salisbury in another connexion, 'with which I daily become more impressed. No movement of any kind can be created by agitation unless there is a substratum of real feeling in there to be agitated.'[5]

[1] Gorst, *The Fourth Party*, pp. 78–79.

[2] (Copy) Northcote to Gorst, 11 Sept. 1880; Gorst to Northcote, 15 Sept. 1880, Iddesleigh MSS. (B.M.), 50041, fols. 32–38.

[3] Balfour MSS. (B.M.), 49695, fol. 176. Wolff to Salisbury, 27 Oct. 1880, Salisbury MSS.

[4] Gorst, *Fourth Party*, pp. 166, 176; Mrs. George Cornwallis-West, *The Reminiscences of Lady Randolph Churchill* (London, 1908), p. 91.

[5] Wolff to Salisbury, 10 Jan. 1884, Salisbury MSS.

The Fourth Party obviously would not have permitted Northcote to let Bradlaugh take the oath without protest. To them Northcote was 'the old goat', and his habitual lack of political pugnacity they attributed not so much to prudence as to a genuine dislike of taking any action which would annoy the Government. Northcote, they believed, feared to lose the high opinion which, he felt, Gladstone had of him.[1] As a matter of fact, Gladstone did not really respect Northcote. After the latter had gone back upon a procedural agreement—presumably at Churchill's behest—Gladstone dismissed his Conservative counterpart as 'flabby and shabby'.[2]

Between Bradlaugh's re-election and the reassembling of Parliament after the spring recess there occurred an event of great significance for the Conservative party, the death of Lord Beaconsfield. In the dark months after the defeat of the previous spring, Disraeli had continued to serve as a focus of unity for his party. He had been able to make the Fourth Party men feel that he sympathized with their fighting spirit without at the same time antagonizing Northcote. Now the revered leader was gone, and the question of the hour became who was to be Disraeli's successor: was it to be Northcote or the new Conservative leader in the House of Lords, the Marquess of Salisbury? Disraeli, though he had played with the idea of resigning the leadership to Salisbury during the previous autumn, had finally done nothing, and in 1880 it was still widely believed that Northcote was the heir apparent.[3] Churchill and Wolff would have preferred an immediate selection of Salisbury as the new party leader. Salisbury, however, was a shrewd politician who had no desire to antagonize the Northcote wing of the party and who saw no need to act hastily.[4]

Salisbury may well have felt that time was on his side, and

---

[1] Balfour, *Chapters of Autobiography*, p. 145. 'He is a loathsome creature,' wrote Wolff privately of Northcote, 'full of small spite and destitute of virility.' Balfour MSS. (B.M.), 49838, fol. 102.

[2] Hamilton Diary (B.M.), 48630, fol. 297; Dilke MSS. (B.M.), 43935, fols. 19–20.

[3] Gower, *My Reminiscences*, ii. 355. Also, Cairns to Northcote, 30 Apr. 1881, Iddesleigh MSS. Gorst, *Fourth Party*, p. 50.

[4] Cairns to Northcote, 30 Apr. 1881, Iddesleigh MSS. (B.M.), 50021, fols. 137–8. Northcote to H. Northcote, 30 Apr. 1883, Iddesleigh MSS.

he worked out an arrangement with Northcote whereby he would lead the party in the House of Lords and Northcote would continue to lead the party in the House of Commons. When the time came for a Conservative Prime Minister to be appointed, Queen Victoria would choose between them.[1] Had the Queen been forced to make such a choice in 1881, there is little question that she would have selected Northcote, but this necessity was not to occur until four years later and by that time circumstances had changed.[2] Whatever other problems it may have raised, Beaconsfield's death made a show of leadership by Northcote in the Bradlaugh case an absolute necessity for him.

In the meanwhile, the Speaker, Northcote, Gladstone, and Bradlaugh were engaged in a stately quadrille, an exchange of courtesies which to a later generation must confirm all its notions of Victorian respectability. Bradlaugh led off by requesting a brief interview with the Speaker in order to discuss certain legal points connected with his claim to take the oath and the course he proposed to take if the claim were not granted. The interview took place, and the Speaker, to his own surprise, found Bradlaugh once again 'frank & respectful. . . . We parted quite amiably.'[3] Northcote in the meantime had politely informed Bradlaugh that he would oppose his right to take the oath. Bradlaugh, with equal cordiality, replied that while he did not quite understand what sort of statement the House of Commons had the right to require from a duly elected member before he took his seat, he was 'at least sure that whatever opposition you think it right to offer will be that of an honourable gentleman & I thank you for the courtesy of your notice'.[4] Gladstone, while at work preparing a counter-motion to meet Northcote's, thoughtfully assured the Conservative leader that no attempt would be made to admit Bradlaugh into Parliament

[1] Sir Erskine May, *The Constitutional History of England*, edited and continued by Francis Holland, iii (London, 1912), 112.
[2] *The Letters of Queen Victoria*, Second Series, ed. G. E. Buckle (New York, 1928), iii. 219.
[3] Bradlaugh to Brand, 20 Apr. 1881, Hampden MSS. The letter is misdated 20 Apr. 1880; Hampden Diary, entry for 25 Apr. 1881.
[4] Bradlaugh to Northcote, 25 Apr. 1881, Iddesleigh MSS. (B.M.), 50041, fols. 52–53.

while a large body of Conservative M.P.s was away attending Lord Beaconsfield's funeral.[1]

And so the next meeting of the House of Commons was postponed until after the funeral, to the evening of 26 April. As Bradlaugh advanced to the Table, Northcote, who had been leaning forward with his hands on his knees like a dog held in leash, rose to interrupt. The Speaker permitted the interruption, and Northcote moved that Bradlaugh, in accordance with the two committee reports and Giffard's resolution of the previous year, 'be not permitted to go through the form of repeating the words of the Oath'. Horace Davey, a Liberal back-bencher, immediately moved to amend Northcote's motion to the effect that 'this House will not, on the ground of information extraneous to the transaction, offer any impediment' to anyone taking the oath.[2]

This time Bradlaugh was given the right to speak at the bar on his own behalf before the crucial vote was taken. He was outwardly calm but within him stirred an immense amount of pent-up feeling, 'almost painful in its silent intensity'.[3] He began by assuring the House once again 'without mental reservation, without equivocation' that he would not go through any form that he did not mean to be binding upon him. Nothing impeached the legality of his recent election, he insisted. There was no charge of bribery, no charge of corruption against him. He suffered from no legal disqualifications. And yet the House insisted upon trying him for his opinions, opinions he had never advanced within the House. 'This', moreover, 'is a political Assembly, met to decide on the policy of the nation, and not on the religious opinions of the citizens.' The law was on his side, Bradlaugh felt sure, even if the House opposed him. 'You think I am an obnoxious man, and that I have no one on my side. If that be so, then the more reason that this House, grand in the strength of its centuries of liberty, should have now that generosity in dealing with one who tomorrow may

[1] (Copy) Gladstone to Brand, G.P. (B.M.), 44544, fol. 162; Gladstone to Northcote, 22 Apr. 1881, Iddesleigh MSS.
[2] *Hansard*, cclx (1881), 1183–8.
[3] London Correspondent, *Freeman's Journal* (Dublin), 27 Apr. 1881, p. 4.

be forced into a struggle for public opinion against it.'[1]
Cheers broke out on the Liberal benches, while the Conservative side of the House was temporarily silent, but the
cheers proved misleading.

The debate went on with all the arguments of the previous
year repeated. The Liberals pointed out that the rights of
Northampton were being violated. 'Is the constituency to
overawe and command Parliament?' was the Conservative
retort. Bradlaugh labours under no legal disqualifications,
contended Sir Henry James, the Attorney-General. Bradlaugh did indeed labour under such a disqualification, replied
Sir Hardinge Giffard; his promises were meaningless because he has never stated that they were 'binding upon his
conscience as an oath'. Suppose Northampton had selected
a woman as its representative, suggested Giffard. 'Are we
to be told that female suffrage is to be immediately established, because a constituency has thought it proper to act
in violation of the law?'[2]

Bradlaugh, declared Gladstone, may be on trial before this
House, 'but the House also, permit me to say it with great
respect, is upon its trial'. The legal nub of the Opposition
case rested on no more than an inference drawn from a statement Bradlaugh made the year before. 'Is it, then, intended',
asked the Prime Minister, 'that for years and years Mr.
Bradlaugh is to be put aside as not being a Member of this
House on the ground of a declaration made by him—I believe
extorted from him. . . . Is he to be prevented from taking the
Oath until there is a recantation?'[3]

That was apparently the case, for Davey's amendment was
defeated, and Northcote's motion was accepted by a vote of
208–175. In the minority were 171 Liberals and 4 Home
Rulers; in the majority, 182 Conservatives, 15 Liberals, and
11 Home Rulers. The Conservatives had sent a very strong
whip, while the Liberals had not made it a party question,
even though Gladstone had privately described the prospect
of defeat 'a moral as well as Parliamentary calamity'.[4] 'A vote

---

[1] *Hansard*, cclx (1881), 1207–12.   [2] Ibid., cols. 1225, 1232.
[3] Ibid., cols. 1213, 1219–20.
[4] Hamilton Diary, 48631 (B.M.), p. 49; (Copy) Gladstone to Hartington,
21 Apr. 1881, G.P. (B.M.), 44544, fol. 159.

of the House of Commons has overridden the law', proclaimed the *Pall Mall Gazette*.¹ Yet 'there is little doubt', was
the ominous comment of *The Times*, that the vote 'represents
the practical judgment of a majority far larger than that which
actually followed Sir Stafford Northcote into the lobby'.²

The House of Commons had once again refused Charles
Bradlaugh the right to take the oath, and once again—as he
had after the defeat of Labouchere's resolution the previous
June—he refused to abide by what he termed an illegal
resolution. The Speaker ordered Bradlaugh to withdraw:
the latter did so only to return to the Table a moment later.
As *Punch* described the scene,

> It was an elaborately-constructed performance, though simple
> in general effect. First, Mr. BRADLAUGH enters, and executes a *pas
> seul* before the Mace. Immediately he is joined by the Sergeant-at-
> Arms, and the two polka down the centre till they reach the Bar.
> Then BRADLAUGH, breaking away from his partner, rushes down
> the stage and strikes an attitude before the foot-lights. His partner,
> Captain GOSSETT, trips gracefully after him; the two embrace, then
> return a few paces, joined by five other members of the ballet,
> when the minuet commences. . . .³

In another vein the *Whitehall Review*, still mourning the
death of Beaconsfield, lamented the same 'melancholy spectacle. . . . Looking upon it one felt almost thankful that
the great guardian of Parliamentary honour, the jealous
custodian of the dignity of the House of Commons, was not
there to see it.'⁴ Northcote announced his willingness again
to move that Bradlaugh be taken into custody—a prospect
to which Bradlaugh did not altogether object—except that
the latter's conduct 'appears to be encouraged and supported
by Her Majesty's Government'. Gladstone indignantly denied the accusation; he was merely abiding by his policy
of the previous year. If his advice was to be rejected by the
House of Commons, it was not his business to relieve the
temporary majority from the dilemma in which it had placed
itself.⁵ Gladstone was equally unwilling to heed the Speaker's

¹ Cited in *N.R.*, 8 May 1881, p. 379.
² 28 Apr. 1881, p. 9.   ³ 30 Apr. 1881, p. 104.
⁴ *Whitehall Review*, 28 Apr. 1881, p. 538.
⁵ *Hansard*, cclx (1881), 1241–50; *N.R.*, 1 May 1881, p. 350.

request that he introduce a resolution to restrain Bradlaugh
physically. At most he was willing to accede to such a resolution if it proved necessary to restore order in the chamber.[1]

The House finally adjourned for the night, but the following day Bradlaugh punctually presented himself again to be
sworn. Another lengthy debate ensued, in the course of which
Labouchere asked Gladstone to introduce immediately a bill
permitting anyone who chose to do so to substitute an
affirmation for an oath. Gladstone agreed, provided that the
Conservatives in turn consented not to oppose the introduction of such a bill. The controversial Irish Land Bill, that
epic piece of legislation whose purpose it was to extend to the
Irish tenant farmers the three F's for which they had long
pleaded—fair rent, free sale, and fixity of tenure—was in
the early stages of its course through Parliament. The bill
embodied Gladstone's hopes of assuaging the conditions
which had led to the necessity of coercion the previous
winter, and the Prime Minister considered it imperative to
proceed with it, even though in the course of the debates
on Bradlaugh hostile Irish members had repeatedly embarrassed the House and obstructed business. Arthur O'Connor
retorted on behalf of the Irish members that 'if it is necessary
[in order] to secure a good Land Bill, or to secure Home
Rule or anything else we desire to secure, that we shall consent to the taking of the Oath by an avowed Atheist, we
cannot and will not consent'.[2] Northcote was equally unwilling to promise not to block an Affirmation Bill. He could
consent to nothing 'in the nature of a bargain'.[3]

Gladstone none the less decided to go ahead with such
a bill, while Bradlaugh pledged himself to stay away from
Parliament pending its passage. The bill, a one-clause affair,
was drawn up at the Cabinet meeting of 29 April 1881—the
original draft was probably Lord Granville's—and it was
decided to attach the names of the Attorney-General, the
Solicitor-General, and John Bright as sponsors.[4]

The bill presented the Conservative party with a new
problem. Both in 1880 and 1881 Northcote and others had

---

[1] Hampden Diary, entry for 27 Apr. 1881.
[2] *Hansard*, cclx (1881), 1252–5, 1291.   [3] Ibid., col. 1262.
[4] G.P. (B.M.), 44642, fol. 176; 44544, fol. 165.

The Protestant Richelieu.

5. "The Protestant Richelieu" (*Whitehall Review*, 19 May 1881)

6. William Ewart Gladstone and Sir Stafford Northcote

argued that the question must be handled not by means of resolutions but by legislation. It was the taking of the oath, Northcote had emphasized on 26 April, not the presence of Bradlaugh as such, to which he objected.[1] Could Northcote now consistently oppose such legislation point-blank? Some members of the Government innocently assumed, indeed, that Northcote would wish to help frame the legal terminology of the bill, and Sir Henry James offered the Conservative leader such an opportunity. Northcote turned it down.

Yet, while objecting to a special 'privilegium' for Bradlaugh and his associates, Northcote suggested privately to Salisbury that the best solution would be 'the entire abandonment of the Oath and the substitution of a single formula of a declaration to be made by every member taking his seat in the House of Commons'.[2] Salisbury immediately warned his colleague not to give any hasty pledges. 'If we were merely devising an abstract policy', he acknowledged, 'I should feel no doubt of the wisdom of allowing the law to be modified in such a manner that this scandal should not arise again. But we are not in the zone of pure reason—or anywhere near it.' For the present, Salisbury proposed a policy of delay, opposition on the basis that the country must first be informed about the proposed changes, and finally an amendment to make the bill inapplicable to any person already elected (thus forcing Bradlaugh, at the very least, to go through another election).[3]

Northcote need not have worried. The bill never came to a second reading. It never even came to a first reading. According to Parliamentary rules, all opposed business had to be introduced by half-past twelve. When Sir Henry James sought leave to bring in the bill on 2 May, he was greeted with a deliberate filibuster led by Lord Randolph Churchill and strongly supported by a group of Irish Nationalists. Churchill attacked the bill as 'a concession to violence and mob law'.

---

[1] *Hansard*, cclx (1881), 1234–6; Hamilton Diary, entry for 28 Apr. 1881 (B.M.), 48631, fol. 51.

[2] Northcote to Salisbury, 20 Apr. 1881, Salisbury MSS.

[3] Salisbury to Northcote, 1 May 1881, Iddesleigh MSS. (B.M.), 50020, fols. 12–15; Cairns to Northcote, 30 Apr. 1881, Iddesleigh MSS. (B.M.), 50021, fols. 138–9.

It merely reflected Gladstone's fear 'that Mr. Bradlaugh would come down every day and turn the House of Commons into a bear garden, and under the protection of the Prime Minister, have a game at romps with the Sergeant-at-Arms'. Lord Randolph virtuously objected to any measure 'placing in the House of Commons brazen Atheism and rampant disloyalty'.[1]

When Gladstone proposed morning sittings for the House so that it might deal with the bill, the enemies of the Bill wrathfully declaimed upon the unworthy purpose of such an innovation. Bradlaugh's opponents were so aghast at the idea of a morning sitting, commented Labouchere ironically, that they 'are prepared to sit up all night to prevent it'.[2] On 6 May and again on 9 May, James was barred from introducing the bill. Time was wasted by repeated votes on motions for adjournment. 'There has seldom been a more shameless case of Obstruction', concluded the Liberal *Scotsman* of Edinburgh.[3] And whether the motive was one of regret in Ireland 'that precedence should be given to this matter over the all-important subject of the Land Law Bill', as one Irish M.P. put it, or whether it was the Conservative desire to impede the Land Bill—'We will put Bradlaugh on their hands and the damned Land Bill is stopped', Lord Henry Lennox is alleged to have said—the result was the same.[4] Gladstone, who had at first been hopeful of the bill's passage, admitted on 13 May 'that we [have] learnt by degrees that our impression did not correspond with the facts'. The Affirmation Bill was to be delayed, therefore, until after the Irish Land Bill had passed.[5]

When Bradlaugh saw the trend of events, he made a further attempt on 10 May to take the oath, only to be halted once again. Northcote, who willingly or not had left the blocking of the Affirmation Bill in Churchill's hands, once again barred the way, and without a division, a resolution was adopted 'that the Sergeant-at-Arms do remove Mr. Bradlaugh from the House, until he shall engage not further to

[1] *Hansard*, cclx (1881), 1557–9.
[2] Ibid., col. 415.
[3] Cited in *N.R.*, 8 May 1881, p. 380.
[4] *Hansard*, cclx (1881), 1568; *N.R.*, 8 May 1881, pp. 372–3.
[5] *Hansard*, cclxi (1881), 426.

disturb the proceedings of the House'.[1] Bradlaugh, in other words, was to be prevented from entering the chamber altogether, even as a visitor, unless he agreed to make no further attempt to take the oath.

While Bradlaugh waited, there occurred a minor incident in Parliament which effectively confirmed his sense of grievance. When on 20 May 1881 the next new M.P. after Bradlaugh came forward to take the oath, Sir Wilfrid Lawson, a Liberal sympathetic to Bradlaugh, rose to interrupt. The new man happened to be one Thomas Collins, a Conservative recently elected at a by-election, and Sir Wilfrid attempted to launch a discussion of Collins's religious beliefs in a manner reminiscent of Wolff's and Northcote's inquiries into Bradlaugh's. The Speaker refused to permit the interruption, explaining afterwards that Collins, a loyal Anglican, had not called attention to his religious opinions in the way Bradlaugh had done.[2] Lawson's purpose, to be sure, had not been to commence a religious inquisition but to illustrate his contention that the distinction drawn by the Speaker lacked legal validity.

The incident, which confirmed Bradlaugh in the same belief, has two curious sidelights. One is that, as we now know, the Speaker was not nearly so certain of his course as he seemed and almost regretted afterwards not having given Lawson the right to interrupt.[3] Secondly, the incident illustrates the perpetual danger of 'guilt by association'. A year later Collins publicly complained that ever since Lawson's attempt to interrupt his oath, he had been receiving letters— some sympathetic, but others strongly hostile—by writers under the impression that his religious views resembled Bradlaugh's. He now wished to declare once and for all that he believed devoutly in the Nicene Creed and was prepared so to swear at any time.[4]

Bradlaugh remained patient while the Irish Land Bill made its tortuous way along the legislative road, a process which was to take much longer than Gladstone had anticipated. In mid-June Bradlaugh attempted to secure a personal

[1] Ibid., cols. 179–82. [2] Ibid., col., 936.
[3] Hampden Diary, entry for 20 May 1881.
[4] N.R., 2 Apr. 1882, p. 280.

interview with Gladstone, but the latter, taking into consideration the extent to which 'Liberal and public interests have been brought into prejudice by untrue suppositions as to communication between you and the Government', denied the request.[1] A week-and-a-half later came further bad news. The Government, Gladstone informed Northampton's representative, had been forced to cancel consideration of many of the bills projected earlier in the year, and the Affirmation Bill was one of them. There was no public expression of regret, though Gladstone's secretary did note in his diary: 'Bradlaugh has behaved so well that I am sorry he has had to go to the wall; but it is inevitable.'[2] Despite a last-minute plea by Labouchere to Chamberlain,[3] the decision to drop the Bill was formally announced to Parliament by Gladstone on 4 July 1881. Bradlaugh was not surprised. He was already contemplating another method of achieving his goal.

[1] G.P. (B.M.), 44544, fol. 183.
[2] (Copy) Gladstone to Bradlaugh, 2 July 1881, G.P. (B.M.), 44544, fol. 189; Hamilton Diary (B.M.), 48631, p. 91.
[3] Thorold, *Life of Labouchere*, p. 145.

XII

STORMING THE RAMPARTS

'IF you place yourselves above the law', Bradlaugh had warned the House in his second speech at the bar, 'you leave me no course save lawless agitation, instead of reasonable pleading.'[1] By July 1881 Bradlaugh was preparing to take more active measures. During late June and early July he had written several long letters to Gladstone, to Northcote, and to the Speaker, further clarifying his position. He reminded Gladstone on 22 June that while an Affirmation Bill was no doubt desirable, the legal right to take his seat had always been his. Now that it appeared unlikely a Bill would pass, 'I cannot in justice to my constituents allow the present unprecedented state of things to continue without one supreme effort.'[2] When Gladstone informed him that no Bill would be forthcoming, Bradlaugh insisted once again: 'This puts upon me the very serious responsibility of taking some definite public step before the session closes to assert my legal right . . . .'[3] Gladstone, who had in the meantime received other warnings as to Bradlaugh's intentions from Joseph Chamberlain, reflected 'We may have awkward days ahead.'[4]

On 1 July 1881 Bradlaugh sent to Northcote a letter—though 'essay' or 'epistle' better characterizes that lengthy document—charging the Conservative leader with having overridden law with force in preventing him from taking the oath in April, with going back on his promise fairly to consider an Affirmation Bill, and with proposing on 10 May that physical force be used to bar a properly qualified and duly elected member from the House. Until then Bradlaugh had looked upon Northcote as a 'fair English Gentleman',

---

[1] *Hansard*, cclx (1881), 1212.   [2] G.P. (B.M.), 44111, fol. 95.
[3] Ibid., fol. 101.
[4] (Copy) Gladstone to Chamberlain, 2 July 1881, G.P. (B.M.), 44544, fol. 189.

but he had since changed his mind. 'Law has been set aside by you by force, and what an undignified and dangerous struggle you provoke. . . . Have you no shame, Sir Stafford Northcote?'

Northcote acknowledged the letter in a brief note in which he insisted that he had acted from a sense of public duty rather than from personal motives and denied that the House had acted illegally. In the first draft of his reply, he added the significant sentence, 'but if there be any illegality in its proceedings, the proper remedy must be found in a Court of Law'. In the letter finally sent to Bradlaugh that passage was eliminated. Perhaps Northcote was fearful of half committing himself again to a course of action he would later be forced to recant.[1]

Bradlaugh's more specific intentions were spelt out in a letter to the Speaker dated 14 July. He would present himself to take his seat on or before 3 August. If the Speaker prevented him from entering the precincts of the House he would be acting illegally, 'and further take Notice that in the event of you or any or every of you using physical force to prevent me from complying with the law, I shall in defence of my lawful right resist such illegal physical force and shall endeavour to overcome the same'.[2] The Speaker was thus given several weeks to prepare. Special squads of police were ordered to the vicinity of Westminster Palace. Brand conferred with the Sergeant-at-Arms and his Deputy and with Sir William Harcourt, the Home Secretary. The Speaker's intention was to have Bradlaugh removed beyond the precincts of the House on the basis of the authority granted him in the resolution of 10 May, and Gladstone agreed that this would be the best course.[3]

For two months Bradlaugh had been touring England addressing meetings, asking for pledges of support, and gathering petitions. There had been one mass meeting at London's St. James's Hall on 9 June, and by the beginning of August petitions bearing over 150,000 signatures had

[1] Iddesleigh MSS. (B.M.), 50041, fols. 58–62.
[2] Hampden MSS.
[3] *N.R.*, 17 July 1881, p. 67; Hampden Diary, entry for 2 Aug. 1881; Brand to Gladstone, 1 Aug. 1881, G.P. (B.M.), 44195, fol. 5; (Copy) Gladstone to Harcourt, G.P. (B.M.), 44545, fol. 4.

been submitted to Parliament.[1] The biggest meeting of all took place at Trafalgar Square on 2 August, the night before Bradlaugh was to make the new and highly publicized attempt to take his seat in the House of Commons. Delegations, aided by the cheap excursion train fares available in midsummer, had been pouring into the city from all over England. A platform was set up at the foot of Nelson's Column facing the National Gallery. Rings of volunteers linked arm-in-arm protected the platform, as a crowd of 15,000 people milled about. The meeting itself was brief because even a Bradlaugh found it difficult to make himself heard with an audience of such size. But as was his custom, he called for a vote of support at the end of the meeting, and only three hands went up in opposition.[2]

Although Bradlaugh asked the crowd to disperse quietly, some 5,000 cheering, excitable people—under the mistaken impression that Bradlaugh would attempt to take his seat that night—streamed down Whitehall into Parliament Square. The police managed to keep them out of the Westminster Palace Yard, but Gladstone found it difficult to leave the House for the night without being recognized and receiving an ovation he did not, on that occasion, welcome.[3]

The next morning Bradlaugh, accompanied by Dr. Edward Aveling, drove from his home in St. John's Wood to the Houses of Parliament in a gleaming hansom cab decorated with the Northampton colours. Its sympathetic owner had lent the cab to Bradlaugh free of charge for the day. Thousands of supporters cheered him as he passed through Parliament Square; hundreds more who, as petitioners, had received permission to enter the Palace Yard and Westminster Hall hailed him as he passed through on his way to the Lobby of the House. How close, one well-dressed lady asked Aveling in Westminster Hall, were they to repeating the events of 1789 in France? Bradlaugh was dressed, as was his custom as M.P., in an elegant black frock-coat. He wore a tall and well-polished hat and carried the ivory-handled and

[1] *N.R.*, 5 June 1881, p. 449; 19 June 1881, p. 481; 14 Aug. 1881, p. 189.
[2] *N.R.*, 7 Aug. 1881, p. 152.
[3] Justin McCarthy, *England under Gladstone, 1880–1884* (London, 1884), p. 151; Gladstone to Grosvenor, 2 Aug. 1881, G.P. (B.M.), 44315, p. 39.

gold-mounted cane which an organization of New York working men had given him in 1874. He left the cane in the Members' cloakroom before entering the House Lobby.[1]

The day's session had not yet begun, but the Lobby, usually empty at such a time, was crowded with small groups of M.P.s waiting for the arrival of the Junior Member from Northampton. Alderman Montague Scott had already climbed a pillar in order to obtain a better view of the proceedings. Bradlaugh, taking note of the fact that the Speaker was not yet in the Chair, halted alone in the centre of the Lobby and impassively faced the door leading to the legislative chamber. By the doorway sat the two doorkeepers and four messengers, two on either side. Beyond these stood four policemen, with Inspector Denning near by. Then, shortly past noon, the Speaker appeared in the usual procession, with the mace carried before him and the train-bearer following behind.[2]

As soon as prayers were over and the Speaker had taken the Chair, Bradlaugh advanced resolutely toward the door. What did Bradlaugh wish, inquired Erskine, the Deputy Sergeant-at-Arms. 'I am here', announced Bradlaugh, 'in accordance with the orders of my constituents, the electors of Northampton; any person who lays hands on me will do so at his peril.' He had orders not to admit Bradlaugh, Erskine replied. Those orders were illegal, retorted Bradlaugh. Then he stepped forward as if to push himself into the Chamber. At Erskine's signal the four messengers closed in and seized Bradlaugh by the arms and the collar of his coat. Bradlaugh fought back, grasping at the collar of the biggest of his assailants and almost choking him. While some one hundred M.P.s stood by and Alderman Fowler yelled 'Kick him out!' the burly messengers began to drag Bradlaugh toward the door.

He resisted every step of the way, kicking out impartially, his hand still fastened tightly on the collar of one of the messengers. At the bottom of the flight of stairs leading to the Members' Entrance Bradlaugh made one violent and

---

[1] *N.R.*, 7 Aug. 1881, p. 153; 14 Aug. 1881, pp. 163–5, 185; O'Connor, *Memoirs*, i. 74.

[2] Lucy, *Two Parliaments*, ii. 193–4; *Punch*, 13 Aug. 1881, p. 65.

almost successful effort to shake off the messengers and remount the steps. At this point, however, the policemen came to the aid of the exhausted messengers, and a force of ten men finally succeeded in propelling the still doggedly resisting Member for Northampton the rest of the way to the doorway leading into the Palace Yard.[1] 'I never saw anything like it before,' recalled one Conservative M.P., 'except the breaking up of a fox after an exciting run.'[2]

Suddenly the vast crowd in the Palace Yard and beyond caught a glimpse of their hero. He was hatless and dishevelled, his coat torn, his face deathly pale, yet his mouth still firmly set, his eyes still fixed upon the doorway through which he had just been expelled. The night before, he had warned Annie Besant to do her share in keeping the crowd from resorting to physical force on his behalf. 'The people know you better than they know anyone, save myself', he told her; 'whatever happens, mind, whatever happens, let them do no violence; I trust to you to keep them quiet.'[3] Now, for a brief moment, it was Bradlaugh himself who was strongly tempted to do otherwise, to call upon those thousands of sullenly murmuring supporters for action.

Brutal force had been used against him, he told Inspector Denning, 'and I shall come again with force enough to overcome it'. 'When?' asked the Inspector. 'Within a minute if I raise my hand', was Bradlaugh's reply. It is the contention of one of Bradlaugh's associates that had Bradlaugh raised his hand, 'the ten policemen would have been tossed aside like chaff by the host of his infuriated friends; the House could have been stormed, and his enemies could have been kicked wholesale into the river'.[4] Whether such an eventuality was indeed possible in the England of 1881 will never be known, because Bradlaugh resisted the temptation, a temptation which would have given him such enormous immediate satisfaction but which was inconsistent with the philosophy of a lifetime and which might have made his eventual entry into Parliament an impossibility. But, 'Oh! if you had let us

[1] Lucy, *Two Parliaments*, ii. 194–5; McCarthy, *England under Gladstone*, p. 151; *The Times*, 4 Aug. 1881, pp. 8–9; *N.R.*, 14 Aug. 1881, p. 172.
[2] Cited in *N.R.*, 1 Apr. 1883, p. 209.
[3] Besant, *Autobiography*, p. 265.
[4] *N.R.*, 4 Aug. 1881, p. 165; Bonner & Robertson, *Bradlaugh*, ii. 287.

go we would have carried him into the House up to the Speaker's chair', one enthusiast told Annie Besant at the time, and what might have happened had the assembled working men used force became a legend in Northampton, a legend not yet dead.[1]

As members inside listened to the ill-tempered roar of the crowd outside, Labouchere loyally introduced a resolution charging the Speaker with having exceeded his instructions in excluding Bradlaugh not merely from the chamber but from the building as well. John Bright was one of the few who came to Labouchere's support; he strongly deprecated the use of force against Bradlaugh. That Bright's speech was 'very injudicious' was the verdict of Gladstone's daughter and of Gladstone's secretary (and probably the opinion of the Prime Minister himself). 'Most mischievous' was the Speaker's judgement.[2] A more sympathetic listener calls it one of the last great speeches of Bright's long career.[3] Gladstone, however, failed to support the resolution, and it was defeated, 191 to 7.

The day ended anti-climactically. Bradlaugh waited outside until news of the outcome of the Parliament discussions was brought to him. Several Liberal M.P.s spoke to him, and Herbert Gladstone shook him warmly by the hand. Inspector Denning brought Bradlaugh a glass of water, while one of the latter's supporters was haranguing an uninterested group of policemen on the constitutional question involved. As an afterthought, Bradlaugh asked Denning to strike him on the chest so that he might be able to obtain a summons charging the inspector with assault. Bradlaugh was fearful that a genuine attempt on his part to re-enter the building—for the primary purpose of instituting a lawsuit—might be misinterpreted by the crowd. Denning co-operated, but the judge, suspecting collusion, afterwards refused to issue a warrant.[4]

---

[1] Besant, *Autobiography*, p. 267; conversation with Alderman Percy Adams in Northampton, 23 Feb. 1957.

[2] *Hansard*, cclxiv (1881), 696, 709; Mary Gladstone Drew Diary (B.M.), 46259, entry for 3 Aug. 1881; Hamilton Diary (B.M.), 48631, p. 111; Hampden Diary, entry for 3 Aug. 1881.

[3] Harry Furniss, *The Confessions of a Caricaturist* (London, 1901), p. 196.

[4] *Tablet*, 6 Aug. 1881, p. 219; *N.R.*, 14 Aug. 1881, pp. 164–7; Lucy, *Two Parliaments*, ii. 195.

From a superficial point of view, the day had been a total loss for Bradlaugh. He had not been able to take his seat. He had gained no Parliamentary support but had instead alienated a number of erstwhile supporters. He had been unable even to use the events as the basis of a lawsuit. All that had happened was that his arm had been injured—a slumbering case of erysipelas (St. Anthony's Fire) had been revived and for weeks one arm had to be swathed in bandages—and his clothes had been torn.[1]

As *Punch* put it:

They fought and they tussled away down the stairs,
    With many a gasp and a guggle,
And poor Daddy Longlegs, who won't say his prayers,
    Lost his collars and tails in the struggle—
        'uggle—'uggle
    Lost his temper and tails in the struggle.

Who profits by this? The reply's not remote,
    Not the Rough, nor the Bobby, nor Gaoler,
But as Mr. BRADLAUGH must have a new coat
    'Tis a capital thing for his tailor—
        'ailor—'ailor,
    A very good thing for the tailor.[2]

The question arises: what had been Bradlaugh's real purpose on 3 August 1881? Primarily it had been to be arrested again, or, at the very least, to be expelled officially from the House of Commons. As Bradlaugh dejectedly wrote to Gladstone on 5 August,

The Leader of the House deems it right to maintain its dignity against a duly elected Member, not by vacating his seat, nor by arrest, but by superior brute force.—Is it quite fair to me to drive me into illegality to maintain the right of my constituents? I do not write this to trouble you for reply nor with a view to publicity nor even with the remote notion that I can now influence you, but I thought it might be a permissible final intrusion . . . .[3]

[1] *N.R.*, 14 Aug. 1881, p. 161; Besant, *Autobiography*, p. 268. 'I was subjected to such brutal injury', wrote Bradlaugh two years later, 'that but for the skill of Drs. Rainskill and Palfrey, the struggle would then probably have ended with my life.' *N.R.*, 30 Sept. 1883, p. 209.
[2] 13 Aug. 1881, p. 12.
[3] G.P. (B.M.), 44111, fol. 110.

But the attempt to storm the ramparts had not been completely in vain. Northampton's stormy petrel had once again succeeded in putting his name in the headlines. He had been successful in dramatizing his contention that the issue was one of law versus brute force. And, finally, he had not misjudged the Prime Minister's mentality as much as he had at first thought. Even before the events of 3 August Gladstone had privately conceded: 'If Bradlaugh resorts to physical force, and mischief results, it will be very difficult to carry on the resistance to him by physical force only.'[1] The Government would have to do something, and within a week after 3 August Gladstone privately promised Bradlaugh that as soon as Parliament re-convened in 1882 the Liberal Ministry would press for a new resolution in his favour.[2] Thus all was not lost; but the events of 3 August ingrained themselves on the minds of Bradlaugh's supporters, and many of them, in retrospect, picked that day as the onset of a physical deterioration which was to bring Bradlaugh's life to a comparatively early end. 'From that fatal day', concluded Annie Besant, 'Charles Bradlaugh was never the same man.'[3]

[1] (Copy) Gladstone to James, 3 July 1881, G.P. (B.M.), 44544, fol. 190.
[2] Cabinet Minutes of 6 Aug. 1881, G.P. (B.M.), 44642, fol. 206; Hamilton Diary, entry for 11 Aug. 1881, (B.M.), 48631, p. 111; Hansard, cclxiv (1881), 1208.   [3] Besant, Autobiography, p. 268.

XIII

A SURPRISE TACTIC

WITH a new assurance of ministerial aid in hand, Bradlaugh
saw his main task during the autumn of 1881 to prepare for
the advent of the new session of Parliament. The repercussions of the incident of 3 August continued, however, to be
felt for several weeks. Annie Besant, for example, advised
Bradlaugh's disappointed followers that they should use
their spare time to join Volunteer Regiments. 'A little drilling would not be bad,' she observed, 'because otherwise
the police have a great advantage over you.' The House of
Commons took notice of the speech, but Gladstone assured
a worried Conservative questioner that the Home Secretary
had ample physical means of supporting the authority of the
House.[1] A parliamentary motion by Labouchere to rescind
the earlier anti-Bradlaugh resolutions was blocked.

In the meantime, Bradlaugh, recovering from the attack
of erysipelas, found time to issue a new manifesto. 'Against
. . . brute force I appeal to public opinion, and to the spirit
of fair play of my fellow-countrymen', he declared. A number
of papers took note of Bradlaugh's illness, some regretting
it, others describing it as a deliberate attempt to gain popular
sympathy, and still others deploring that the illness had not
proved even more serious. 'Can it be denied', asked the
Gloucester Journal, 'that a great many persons who cultivate
a character for humane feeling, would hear of Mr. Bradlaugh's death without regret—perhaps with a sense of
gratitude to Providence for having thus solved a nauseous
difficulty?'[2]

Bradlaugh was still very much alive, however, when
Parliament re-convened the following February. He had been
even busier than before in soliciting petitions in his favour,

[1] *Hansard*, cclxiv (1881), 1385-6.
[2] Cited in *N.R.*, 4 Sept. 1881, p. 225; 28 Aug. 1881, p. 215.

and over 1,000 petitions with a total of 241,970 signatures were to be submitted on his behalf during the first week of the new Parliament.[1] Bradlaugh had announced three weeks beforehand that on 7 February, the opening day of the 1882 session, he would appear once more to take the oath, the resolutions of the previous year having expired.[2] Sir Stafford Northcote was similarly preparing to renew the conflict, though as usual he was worried—worried on this occasion that Bradlaugh would alter his announced plans and 'that there should be . . . a surprise and a scare at the last moment'.[3] Speaker Brand, less troubled on this score, used the occasion to appeal once again to the Conservative leader to permit Bradlaugh to take the oath and thus 'let Bradlaugh discredit himself with his supporters. . . . We might lift him into popularity by exclusion while he would sink to his natural low level by admission.'[4] Brand's arguments were fruitless, however, for by this time Northcote's attitude, originally the result of pressure from the militants in his party, had been buttressed by the passage of time, and it would have required much greater courage and initiative on Northcote's part to alter his course than to continue the previous year's policy. And so Northcote issued a special whip requiring all Conservatives to be present on the opening day.[5]

Northcote had in any case received fresh ammunition, a pamphlet by Charles Wharton addressed to all Members of Parliament in a fashion similar to Varley's the previous April. Wharton was less interested in citing passages from Bradlaugh's pamphlets—though he did take time to dub the Northampton representative 'an inhuman monster'—than he was in refuting Bradlaugh's reasoning. Bradlaugh claimed to be willing to take the oath, but as an atheist this was necessarily impossible for him because an oath had a religious meaning. For Bradlaugh to claim to take the oath was as absurd as it would be for a man to say 'I will lift my right arm' if he had no right arm.

There was, in any case, Wharton observed, but one incentive

[1] *The Times*, 17 Feb. 1882, p. 3.
[2] *N.R.*, 15 Jan. 1882, p. 34.
[3] Northcote to Brand, 4 Feb. 1882, Hampden MSS.
[4] Hampden Diary, entry for 7 Feb. 1882.
[5] *N.R.*, 22 Jan. 1882, p. 50.

to abide by an oath of allegiance (since treason was a separate crime and treason laws were applicable to swearers and non-swearers alike) and that was the hope of future reward in heaven or the fear of future punishment in hell. Since Bradlaugh believed·in neither, he might go back upon his oath at will. To deprive Bradlaugh of his seat, Wharton went on, was not unjust, because the English Constitution antedated the rights of Northampton, and so long as the monarch of England was styled 'Defender of the Faith', so long as England had an Established Church, so long as meetings of Parliament commenced with prayers, then so long was religion 'part and parcel of the Constitution of England'. Wharton's own solution to the Bradlaugh imbroglio was an Act of Parliament specifically denying the right of member-ship to avowed atheists. That would put Bradlaugh in his place and keep him from making further difficulties.[1]

Gladstone in the meantime had decided to meet the opposi-tion to Bradlaugh's admission by means of a Parliamentary manœuvre. When Northcote interrupted with a repetition of earlier resolutions, Gladstone would move 'the previous question', a method, if approved, whereby the House of Commons might decline to exercise any jurisdiction in the case and leave Bradlaugh free to act upon his own responsi-bility. That had been the decision of the Cabinet the previous August—possibly upon the Speaker's suggestion—and the decision was confirmed in January 1882. John Bright sug-gested a different counter-resolution, one instructing the Speaker to ask Bradlaugh whether he felt morally bound by the oath. If he replied in the affirmative, the question would have settled itself. The Cabinet of 7 February 1882 decided, however, to abide by the 'previous question' formula.[2]

The 7th of February once again saw a stern-faced Brad-laugh move through Parliament Square and the Palace Yard amidst the roars of his supporters and of vendors selling Bradlaugh portraits and free-thought pamphlets.[3] Once again

---

[1] Charles H. M. Wharton, *Mr. Bradlaugh and the Oath* (Manchester, 1882), *passim*.

[2] G.P. (B.M.), 44642, fol. 206; G.P. (B.M.), 44643, fols. 2, 16, 30, 40; (Copy) Gladstone to Bradlaugh, 18 Feb. 1882, G.P. (B.M.), 44545, fol. 100; Hamilton Diary, entry for 3 Feb. 1882 (B.M.), 48631, p. 245.

[3] *N.R.*, 12 Feb. 1882, p. 115; *Freeman's Journal* (Dublin), 8 Feb. 1882, p. 5.

Bradlaugh advanced toward the Table to take the oath. Once again Northcote interrupted with a resolution forbidding him to do so. Gladstone had not yet arrived in the House, and it was therefore Sir William Harcourt who moved 'the previous question' on his behalf. Gladstone came in time to defend the motion as one which would assure Bradlaugh the opportunity of having his oath tested in the law courts just as his affirmation had been tested a year before.

Once again Bradlaugh was granted the opportunity to speak in his own behalf. In some respects this third speech was less well organized than his earlier speeches at the bar, as Bradlaugh took time to reply to a variety of specific attacks made upon him both within and outside the House. He had been accused of so many things—he had been 'a red rag to a wild Conservative bull'—yet, he pleaded, if he were to be tried for his opinions, 'at least let me be tried for the opinions I hold and the views I express'. Again, even more forcefully than before, he promised to regard the oath as binding upon his conscience in the fullest degree, but, he regretfully admitted, 'I have found myself so harshly judged, so unfairly dealt with, that one feels a difficulty in understanding whether any form of words, however often repeated, would convey any kind of conviction to some minds.' If the House would consider a new Affirmation Bill, he would willingly wait. He was even willing to fight still another election so that a relief measure could not be tagged a Bradlaugh Relief Bill. 'I have no fear. If I am not fit for my constituents, they shall dismiss me; but you never shall. The grave alone shall make me yield.'[1]

Opinion on the speech was divided. Gladstone's secretary considered it coarse, in bad taste, and far less effective than the earlier speeches. The usually hostile Catholic *Tablet*, on the other hand, called it 'studiously moderate and calculated to give no offence'.[2]

The previous autumn Gladstone had felt sure that the 'previous question' motion would settle the problem; it would compel his partisans to uphold no controversial doctrine nor force them to support Bradlaugh directly. But even

[1] *Hansard*, cclxvi (1882), 70–75.
[2] Hamilton Diary (B.M.), 48631, pp. 247–8; *Tablet*, 11 Feb. 1882, p. 197.

before the vote of 7 February the Cabinet half expected defeat. It was only the size of the defeat which caused surprise, a vote of 286 to 228.[1] The majority was made up of 222 Conservatives, 25 Liberals, and 39 Home Rulers, the minority of 227 Liberals and one solitary Home Ruler. Only 14 Conservatives had been absent, but so had 76 Liberals.

Criticism of the Government was widespread. The Bradlaughites considered the defeat deserved in view of the half-hearted manner in which the matter had been taken up. They condemned the 'previous question' resolution as a 'tricky fashion of shelving principle [which] invited and merited defeat'.[2] The *Spectator* considered the division list 'very discreditable' to Liberal Members. The Liberal *Daily Chronicle* depicted the vote as one that 'strikes a blow at popular Government'. The more moderate *Daily News* was equally unhappy but thought that Bradlaugh, while not wholly to blame, had increased the difficulties of the situation. *The Times* too blamed Bradlaugh for raising the question but still wished that some solution might be found. The Conservative *Morning Advertiser* felt sure the decision deserved 'the grateful acknowledgment of the nation', while the independent *Daily Telegraph* termed the vote 'a severe defeat in the first hours of the Session' for the Government.[3] The *Freeman's Journal* agreed: 'It may be that the question is an open one'—the Government had once again refused to make the vote a party question—but 'the debate had all the well-known features of a party one, and . . . when men like Mr. Gladstone and Sir William Harcourt intervene in such a discussion, take a foremost part in the fray, strain every nerve to win, and are beaten, it is on the Ministry and not on the individual that the blow falls.'[4]

Charles Bradlaugh's road appeared to have come to a dead end. It had been all very well for Gladstone to discourse on the desirability of Bradlaugh's having his oath tested in the law courts, but how was that to be possible if the House of

[1] Hamilton Diary (B.M.), 48631, pp. 111, 248; Dilke MSS. (B.M.), 43924, fol. 70.
[2] *N.R.*, 12 Feb. 1882, p. 99.
[3] Cited in *N.R.*, 19 Feb. 1882, p. 134; 12 Feb. 1882, pp. 123, 124.
[4] 8 Feb. 1882, p. 4.

Commons barred him from ever taking the oath in the first place? Gladstone, moreover, bluntly informed Bradlaugh on 18 February 1882 that, the 'previous question' manœuvre having failed, he was not prepared to offer any additional remedy.[1] Since 7 February Bradlaugh had been visiting the House regularly without making any further efforts to take the oath, thus—*Punch* reported ironically—disappointing the gallery visitors. It was 'like going to the play and finding Hamlet's mother and stepfather alive when the curtain falls'.[2] But Bradlaugh was apparently not at a complete loss for ideas. As he confided to his fellow secularists on 19 February, 'I do not intend the matter to rest many days in the present state'.[3]

On 21 February Henry Labouchere surprised the House by proposing the issue of a new writ for Northampton, so that a Member of Parliament might be elected 'in the place of Charles Bradlaugh, Esquire, who by resolution of the House has been prevented from taking and subscribing the oath provided by law'. Gladstone saw no reason to favour the proposal, which amounted to a vote of expulsion, since the Liberals had no desire to expel Bradlaugh (even though the latter apparently wished to be expelled).[4] Conservatives were placed in something of a dilemma; if they voted for the resolution, they opened the way to the strong possibility of Bradlaugh's re-election. If they voted against the resolution, they were voting, by implication, that Northampton did not have the right to full representation in Parliament.

Lord Randolph Churchill, for one, approved expulsion but offered an amendment to Labouchere's resolution to make the last phrase read: 'in the place of Charles Bradlaugh, Esquire, who is disqualified by law from taking his seat in the House.' This analysis seemed too extreme for a majority of the House, and the amendment was defeated, whereupon the next question—that Labouchere's original phrase be kept—was similarly voted down. Labouchere's resolution had now been truncated so that it simply ended with the

---

[1] (Copy) Gladstone to Bradlaugh, 18 Feb. 1882, G.P. (B.M.), 44545, fol. 100.   [2] *Punch*, 18 Feb. 1882, p. 76.
[3] *N.R.*, 19 Feb. 1882, p. 129.
[4] James to Gladstone, G.P. (B.M.), 44219, fol. 58.

words 'in the place of Charles Bradlaugh, who—'. This rather meaningless resolution was itself thereupon defeated, 307 to 18.[1]

As the announcement of the vote was completed Bradlaugh left his seat under the gallery and began to walk toward the Table. It was a familiar promenade, and few members exhibited any great interest in the junior Member for Northampton but turned instead towards the Speaker, expecting him to make the usual request that Bradlaugh withdraw. All of a sudden it became clear that Bradlaugh had brought a book with him—the New Testament—and was, moreover, distinctly reciting the words of the Parliamentary oath. He was administering the oath to himself, and in accordance with custom, he thereupon kissed the Bible and inscribed his name upon a sheet of paper he had also brought along. 'I tender that as the oath I have taken according to law.' Finding no clerk to whom he might hand the paper, he carefully laid it on the Prime Minister's dispatch-box.

It was all over in less than a minute. The House was literally stupefied. The Speaker half rose to call out 'Order!' but then sat down. Sir Stafford Northcote rose, but unable to think of anything to say, also sat down again. In the meantime stunned surprise had given way to howls of outrage from all parts of the chamber. The Speaker finally collected himself sufficiently to order Bradlaugh to withdraw below the bar. Bradlaugh courteously complied and then quietly seated himself on the Liberal benches with the complacent appearance of a man who had now succeeded in satisfying all scruples and pleasing all parties.[2]

Lord Randolph Churchill was the first man in the astonished chamber to recover his self-possession. Perceiving the frustrated anger of the House he proposed Bradlaugh's immediate expulsion. The House adjourned for the night, however, before taking any action, and a special Cabinet meeting was summoned for the following afternoon at 1 p.m.

[1] *Hansard*, cclxvi (1882), 1234–51.

[2] The following accounts of the incident all substantially corroborate one another: London *Daily News*, 22 Feb. 1882, cited in *N.R.*, 26 Feb. 1882, p. 164; Lucy, *Two Parliaments*, ii. 212; McCarthy, *England under Gladstone*, p. 171. Also (Copy) Gladstone to Granville, 23 Feb. 1882, G.P. (B.M.), 44545, fol. 102.

In the meantime great pressure was being brought to bear upon the Prime Minister to alter his course of studious legal impartiality. Edward Hamilton, one of his secretaries, was only one of several aides and colleagues who attempted to persuade Gladstone that Bradlaugh had flagrantly insulted the House and that Gladstone should now take the lead in asking Bradlaugh's immediate expulsion. The bulk of the Liberal party, he was assured, would enthusiastically follow the Prime Minister's lead.[1] The Speaker strongly urged Gladstone to do the same. And so did a majority of Gladstone's Cabinet.

The Cabinet was split three ways. All but three men wanted the Government to take the initiative. Childers, the Secretary of War, Harcourt, the Home Secretary, and Dodson, the President of the Local Government Board, merely desired a resolution reminiscent of the previous year, excluding Bradlaugh from the precincts of the House. Six other members, headed by Lord Hartington, the Secretary of State for India, wanted the Government to propose immediate expulsion. Only Chamberlain, Bright, and Gladstone wished to remain consistent and do nothing. Bright was at home with a cold that day, but he advised the Prime Minister that now that the oath had been taken, 'tho' with some irregularity', Bradlaugh should be allowed to take his seat and that the Speaker should urge any person who disputed the legality of the act to take his case to the courts.[2] Gladstone could not view the proceedings quite so lightly as that. He had privately described Bradlaugh's self-swearing as 'an extraordinary scene of the utmost scandal', and yet when all but one of his colleagues urgently pressed him to take the lead against the infidel, Gladstone remained adamant. 'I cannot', he insisted.[3] The Cabinet meeting broke up in complete disagreement.

There is no question that numerous Liberals hitherto sympathetic to Bradlaugh had been antagonized by his latest action—the press was uniformly hostile—though, as the

---

[1] Hamilton Diary (B.M.), 48631, p. 266.

[2] G.P. (B.M.), 44643, fols. 54–57; Bright to Gladstone, 22 Feb. 1882, G.P. (B.M.), 44113, fol. 170.

[3] Dilke MSS. (B.M.), 43924, fol. 76. Diary entry for 22 Feb. 1882.

Pall Mall Gazette no doubt aptly observed, 'there are only too many people who, lending a ready ear to the counsels of cowardice, seek to clear themselves from the social unpopularity attaching to their support of the principle that he represents by denouncing in unmeasured language the steps by which he has attempted to vindicate it'.[1] Bradlaugh himself was by no means wholly blind to these feelings; he looked upon the self-swearing—a step which Labouchere may well have suggested to him[2]—as an unfortunate last resort, and he could understand, if not agree with, 'the state of feeling which applies the word "outrage" to what I did . . .'.[3]

When the House convened again, Northcote rose to move a new resolution merely requesting the Sergeant-at-Arms to take steps to keep Bradlaugh from re-entering the House. It was a resolution much milder than anything either Churchill among the Conservatives or Hartington among the Liberals had advocated. It was only when Bradlaugh entered the House and deliberately seated himself again inside the chamber that Northcote amended his own motion to read: 'that Charles Bradlaugh, . . . having in contempt of the authority of the House, irregularly and contumaciously pretended to take and subscribe the Oath required by law, be expelled from this House'. Bradlaugh himself entered the Lobby, with Chamberlain and Mundella on either side, to vote against his own expulsion.[4] The resolution was approved, however, by a vote of 297 to 80. The majority was made up of 192 Conservatives, 78 Liberals, and 27 Home Rulers, the minority of 77 Liberals and 3 Home Rulers. Gladstone and many of the other Liberals deliberately abstained. Of the Cabinet members in the House of Commons only Chamberlain voted against expulsion, though Bright also would presumably have done so had he not been ill.

Bradlaugh took the result—hardly an unexpected one—with good grace and left the House without further ado. There was another legal case to be fought, and since, by

---

[1] Cited in *N.R.*, 26 Feb. 1882, p. 163.
[2] Thorold, *Life of Labouchere*, p. 145.
[3] *N.R.*, 26 Nov. 1882, p. 369.
[4] *Hansard*, cclxvi (1882), 1314–48; *Tablet*, 25 Feb. 1882, p. 302.

tradition, expulsion from Parliament did not legally bar a man from standing again—there was another election to be won. And so, Charles Bradlaugh, for the sixth time in his life, and for the third time in three years, offered himself as a candidate to the voters of Northampton.

XIV

THE CAMPAIGN CONTINUES

BRADLAUGH embarked upon a hectic week of campaign-ing. His opponent was the same Edward Corbett he had managed to defeat the previous year, but the 1882 contest was on the whole a more fiercely fought and less gentlemanly affair than the election of the year before. Certainly Corbett ignored political issues almost entirely in order to con-centrate upon Bradlaugh's 'subversive' religious and social doctrines. Bradlaugh was termed a 'monster' who 'mocks at the sanctity of the marriage tie' and was attempting to turn English homes into brothels.[1]

Corbett had the assistance of a number of groups including the Roman Catholics, represented by Cardinal Manning, the Irish Home-Rule Party, represented by John Redmond, M.P., and dissident Liberals, such as a Samuel Morley, M.P. for Bristol. This leading Baptist layman, who in 1880 had supported Bradlaugh's election (although subsequently regretting this step), publicly came out for Corbett in 1882 'as an act of allegiance to God'. He wrote: 'The loss of a Liberal Vote is as nothing compared to the shame which will attach to the Town if with all we know now the former mistake is repeated.'[2] At the same time, large posters signed 'Gladstonian' described Bradlaugh as a great embarrassment to the Government, and a reporter for the *Manchester Guardian* professed to see many signs that Northampton Liberals were wearying of Bradlaugh and the conflict in which he was involved.[3]

Bradlaugh's supporters counter-attacked with vigour, and some of their practices indicated clearly that Bradlaugh was

[1] *N.R.*, 5 Mar. 1882, p. 181; 12 Mar. 1882, pp. 211–12; Northampton Library collection of election clippings.

[2] *N.R.*, 12 Mar. 1882, p. 211; 5 Mar. 1882, p. 197; Northampton Library collection of election clippings.

[3] *N.R.*, 5 Mar. 1882, pp. 197, 188.

fearful of defeat. Numerous Corbett election meetings were broken up by fist fights; and Samuel Morley's 1880 telegram of support, long since repudiated, was reproduced as if newly sent.[1] Labouchere did his best to counter the impression that Gladstone was hostile to Bradlaugh's re-election. 'I can only say this,' he assured the Northampton electorate, 'that I truly believe that there is not one man in the whole House of Commons so strong in supporting Mr. Bradlaugh as Mr. Gladstone.'[2] Bradlaugh gathered as many Nonconformist ministers as he could find to speak in his behalf. One of these, the Reverend Arthur Mursell, observed that 'Mr. Bradlaugh owed a higher obedience and a more sacred loyalty to his masters, the people, than he did to the people's servants, the members of the House of Commons.' W. Griffith, another clergyman, suggested that, in line with the principle of 'no taxation without representation' maintained by the Bostonians of the eighteenth century, Bradlaugh ought either to be seated or else Northampton should be exempted from national taxation.[3]

As always there were election songs and poems to commemorate what had happened:

> Up at St. Stephen's Hall
> The members may shout and brawl,
> 　　There never was yet such a bigoted set
> 　　And you may be sure they'll have cause to regret
> 　　What they did one night when Parliament met
> Up at St. Stephen's Hall.

and to advise what was to be done:

> 　　Shoulder arms! and prepare for the charge,
> 　　Northampton's in front! once again;
> 　　They've turned back your member and now
> 　　Do your duty and send him again.[4]

The poll took place on 2 March. The result: Bradlaugh 3,796 votes, Corbett 3,688. By the slim margin of 108 votes,

---

[1] N.R., 12 Mar. 1882, p. 211; Northampton Library collection of election clippings. 　　　　[2] Cited in N.R., 5 Mar. 1882, p. 197.
[3] Northampton Guardian, 28 Feb. 1882; Northampton Mercury, 18 Feb. 1882.
[4] Northampton Library collection of election clippings.

the narrowest of his three victories, Bradlaugh had been re-elected. If Conservatives were disappointed, moderate Liberals felt worse. While the Conservative London *Standard* was declaring that 'the offence that justified expulsion is not in any degree purged by the act of the constituency in re-electing the expelled person', Hamilton wrote in despair: 'We shall accordingly be confronted once more with this infernal business.'[1] All over England crowds had assembled in front of newspaper offices to hear the election returns as well as the unexpected report that an unsuccessful attempt had been made that day to assassinate Queen Victoria. Speaker Brand faithfully noted the coincidence of the two events in his diary:

At 7.30 news of assassination attempt on Queen.

At 8—News came of Bradlaugh's return! which might have been prevented by better management!

This is indeed bad News![2]

By that time Edward Corbett had already departed from Northampton, having announced in disgust: 'I shan't come back to this dirty town any more.'[3]

Even before the victor's return to London, Northcote had announced his intention to block Bradlaugh's oath once again, and he accordingly informed Bradlaugh that he was preparing a new Parliamentary motion. Bradlaugh chose deliberately to misunderstand the type of motion Northcote was preparing, and replied in his most scathingly ironic vein:

You do not say what is the nature of the motion of which you intend to give notice on Monday but presuming that it is one intended to promote the legislation which you have frequently suggested ought to take place and thereby to avoid further lawlessness on the part of the curiously composed majority you temporarily lead—and that such motion will probably be for leave to bring in a bill to substitute affirmation of allegiance for oath—I can only say that I congratulate you on the return of, at least, yourself, to some respect for the law & beg to assure you that I will in such case do my best to help you avoid further

[1] Cited in *N.R.*, 19 Mar. 1882, p. 241; Hamilton Diary (B.M.), 48632, p. 2.
[2] Hampden Diary, entry for 2 Mar. 1882.
[3] Cited in *N.R.*, 12 Mar. 1882, p. 211.

embittering a conflict of which I am sure you must feel heartily ashamed.[1]

Gladstone's Cabinet was again divided and could agree on no better method of resisting Northcote's new motion to prevent Bradlaugh from taking the oath than once more asking for 'the previous question'.[2] It was only upon the suggestion of a Liberal newcomer, Edward Marjoribanks, that a different method was employed. Marjoribanks belonged to the right wing of the Liberal party and had long been a less than enthusiastic supporter of Bradlaugh's admission. He favoured Bradlaugh's right to affirm, but he considered the House justified in not granting him the right to swear, and he had voted for Bradlaugh's expulsion two weeks earlier. Marjoribanks proposed that the Liberals amend Northcote's motion to the effect that an Affirmation Bill was desirable. Gladstone approved the idea, though he at first suggested that George Joachim Goschen, a more widely known Whig who had served as First Lord of the Admiralty during Gladstone's First Ministry, move the amendment in Marjoribanks' place.[3] Gladstone's suggestion did not work out, however, and when, even before Bradlaugh had presented himself to take the oath, Northcote introduced his motion, it was Marjoribanks who proposed the amendment. He did so, moreover, in a speech so hostile to Bradlaugh personally that Labouchere felt impelled to protest.

Gladstone supported Marjoribanks's amendment, but he refused to give a direct promise that, should it pass, the Government would promptly introduce a new Affirmation Bill. The lack of such a promise no doubt hurt the Liberals as did the unpreparedness of the Liberal Whips; yet the Conservative and Irish members seemed fearful they would lose.[4] After a debate of several hours, it was Marjoribanks's amendment, however, which was defeated, and once again the joy of the relieved Opposition 'knew no bounds'.[5] The

[1] Iddesleigh MSS (B.M.), 50041, fols. 96–97.

[2] G.P. (B.M.), 44643, fol. 66; Dilke Diary (B.M.), 43924, fol. 78.

[3] Gladstone to Hartington, 6 Mar. 1882, G.P. (B.M.), 44146, fol. 15.

[4] Hamilton Diary (B.M.), 48632, pp. 8–9; *Daily News*, 7 Mar. 1882; Northampton *Weekly Reporter*, 10 Mar. 1882.

[5] *Freeman's Journal* (Dublin), 6 Mar. 1882, p. 5.

vote was 257 to 242, the closest significant division yet in the two-year-old contest. The majority was made up of 220 Conservatives, 12 Liberals, and 25 Home Rulers, the minority of 237 Liberals and 5 Home Rulers.

Bradlaugh made no further attempt during the spring and summer of 1882 to take his seat in the House of Commons. He was once again permitted to sit within the chamber, though outside the bar, on the condition that he made no attempt to pass this barrier. In July of that year, Labouchere made an attempt to enable Bradlaugh to become a member of a Parliamentary Committee as well—the case of Baron Rothschild provided a precedent for such a step—but the motion was defeated, 120 to 35.[1]

In the course of the year the focus of attention in the Bradlaugh case moved temporarily from the House of Commons to the House of Lords. In March, Lord Redesdale, a Conservative, brought in a bill requiring every member of Parliament publicly to declare 'I believe in an Almighty God'. The bill was defeated on 23 March, when a fellow Conservative, Lord Shaftesbury, successfully moved 'the previous question'.[2] 'The notion of imposing a new theological test at this time of day has caused some amusement', noted James Bryce, M.P., then London correspondent of the American *Nation*, but he was forced to concede that the House of Commons, by means of resolutions, had in effect already imposed such a test. Bradlaugh found some comfort in both the bill and its defeat, which seemed to be an implicit admission on the part of Conservatives that atheists were not already legally disqualified from election.[3]

In June 1882 the Duke of Argyll introduced an Affirmation Bill in the House of Lords. The bill was not in any sense a Government measure, though the Duke was a Liberal. He had served as Gladstone's Secretary of State for India from 1868 to 1874 and as his Lord Privy Seal in 1880 but had resigned during the following year because he could not agree to the Irish Land Act. After careful consideration the Conservatives moved to oppose the bill, not so much on the ground

[1] *Hansard*, cclxxii (1882), 966–72; McCarthy, *England under Gladstone*, p. 177. [2] Ibid., p. 178.
[3] *The Nation*, xxxiv (1882), p. 293; *N.R.*, 19 Mar. 1882, p. 241.

that the retention of the Parliamentary oath was intrinsically desirable as on the ground that it was inexpedient for the House of Lords to take action on a matter with which the House of Commons had not yet seen fit to deal.[1] The Duke of Argyll's bill was thereupon defeated, 138 to 63, an indication of considerable interest in the House of Lords. Only a small fraction of its 521 members attended ordinarily. Hamilton looked upon the vote as a sign of the difficult prospects which even an Affirmation Bill approved in the Commons would face in the Lords, but Bradlaugh himself was both pleased and surprised that, in a legislative chamber whose abolition he had long urged, over sixty members could be found to support a measure directly benefiting him.[2]

Bradlaugh had not been directly involved in the House of Lords debate, even though the Duke of Argyll had made a number of hostile personal references to him, but he was hardly neglecting other avenues in his battle for admission. He not only pursued a number of legal cases but also gave lectures and held public meetings. The largest of these meetings took place in London, where a huge gathering in Trafalgar Square on 10 May 1882 was followed by a mass demonstration in Hyde Park four days later. Newspaper reporters estimated that between 30,000 and 60,000 people participated in the latter event.[3] His supporters had signed numerous petitions urging his admission to Parliament, and Bradlaugh could take satisfaction in the fact that in the course of the entire Parliamentary session of 1882 there had been submitted petitions bearing 263,259 signatures favouring his admission as contrasted to a mere 72,953 opposing him.[4] In October 1882 Bradlaugh issued another appeal to the electors urging them to put new pressure upon their representatives to support his cause, and he made repeated journeys to Northampton to revive flagging spirits and to induce his followers to hold meetings at which the Northampton electorate pledged itself 'to use every legitimate means to

[1] e.g. Shaftesbury to Salisbury, 26 June 1882, Salisbury MSS.
[2] Hamilton Diary (B.M.), 48632, p. 175; N.R., 16 June 1882, p. 34.
[3] N.R., 21 May 1882, pp. 385, 386, 392.
[4] Report of the Committee on Parliamentary Petitions, 1882.

return him again and again—aye, and again—if required, as the honoured member for Northampton'.[1]

Nor had the public at large lost interest in the case. One manifestation of the great interest the average Englishman took in Parliamentary affairs in general during the late nineteenth century was the existence of over two hundred local Parliamentary Debating Societies with some 50,000 members in all. Each had its own 'Government' and 'Opposition', and each debated the issues then exciting interest at Westminster. The first such society had been founded in Liverpool in 1861, and during the 1880's these organizations reached their peak of popularity. Not surprisingly, a favourite topic during these years was Bradlaugh's admission to Parliament, and more often than not the debate would go in Bradlaugh's favour. The *National Reformer* reported these moral victories with almost as much relish as a victory in the actual Parliament produced. In his *Autobiography* Moncure Conway has recorded the details of such a debate at the Cambridge Union. Some four hundred students were present, he reports, not counting the gallery visitors. The debate, 'Should the Parliamentary Oath be Abolished?', was conducted in accordance with House of Commons rules. When one member of the 'Opposition' spoke of atheists as 'disgusting' and 'despicable', he was called to order by the Chairman on the ground 'that no person could be permitted to use such language concerning the opinions of members of this House'.[2]

When, upon Gladstone's advice, an autumn session of the Commons was convoked to debate and pass curbs on unrestricted Parliamentary debate, Bradlaugh, through Labouchere, asked for time to be heard again at the bar. The Attorney-General advised Gladstone to deny the request on the ground that Northcote's motion of March was still on the books and that an attempt to rescind it would involve 'long and acrimonious debate'. The autumn session, moreover, had been called for a particular purpose, and to make an exception for Bradlaugh would lead to similar pleas by other members. The Cabinet accordingly voted to turn

[1] *N.R.*, 1 Oct. 1882, p. 225; 19 Nov. 1882, p. 353.

[2] Letter in *Radio Times*, 8 Mar. 1957; *N.R.*, 11 Dec. 1881, p. 455; 22 Apr. 1883, p. 295; Moncure D. Conway, *Autobiography* (London, 1904), ii. 343.

down Bradlaugh's request.[1] Bradlaugh was disappointed but immediately began preparations for a new petition drive and for a 'Great National Demonstration' to be held on 15 February 1883, when the next session of Parliament would begin.[2]

If the necessity of continually organizing meetings, sponsoring petition drives, and making speeches in order not to be forgotten created a problem for Bradlaugh, then Bradlaugh, in turn, represented a continuing problem for the Liberal Party. For one thing there was the effect of the Bradlaugh case upon by-election results. Conservatives boasted and Liberals complained time and again that the case was hurting the Liberal party. Edward Hamilton noted in his diary in 1882: 'The beastly business . . . is doing incalculable harm to the party in the country.'[3] The word 'incalculable', literally defined, is appropriate since, if it is difficult in any free election to isolate one particular issue and term it decisive, this was even more true in an age before public-opinion polls.

The Liberal Party had suffered a net loss of five seats in by-elections in 1880 and five more in 1881. It did not, on balance, lose any additional seats in 1882, a year during which only four seats changed hands, but its share of the vote declined in seven out of that year's eight contests.[4] Such a decrease in Liberal strength was not altogether surprising; it has been the customary, if not universal, experience whenever one party wins a general election by a commanding majority. Nor was the Bradlaugh case the only issue at stake. What can fairly be concluded, on the basis of a survey of these by-elections, is that wherever Bradlaugh was made an issue the Liberal Party lost votes. Many Conservative platform speakers seemed to be suffering from 'Bradlaugh on the Brain',[5] and no quick cure was in the offing. As early as July 1880 an Anglican clergyman had taken the lead in supporting

---

[1] Memorandum by Henry James, 14 Nov. 1882, G.P. (B.M.), 44219, fol. 76; G.P. (B.M.), 44643, fol. 184.

[2] *N.R.*, 3 Dec. 1882, p. 385; 21 Jan. 1883, p. 34.

[3] Hamilton Diary (B.M.), 48631, p. 248.

[4] All summaries of by-election results are based upon an analysis of results given in the annual issues of *Dod's Parliamentary Companion*, 1881–5.

[5] *N.R.*, 19 Dec. 1880, p. 433.

the Conservative candidate in a by-election in Scarborough. He had nothing against the Liberal candidate personally, he declared, 'but this I feel (as I am sure do many others) that every vote given to keep Bradlaugh's friends in power is a nail in the coffin of English Christianity'.[1] The Conservatives had flooded the constituency with 3 in. × 2 in. blue cards bearing the following inscription: 'Fathers of Scarborough. Do you want your children to be defiled by Bradlaugh's filth? If not, Vote for DUNSCOMBE.' Despite these tactics, the Liberals retained the seat but their majority of 595 in April was reduced to 222 three months later.

The situation had been different in North Berwick and Wigton; in both boroughs Bradlaugh's name was widely used, and in both towns Liberal victories at the general election of April 1880 were reversed in July. Admiral Sir John C. D. Hay, the Conservative victor at Wigton, was especially fond of citing the *Fruits of Philosophy* legal case. 'Mr. Bradlaugh was an Atheist,' observed Hay in one speech, 'and had published a book which showed how the Seventh Commandment might be broken without adding to the population of the country. . . . Mr. Bradlaugh travelled about with a lady, and had published a book which he supposed was the fruits of their experimental philosophy.' Bradlaugh protested both publicly and privately (to Northcote) against Hay's 'grossly foul and infamous suggestions', but the Opposition leader replied politely that he could not undertake to be responsible for every statement made by a Conservative candidate 'however much I may disapprove . . .'.[2]

Though the tide against the Government was halted temporarily in the winter of 1880–1, five additional seats were lost in rapid succession during the spring and summer of 1881, and James Knowles, the editor of the *Nineteenth Century*, deemed Bradlaugh and 'fair trade' (a revived protectionism) the two issues most damaging to the Liberals that year.[3] The Bradlaugh case aroused much concern in a by-election in the

---

[1] Cited in *N.R.*, 8 Aug. 1880, p. 138. Iddesleigh MSS. (B.M.), 50041, fol. 26, contain sample copy of card.

[2] Iddesleigh MSS. (B.M.), 50041, fols. 23–31; *N.R.*, 15 Aug. 1880, p. 149.

[3] Hamilton Diary (B.M.), 48631, p. 131.

North Riding of Yorkshire in January 1882. No other question generated greater interest among the voters, according to Guy Dawnay, the Conservative candidate, and even a last-minute reversal of his pro-Bradlaugh stand by the Liberal nominee failed to save him from defeat.[1] Only two months later Sir Thomas Dyke Acland, whose son was contesting East Cornwall, wrote bitterly to Gladstone that the Bradlaugh issue was being used effectively against his son, a situation for which he held the Prime Minister personally responsible. Gladstone did his best to comfort Acland, though readily acknowledging the damage the case was doing.[2] The younger Acland did ultimately retain the seat for the Liberals, though the party's percentage of the vote plummeted from 60 per cent. in 1880 to 51 per cent. two years later.

It is against this background that the prevailing attitude of Liberal M.P.s toward the case must be understood. An analysis of the Liberal vote in thirteen key roll calls indicates that 69 per cent. of the party's members tended generally to vote in favour of Bradlaugh's admission, 23 per cent. tended to abstain, and 8 per cent. tended to oppose his admission. Although the Conservative *Saturday Review* considered the Parliament of 1880 'the most mechanically elected and the most mechanically drilled Parliament that England has yet seen',[3] party discipline was still relatively lax by twentieth-century British standards.

Many of the Liberals who did support the Northampton M.P.'s constitutional claims did so apologetically and with a notable absence of enthusiasm. When A. J. Mundella, a Liberal minister, voted against Bradlaugh's expulsion in February 1882 he felt compelled to write an immediate letter of explanation to the chairman of his constituency's party organization.[4] Overt anti-clericals like John Dick Peddie, who bluntly asserted on one occasion that 'there can be no worse index to the opinion of any country than the opinions of the churches',[5] were very rare indeed. A Scottish colleague,

[1] *Daily News*, 2 Feb. 1882. [2] G.P. (B.M.), 44545, fol. 113.
[3] 19 Jan. 1884, p. 68.
[4] Mundella to Leader, 22 Feb. 1882, Mundella MSS.
[5] *Hansard*, cclxxxviii (1883), 1205.

Dr. Charles Cameron of Glasgow, did, to be sure, venture even further on one occasion:

I have voted [he declared] against the exclusion of clergymen of the Established Church, I have voted against the exclusion of Mr. Bradlaugh, and I would vote against the the exclusion of Beelzebub himself if any constituency thought fit to return him to Parliament as its accredited representative. . . . And I should do so totally regardless of the political or religious opinions of the respective parties—in the conviction that the clergymen and Beelzebub, if admitted, would take their seats on the Opposition benches, the latter probably in the ranks of the Fourth Party, and show themselves determined enemies of anything savouring of Radicalism or reform.[1]

While 'Radical' M.P.s tended to vote more consistently for Bradlaugh than other Liberals (83 per cent. as compared to 67 per cent.), not all self-styled Radicals showed equal sympathy to the man or his case. John Morley of the *Pall Mall Gazette* and Joseph Cowen of the Newcastle *Chronicle*, though supporters of Bradlaugh's admission, were often distinctly critical of his character and his tactics. Samuel Morley's attitude has been noted above, while W. McCullagh Torrens, a Radical from Finsbury (in Greater London), had by 1883 emerged as one of Bradlaugh's leading Liberal opponents and an expert organizer of a petition campaign against an Affirmation Bill.[2] Joseph Chamberlain, popularly a Unitarian though privately an agnostic and non-church-goer, was reluctant to use the National Liberal Federation— an outgrowth of the famous Birmingham caucus—as a propaganda vehicle on Bradlaugh's behalf, and Charles W. Dilke was equally reluctant to do more than vote for Bradlaugh.[3] When Bradlaugh sought admission, as a Liberal M.P., to the National Liberal Club, its chairman, William C. Borlase, was deeply perplexed: 'To elect him', he warned Herbert Gladstone, 'would cause *hundreds* to withdraw; to reject him

---

[1] Cited in *N.R.*, 22 Jan. 1882, p. 49.
[2] See Torrens's autobiography, *Twenty Years of Parliament* (London, 1893), pp. 313–15.
[3] See (Copy) Dilke to Chamberlain, 9 Jan. 1883, Dilke MSS. (B.M.), 43886; also 43892, fol. 23. For Chamberlain's religious views, see his letter to Dilke, 43887, fol. 76.

would cause *tens* to do so.'[1] The application was discreetly withdrawn.

Bradlaugh's obvious unpopularity among his fellow Liberals helps to explain the relatively indulgent attitude of the Cabinet towards 'weak-kneed' back-benchers. When Frederick Grafton of Lancashire was criticized for opposing Bradlaugh's admission on the basis that 'a Christian country should be governed by Christian men' his Liberal colleague, the Marquess of Hartington, came to his support. Hartington, the leading Whig in the Cabinet, had a 10–1 pro-Bradlaugh record on thirteen key divisions, but he freely defended Grafton's right to follow his own dictates of conscience.[2] Other Liberals opposed or abstained not for reasons of principle but because they feared their constituents would not distinguish between atheism and the just treatment of an atheist. Alexander McArthur of Leicester was perhaps the most honest of all. Asked to explain his failure to support Bradlaugh's position during a highly significant division, he declared that, while he had never questioned Bradlaugh's right to his seat, he had abstained 'as a matter of expediency'.[3]

If not all Radicals were strong Bradlaugh supporters, then neither were all Whigs his opponents. The vindication of the rights of constituencies to select their own representatives was, after all, much more a traditional Whig principle than was government interference with the prerogatives of land ownership. Thus the Duke of Argyll, a man who had resigned from the Cabinet on the issue of the Irish Land Act, could consistently sponsor an Affirmation Bill in the House of Lords. Lord Selborne, the Lord Chancellor, another Whiggish Cabinet member who often wondered how long he could continue to reconcile himself with the direction in which his party was moving, publicly declared his complete agreement with his Cabinet colleagues in defence of Bradlaugh's right to his seat.[4]

Perhaps the most cogent argument against the whole philosophy of oath-taking written in connexion with the

[1] Viscount (Herbert) Gladstone MSS. (B.M.), 46049, fol. 314.
[2] Cited in *N.R.*, 4 Dec. 1881, p. 433; 28 Jan. 1883, pp. 52–53.
[3] Cited in *N.R.*, 2 Nov. 1884, p. 291.
[4] Granville MSS., Box 30/29, fol. 141; *N.R.*, 15 May 1881, p. 392.

Bradlaugh case was set forth in an article by still another Whig, Robert Lowe, Viscount Sherbrooke, in the August 1882 issue of *Nineteenth Century*. Lowe had been one of the leading opponents of the Reform Bill of 1867, though he had afterwards served successively as Gladstone's Chancellor of the Exchequer and Home Secretary.[1] By 1880 he was too far out of sympathy with the Radical element in the Liberal party to re-enter the Cabinet, and he retired to the House of Lords. Yet Sherbrooke sounds like a staunch reformer when he takes issue with the upholders of Parliamentary oaths, that 'perilous and ungrateful subject'. There were two distinct types of oaths, Sherbrooke observed, assertory oaths which dealt with events of the past and promissory oaths which were an undertaking 'for all time to come'. Both oaths represented an appeal to a supernatural power, and yet a man like Bradlaugh was permitted to substitute an affirmation for the first type of oath—as a legal witness—but not for the second. This was obviously inconsistent. Sherbrooke then went on to question the intrinsic value of promissory oaths. Why should a Peer or a Member of Parliament undertake by oath a duty he was already bound by the laws of his country and by 'the clearest mandates of morality' to perform? 'All the execrations in the world cannot make it more binding; all the promises that can be uttered add nothing to its force.' If such oaths were more than empty forms—if they imposed any duty not already binding—'the result must necessarily be that no one could be punished for disobeying a law which he had never formally promised to obey'.

In any case the attempt to create a religious barrier out of a promise of fidelity should be given up at once. Bradlaugh had been deprived of his rightful seat 'by the arbitrary and illegal action of the House of Commons. . . . It is a melancholy exhibition of the tyranny of orthodoxy when we see one branch of the legislature taking upon itself to nullify laws which the whole legislature itself has sanctioned.' (For perhaps the only time in the course of Bradlaugh's struggle, his exclusion was interpreted as an implied affront upon the House of Lords.) Why should any man be forced to state or

[1] See, for example, 'Robert Lowe and the Fear of Democracy', in Asa Briggs, *Victorian People* (Chicago, 1955).

intimate that he had conscientious objections to promissory oaths? Why should they not be ended altogether, since they served to set up a conception of two types of truth and to create the impression that lies not accompanied by judicial formalities were insignificant misdemeanours? Promissory oaths, concluded Viscount Sherbrooke, were 'immoral and degrading', and the sooner they were abolished the better.

The enthusiasm of a Sherbrooke was not necessarily infectious, however, and most Liberals at the end of 1882 were fearful of a future clouded by new incidents in an apparently unending Bradlaugh case. It was a most unhappy prospect.

XV

THE AFFIRMATION BILL

ONE conclusion concerning the Bradlaugh case which has never been questioned is that it troubled Gladstone. It was, wrote John Morley, 'a controversy that was probably more distasteful to him than any other of the myriad contentions, small and great, with which his life was encumbered'.[1] It cannot but have been unpleasant for him to find himself and his views repeatedly misrepresented, to see newspapers write of an openly avowed 'Bradlaugh–Gladstone alliance', of 'Gladstone's patronage of an atheist', of Gladstone and Bradlaugh as a political partnership, of Gladstone 'taking the Atheist by the hand'.[2] It seemed most unfair to a man who saw himself charting a straightforward judicial path through the thicket of political and religious emotionalism the case had provoked.

Over the years there was a host of reports attesting to the Prime Minister's distress. This 'peculiarly odious worry', remarked Gladstone's niece in May 1881 has 'lately made Uncle W[illiam] ill'.[3] In August 1881 Gladstone himself referred to Bradlaugh as an impediment to Parliamentary business;[4] and in December 1881 Chief Justice Coleridge noted that Gladstone had spoken to him 'rather despondingly of the Bradlaugh row'.[5] 'It is the one thing of all others', observed Hamilton, one of the Prime Minister's secretaries,

---

[1] *Gladstone*, iii. 11.

[2] e.g., *England*, 3 July 1880, p. 1; 30 Apr. 1881, p. 8; *Whitehall Review*, 1 July 1880, p. 155. By countenancing Bradlaugh, wrote an anonymous pamphleteer, Gladstone 'has upset the religious morality of the people more than all the religious sects put together have done to improve the people the last 50 years . . .'. *Otherwise: or Quite Another Tack* (London [1882]), p. 12.

[3] *The Diary of Lady Frederick Cavendish*, ed. John Baily (London, 1927), ii. 286.

[4] *Gladstone to His Wife*, ed. A. Tilney Basset (London, 1936), p. 236.

[5] Cited by Ernest Hartley Coleridge, *Life and Correspondence of John Duke, Lord Coleridge* (London, 1904), ii. 309.

in February 1882, 'which is genuinely disagreeable and distasteful to Mr. Gladstone.'[1]

Gladstone's position, as has been noted earlier, was to see the question of Bradlaugh's oath as lying essentially outside the jurisdiction of the House of Commons. This attitude of being above the battle, of viewing the matter as little more than a technical legal question to be determined in the law courts, was one that appealed neither to the Opposition, which regarded the House of Commons as fully competent to deal with Bradlaugh, nor to many Liberals, who preferred to cope with the issue by legislation rather than by a Parliamentary resolution designed to create a legal case. For three years, however, Gladstone consistently opposed new legislation as an appropriate solution. He weakened briefly in April and May 1881, when what may be termed the first Affirmation Bill was proposed by Sir Henry James; but the subsequent success of the Opposition in blocking even the formal introduction of the bill convinced him once again that legislation was not the answer.

This was not the attitude, however, of the more influential newspapers. 'The only logical course', commented *The Times* in February 1882, 'is to legalize the alternative of affirmation.'[2] The *Daily News* agreed, and even the Conservative *Saturday Review* predicted in November 1881 that, unless Bradlaugh were allowed to take the oath at the commencement of the next session, 'the Government must try to give him the measure of general relief which it has promised him'.[3] As late as October 1882 the *Nottingham Journal* expressed its confidence that 'such a measure might reckon on the warm support of the great bulk of the Liberal party' as well as of a minority of Conservatives.[4]

The question then arises: why did Gladstone oppose new legislation so consistently? Political expediency provides a partial answer in that he saw more vividly than did some of his more enthusiastic supporters the pitfalls such a bill faced not merely in the House of Commons but also in the House of Lords. Gladstone was conscious of the reservations held

[1] Hamilton Diary (B.M.), 48631, p. 249. [2] 8 Feb. 1882, p. 10.
[3] Cited in *N.R.*, 13 Nov. 1881, p. 385.
[4] Cited in *N.R.*, 15 Oct. 1882, p. 263.

by many Liberals and as aware as the staunchly Liberal *Daily Chronicle* that the exclusion of Bradlaugh, however ill-advised, was not looked upon by the constituencies 'as worthy of being called a party question'.[1] Nor could he altogether overlook Queen Victoria's opposition to any action which might be interpreted as promoting atheism. Only the year before she had successfully used her influence to bar Sir Charles Dilke from the Chancellorship of the Duchy of Lancaster, and as Gladstone in 1883 confided to his secretary concerning the Queen, there was 'no greater Tory in the land'.[2] It is not surprising that in view of Gladstone's apparent opposition to an Affirmation Bill, both the opponents and the more ardent supporters of Bradlaugh's admission should have interpreted the Prime Minister's attitude as one of shrinking from 'this public concession to Atheism . . .'.[3]

Such an assessment would be wide of the mark, however, conflicting as it does with Gladstone's heroic refusal to heed the majority of his Cabinet in February 1882 and sponsor a motion of expulsion. At that time the Attorney-General had advocated that the Government should wash its hands of the case and grant Bradlaugh no further Parliamentary support whatsoever; yet Gladstone had refused.[4] 'I never was more convinced that a political mistake was made', wrote Edward Hamilton. 'Any strong action of the Government [against Bradlaugh] would have been supported enthusiastically by the bulk of the Liberal party.'[5] No, Gladstone's course can hardly be explained solely on the basis of political expediency. Gladstone had solved the issue in the summer of 1880 by means of a resolution affording a court test of Bradlaugh's right to affirm. The test had gone against Bradlaugh. What Gladstone now wanted was a similar opportunity for Bradlaugh to test the legal validity of his oath in the

---

[1] Cited in *N.R.*, 31 Dec. 1882, p. 483. See also G.P. (B.M.), 44546, fol. 23.
[2] Hamilton Diary (B.M.), 48634, p. 24.
[3] *Tablet*, 3 Mar. 1883, p. 322. 'Everybody knows', wrote the Radical *Weekly Dispatch* in December 1884, 'that he could have secured Mr. Bradlaugh in the possession of his rights long ago, had he been courageous enough to set himself the task.' Cited in *N.R.*, 28 Dec. 1884, p. 460.
[4] G.P. (B.M.), 44219, fol. 57.
[5] Hamilton Diary (B.M.), 48631, p. 266.

courts, but it was impossible for Bradlaugh to gain such an opportunity until Parliament first granted him the right to swear. It all seemed simple and straightforward to Gladstone. He was willing to concede that Bradlaugh was acting in bad taste in wishing to take the oath in the first place, but he was equally certain that the House of Commons could not constitutionally bar him from so doing.

As he explained to one of his critics, either 'Bradlaugh has fulfilled the law, or he has not. If he has, he should sit. If he has not, the courts should correct him.'[1] This was no more than justice toward Bradlaugh; and as Gladstone observed to another critic, 'though you disapprove my action, I am sure you accept its principle, which is that of doing justice at the cost of every kind of misapprehension and political inconvenience'.[2] Indeed, Gladstone was in good company. Such legal authorities as Frederick Pollock fully agreed that the attempt to use the Parliamentary oath as a religious test 'has nothing to justify it in English history, or in the traditions of English politics. It is an unhappy example of the ignorance and confusion of mind concerning the institutions of their own country which are still common among English legislators.'[3]

Gladstone's position may thus be described as the truly legal and the truly conservative one; but what if the House of Commons refused to agree with him as it had time and again over the years? Then he had no solution to offer except temporary abdication of leadership, a role the hostile *Freeman's Journal* interpreted as 'Achilles sulking in his tent'.[4] Judicial impartiality under these circumstances became no more than lack of leadership. The Liberal ship was buffeted every few months by the storm from Northampton, yet Gladstone provided no firm hand at the tiller. Throughout 1882 Gladstone remained consistent, however; and when in December 1882 the Cabinet began to plan the legislative

---

[1] (Copy) Gladstone to J. G. Hubbard, 11 June 1881, G.P. (B.M.), 44544, fol. 179.
[2] (Copy) Gladstone to W. H. Farquhar, 10 Feb. 1882, G.P. (B.M.), 44545, fol. 100.
[3] *Essays in Jurisprudence and Ethics* (London, 1882), p. 197.
[4] 7 Mar. 1882, p. 4.

programme of the session to come, no Affirmation Bill was on the agenda.[1]

In February 1883 the Gladstone Ministry did, however, decide to add an Affirmation Bill to the legislative programme of the coming session of Parliament. The impression created in most biographies of Gladstone[2] is that this decision was consistent with the Prime Minister's previous policy and that Gladstone was primarily responsible for it. As should now be evident, this shift in policy was inconsistent with Gladstone's previous stand. It was, moreover, decided upon by the Liberal Cabinet in Gladstone's absence. For reasons of ill health[3] Gladstone had departed for Cannes in mid-January, and he did not return to London until early March, by which time the new session was well under way.

On the day after Gladstone had left for Cannes, Bradlaugh called upon Speaker Brand to inform him that, as soon as the session began, he intended to present himself once again to take the oath, unless the Government first agreed to introduce an Affirmation Bill. Both the Speaker and Hamilton tended to favour such a bill as the lesser of two evils.[4] The Liberal Cabinet, which had been informed of Bradlaugh's hardly surprising intentions, met on several occasions in late January and early February, with Lord Granville, the Foreign Secretary, presiding in Gladstone's absence. The Bradlaugh question was discussed at the Cabinet meetings of 9, 13, and 17 February. There was an immediate consensus that new legislation was necessary, and Cabinet disagreement on other measures to be included in the programme for the session made a bill dealing with the Bradlaugh case more palatable. Lord Selborne, the Lord Chancellor, and William Harcourt, the Home Secretary, preferred the complete abolition of the oath; but a majority of the Cabinet, including Chamberlain, chose to limit the bill to giving the option of affirmation to all who desired it. Over the strong objections

---

[1] Hamilton Diary (B.M.), 48633, p. 60.

[2] Cf. Magnus, *Gladstone*, p. 278, and Eyck, *Gladstone*, p. 293.

[3] The Home Secretary, William Harcourt, was one of several members of the ministry who thought Gladstone so ill that he might never return. Dilke MSS. (B.M.), 43937, fol. 7.

[4] Hamilton Diary (B.M.), 48633, p. 99; Hampden Diary, entry for 15 Feb. 1883.

of Granville and Hartington, the Bill was made retrospective; it would, in other words, apply to Bradlaugh immediately upon enactment.[1]

Granville informed both Queen Victoria and Gladstone on 9 February that an Affirmation Bill would be introduced on the first day of the session. In his reports to the Queen, he did his best to make the decision appear a routine one, but Gladstone was fully aware of its significance. 'I am not at all surprised or dissatisfied at the decision to introduce an Affirmation Bill under the present circumstances', was his reply. The delay in other legislation which the bill would cause might of course 'seriously affect the plan of business for the whole Session'. The matter was, in any case, 'probably better out of my hands than in them', since he had always maintained that a new law was unnecessary.[2]

By this time Gladstone's health had improved and he had become impatient with the holiday his solicitous associates had imposed upon him. His Riviera neighbour, Lady Queensberry, when invited to have tea with the Prime Minister, had brought with her a seven-year-old girl to whom she introduced Gladstone as the 'governor of England'. 'But how can he govern England and eat bread & butter here with me?' asked the little girl. Gladstone strongly felt the force of the remark.[3] He was with difficulty prevailed upon to remain in southern France a few weeks longer.

In the meantime, Charles Bradlaugh, ignorant thus far of the Cabinet's decision, was preparing for the opening day of Parliament another gigantic meeting in Trafalgar Square, a 'National Demonstration to protest against the Continued Violation of Northampton's Constitutional Rights'. Some 30,000 supporters had gathered by the time Bradlaugh and a few close associates arrived at 12.45 p.m. on 15 February 1883. The man who introduced a resolution that the meeting protest against the 'flagrant wrong' done Northampton was, characteristically, a Dissenting minister, a Mr. Sharman. Joseph Arch, the farm-labour leader, seconded the motion.

[1] Dilke MSS. (B.M.), 43925, fols. 43, 45, 46; 43937, fols. 51, 55, 63.
[2] Granville MSS., Box 30/29/29A, and G.P. (B.M.), 44175, fol. 79; (Copy) Gladstone to Granville, 17 Feb. 1883, G.P. (B.M.), 44546, fol. 80. See also Hampden Diary, entry for 25 Mar. 1883.
[3] G.P. (B.M.), 44546, fol. 81.

Then Bradlaugh himself, 'the Tribune of the People', made a few remarks to the vast assembly. He was perhaps the only one who could make himself heard. He congratulated the crowd for ignoring a steady downpour in order to assemble. 'Inclement as the weather is . . . you are gathered, called by no power save that of principle.' The meeting was adjourned to permit Bradlaugh to enter the House of Commons for his avowed purpose of once again attempting to take the oath. More than an hour elapsed, and the crowd was beginning to grow restless, when a triumphant Bradlaugh emerged from Westminster Palace to announce that Lord Hartington had just pledged the Government to introduce an Affirmation Bill the very next day. What 'a very glorious ending to a very painful struggle'.[1]

The Cabinet's initial decision to introduce an Affirmation Bill had not been publicized except for 'an indiscreet paragraph' in the *Daily News*. Only on 14 February did the Government decide to inform Bradlaugh directly of its intentions.[2] Whether Bradlaugh had been notified at the time of the big demonstration the following day remains therefore debatable. The popular impression was that the Government had been swayed by the Trafalgar Square meeting. The Radical *Weekly Dispatch* was as sure of this as was the Conservative *Morning Post*, which condemned the Government's promise as a concession to mob rule. 'To the eternal and lasting disgrace of the executive of a civilized country, the advisers of the Crown yielded to this brutal and vulgar menace.'[3]

The introduction of the bill had obviously been mishandled. Equally difficult to defend was the failure of the Cabinet to include the Affirmation Bill, so obviously a Government measure, in the Queen's Speech, which referred to numerous bills of lesser political importance. As even one of Gladstone's secretaries privately conceded: 'The omission is rather awkward; and I don't quite know how it is to be justified. But I presume the Cabinet thought the mention of

---

[1] *Evening Standard*, 15 Feb. 1883, and *Pall Mall Gazette*, 16 Feb. 1883, cited in *N.R.*, 25 Feb. 1883, pp. 116–17; *N.R.*, 18 Feb. 1883, p. 97.
[2] G.P. (B.M.), 44175, fols. 79, 83.
[3] Cited in *N.R.*, 25 Feb. 1883, p. 122.

it would look too much like submission to dictation by Bradlaugh. Of course the great aim is to dissociate the measure from a Bradlaugh Relief Bill.'[1] Gladstone himself, upon his return to London, seemed less happy than ever with the measure. The Affirmation Bill, he confided to his Cabinet, 'is a stone round our necks'.[2]

[1] Sir Henry Ponsonby MSS. (B.M.), 45725, fol. 59.
[2] Dilke MSS. (B.M.), 43925, fol. 50.

XVI

THE GREAT CRUSADE

FOR the majority of religious organizations in the United Kingdom the Affirmation Bill represented at once an affront and a challenge. 'Not alone the forces of religious orthodoxy,' wrote *The Times* in late April, 'but all the associations and traditions connected with every form of Christianity have been called into action.'[1] The appraisal is, by and large, a just one. Yet it would be an error to regard the attitude of all religious denominations as identical or to conclude that no differences of opinion existed within each denomination. If one were to paint a religious spectrum ranging from agnosticism and Unitarianism at one end to Roman Catholicism at the other, then one would find in general that those with convictions closer to Bradlaugh's own were more sympathetic to his cause. Yet there remain a number of significant exceptions to such a generalization.

George Jacob Holyoake, whose British Secular Union was an unsuccessful rival to Bradlaugh's National Secular Society, was certainly a strong advocate of the Affirmation Bill, but until the two men were partially reconciled in 1883, he scoffed at Bradlaugh's willingness to take the Parliamentary Oath. 'Do not the unsympathising churches scream with merriment', he asked rhetorically on one occasion, 'at the comic spectacle of an Atheist, smitten with devotion and remorse, fighting his way to kiss the Bible?'[2] The honorary president of the British Secular Union, the Marquess of Queensberry, was more sympathetic, and in 1881 he contributed £50 to Bradlaugh's Constitutional Rights League and spoke on his behalf at a St. James's Hall meeting. Queensberry, whose historical reputation today is more closely identified with boxing than with free thought, was, however, far more concerned with efforts to regain his own place in the

[1] 24 Apr. 1883, p. 9.　　　　[2] Cited in *N.R.*, 22 Jan. 1882, p. 60.

House of Lords than with Bradlaugh's possible entry into the House of Commons. He had served as a representative Scottish peer until 1880, when he had been displaced, he asserted, because of his anti-religious views.[1] Frederic Harrison, England's leading positivist, and T. H. Huxley, the coiner of the term 'agnostic', tended to be more concerned with distinguishing their own convictions from outright atheism than with becoming involved in Bradlaugh's parliamentary struggle. 'We warmly repudiate the arid conceit of Atheism', insisted Harrison in his autobiography.[2] Huxley took no public stand on the case. An emphasis by agnostics upon the gulf between their own views and atheism—in order to claim a place beneath the mantle of Victorian respectability—seemed all the more desirable at a time when numerous observers were detecting signs of a religious revival. 'Whether the civilized world be in its actual practice manifesting an increased regard for morals and religion,' wrote F. W. H. Myers in 1881, 'there seems at least to be no doubt that those subjects occupy now a larger space in its thoughts than has been the case since the Reformation.'[3]

One apparent free thinker who quite obviously damaged Bradlaugh's cause was an anonymous letter-writer to the Newcastle *Daily Chronicle* who repeatedly applauded the co-operation of atheists and Nonconformists in furthering the Affirmation Bill. He looked forward to several generations of secular education after which 'will dawn upon old England that happy time which the Freethought philosophers have foretold when the little child will repeat to its approving parent Shelley's dictum, "There is no God"'. The letters were prominently reprinted in the London press in April 1883 and cited in Parliament as an example of atheistic morality. Bradlaugh himself described the letters as 'exceedingly crafty', and only after the fate of the Affirmation Bill had been decided did their author reveal himself as a Tory churchgoer.[4]

[1] *N.R.*, 29 May 1881, p. 439; 27 Aug. 1882, p. 155; *Tablet*, 18 June 1881, p. 964.

[2] Frederic Harrison, *Autobiographical Memoirs* (London, 1911), ii. 276.

[3] 'M. Renan and Miracles', *Nineteenth Century*, July 1881, p. 91.

[4] *N.R.*, 13 May 1883, p. 353; 30 Mar. 1884, p. 218; *Tablet*, 7 Apr. 1883.

Not all agnostics were personally unfriendly to Bradlaugh. Leslie Stephen, for one, contributed a sympathetic article to the *Fortnightly Review*,[1] and Moncure D. Conway, the American expatriate, was both a friend and staunch supporter.[2] Among the major periodicals, the *Westminster Review*, whose rationalist proclivities descended from the times of Jeremy Bentham, was most obviously in Bradlaugh's corner and willing, on occasion, to make light of the gravity with which many clergymen treated Bradlaugh's assaults upon the Parliamentary oath. 'The Devil might come into Parliament under the Affirmation Bill', it quoted one clergyman as having warned. He was thereupon reminded that 'the Devil, being a most convinced *Deist*, might be, and possibly is, a member of that enlightened assembly as the law now stands'.[3]

Both Unitarians and Jews tended strongly to favour the Affirmation Bill. Baron de Worms, a Conservative M.P. of Jewish origin, had been criticized so often by Bradlaugh's *National Reformer* that on one occasion Bradlaugh found it necessary to correct the prevalent misapprehension 'that the Jews as a body have been hostile to my admission to Parliament'. Both Serjeant Simon and Arthur Cohen, Liberal M.P.s professing Judaism, spoke warmly in Bradlaugh's favour, and the *Jewish World* reminded its readers in 1883 that 'people have in the personality of the man lost sight of the cause he is really fighting—the cause of religious liberty, which should be held to include the liberty to believe little as well as much'.[4]

Though the Nonconformist denominations had been perplexed by Bradlaugh's willingness to take the oath, a majority of their members consistently favoured an Affirmation Bill. John Bright, who continued to make his influence felt even after his resignation from the Cabinet in 1882 over a foreign policy issue, was, as a Quaker, necessarily a fervent advocate of the Affirmation Bill of 1883. '. . . probably there is nothing in the New Testament more especially condemned and forbidden than oaths', he reminded his fellow Christians. 'To

[1] *Fortnightly Review*, August 1880, cited in *N.R.*, 8 Aug. 1880, p. 141.
[2] *N.R.*, 30 Apr. 1882, p. 342.   [3] *Westminster Review*, July 1883, p. 230.
[4] Cited in *N.R.*, 13 May 1883, p. 364. See also *N.R.*, 4 Mar. 1883, p. 129.

those who do not care about the New Testament', he added tartly, 'this fact will be of no weight.'[1] All but one of the seven Baptists in Parliament were equally favourable to Bradlaugh's admission and the Affirmation Bill. The Protestant Dissenting Deputies, an organization representing Presbyterian, Independent, and Baptist congregations in the London area, whose chairman was Henry Richard, a Liberal M.P., also came out strongly in favour of the bill.[2]

The Congregationalist Union similarly expressed its formal approval of the Affirmation Bill, though individual Congregationalist ministers and an occasional Baptist might well feel otherwise. 'I shall deeply regret that any constituency c[oul]d so dishonour itself as to take him [Bradlaugh] for a representative,' wrote a leading Baptist preacher, 'but if they will do so I see more danger in denying the man's right than in allowing it.'[3] The point of view is typical.

Presbyterians tended to be more divided on the question than the denominations cited above. English Presbyterians were generally favourable toward Bradlaugh's claims, but the Kirk of Scotland and the Presbyterians of Ulster, whose Orange associations co-operated with Roman Catholics in gathering anti-Bradlaugh petitions, were not.[4] In 1881 the General Assembly of the Church of Scotland approved by a vote of 177 to 19 a resolution to petition Parliament against an Affirmation Bill. The decision was re-confirmed in 1883.[5]

Whether Methodists ought to be classified as Nonconformists remains debatable today and was equally so in 1880. The *Nonconformist* complained that year: 'Wesleyans are included under the general description of Nonconformists when this can be made to tell for Tory or Church purposes, but Wesleyans are not the Nonconformists who won the Liberal victory, and who constitute the real Nonconformist party.'[6] The denomination was certainly less closely tied to

[1] *The Public Letters of the Rt. Hon. John Bright, M.P.*, ed. H. J. Leach (London, 1885), p. 278.
[2] The Protestant Dissenting Deputies, MS. Minute Books, 1881–90, pp. 108, 301.
[3] C. H. Spurgeon to C. N. Newdegate, 30 June 1880. Newdegate MSS.
[4] *N.R.*, 3 July 1881, p. 42.
[5] *N.R.*, 5 June 1881, p. 456; 11 Mar. 1883, p. 152.
[6] *Nonconformist*, cited in *Rock*, 2 July 1880, p. 505.

Gladstone's party than were the Baptists and Congregationalists. Thus it is not surprising that the Wesleyan Conference
of 1880 should have protested against Bradlaugh's admission
to Parliament and that the Conference of 1883 should have
found itself perplexed by the Affirmation Bill. At the urging
of its president, the Rev. Charles Garrett, the assembly resolved that the bill did not lie within the scope of questions
it had convened to determine. More than a thousand members
of the Wesleyan Conference signed petitions opposing the
bill as private citizens, but the president preserved a public
neutrality. 'I have done all in my power', he piously declared,
'to prevent agitation in Methodism on this subject, and,
though strongly tempted, I avoided any expression of my
opinion.' Only after the bill had been voted upon in Parliament did Garrett admit his approval of its provisions.[1]

All the Nonconformists combined made up only a small
minority of the British population, and in the ranks of the
dominant Church of England there was much less hesitation
when it came to condemning both Bradlaugh's admission to
Parliament and the Affirmation Bill of 1883. Yet, here too,
there were exceptions. Certain High Church 'ritualists'
favoured the Affirmation Bill. So did an independent clergyman like Canon Malcolm MacColl, who protested publicly
that Christians should not impose oaths upon non-believers.
Is it 'altogether wise', he asked, 'on the part of the clergy to
be always exhibiting themselves in the attitude of opposition
to popular reforms and civil rights'?[2]

An even more striking exception to Anglican unanimity
was the Reverend Stewart Headlam, a man who not only
favoured Bradlaugh but was indeed a personal friend of the
notorious atheist. From the beginning of his clerical career
Headlam had found himself at odds with a majority of his
colleagues. He first became notorious in church circles for
giving religious sanction to performances in theatres and
music halls and for consistently opposing legal barriers
against working-class recreation on Sundays.[3] He became

[1] Cited in Bradford *Chronicle & Mail*, 8 June 1880; cited in *N.R.*, 15 Apr.
1883, p. 248; 13 May 1883, p. 360; *Hansard*, cclxxviii (1883), cols. 1453, 1454.
[2] Letter to *Manchester Guardian*, 7 Apr. 1883 (clipping in Cardinal Newman
MSS.); also the *Rock*, 11 May 1883, p. 339.
[3] See, for example, *N.R.*, 21 Oct. 1883, p. 259.

acquainted with Bradlaugh during the 1870's when curate of St. Matthew's, Bethnal Green, not far from Bradlaugh's Hall of Science. Finding it difficult to interest the older boys of his congregation in Sunday School and attributing the religious laxity of his neighbourhood to Bradlaugh's success in casting doubt upon Biblical traditions, he decided that Bradlaugh's boldness and eloquence ought to be matched by that of a spokesman for Christianity. In 1875 he began to read the *National Reformer* and to attend lectures at the Hall of Science. Soon he participated in the programme there, ever intent upon remaining reasonable and courteous toward his antagonists in contrast to many of the clergymen sent by the fundamentalist Christian Evidence Society to debate with the secularists.[1]

He was impressed from the first with Bradlaugh's personality and with the practical humanitarianism for which Bradlaugh seemed to stand, which he contrasted favourably with the efforts of contemporary fundamentalist revivalists and the methods of the Salvation Army. 'How much nearer to the Kingdom of Heaven are these men in the Hall of Science', he noted in 1876, 'than the followers of Moody and Sankey!'[2] He soon acknowledged that it would be impossible to convert Bradlaugh, but he did feel—probably rightly—that he could modify the loathing many of the rank and file secularists expressed for the Christian creed. When, however, he began to make statements such as the following: 'The Secularists have, in fact, absorbed some of the best Christian Truths which the Churches have been ignoring...', some of Headlam's fellow Anglicans began to wonder whether he was not becoming a convert to atheism.[3]

Headlam never became a convert. Instead he founded in 1877 the Guild of St. Matthew, an organization pledged to work for the reconversion of secularists to Christianity. Its formal objects were three:

I. To get rid, by every possible means, of the existing prejudices, especially on the part of 'Secularists', against the Church—

---

[1] F. G. Bettany, *Stewart Headlam: A Biography* (London, 1926), pp. 44–50.
[2] Cited ibid., p. 50.
[3] Stewart D. Headlam, *The Sure Foundation: An Address given before the Guild of St. Matthew, at the Annual Meeting 1883* (London, 1883), p. 10.

her Sacraments and Doctrines; and to endeavour to justify GOD to the People.

II. To promote frequent and reverent Worship in the Holy Communion and a better observance of the teaching of the Church of England as set forth in the Book of Common Prayer.

III. To promote the Study of Social and Political Questions in the light of the Incarnation.[1]

The Guild published a journal, *The Church Reformer*, preached to secularists, and, in addition, held numerous debates and discussions at which, as Bradlaugh readily conceded, 'the fullest and freest discussion is invited and allowed'.[2] Fellow Anglicans remained sceptical: 'Let us give our prayers and Eucharists,' wrote one clergyman in 1881, 'though we may perhaps withhold our shillings till we have watched their further action.'[3] Headlam resented such an attitude. It was difficult enough, he complained, to listen patiently to the scornful attacks of the secularists 'without the additional risk of being shot in the back by our episcopal generals'.[4]

The Guild of St. Matthew never did establish a secure place for itself within the Church of England—even at its height during the 1890's its membership barely exceeded two hundred, seventy of them in Holy Orders—partly because by the middle 1880's it was veering more definitely toward socialism (and publishing books by William Morris and Henry George) and partly because by that time much of its energy was taken up in defending Bradlaugh on the political scene. The affectionate nickname which Bradlaugh's followers had coined for the Guild of St. Matthew was 'The Society for the Prevention of Cruelty to Atheists'.[5]

By 1880 Headlam knew Bradlaugh well enough to permit his name to be added to the Bradlaugh election committee in Northampton.[6] When Bradlaugh's efforts to enter Parliament in the summer of 1880 led to his temporary imprisonment in the Clock Tower, Headlam was among the first to telegraph his good wishes: 'Accept my warmest sympathy;

[1] Ibid., p. 2. [2] *N.R.*, 25 Sept. 1881, p. 282.
[3] Cited in *N.R.*, 8 Jan. 1882, p. 23.
[4] Headlam, *The Sure Foundation*, p. 7.
[5] Stewart D. Headlam, *Charles Bradlaugh, An Appreciation* (London, 1907), p. 14. [6] *N.R.*, 1 Feb. 1880, p. 75.

I wish you good luck in the name of Jesus Christ, the emancipator, whom so many of your opponents blaspheme.'[1] From then on, Headlam aided Bradlaugh on many an occasion. He participated in Bradlaugh's 'League for the Defence of Constitutional Rights'. His continual theme was that the persecution of Bradlaugh was hurting rather than aiding Christianity. '. . . the result of the action of the religious party in the House', he declared in 1881, 'has been to make the religion of Jesus Christ to stink in the nostrils of the people.'[2] In 1882 Headlam began lecturing throughout the country on the subject 'A Christian View of the Bradlaugh Case'. 'As far as I understand the life and character of Jesus Christ,' declared Headlam in this lecture, 'he was far more of a secularist than many religious people seem to think.' His Kingdom of Heaven was much less in the clouds than a righteous society on earth. He associated, moreover, with the outcasts of his society while boldly rebuking the vices of contemporary clergymen and social leaders. He was willing to work with any man trying to make the world better rather than troubling himself about theological doctrines.

Headlam therefore favoured Bradlaugh as a fellow reformer, as a man with a following large enough to deserve representation in Parliament, and as a man willing to speak his mind plainly and fearlessly. Headlam dismissed the question of blasphemy as nonsense by definition. 'How can an Atheist blaspheme?' he asked; only a believer could do that. On constitutional, social, and religious grounds alike, Bradlaugh's admission to Parliament was fully justified.[3] Headlam and the Guild of St. Matthew petitioned earnestly in favour of the Affirmation Bill, and Headlam joined Mr. Sharman, the Unitarian minister, in an Association for the Repeal of the Blasphemy Laws.[4]

Bradlaugh's notoriety during the 1880's caused Parliamentary publicity to be given to the fact that, when school classes had first been organized in the Hall of Science in 1879, Bradlaugh had asked Headlam for assistance. In order to

[1] N.R., 4 July 1880, p. 39.
[2] Cited in N.R., 19 June 1881, p. 492.
[3] Cited in N.R., 24 Dec. 1882, pp. 453–4.
[4] N.R., 17 Dec. 1882, p. 439.

obtain a government education grant, Bradlaugh required either a Justice of the Peace or a clergyman on his School Committee. Unable to obtain the agreement of a Justice of the Peace, Bradlaugh eventually received Headlam's consent to serve. This Headlam did faithfully, often appearing on the annual prize-giving day programme. In an address to the Hall of Science students in 1882, he urged them indeed to bring to bear the scientific spirit upon all subjects connected with the welfare of man, social, political, and theological, in order to assure 'true progress'.[1] The Bishop of London sent a stiffly worded letter to Headlam, then Curate of St. Michael's, Shoreditch. 'Surely no laws of toleration or charitable hope can justify a Christian, still less a clergyman, in placing the teaching of the young in the hands of avowed Atheists', protested the bishop: Headlam's action had been indefensible.

Headlam replied in kind:

Personally, I think an 'Atheist' is kept for the time out of harm by being set to teach or learn purely scientific subjects. I am Chairman of the Committee of the Old Street Classes; the students are not any of them children, most of them grown men and women; the discipline which their study gives them, as well as the information they receive about GOD's wonderful physical world, must (I thought when I became chairman) do them some good in many ways, and make them, sooner or later, more careful in their theological and biblical studies than most 'Atheists' are at present. . . . It would be absurd to say that my action in the matter is worthy of the attention of the great council of the nation. But in any case I could hardly expect your lordship to defend me. Defence, my lord, is about the last thing which I, myself especially, and any priests who go a little out of the ordinary way in trying to fetch the wanderers home to the flock, have learnt to expect from their bishops . . . .[2]

In December 1882 Headlam was forced to resign his curacy in Shoreditch. 'I have been on very good terms with my Vicar,' Headlam explained, 'but he finds my political teaching is too strong for his friends, so we have to part.' On a subsequent occasion, Headlam explained the matter

[1] Headlam, *Charles Bradlaugh*, p. 5; *N.R.*, 8 Oct. 1882, p. 242.
[2] The correspondence is reprinted in *N.R.*, 13 Aug. 1882, p. 116.

more simply: 'What cost me my curacy was my defence of Bradlaugh.'[1]

It is not surprising that in Bradlaugh's circle Headlam became a hero, one of the very few clergymen to attain such a distinction. Bradlaugh publicly admired Headlam's 'splendid humanitarianism', willingly announced Headlam's lectures in the *National Reformer*, and frequently counted upon Headlam's support in his struggle to enter Parliament.[2] Annie Besant was even more fervent in her admiration: 'Let us reverently and gratefully admit the nobility of men like the Rev. Stewart D. Headlam', she wrote in 1881. '. . . our aims are one although our creeds are different', she added a year later. 'For beneath the rough turmoil of our controversies, deeper than the wrangling of our shibboleths, is the firm underlying rock of unity and brotherhood between all who recognise duty, love, and work as the three great foundation stones of all noble human life.'[3]

As a matter of fact, by the middle 1880's Headlam's political opinions were beginning to diverge significantly from Bradlaugh's. Convinced by Henry George of the desirability of the nationalization of all land, Headlam was becoming more openly a socialist. As early as 1882, in a sermon in Westminster Abbey, Headlam described Christ as 'a socialistic carpenter'. In an address to the Guild of St. Matthew the following year Headlam pictured Christ as 'the greatest of all secular workers, the founder of the great Socialistic society for the promotion of righteousness, the preacher of a Revolution, the denouncer of kings, the gentle, tender sympathiser with the rough and the outcast, who could utter scathing, burning words against the rich, the respectable, the religious'.[4] In 1883, Headlam began publishing *The Christian Socialist*, and in due course he joined the Fabian Society. The Guild of St. Matthew lasted until 1909, and Headlam himself outlived Bradlaugh by thirty-four years, but he long cherished his memories of the great

[1] Cited in *N.R.*, 24 Dec. 1882, p. 455; Bettany, *Headlam*, p. 77.
[2] See Bradlaugh to Adams, 30 Sept. 1882, Thomas Adams MSS. Also Bettany, *Headlam*, p. 49; *N.R.*, 25 Sept. 1881, p. 282.
[3] *N.R.*, 30 Oct. 1881, p. 355; 10 Dec. 1882, p. 407.
[4] Stewart D. Headlam, *The Service of Humanity and Other Sermons* (London, 1882), cited in *N.R.*, 10 Dec. 1882, p. 407; Headlam, *The Sure Foundation*, p. 6.

iconoclast. 'Bradlaugh may not know God,' he once told Sidney Webb, 'but God knows Bradlaugh.'[1]

Anglican clergymen like MacColl, Headlam, and the Reverend C. Williams, Vicar of Coalville, whose *Reasons for the Affirmation Bill Becoming Law (Though Involving Bradlaugh Sitting)* remains the most eloquent of the pro-Bradlaugh pamphlets written from a professedly religious point of view, remained a small minority. More representative was the Church of England priest who pleaded almost despairingly in July 1880 that Gladstone might at least publicize the loathing he must feel for Bradlaugh's unbelief.

Last Sunday night [he went on] when I read the Prayer for Parliament in my Church, I felt it almost bordering on profanity to ask for the blessing of God upon Parliament, and that HE would direct and prosper all its Consultations to the advancement of HIS Glory, and the good of HIS Church, while at the same time a man who openly denies God has been lawfully allowed to take his seat as one of its Members. This admission of an Atheist into the Parliament of a Christian Country, has shattered my political creed, and almost wrecked all my former views upon Liberalism and Conservatism.[2]

The theme was often to be repeated. By admitting Bradlaugh, the Reverend David Lewis of Wales urged in 1881, the Liberals 'will do more harm to themselves than the loss of fifty elections could do them'.[3] The *Protestant Times* went so far, indeed, as to sponsor a prize essay contest on the subject 'Liberalism in England and its Demoralizing Effects on Our National Religion and Liberties'.

The great majority of observations by Anglican clergymen recorded in the public press were hostile to Bradlaugh's admission into Parliament under any circumstances, though the grounds mentioned were often based less on religion, strictly defined, than on Bradlaugh's violations of contemporary canons of respectability. Both the Archbishop of York and the Bishop of Manchester took the opportunity at the annual Church Congress of 1881 at Newcastle upon Tyne to refer to 'the terrible immoral influences that accompanied the

[1] Cited in Bettany, *Headlam*, p. 138.
[2] G.P. (B.M.), 44465, fol. 74.
[3] Cited in *N.R.*, 10 July 1881, p. 56.

preaching of Atheism and Secularism in these later days'. The Archbishop scorned secularism, whose 'principles are, according to its most representative interpreter, "Atheistic, Republican, and Malthusian", the practical rendering of which would be, "No God, no King, and at least for the present—as few people as possible"'. According to the Bishop of Manchester the doctrine secularists preached in regard to family life was that 'the woman with whom the man cohabited could be put aside as soon as she became sick or otherwise disagreeable'. The purity of family life, upon which English greatness depended, was obviously in grave danger.[1] There were numerous direct or indirect references to *The Fruits of Philosophy*, a book which, according to the Fundamentalist *Rock*, 'proclaimed opinions and advocated practices which ... would if they were adopted reduce men and women below the brutes'. It was, indeed, 'too revolting even for remote reference in decent society'.[2]

Other clergymen made frequent reference to Bradlaugh's supposed desire to stir up social revolution. The Northampton representative had boasted publicly, according to one clergyman, that he sought entry into the House of Commons in order 'to insult its members and all its past glorious history and level it, if possible, with its Sister House to the ground'.[3] Another clergyman who had witnessed an anti-Bradlaugh meeting disrupted by a band of Bradlaugh supporters, afterwards recalled the scene vividly. He had observed in that hall, he solemnly reported, 'what he had seen in the pages of history before—the Red Republican, whose pale face, long hair, open mouth, and ferocious look meant blood'.[4] In order to document the reality of the danger, still another clergyman cited an encounter by a Northampton lady who had graciously given aid to one of her poorer neighbours. 'Oh, but there's going to be a change', the neighbour had declared. 'You're going to be the woman, and I am to be the lady; and when Bradlaugh gets in the Queen'll have to do her own washing.'[5]

[1] Cited in *N.R.*, 16 Oct. 1881, pp. 321, 323; 23 Oct. 1881, p. 339.
[2] 18 June 1880, p. 456.
[3] Letter to editor of *Scotsman*, cited in *N.R.*, 10 Dec. 1882, p. 401.
[4] Cited in *N.R.*, 5 June 1881, p. 453.
[5] Cited in *N.R.*, 18 June 1882, p. 458.

If 'High Church' ritualists tended to feel less strongly on the subject, and if the *Guardian*, a 'High Church' journal, went so far in 1883 as to support the Affirmation Bill, then the 'Low Church' *Rock* represented a diametrically opposed point of view. Not that Bradlaugh was the *Rock*'s only *bête noire*. It advertised itself as 'A Church of England Family Newspaper' opposed to Romanism, Ritualism, and Rationalism, and preached instead a 'return to the old principles of the Reformation' at a time when 'Popery, Ritualism, and revolutionary principles are doing all the mischief in their power by secret combinations against constituted authority'.[1] Initially, the *Rock* found Bradlaugh handy as a stick with which to beat the 'Ritualists'; 'if there are blatant Atheists among us . . . who is to blame but the Church of God for her neglect of the masses?' Secularists might be seditious, blasphemous, and immoral, yet 'the idea of Ritualism putting down infidelity is absurd in the extreme'. Secularists never tired of pointing to the Ritualists 'and holding up their mummeries to ridicule. . . . In this the infidels are at least straightforward.'[2]

Once the *Rock* became certain, in June 1880, that Bradlaugh as M.P. was a greater menace to English society than Lord Ripon as Viceroy of India, it entered the fray with relish. 'It is not too much to affirm that the eyes of the civilised world have been anxiously awaiting the issue of the BRADLAUGH case. . . . It is not a mere political test. It is a national, an imperial question involving the stability of the throne, and the very existence of the empire . . . .'[3] From that time on, the *Rock* steadfastly opposed all attempts to enable Bradlaugh to enter Parliament.

The campaign was kept up during 1881 and 1882 and reached its climax as the Affirmation Bill of 1883 came to the fore. Week after week, during March and April of 1883, the *Rock* continued the attack: 'To set up the will of a portion— chiefly the illiterate portion—of one constituency against the will of millions is simply preposterous tyranny', the journal emphasized. By the end of April it was pleased to observe

[1] The *Rock*, 12 Mar. 1880, p. 168.
[2] Ibid., 16 Apr. 1880, p. 264; 30 Apr. 1880, p. 297.
[3] Ibid., 14 May 1880, p. 379; 25 June 1880, p. 465.

'that there is manifested, throughout the country, an ever growing repugnance to the measure'. It was indeed '*the* "burning question" of the hour'.[1]

More than one contributor to the *Rock* detected examples of direct Divine intervention in the Bradlaugh case. The *Whitehall Review*, which intimated a similar direct acquaintance with the feelings of the Deity, did, to be sure, suggest in the summer of 1880, 'that God has such a contempt for those who take His Holy name in vain that He does not care to molest them—regarding all atheists as too infinitely little to occupy a second's thought . . . not caring Himself to soil His Hands with them'.[2] The writer of a letter to the *Rock*, published in April 1880, was less sure. The election of an atheist 'certainly appears, to my mind,' he wrote, 'one of those signs which we have been foretold shall precede the millennium, a time in which the devil will make great havoc, because his time is short'.[3] Preaching a year later, the Reverend Canon Garratt of Ipswich saw such signs confirmed. A year ago, he was reported as saying,

we had every promise of prosperity, we had peace in Ireland, success in our wars, and every promise of a good harvest. Not long after, the disaster at Maiwand occurred, Ireland was thrown into a state of anarchy, and the rains of July spoilt our harvest. . . . What was the case of this sudden change? Mr Garratt suggested that it was the manifestation of divine displeasure at the appointment of a Roman Catholic to represent the Queen in India, and at Mr. Bradlaugh's attempt to force himself into the House of Commons.[4]

The *Christian Herald* agreed that 'the recent disasters and calamities that have befallen Britain' might well be 'judgments from God for the favour and patronage thus shown by the British Government to Popery and Atheism'.[5] Numerous comparable suggestions were made in 1882 and 1883. With the Northampton electors insistent upon repeatedly

[1] The *Rock*, 2 Mar. 1883, p. 141; 4 May 1883, pp. 297, 301.
[2] *Whitehall Review*, 24 June 1880, p. 141.
[3] The *Rock*, 16 Apr. 1880, p. 260.
[4] *Suffolk Chronicle*, cited in *N.R.*, 5 June 1881, p. 458.
[5] *Christian Herald*, 15 June 1881 (clipping in G.P. (B.M.), 44470, fol. 204).

returning Bradlaugh, observed a rector's wife in Kettering, 'it was no wonder we had wet harvests'.[1]

The single most active and influential body gathering petitions against the Affirmation Bill was the Church Defence Institution, an Anglican organization which had been founded in 1860 in order to combat movements favouring Disestablishment and which published pamphlets on church questions 'and also on measures which are likely to come under the cognizance of Parliament'.[2] Formally headed by the Archbishop of Canterbury, the Church Defence Institution and its various branches heard speeches opposing Bradlaugh's admission, and sponsored in June 1881 a meeting in Exeter Hall with the theme: 'Is England to Remain a Christian Kingdom?' It passed resolutions and urged petitions. In March 1883 it sent a form for signatures against the Affirmation Bill, with stamped return envelope enclosed, to every clergyman in the Church of England. More than 13,000 signed.[3]

Numerous diocesan conferences expressed their opposition to Bradlaugh's admission. The resolution passed unanimously in October 1881 by the Bath and Wells Church of England diocesan conference is representative:

> That in view of the expressed determination to make a fresh effort to force Mr. Bradlaugh into Parliament at its next session this Conference pledges itself to use its utmost power and influence to defeat such determination, and calls upon its members who possess seats in either the House of Commons or the House of Lords to give their active opposition to any measure tending to the admission of professed infidels into Parliament.[4]

The Church Convocation which met at Canterbury in April 1883 found the pending Affirmation Bill a most controversial topic. Some clergymen spoke for the bill, but others such as Archdeacon Denison insisted that the bill could not be separated from the man who would benefit

[1] Cited in *N.R.*, 5 Nov. 1882, p. 314.
[2] The Church Defence Institution, *The Church Defence Handy Volume* (London, 1885), p. 1; see also Canon MacColl to Newman, 27 Apr. 1883, Cardinal Newman MSS.
[3] G.P. (B.M.), 44095, fol. 291; *N.R.*, 12 June 1881, p. 477; 17 July 1881, p. 74; 1 Apr. 1883, p. 209; 15 Apr. 1883, p. 248.
[4] Cited in *N.R.*, 23 Oct. 1881, p. 337.

from its provisions. By a vote of 66 to 11, the Convocation's Parliamentary Committee chose to oppose the measure, and the Lower House of Convocation subsequently confirmed the committee's decision and voted to request the bishops in the House of Lords to oppose the Bill 'to the uttermost'.[1]

What about the views of the Archbishop of Canterbury himself? Sir Philip Magnus contends in his biography of Gladstone that the latter took 'the bull by the horns' in 1883 by winning round the Archbishop of Canterbury to his point of view of the Bradlaugh case.[2] The statement is misleading, if only by failing to make clear that two archbishops were involved. Archbishop Tait, who died in December 1882, had been hostile toward Bradlaugh, although he had taken no personal role in the anti-Bradlaugh agitation. His successor —and Gladstone's choice—was Edward White Benson, formerly Bishop of Truro. Benson, in his letter of acceptance, noted how deeply gratified he was that the Prime Minister who had nominated him was Gladstone, whose 'heart-deep love of the English Church, and [whose] devotion to her work and her Life,' he duly recognized.[3] Yet Benson was hardly the man to tolerate a man like Bradlaugh. Religion was for him '*the* absorbing fact of life' notes his son and biographer. 'People of diametrically opposite views he could not really tolerate. Cordiality with them was out of the question. . . . With certain politicians he had so little in common that he thought of them as dangerous and deadly enemies, not as rational and serious opponents.' He approved of Gladstone's piety, and the two men were personal friends, but Benson was often severely critical of Gladstone's political principles. Benson did make one statement on the Affirmation Bill in April 1883, which seemed to indicate that he was leaning toward Gladstone's point of view, but this did not keep him from signing memorials against the bill, and when he was asked point-blank whether he would vote for or against the bill were it to reach the House of Lords, he assured the questioner that he would vote against it.[4]

[1] *N.R*, 22 Apr. 1883, pp. 300–1.

[2] Magnus, *Gladstone*, p. 278.

[3] Arthur Christopher Benson, *The Life of Edward White Benson* (London, 1899), i. 548, 553.

[4] Ibid., pp. 591–2; the *Rock*, 27 Apr. 1883, p. 265.

Benson in no way interfered with the clerical agitation against what the Bishop of Lincoln had termed 'an act of national apostasy'. The resulting campaigns were, from the point of view of publications such as the *Rock*, deeply gratify-fying. 'The present crisis has called forth a deep and wide-spread expression of religious conviction and a warm protest from the country. Let not this be suffered to die away with the special cause which has evoked this question.'[1]

[1] *N.R.*, 29 Oct. 1882, p. 289; the *Rock*, 11 May 1883, p. 337.

XVII

CARDINAL MANNING

A HIGHLY significant participant in the great crusade against the Affirmation Bill of 1883 was Cardinal Manning, Archbishop of Westminster and since 1865 the head of the Roman Catholic hierarchy in England. Manning had not participated in the Bradlaugh case during the spring and early summer of 1880, because he had been in Rome, and his 'Englishman's Protest' after Bradlaugh's admission later in the year must have seemed fruitless to many. Yet, once the case was reopened by the judicial decision depriving Bradlaugh of his seat, Manning returned eagerly to the polemical wars. His motives were to him self-evident; it was the business of the head of the Catholic hierarchy to frustrate the encroachments of blatant atheism. Manning had himself acknowledged only a decade earlier that the English people had come 'to tolerate the Catholic religion as religion in the spiritual sphere; but the slightest contact of the Catholic Church in matters of politics rouses suspicion and opposition'.[1] Yet he was to take this risk, in part because he felt sure of his legal ground and in part because he saw the Bradlaugh case as an excellent opportunity for the Church to lead a politically popular drive in favour of morality and respectability. Englishmen would come to see the Church as the citadel of true conservatism rather than associating it, as they often did, with Irish agitation and violence. After all, of the 1,200,000 Roman Catholics in the England and Wales of 1881 one million were of Irish extraction.[2]

There was a related reason, Manning's personality. His father had served as Member of Parliament, and he was—if one may use the phrase—a politician by instinct. Few tasks

[1] Cited by Shane Leslie, *Henry Edward Manning: His Life and Labours* (London, 1921), p. 292.

[2] Manning to Gladstone, 25 Sept. 1887, G.P. (B.M.), 44250, fol. 254. The figures in the *Saturday Review*, li (1880), 44, are comparable.

in his life gave him greater pleasure than to serve in 1884 under Sir Charles Dilke as a member of the Royal Commission on the Housing of the Working Classes. Were he not Cardinal Archbishop, he once confided to Dilke, he would stand for Parliament as a Radical. An 'Old Testament Radical' was his favourite description of himself,[1] and indeed on such questions as slum clearance and trade-union organization he *was* a radical (or, perhaps, paternalistic) reformer. Manning and Bradlaugh had first met, indeed, in 1872, when both lent their support to Joseph Arch's Agricultural Labourers' Union. Their meeting had been a brief one, to be sure, since as soon as Bradlaugh ascended the platform Manning had stalked off.[2] Manning's advocacy of social reform and acceptance of political democracy in no way implied a departure from theological orthodoxy or from an insistence upon the unquestioned supremacy of the Church in such fields as education. And Bradlaugh's admission to Parliament impressed him as a theological question which might well have the practical consequence of hastening the establishment of a completely secular national school system.

Manning fought Bradlaugh's admission and the passage of an Affirmation Bill in four ways: by writing public articles; by conducting private correspondence and negotiations with Liberal ministers and with the leaders of the Conservative Party; by using his direct influence upon Roman Catholic Members of Parliament; and by organizing petition drives. Each of these methods will be examined in turn.

Most of Manning's articles were published in 1881 and 1882. In April 1881 appeared one article entitled 'The Parliamentary Oath and the Government', and in June of that year another entitled 'Atheism and the Constitution of England'. Had it not been for the accident of the recent legal decision, argued Manning, a profound change in the character of the English Constitution would have been 'filched or stolen from the Legislature'. Nor could a Government-sponsored

---

[1] Stephen Gwynn and Gertrude M. Tuckwell, *The Life of the Rt. Hon. Sir Charles W. Dilke* (London, 1917), i. 292; Mahon MSS., file 10, fol. 13.

[2] Edmund S. Purcell, *Life of Cardinal Manning: Archbishop of Westminster* (London, 1895), ii. 640-1.

bill legalizing the option of affirmation be regarded as a suitable remedy. Even if some Nonconformists favoured such a step, it seemed obvious that a majority of the Church of England opposed it, and, as for the Roman Catholics, they 'may be taken as one man against the Government on this matter'. At the very minimum the question ought to be put to the test of a general election.[1]

A subsequent article in the *Contemporary Review*, 'Without God, No Commonwealth', urged that an England which permitted atheists as legislators would disintegrate morally:

What should restrain such a Legislature from abolishing the legal observance of Christmas, of Good Friday, and of Sunday; of rescinding all restraints on the employment of women and children in mines, factories, and poisonous trades; thereby destroying what remains of home-life among the poor? What shall hinder the multiplication of causes justifying divorce by the adoption of foreign and Oriental codes?[2]

Such warnings might be deemed exaggerations, Manning conceded. Would the abolition of the Parliamentary oath truly have consequences so profound? Yes, replied Manning, just as the loss of a single bolt might in due course sink a great ship.

In a second 'Englishman's Protest', in the issue of the *Nineteenth Century* for March 1882, Manning re-entered the fray with a point-by-point refutation of six arguments used by supporters of Bradlaugh's admission. They charged that an inquisition had been opened into Bradlaugh's beliefs; this was not so, for Bradlaugh had publicly paraded his beliefs. They asserted that it was bigotry to require a profession of belief for entry in the House of Commons; untrue, since the laws of England explicitly held the Bible to be the word of God. They contended that the decision of the constituency was binding; incorrect, in that all prospective candidates had to fulfil the law and the law comprised the oath as well as the election, and it was impossible for Bradlaugh to take an oath. They urged that since Bradlaugh was willing to take the oath, the House of Commons ought to accept it. But Bradlaugh's oath was not an oath at all; rather it was 'an outrage

---

[1] Edward (Cardinal) Manning, *Miscellaneous Works*, iii (London, 1888), 108–17.   [2] Ibid., p. 163.

in morals and null in law'. Gladstone's contentions notwithstanding, Bradlaugh had no right to his seat. The impasse in which the House of Commons found itself was made by Bradlaugh and not by the Opposition leaders who had merely been defending 'the law of the land' and 'the moral order of nature'.[1] Once again quoting Coke and Blackstone 'as though they were early Fathers'[2] Manning sought to demonstrate that the propagation of atheism remained an indictable offence under English law.

Manning felt called upon to rush into print again later that year after Viscount Sherbrooke had, in the issue of the *Nineteenth Century* for August 1882, questioned the utility of oath-taking generally. Sherbrooke was mistaken, replied Manning. The fear of punishment by God was a 'higher motive than the fear of any punishment by human law'. Two such motives were, in any event, preferable to one. Since the Parliamentary oath carried with it no secular sanctions but only supernatural ones—and since Bradlaugh did not acknowledge the latter—it would be impossible to bind Bradlaugh to observe such an oath. Manning failed to see that he was wielding a double-edged metaphysical sword; how was it possible for Bradlaugh to violate the Parliamentary oath without at the same time violating the ban on treason, a prohibition Bradlaugh was responsible for obeying whether he took the Parliamentary oath or not? Manning concluded this latest essay with still another eloquent warning against 'this intellectual and moral anarchy' into which England was descending.[3]

Charles Bradlaugh, while not unaccustomed to attacks by Roman Catholics, was increasingly aroused by Manning's campaign. His own *National Reformer* afforded him the opportunity to comment carpingly on Manning's articles, but he was frustrated in all attempts to obtain space for reply in the pages of the *Nineteenth Century* itself. Despite the fact that the prospectus of the journal defined its policy as 'absolutely impartial and non-sectarian' the editor refused

[1] Edward (Cardinal) Manning, 'An Englishman's Protest', *Nineteenth Century*, March 1882, pp. 488–92.

[2] Leslie, *Manning*, p. 318.

[3] Edward (Cardinal) Manning, 'Parliamentary Oaths', *Nineteenth Century*, September 1882, pp. 474–80.

point-blank.[1] In the autumn of 1882 Bradlaugh's ire finally exploded in a savage reply in pamphlet form entitled *A Cardinal's Broken Oath*.

'Three times your Eminence has—', Bradlaugh began, 'through the pages of the *Nineteenth Century*—personally and publicly interfered and used the weight of your ecclesiastical position against me', although Manning was neither a voter in Northampton nor 'even a co-citizen in the State to which I belong'. If Manning could quote Parliamentary statutes, so could Bradlaugh, and the latter pointed out accurately enough that according to a statute of the reign of George IV still on the books, Manning was liable to indictment for misdemeanour as 'member of a society of the Church of Rome'. It was all very well for Manning to denounce Bradlaugh's iniquity and to refer to him and his followers as 'cattle'.

But who are you, Henry Edward Manning, that you should throw stones at me . . . ? Is it the oath alone which stirs you? Your tenderness on swearing comes very late in life. When you took orders as a deacon of the English Church, in presence of your bishop, you swore 'so help me God' that you did from your 'heart abhor, detest, and abjure,' and with your hand on the 'Holy Gospels' you declared 'that no foreign prince, person, prelate, state, or potentate . . . ought to have, any . . . authority, ecclesiastical or spiritual, within this realm.'. . . . The oath you took you have broken. . . . Then, to move the timid, you suggest 'the fear of eternal punishment' as associated with a broken oath. Have you any such fear? . . . Have you no personal shame that you have broken your oath? Or do the pride and pomp of your ecclesiastical position outbribe your conscience?[2]

So it went, page after page. While there is no direct evidence that Cardinal Manning ever read the pamphlet, a Catholic cleric hostile to Manning translated it into Italian and distributed it among the Vatican hierarchy, and it remains significant that Manning thereupon ceased to write articles about the Bradlaugh case for the monthly press.[3]

Behind the scenes, however, Manning remained as active as ever. He wrote numerous letters to clerical subordinates

[1] *N.R.*, 26 Mar. 1882, p. 257; G.P. (B.M.), 44232, fols. 171, 172.
[2] Charles Bradlaugh, *A Cardinal's Broken Oath* (London, 1882), *passim*.
[3] Bonner & Robertson, *Bradlaugh*, ii. 312.

and laymen opposing Bradlaugh's admission to Parliament. While discussing school business with A. J. Mundella, the member of Gladstone's ministry responsible for education, he urged upon him the desirability of excluding from both Houses of Parliament all men who did not profess Christianity.[1] It was with Sir Stafford Northcote, however, that Manning was more significantly concerned. 'Let me thank you', wrote Manning to Northcote in 1882, 'for all you have done in this Session to avert the desecration of the Commonwealth of England.'[2] Northcote replied in characteristically pessimistic terms. True, Bradlaugh had been officially expelled from Parliament, but he might be re-elected, and if so 'our contention then will be with the constituency much more directly than with him. Of course we must strive to maintain our ground . . . .' If only Bradlaugh could be defeated at Northampton! Perhaps Manning might help in a more specific manner, Northcote thought, and he began to write: 'If you can in any degree influence the Roman Catholic portion of the Electorate at Northampton (I don't know whether there are many or few) to put . . .' Then the Conservative leader hesitated. Perhaps he was going too far. Perhaps it was unwise to seem to be plotting election tactics with the leader of the Roman Catholic hierarchy. Perhaps it was unethical. Perhaps it was unnecessary. In any event, Northcote crossed out the last sentence, and concluded his letter in more general terms: 'I can only trust that men will find the necessity of putting the cause of religion before that of politics in this contest. The wave of infidelity can only be checked, under God's blessing, by the determination of religious men of various denominations and shades of opinion to stand firmly together in resisting it.'[3]

Northcote's hints were unnecessary. Whatever political influence the Roman Catholic hierarchy could exercise in Northampton it had long since brought to bear. Canon Scott of the Catholic Cathedral in that borough had cautioned his parishioners against Bradlaugh time and again. Should he

[1] A. J. Mundella to Robert Leader, 16 May 1881. Mundella MSS. Mundella's official title was Vice-President of the Council.

[2] Iddesleigh MSS. (B.M.), 50041, fol. 88.

[3] (First Draft) Northcote to Manning, 22 Feb. 1882, Iddesleigh MSS. (B.M.), 50041, fol. 91.

succeed in his quest for a seat in Parliament, Scott had warned in 1880, Bradlaugh would 'obtain a vantage ground for the better prosecution of the great project of his life. And what is that? The same as that of the Communist, the Socialist, and the Nihilist . . . .'[1] Canon Scott was equally definite on the occasion of the 1882 by-election. The issue was simple : 'God was to be expelled that the blasphemer might be admitted. He [Scott] need not tell them, his flock, what would be their duty in the coming week. They knew it well, and they were not likely to be deluded by the specious cries . . . of Constitutional liberties.' Unfortunately for Scott and Manning the Roman Catholic diocese of Northampton was geographically the most scattered and financially the poorest diocese in England. Even the *Tablet* was forced to concede that the Catholic proportion of Northampton's population was exceedingly small.[2]

Manning's efforts did not go unappreciated in Conservative circles. 'The whole country—indeed the whole Christian world—ought to thank you', wrote one Tory editor. One of Manning's articles, wrote a Methodist minister, had served as a 'trumpet blast', causing the barriers of creed to fall in the face of 'this important crisis'.[3] Not only did Tory newspapers more frequently than before refer to the Cardinal as a man of significant political influence, but when in August 1882 he paid an official visit to the apparent hotbed of infidelity itself, he was formally received by the Tory Mayor of Northampton in his robes and chain of office. There was no modern precedent for such a reception, and the Catholic *Weekly Register* hailed the event as 'a sign of hope and a happy augury for the state of religion in [our] native land'. It was an example of the sympathy Protestants were now offering the Catholic Church, 'the one organisation able to cope with the common enemy'.[4]

Manning's correspondence with Northcote continued intermittently, reaching its crescendo in the course of the

[1] Cited in Northampton *Mercury*, 20 Mar. 1880, p. 6.
[2] *Tablet*, 4 Mar. 1882, p. 319; 27 Nov. 1880, p. 692; 10 Apr. 1880, p. 452.
[3] Edward Legge, editor of *Whitehall Review*, to Manning, 27 Feb. 1882; Rev. Thomeley Smith to Manning, 6 Mar. 1882, Manning MSS.
[4] *N.R.*, 17 Sept. 1882, p. 195. *Weekly Register* cited in *N.R.*, 3 Sept. 1882, p. 161.

campaign against the Affirmation Bill of 1883. Manning repeatedly fortified Northcote's resolution, exhorting him to treat the Bradlaugh affair not as 'a difficulty to be got rid of' but rather as 'a broad issue of Constitutional law . . .'.[1] Fearful that Gladstone's eloquent defence of the bill might sway Northcote unduly—the letters reveal that it did—Manning reminded Northcote that there was no possible comparison between the admission of religious minorities such as Catholics and Jews to Parliament and the admission of atheists. The result would be 'the pure anti-Christian & anti-social Revolution: the solvent of all that Christian civilisation has done for mankind'.[2]

Manning had a third method at his disposal, to use his influence directly upon Roman Catholic Members of Parliament. One difficulty with this task lay in the fact that while the House of Lords of 1880 included thirty-two Roman Catholic peers, the House of Commons elected that year included not a single English, Welsh, or Scottish Roman Catholic. When a member of an old Catholic family, Hubert Jerningham, was chosen Liberal candidate for the by-election in Berwick-on-Tweed in 1881, the immediate reaction on the part of the Catholic press was therefore one of unfeigned delight. As one writer of a letter to the editor of the *Tablet* phrased it: 'We are all, I hope, Catholics *first*, and Liberals or Conservatives afterwards. . . .'[3] The fly in the ointment was that in his election programme Jerningham had pledged full support to the policy of the Liberal leadership of seeking to permit Bradlaugh to take his seat. He was not, Jerningham insisted, in favour of atheists in Parliament; he merely believed that Bradlaugh had been fairly elected and ought therefore to be seated.[4] Torn by conflicting aims, the editors of the *Tablet* came out in support of Jerningham, even after a local Roman Catholic priest in Berwick had denounced the candidate and after a puzzled reader had pleaded vainly for guidance in distinguishing theology from politics.[5]

Once Jerningham had been elected the *Tablet* was too jubilant over the victory of a Catholic M.P. to concern itself

---

[1] Iddesleigh MSS. (B.M.), 50041, fol. 92.   [2] Ibid., fol. 181.
[3] *Tablet*, 19 Nov. 1881, p. 820.   [4] Ibid., 5 Nov. 1881, p. 742.
[5] Ibid., 19 Nov. 1881, p. 819; 29 Oct. 1881, p. 700; 12 Nov. 1881, p. 781.

with the philosophical problems of its readers. Thus far, after all, Jerningham had merely issued an election address; he had not yet participated in a Parliamentary division. And though *The Times* hailed Jerningham's triumph as a sign that the working classes wished to see the Bradlaugh case 'settled on a Liberal basis without delay',[1] its hopes were disappointed. After the *Tablet* had bluntly warned in January 1882 that any M.P. who co-operated with Gladstone in favouring Brad laugh's admission 'makes himself a partaker of crime against religion'[2] Jerningham reconsidered. He did cast one tentative pro-Bradlaugh vote in March 1882, but from then on he consistently opposed Bradlaugh's position, and when it came to the all-important Affirmation Bill of 1883, Jerningham proved to be one of a handful of Liberals to vote against it. The pressures of his church had obviously been too great. The *Tablet* might piously declare that 'religion in England is one thing; politics are quite another',[3] but like most generalizations, this one would appear to have had its exceptions.

Though only one Englishman in the House of Commons of 1880 was a Roman Catholic, this distinction was held by 56 of Ireland's 103 representatives.[4] Manning was on excellent terms with many of the Irish members and a frequent visitor to the House of Commons, where he might be found in the Lobby 'with a little circle of Irish members gathered around him who had intercepted him, perhaps on his way into one of the galleries'.[5] Manning's success in influencing the Irish vote will be analysed below.

For the moment Roman Catholics could concentrate, as did the Church of England's Church Defence Society Institution, on gathering petitions to Parliament. In the late nineteenth century the power of petitions to influence votes was still widely held to be significant. Though not read aloud, each petition was deposited by a member in a bag behind the Speaker's Chair; from there they were sent to a Select Committee on Parliamentary Petitions, which scrutinized them for propriety and issued weekly reports

---

[1] Cited in *N.R.*, 6 Nov. 1881, p. 369.
[2] *Tablet*, 28 Jan. 1882, p. 131. [3] Ibid., 29 July 1881, p. 162.
[4] Ibid., 25 June 1881, p. 1014.
[5] Justin McCarthy, *Reminiscences* (London, 1899), ii. 171.

listing the source of each petition and the number of signatures. In addition, it tabulated the number of petitions
and signatures received in favour of or against any major
proposal.

Bradlaugh was, of course, as aware as any of his opponents
of the desirability of garnering petitions, and during the
early 1880's the local chapters of the National Secular Society
were kept busy with repeated appeals for petitions. From
time to time he would receive aid also, solicited or not, from
local Liberal clubs, Unitarian churches, and others. As the
hostile *Saturday Review* put it on one occasion, 'Cobden Clubs
and Three Hundreds and Liberal Federations and other
gatherings of political tagrag and bobtail throughout the
country have been resolving and petitioning with some
vigour on Mr. Bradlaugh's side . . . .'[1]

Yet by and large Bradlaugh's efforts failed to make the
impact he desired. Even his success in gathering over 260,000
pro-Bradlaugh signatures in the course of 1882 seemed to
change his status but little, and by the end of that year he
announced that no further petitions would be asked for. The
previous ones, he complained, had been treated as 'waste
paper'.[2] But by March of 1883 Bradlaugh was forced to
change his stand. Conscious of the tremendous drive against
the Affirmation Bill under way, he exhorted his own supporters into renewed activity.[3] His efforts were overshadowed, however, by the exertions of his opponents. The
success of the drive for petitions against the Affirmation Bill
can best be understood in the form of a brief statistical table.[4]

YEAR	NUMBER OF SIGNATURES	
	Pro-Bradlaugh	*Anti-Bradlaugh*
1880	44,840	41,252
1881	179,348	300,829
1882	263,674	73,179
1883	174,667	710,298

Of the various issues before the public during the 1880's,
many others aroused petition drives of considerable pro-
portions—vivisection, school taxes, the question of whether

[1] *Saturday Review*, 10 Feb. 1883, p. 172.
[2] *N.R.*, 24 Dec. 1882, p. 452.   [3] *N.R.*, 4 Mar. 1883, p. 129.
[4] *Reports of the Select Committee on Parliamentary Petitions*, 1880–3.

museums ought to be opened on Sundays. But only one—using the number of signatures as a yardstick—aroused more public interest than did the Affirmation Bill. That was the perennial question of whether liquor should be sold on Sundays.[1]

A representative selection of the sources of petitions on a single day illustrates the striking importance of religious bodies in petitioning for or against the Affirmation Bill. On 30 April 1883, for example, while petitions favouring the bill were received from Unitarian and Congregationalist groups and from one Church of England organization, petitions opposing the bill came in from the Church of Scotland, from the Anglican clergy of Gloucester, from the Church of England Sunday School Teachers' Association, from members of the congregation of the Church of Ireland in Wexford, Westmeath, Donegal, and Dublin, from various Methodist, Presbyterian, Roman Catholic groups, and from one Baptist organization as well.[2]

Bradlaugh attempted to discount the number of hostile petitions flooding Westminster, either by emphasizing the power of the clergy, or by attempting to show that signatures were being collected by unfair methods. From time to time he cited examples of children under fourteen being forced to sign petitions in Sunday Schools, of forewomen in a London department store putting pressure upon their shop assistants to sign, of office boys in factories instructed to gain signatures, of customers boycotting merchants who had refused to sign, and of a Church of England clergyman who left a stamped and addressed envelope with a blank petition form in every house of his parish.[3] One English girl studying in Germany wrote home: 'What is this Affirmation Bill? The English chaplain brought in a petition against it, and we all had to sign.'[4]

But not all the signatures were involuntary, and the signatories included the mighty as well as the poor, peers and commoners, five hundred members of the London Stock

[1] *Reports of the Select Committee on Parliamentary Petitions*, 1880–3.

[2] Ibid., 1883, pp. 572–88.

[3] *N.R.*, 26 June 1881, pp. 17, 25; 29 May 1881, p. 490; 12 Feb. 1882, p. 113; 1 Apr. 1883, p. 209.   [4] Cited in *N.R.*, 8 Apr. 1883, p. 216.

Exchange, dozens of bishops and thousands of lesser clergy-men. When a renegade Liberal, W. McCullagh Torrens, organized a petition drive on behalf of a committee of Lords and Commoners, he approached Cardinal Manning before anyone else. Manning was characteristically gracious and diplomatic. He gave Torrens his permission to affix his signature whenever Torrens should find the step expedient. To sign immediately, the Cardinal suggested politely, might 'tend to deter those whose names it would be more impor-tant to obtain'.[1] Few were deterred, and late in April 1883 Torrens could exult in Parliament that 'for the first time in the religious history of the country, the best men of rival communions' had felt it 'consistent with their honour and their duty' to sign the same petition. Anglicans and Dissenters had signed and so had 'the whole of the Bishops of the Catholic Church in England and in Ireland'.[2] The flood of petitions, most under the auspices of religious organizations, helped convince Liberals, Conservatives, and Irish National-ists alike—and justly so—that the country was hostile to the Affirmation Bill.

[1] Cited in W. McCullagh Torrens, *Twenty Years of Parliament*, pp. 313–14.
[2] *Hansard*, cclxxviii (1883), 938–9.

XVIII

GLADSTONE AS ADVOCATE

EARLY in the April of 1883 Gladstone began to take a personal interest in the Affirmation Bill, the provisions of which had been agreed upon in his absence. He began to refresh his memory of the details of the case and to ask his secretaries to obtain relevant library books for him. Gladstone bombarded Sir Henry James, the Attorney-General, with requests for information about oaths and affirmations, even though Sir Henry would have preferred to concentrate his attention upon the Corrupt Practices Bill, a measure designed to reform the conduct of elections. Gladstone's request for a long memorandum on the history of oaths was entrusted by James to his young legal assistant, Herbert Asquith. Gladstone described the result as a 'magnificent statement', and Asquith, the future Liberal Prime Minister, was consequently introduced to Gladstone for the first time.[1]

Gladstone did a good deal of homework on the subject himself. In the summer of 1880 he had copied in his own hand an account of comparative Parliamentary oaths in other countries; and a year later Lord Granville had requested British ministers and ambassadors throughout Europe to report on the customs relating to such oaths in their respective countries. An amazing variety of practices emerged from this study. Nations such as Greece, Serbia, and Portugal required oaths far more complicated than that of the United Kingdom. A Greek member of Parliament, for example, had to 'swear in the name of the Holy and Consubstantial and Indivisible Trinity', while a Portuguese had to be 'inviolably faithful to the Catholic Apostolic Roman Religion'. In other countries, oaths were shorter and the alternative of affirmation was conceded to the non-believer. Switzerland, the Netherlands, and the United States fell into this category. As for France,

[1] G. R. Askwith, *Lord James of Hereford* (London, 1930), pp. 120–5.

Germany (on the national level), Hungary, Rumania, and Sweden, they required neither oaths nor affirmations from their deputies. The British minister to Montenegro found it somewhat difficult to know how to reply to the Foreign Secretary's query. 'I have the honour to reply', he finally wrote, 'that the Principality of Montenegro is not endowed with a Legislative Assembly.'[1]

The more Gladstone studied the matter the more involved he became in it, and for perhaps the first time the Bradlaugh case became in his mind not a technical legal question involving a distasteful individual, but a question of general principle, a principle very closely intertwined in the Liberal tradition. As Lord Bryce has sagely observed, Gladstone's sympathy 'was keener and stronger for the sufferings of nations or masses of men than with the fortunes of an individual man'.[2] And Gladstone in the spring of 1883 began to see in the Bradlaugh case a matter involving injustice to a sizeable proportion of the British population. Thus at the very time that hostile petitions were flooding Parliament, Gladstone convinced himself that the proposal his colleagues had agreed upon in his absence deserved not only his support but his leadership. The battle of the Affirmation Bill was a question of principle to be fought through to the finish.

The debate on the second reading of the Affirmation Bill began on 23 April 1883, when the proposed law was introduced with a thoughtful historical exposition by the Attorney-General. From the first the opponents of the measure were far more vocal than its supporters. Conservative back-benchers, aware that a major speech by the Prime Minister was in preparation, amused themselves by searching through old volumes of *Hansard* in order to find ammunition against the proposal in Gladstone's own words. Had not Gladstone, then a youthful Tory, told Parliament in 1835: 'If in the administration of this great country the elements of religion should not enter—if those who were called to guide it in its career should be forced to listen to the caprices and

---

[1] G.P. (B.M.), 44111, fols. 80–81; Great Britain, *Parliamentary Papers*, 1882, lii. 459–506.
[2] James Bryce, *Studies in Contemporary Biography* (London, 1903), p. 424.

to the whims of every body of visionaries, they would lose that station all great men were hitherto proud of.'[1]

It was on the night of Thursday 26 April that Gladstone rose to rally his forces in support of the bill. The house was packed, the audience expectant. Gladstone commenced by attempting to refute a number of frequently voiced objections to the bill. One was that atheists were by law prevented from sitting in the House of Commons. Gladstone denied anew that this was the case. But though there was no legal need for an Affirmation Bill, the Cabinet had decided, for the sake of the dignity of the House and in the best interests of the country, 'that this painful controversy which has subsisted so long should be brought to a close, and that there should be no longer the temptation which has existed in this House to deal with matters strictly judicial in a temper and with indica-tions not always presenting the best features of the judicial character'. Another frequently heard objection was that the law should not be altered for the sake of one person. 'But it so happens', replied Gladstone, 'that these laws are commonly altered for the sake of one person.' The cases of O'Connell and Rothschild served as examples. It was held by some, acknowledged the Prime Minister, that atheists were in the position of aliens, peers, and felons in being excluded from the House of Commons on the basis of the Common Law. Gladstone denied that the disqualification of the unbeliever had a comparable historical basis, since religious oaths had not been employed before Elizabeth's time and since they were introduced as tests of loyalty rather than as religious barriers.

Gladstone then turned to a far more potent argument, that the Bill was intimately connected with a man associated with causes distasteful to a great majority of Englishmen:

Do you suppose [asked Gladstone] that we do not feel pain? Do you suppose that we are unaware how difficult—how all but impracticable—it has become to do what we believe to be strict justice in the face of such associations?... Sir, I believe that every one of us intending to vote for this Bill feels that it is indeed difficult to do justice under such circumstances. But the difficulty is the measure of the duty, and the honour; and just as if we were

[1] Cited in *Hansard*, cclxxviii (1883), 964–5.

in the jury-box, and a person stood before us under a criminal charge, we will put a strong hand of self-restraint upon ourselves, and we will take care that full justice—nothing more and nothing less—shall be awarded to every citizen of England.

What of the petitions, which seemed to indicate a public opinion strongly hostile to the bill? To Gladstone, a statesman who had become by 1883 in every sense a convinced democrat, this proved a somewhat perplexing problem. He could sympathize, he observed, with the honest 'religious instincts' of the bill's opponents, yet on this occasion they were mistaken.

In my opinion, upon broad questions of principle, which stand out disentangled from the surrounding facts, the immediate instincts and sense of the people are very generally right. . . . But I cannot say that this is a uniform and unbending rule. It does, unfortunately, sometimes happen that, when broad principles are disguised by the incidents of the case, the momentary opinion, guided by the instincts of the populace . . . is not a safe guide. . . . I should trust them far more upon questions where their own interests are concerned than on questions where the prepossessions of religion are concerned. The latter is a class of questions on which we must be careful against taking momentary indications of public feeling for our guide.

The history of the Jewish Naturalization Bill of 1753 and of the Catholic Emancipation Bill of 1829 illustrated that thesis.

The Opposition accused the Liberal Goverment of bowing to mob violence, Gladstone went on, but it was clear that the hope of political profit could hardly be the party's motive in this instance.

Do you suppose that we are ignorant that, in every contested election that has happened since the case of Mr. Bradlaugh came up, you have gained votes and we have lost them? . . . Sir, the Liberal Party has suffered, and is suffering, on this account. It is not the first time in its history. It is the old story over again. . . . Sir, what I hope is this—that the Liberal Party will not be deterred, by fear or favour, from working steadily onward in the path which it believes to be the path of equity and justice. There is no greater honour to a man than to suffer for what he thinks to be righteous; and there is no greater honour to a Party than to suffer in the endeavour to give effect to the principles which they believe to be just.

At this point Gladstone came to what he considered the heart of the question: whether or not the Opposition was correct in asserting that 'the main question for the State is not what religion a man professes, but whether he professes some religion or none', that every previous legislative step toward toleration had approached the precipice but that only the Affirmation Bill would fall into the abyss. Gladstone rejected this proposition as offering no 'good solid standing-ground for legislation'.

First of all it violated the now accepted British principle that there should be a total divorce between religious belief and civil privilege and power. Secondly, the proposition was highly disparaging to Christianity. The Opposition implied

that you may go any length you please in the denial of religion, provided only you do not reject the name of the Deity. They tear religion—if I may say so—in shreds, and they set aside one particular shred of it, with which nothing will ever induce them to part. . . . They divide, I say, religion into what can be dispensed with and what cannot be dispensed with, and then they find that Christianity can be dispensed with . . . .

The line drawn by the Opposition was merely one which separated the abstract denial of God from the abstract admission of the Deity. 'My proposition is', Gladstone's voice rang out, 'that your line is worthless. There is much on your side of the line which is just as objectionable as the Atheism on the other side.' The acknowledgement of the providence of God and man's responsibility to God were far more important than the mere abstract acknowledgement of the kind of deity envisioned by Lucretius. And Gladstone began to quote, from memory, the words of the Latin poet.

> Omnis enim per se divôm natura necesse est,
> Immortali aevo summa cum pace fruatur;
> Sejuncta a nostris rebus, semotaque longe.
> Nam privata dolore omni, privata periclis,
> Ipsa suis pollens opibus, nihil indiga nostri,
> Nec bene promeritis capitur nec tangitur ira.[1]

[1] 'For the very nature of Divinity must of necessity enjoy immortal life in the profoundest peace, far removed and separated from our troubles; for without any pain, without any danger, itself mighty by its own resources, needing us not at all, it is neither propitiated by services nor touched by wrath.'

The chief evil of the age, Gladstone went on, was not 'blank Atheism' but agnosticism, and that mischief was unaffected by the bill. 'Whether we be beaten or not', declared Gladstone, 'we do not decline the battle', nor are we 'going to allow it to be said that the interests of religion are put in peril, and that they are to find their defenders only on the opposite side of the House.' Before closing the Prime Minister advanced a related argument, that the proposed legislation would advance the cause of morality:

A seat in this House is to the ordinary Englishman in early life, or, perhaps in middle or mature life, when he has reached a position of distinction in his career, the highest prize of his ambition. But if you place between him and that prize not only the necessity of conforming to certain civil conditions, but the adoption of certain religious words, and if these words are not justly measured to the condition of his conscience and of his convictions, you give him an inducement—nay, I do not go too far when I say you offer him a bribe to tamper with those convictions—to do violence to his conscience in order that he may not be stigmatized by being shut out from what is held to be the noblest privilege of the English citizen—that of representing his fellow-citizens in Parliament.

The immediate purpose of the bill admittedly was to bring the Bradlaugh case to a close. 'I have no fear of Atheism in this House', thundered Gladstone. 'Truth is the expression of the Divine mind; and however little our feeble vision may be able to discern the means by which God will provide for its preservation, we may leave the matter in His hands' and confine ourselves to doing justice on earth. And here on earth, religion was damaged rather than aided by the fact that the citizens of Northampton and thousands of other Englishmen had been led to associate religion with that they deemed injustice. The result was that unbelief attracted unwonted sympathy. What was the upshot? The impairment of 'that religious faith, the loss of which I believe to be the most inexpressible calamity which can fall either upon a man or upon a nation'.[1]

The speech produced a profound impression upon its listeners and for the moment literally stunned the Oppositon

[1] *Hansard*, cclxxviii (1883), 1174-96.

into silence. Many of Gladstone's family and colleagues considered it the greatest oration of a long career, while the lines from Lucretius 'thrilled the imagination of the audience and held it spellbound, lifting for a moment the whole subject of debate into a region far above party conflict . . . '.[1] One loyal Gladstonian wrote a sonnet in honour of the oration:

> Philosopher & Statesman both unite
> In thee, whose fame, when Albion's sun has set
> Shall shine with fuller lustre in her night
> Than do the noblest Greeks . . . .[2]

The speech so stirred young Herbert Asquith that over forty years later he devoted almost an entire chapter in his autobiography to that event.[3] 'It was the voice and manner,' wrote Lord Bryce, 'above all the voice, with its marvellous modulations, that made the speech majestic.'[4] Yet the purpose of Parliamentary speeches during the 1880's was not merely to adorn reputations but to sway votes, and while Gladstone's daughter, for one, was convinced 'the Bill w[oul]d now swim in', more experienced politicians were less certain.[5]

The precepts of dramatic unity might dictate an immediate division on the bill, but the realities of practical politics caused the debate to drag on for another week. Though Gladstone's oration had bought to a halt the yells and hoots with which the Opposition greeted most arguments for the bill, the respite proved to be a brief one. The same contentions were soon put forward again, the same accusations were levelled, the same doom for a Godless England was predicted. As Lord Randolph Churchill candidly admitted, by 1883 'they had all gone too far to recede from the respective positions which they had taken up'.[6] For the Opposition the question, as before, was that of God versus Bradlaugh, of whether or not 'to dethrone the Supreme Being in this

---

[1] Bryce, *Studies*, p. 437; G.P. (B.M.), 44198, fol. 50.
[2] Edward G. Foskett to Gladstone, 30 Apr. 1883, G.P. (B.M.), 44480, fols. 261–2.
[3] Earl of Oxford and Asquith, *Fifty Years of Parliament* (London, 1926), i. 68 ff.   [4] Bryce, *Studies*, p. 437.
[5] *Mary (Gladstone) Drew: Diary and Letters* (London, 1930), p. 288; Hamilton Diary (B.M.), 48633, pp. 180–2.
[6] *Hansard*, cclxxviii (1883), 1439.

MEETING THE DIFFICULTY.

GLADSTONE.—YOU WON'T BE ALLOWED TO PASS IN THERE. DON'T BOTHER ANY MORE AT THAT NARROW OLD STILE; THERE'LL BE A BROADER WAY PRESENTLY.

7. "Meeting the Difficulty" (*Funny Folks*, 14 May 1881)

EXIT CALIBAN

(*After "The Tempest"*).

CALIBAN	Mr. BR-DL-GH.	
	ARIEL	LORD R-ND-LPH CH-RCH-LL.

[*Act IV. Sc. 1.*]

House, and to wipe out the name of God from the records of Parliament'.[1] Henry Chaplin, a Conservative M.P. and a noted devotee of horse racing, confidently assured the House that the proposed measure

shocks, horrifies, and outrages every sentiment and every feeling nearest and dearest to the hearts of the people, in every family, in every home, by every fireside, from the palace of the noble and the rich to the dwellings of the poor and the lowliest cottage in the land—aye, and to millions upon millions of our race besides— wherever the English tongue is spoken on the face of the civilised globe.[2]

The Liberals were no longer the party of 'Peace, Retrenchment, and Reform' but rather the party of 'Bradlaugh and Blasphemy'. Not once during the three-year controversy had they been 'on the side of morality, of religion, or of justice'.[3] The question at issue was one not of religious liberty but of religious licence; it was indeed not a question of religion at all but a question of irreligion. Nor was it a question of constituency rights. 'If the people of Northampton . . . choose to elect a man whom they know the House will not admit, it is their affair, and not that of the House', explained William McCullagh Torrens, a Liberal who supported the Opposition on this issue. Neither was the Opposition mollified by being told that non-believers such as Edward Gibbon and Lord Bolingbroke had sat in Parliaments protected by oaths much more elaborate than the present one. This might well have been the case, conceded Torrens. 'The brake does not always prevent the train from running off the line; but what will be said of the guard who is willing to place in the hands of some crazy third-class passenger the instrument on which is believed to depend the safety of all?'[4] It was indeed 'absurd' to contend, argued Baron de Worms, that the law on the books did not disqualify Bradlaugh from sitting. 'The conditions which the House has laid down . . . are as much of a disability in the case of Mr. Bradlaugh as in the case of a felon, a lunatic, or a woman.'[5]

Was Bradlaugh, in any case, worth all this trouble? He was

[1] Ibid., col. 1478.   [2] Ibid., cols. 1750-1.   [3] Ibid., cols. 963, 1768.
[4] Ibid., cols. 939-41.   [5] Ibid., col. 962.

but one man 'representing, as far as we know, only himself'. The number of people agreeing in all things with Bradlaugh, estimated William O'Brien, 'is not much greater . . . than the number of people who would like to go about the streets naked, and I do not apprehend that in this climate the one creed is ever more likely to be popular than the other'. Whatever supporters the Northampton heretic might boast were 'more deserving of the attention of the police court than of the legislature of the land'.[1] The bill was obviously unpopular, all Opposition speakers agreed. 'Is it wise', asked Edward Gibson, 'to outrage, to ignore, or even to outrun the general opinion of our people on a question which so deeply stirs all their strongest feelings?'[2]

While not all Conservative M.P.s remained in a perpetually high state of dudgeon on the issue, not a single Tory M.P. dared oppose his party's stand. A local Conservative Club in Salford did support the bill; and the outrage felt by still other Conservatives was tempered by amused detachment. When asked to subscribe funds for a Northampton Horticultural Show, Lord Winchelsea replied: 'A town which enjoys the flowers of Mr. Labouchere's oratory and the fruits of Mr. Bradlaugh's philosophy can need no further horticultural exhibition.'[3]

Each of the leaders of the Conservative party treated the Affirmation Bill in his own characteristic manner. Lord Salisbury, who had little direct responsibility for dealing with the Bradlaugh question except at the time of the Duke of Argyll's 1882 Affirmation Bill, spoke in general terms only. In 1882 he had alluded to the solemn issue 'whether we as men, whether we as nations, shall bow before a supernatural authority or not'. Though conceding that many Liberals were religious men, the Conservative leader had gone on to emphasize that it was to the Liberal side in politics that 'those who challenge the supernatural goverment of the world turn for counsel and support'.[4] In the spring of 1883 Salisbury spoke in a similar vein of the overriding issue of 'whether the

[1] *Hansard*, cols. 1441, 1761, 1595.   [2] Ibid., col. 1213.
[3] Cited by Gwynn and Tuckwell, *Life of Dilke*, i. 422; *N.R.*, 15 Apr. 1883, p. 248.
[4] Cited in *N.R.*, 30 Apr. 1882, p. 337.

State shall be atheistic or not'.[1] On one occasion, to be sure, when he had gone so far as to bracket Gladstone and Bradlaugh by name, he was reproved by Lord Granville and excused himself by blaming his secretary for the controversial turn of phrase.[2]

As for Northcote, that 'gentlest of human beings',[3] he had begun to take quiet satisfaction in the leadership of the anti-Bradlaugh campaign, which many Conservatives attributed to him. Actual encounters with Bradlaugh made him distinctly uncomfortable, but in retrospect Northcote could take some pride in his repeated successes. Bradlaugh had been barred from the House of Commons, observed the Conservative leader at Manchester in 1881, and 'I may say we get on very well without him'.[4] A Scottish Conservative meeting in Glasgow in October 1882 could find only two issues on which to congratulate the visiting Northcote formally: his resistance to *clôture* (the curbs on House of Commons debates being imposed in response to Irish Nationalist tactics) and the 'firm stand against the admission of an avowed Atheist to Parliament made by the leader of the Opposition'.[5] The very fact that the Bradlaugh case appeared to be the most popular weapon in the Conservative arsenal made Northcote the prisoner as well as the leader of a cause of whose transcendent value he was never completely convinced.

Northcote's leadership, moreover, was by no means secure. 'One can never dine in Tory company', noted Edward Hamilton in 1884, 'without hearing Sir S[tafford] Northcote slighted.'[6] And indeed the wounds opened by the Fourth Party in 1880 had not been healed during the succeeding years. For Lord Randolph Churchill these were years in which he won increasing acclaim—or notoriety—as he zestfully attacked Gladstone's ministry both in and out of Parliament for its errors abroad, its blunders in Ireland, and its attachment to atheism. A letter written to Wolff in November 1881 is

[1] Cited in *N.R.*, 8 Apr. 1883, p. 232.
[2] Hamilton Diary (B.M.), 48632, pp. 22, 23.
[3] Sir Herbert Maxwell, *The Life and Times of the Right Honourable William Henry Smith, M.P.* (Edinburgh, 1893), ii. 57.
[4] Cited in *N.R.*, 12 June 1881, p. 465.
[5] Cited in *N.R.*, 15 Oct. 1882, p. 257.
[6] Hamilton Diary (B.M.), 48636, p. 26.

indicative. 'Well! Hull was a triumph. I never had such a success with a large audience. Every point told surprisingly. In my second speech my reference to your successful contest with Bradlaugh provoked the greatest enthusiasm.'[1]

It was not until the spring of 1883, however, that an open break with Northcote came. It was precipitated by the selection of Northcote rather than Salisbury to unveil a newly completed statue of Disraeli, a choice which appeared to make the former the leading contender for the party succession. Churchill thereupon wrote two devastating letters to *The Times* in which he denounced Northcote for his 'pusillanimity, vacillation, and discouragement of hard-working followers'. Northcote's handling of the Bradlaugh case in 1880 was cited in evidence. This was followed by an article, 'Elijah's Mantle', in the *Fortnightly Review*, an espousal of Tory democracy which emphasized once again that, whoever in the party was fit to wear Lord Beaconsfield's cloak, Northcote was not the man.[2]

Northcote was, not surprisingly, annoyed by these and other manifestations of Lord Randolph's scorn. 'It is becoming necessary to bring our young friend to his bearings,' he wrote to Salisbury, 'otherwise the party will be quite disorganized.'[3] Northcote protested in similar vein to Churchill directly, but the latter—whose London house in St. James's Park curiously enough adjoined Northcote's—remained obdurate.

Since I have been in Parliament [he wrote to Northcote], I have always acted on my own account and shall continue to do so, for I have not found the results of such a line of action at all unsatisfactory. . . . The numerous letters which I have for some time received, and which I continue to receive from all parts of the country & from all sorts of individuals & bodies, enable me to be confident that my political actions & views are not so entirely personal as you w[oul]d seem to imagine.[4]

[1] Cited by Winston S. Churchill, *Randolph Churchill*, i. 163.
[2] May, *The Constitutional History of England*, continued and edited by Francis Holland, iii (London, 1912), 107; Churchill, *Churchill*, i. 246, and *passim*.
[3] Northcote to Salisbury, 9 Mar. 1883, Salisbury MSS.
[4] Churchill to Northcote, 10 Mar. 1883, Iddesleigh MSS. (B.M.), 50021, fol. 84.

'The anarchy is great in the opposition', wrote Granville, with evident satisfaction, to Gladstone in Cannes.[1] This 'anarchy' proved not at all in evidence during the Affirmation Bill debate, however, except in so far as Churchill saw himself rather than Northcote as the man who might most appropriately reply to Gladstone's masterful oration. The result was an excellent example of Churchill's own oratorical gifts, which at the same time highlighted the elements in the Bradlaugh case which the Tory party continued to regard as a political goldmine.

Churchill began by paying mock tribute to the Prime Minister, whose theological subtleties he compared to those fashioned by medieval schoolmen. His own task, Lord Randolph explained, was to strip the bill of all flimsy disguises and to place it 'naked before the Parliament and before the country— a Bill for the admission of avowed Atheists into the House of Commons'. And who were the supporters of atheism in England? Not 'the religious, the moral, the law-abiding, and the industrious', but 'for the most part, they were the residuum, the rabble, and the scum of the population'. For, hard as the Prime Minister might try to do so, the measure could not be separated from the person who would be the first to take advantage of it. This was not a measure of general application, like the Oaths Act of 1866, introduced to simplify the law. It was for the sole benefit of one man, a man whose initial action in claiming to affirm had been 'a deliberate and premeditated avowal of Atheism to the assembled House of Commons, and a declaration of war against Christianity'. And the proposed bill to repudiate the Parliamentary oath was in reality Bradlaugh's first attack upon that spiritual fortress. For, despite all that Gladstone had said, Christianity was still part and parcel of the law of England. In Churchill's opinion, it was not at all true that the admission of Jews had altered that state of affairs, and in order to substantiate this contention, Lord Randolph began to delve into early Church history with an apparent proficiency that left Gladstone and some of his colleagues in a state of bemused wonderment.[2]

---

[1] G.P. (B.M.), 44175, fol. 94.
[2] T. P. O'Connor, *Gladstone's House of Commons*, p. 331.

Judaism and Christianity, insisted Churchill, shared similar moral sanctions, a belief in a Supreme Being and in a future state of rewards and punishments, and the same Ten Commandments. 'The God of the Christians and the God of the Jews was one and the same.' Indeed, Judaism was separated only by a small degree from Arianism, and it was historical accident primarily which had caused the Council of Nicaea of A.D. 325 to reject Arianism as the official doctrine of the Church. Churchill cited Disraeli as to the great spiritual debt which Christianity owed Judaism and then went on to look forward hopefully to a time when Jews, like Christians, would recognize the doctrine of the Trinity. In any case, he 'ventured to say that if any member of the House advocated the claims of Mr. Bradlaugh by comparing them with the claims of the Jews, he inflicted upon that ancient people a fouler insult and a crueler wrong than was ever devised by mediæval fanaticism'.

Churchill went on to consider the possible social effects of this proposed Parliamentary acknowledgement of atheism:

Could they contemplate without alarm the revulsion that such an Act might occasion among those masses of the people who, with some hope of a happier state hereafter, were toiling their weary way through the world, content to tolerate, for a time, their less fortunate lot—the revulsion that would occur should they infer from the action of the Legislature that it was even possible that their faith was false? Surely the horrors of the French Revolution should give some idea of the effect on the masses of the State recognition of Atheism.

This was not a question of religious liberty but rather one of common prudence and common sense. To think that the banner of religious liberty, which had been triumphantly and justifiably carried to victory in the emancipation of Catholics and Jews, should now be flourished on behalf of a man 'to whom religious liberty was nothing more than superstitious licence, and to whom religion itself was but as a mania, as a disease, almost as a crime, to be combated, scoffed at, insulted, and profaned on every convenient or conceivable opportunity'.

And in the face of all this, the Prime Minister asked them to disregard the feelings of the people. Had Disraeli ever suggested such a step, what a torrent of denunciation would have been Gladstone's rejoinder. But the people were against the bill, by a margin of four to one. Petitions with 597,000 signatures had been submitted opposing the bill; petitions with but 153,000 signatures were in its favour. In spite of this fact, Churchill conceded, the Opposition might yet be defeated on the issue. Should that happen

and should the time arrive, as in that case it most certainly would, when *The Fruits of Philosophy* should become the Bible of the people, and when the age of so-called 'Reason' should have supplanted the age of Christian morality, at any rate it should then be recognized by a suffering posterity that their great principles were not sacrificed, and that their great cause was not lost, except after the bitterest conflict which could be recorded in the annals of a Parliament or in the history of a people.[1]

Challenges like those of Churchill did not go completely unanswered. 'Sir, I think we can afford to be fair, even to an Atheist', declared Edward Leatham, and the statement typifies the attitude of those Liberals who chose to speak on the issue.[2] 'It must be remembered', said Lyulph Stanley, an Anglican, 'that religious freedom does not mean merely freedom for religious people.' William Edward Baxter, a Scottish Presbyterian, introduced an anti-clerical note. He defended the bill as a climactic step in a long Liberal tradition; 'the legislation of England never goes back,' he insisted, 'and it is no more in the power of those narrow ecclesiastical bodies—Roman Catholic and Protestant—Established and Dissenting—to prevent the passing of a measure like this than it was in the power of their predecessors to convince mankind that the world was not round'.[3]

Such protests did little but interrupt temporarily the long orations with which Conservative and Irish speakers filled the air night after night. Finally, late on the night of 3 May the decisive vote came. Gladstone was by no means overconfident. Lord Richard Grosvenor, his chief Whip, could promise at most a margin of ten votes, hardly enough 'to float the Bill through the House of Lords'.[4] Not that the

[1] *Hansard*, cclxxviii (1883), 1439–55.   [2] Ibid., col. 1481.
[3] Ibid., cols. 1476, 948.
[4] Hamilton Diary (B.M.), 48633, p. 185; Hampden Diary, entry for 23 Apr. 1883.

Conservatives were certain of success, either; in three years they had failed to defeat the Government on any legislation of consequence.

The division began; Government supporters began to file into one lobby, Opposition members into the other. A large cartoon had been hung on the wall of the latter depicting Gladstone and Bradlaugh both embracing a female figure labelled 'Atheism' whose features had been drawn to resemble those of Annie Besant. Only after one athletically inclined Liberal M.P. threatened to sprint into the Opposition lobby and tear the picture down did a Conservative Whip remove it.[1] Gladstone himself returned to the Government bench to await the tally, nervously grasping the blotting pad on which he wrote his nightly report to Queen Victoria. 'If it had been the Premier's first critical division, on which all his political prospects depended', noted one veteran Parliamentary reporter, 'he could not more plainly have shown the anxiety that possessed him.'[2]

Then the results were announced: Ayes 289; Noes 292. Bradlaugh had been beaten once again. Gladstone and one of the most powerful British ministries of the nineteenth century had been defeated as well. The throng of members on the Opposition benches broke up into a confused mass of outstretched arms, waving hats, flashing handkerchiefs, and flushed, hoarsely-cheering faces. In the midst of this frantic excitement Gladstone sombrely returned to writing his nightly letter to the Queen.[3]

[1] Hamilton Diary (B.M.), 48633, p. 204; G.P. (B.M.), 44189, fol. 221.
[2] Lucy, *Two Parliaments*, ii. 329.
[3] Ibid., p. 331; London *Daily News*, 4 May 1883.

XIX

THE ROLE OF
THE IRISH NATIONALISTS

How can the defeat of the Affirmation Bill be explained? Almost all contemporary observers agreed that the defeat of the bill on its second reading discredited the Gladstone ministry. Yet to look primarily to defectors within the Liberal Party would be a mistake, since of the 328 Liberals then in Parliament, 286 had voted in favour of the bill, only 33 had been absent or had deliberately abstained, and a mere 9 had voted against the measure. Taking into consideration the pressure of public opinion and contemporary standards of party discipline, the result was a tribute to Gladstone's powers of persuasion. Not that Gladstone had made the question one of confidence. He had been only too aware of the possibility of defeat, and he had no desire to fight a general election on the issue. At least one Conservative M.P. accused the Prime Minister of playing 'the confidence trick', of acting for all purposes as if the bill were a major Government measure, except in case of defeat. On the morning of 4 May at least one M.P. inquired at Number Ten Downing Street whether the Government's resignation had been submitted to the Queen.[1]

If Liberal defectors had been few, then Conservatives defectors had been still fewer. Of the Conservatives, 239 had voted against the bill, none had voted in favour, and only 6 had been absent. Among these six, only one deliberate abstention, that of Percy Windham, is known. The Irish Nationalists, with three votes in favour, 16 abstentions, and 45 votes against the bill, had swung the balance.

These statistics are significant in a number of respects. They are remarkable, first of all, for the large number of Members of Parliament personally participating in the division.

[1] *Hansard*, cclxxviii (1883), 955; Mary (Gladstone) Drew MSS. (B.M.), 46261, fol. 13.

On only one other occasion during the 1880–5 Parliament did the total vote go higher.[1] It was higher than any division recorded during the 1874–80 Parliament and higher than the controversial Irish Universities Bill upon which Gladstone had been defeated in 1873 by a vote of 287 to 284. Secondly, the vote illustrates how costly the by-election defeats since 1880 had proved. A net loss of some eleven seats had left the Liberal majority over Conservatives and Home Rulers combined at not much over twenty seats.[2] This is another way of saying that had an Affirmation Bill been pushed through the House of Commons with comparable vigour in 1880 or 1881, it might well have passed, but by 1883 it was too late.

Where then does the responsibility for the defeat lie? It lies, for one thing, in the enthusiasm engendered in Tory ranks by the conviction that they were not only on the morally correct but on the popular side. This enthusiasm is attributable in large part not only to the efforts of Lord Randolph Churchill but also to the success of the petition drive which had been led by the Church of England with the partial support of Dissenting Protestants and with the whole-hearted support of the Roman Catholic Church under Cardinal Manning. It lies, secondly, in the related role of the Irish Members of Parliament, not merely the Home Rulers but the Irish Liberals as well. Uniting as they did the political power of the churches with the vitality of the Fourth Party and the vigour of the Irish Nationalists, 'the forces allied for the moment were so strong, that the smallness of the majority was more remarkable than the fact that there was a majority against the Government'.[3]

The Irish Nationalists played a crucial role in the Affirmation Bill battle and the Bradlaugh Case generally. According to *Dod's Parliamentary Companion*, of the 103 M.P.s Ireland sent to Westminster in 1880, 63 were pledged to Home Rule,

---

[1] The sole exception was the vote on an amendment to the Parliamentary *clôture* resolution of 1882, which had been defeated, 318 to 279. *Daily News*, 5 May 1883; G.P. (B.M.), 44629, fol. 89.

[2] The uncertainty of such statistics results from the ambiguous status of certain Irish M.P.s, who according to some reckonings are classified as Home Rulers and according to others as Liberals. See, for example, G.P. (B.M.), 44643, fol. 152.

[3] McCarthy, *England under Gladstone, 1880–1884*, p. 260.

15 were Liberals, and 25 were Conservatives. This analysis is unfortunately more specific than was the reality, because the Home Rulers of the second Gladstone Ministry were by no means a unified, tightly-knit party. They immediately split, indeed, upon a fundamental issue, whether to move with the Liberals from the Opposition to the Government benches or to join the Conservatives in opposition. At a meeting in Dublin on 17 May 1880 they chose between William Shaw, the moderate who had succeeded Isaac Butt as the party's official leader in 1879, and Charles Stewart Parnell, the man who had become closely identified with the tactic of deliberate obstruction of Parliamentary business as a method of gaining influence. Largely because several moderates were absent, Parnell was elected by a vote of 23 to 18. Parnell's adherents chose to remain in opposition, while Shaw's contingent joined the Liberals. The number of Irish M.P.s directly pledged to Parnell's leadership was to wax and wane frequently during the years that followed, but by 1885 his ascendancy was generally acknowledged.[1] It was, moreover, during the second Gladstone Ministry that both Liberals and Conservatives came to acknowledge that a true third party had taken its place in their midst. Until February 1881, for example, Liberal Whips continued to issue circulars even to Home Rule members sitting on the Opposition benches.[2]

Irish Nationalist M.P.s took an immediate interest in the Bradlaugh case, and except on the vote to set up a select committee to inquire into Bradlaugh's right to affirm, a majority of Home Rulers was to vote in opposition to Bradlaugh. Frank Hugh O'Donnell, who fancied himself better than anyone to lead the Irish third party, was the first M.P. to make a direct reference in debate to Bradlaugh's atheism and his role as publisher of *Fruits of Philosophy*, the birth-control pamphlet. The latter was, in O'Donnell's opinion, 'the gravest bar' to Bradlaugh's admission and 'the ground of the determined hostility of the majority of the House'.[3]

[1] T. P. O'Connor, *Charles Stewart Parnell: A Memory* (London, 1891), pp. 79–89. Gladstone estimated the number at 35 to 40 in January 1883. Hamilton Diary (B.M.), 48633, p. 106.
[2] *Freeman's Journal* (Dublin), 9 Feb. 1881, p. 5.
[3] Frank Hugh O'Donnell, *A History of the Irish Parliamentary Party* (London, 1910), i. 491. O'Donnell relates that 'as I was going down to

Arthur Moore, Sir Patrick O'Brien, A. M. Sullivan, William Corbet, and James McCoan all spoke forcefully against Bradlaugh. They deemed the Liberals' comparison of Bradlaugh's position in 1880 with that of the Roman Catholics at the time of the Catholic Emancipation Bill of 1829 'as in the highest degree offensive to the Catholic population'.[1] 'Because it was just to allow Catholics who had been unjustly excluded from the House to enter, does it follow that it is just to allow an unbeliever, an Atheist, contrary to all usage and precedent to do so?' Moore's answer was a defiant 'No!'[2]

There was obviously a close connexion between religion and politics in the stand taken up by the majority of the Home-Rule members. The election of 1880 had produced the first Irish parliamentary contingent in Westminster which even roughly reflected the religious distribution of Ireland. Fifty-six of Ireland's 103 members were now Catholics—for the first time a majority—while according to the religious census of 1881 Catholics made up 76·62 of the total population.[3] As Conor Cruise O'Brien demonstrates in *Parnell and His Party, 1880–1890*, by far the ablest study of the subject, the Catholic Church had a vast influence upon Irish elections, so that 'the home rule nomination was often in practice decided by meetings of "the bishop and clergy" of the diocese in which the constituency was situated'.[4] Most Home-Rule members were Catholics 'of unchallenged orthodoxy',[5] and there was, as has been suggested above, a reasonably close connexion between the English Catholic Church headed by

Charing Cross Station on my way to the House one afternoon, first one, then another, and then other children and young boys and girls came running up to me and other passers-by crying: "Here you are, sir. The 'Fruits of Philosophy' for sixpence. Nothing left out. Only sixpence. Only sixpence." Bradlaugh had published a cheap edition of the beastly and abominable "Guide to Safe Lust" and had given it to swarms of children of the newspaper-boy and flower-girl class to sell at the London railway stations.' (Ibid., p. 480.) O'Donnell has a deserved reputation for unreliability, but the account is given partial substantiation by Annie Besant, who later recalled that 'when we found that the street-boys were selling the pamphlet at a price higher than its published one, and in an offensive way, we refused to supply them, instead of printing for them bills of the most prurient suggestiveness'. (*N.R.*, 26 July 1885, p. 55.)

[1] *Hansard*, ccliii (1880), 513.
[2] Ibid., col. 599.   [3] *Tablet*, 25 June 1881, p. 1014.
[4] O'Brien, *Parnell and his Party*, p. 42.   [5] Ibid., p. 28.

Cardinal Manning and some of the Home-Rule members, such as Frank Hugh O'Donnell and Justin McCarthy.

And yet not all the Irish Home Rulers sided with their Church—or what seemed to be the interest of their Church—in the spring and summer of 1880. Lysaght Finigan, for one, defended Bradlaugh. 'As an Irish member sent to the House for the purpose of obtaining guarantees for the liberty and freedom of Ireland' he could not understand how he was supporting the principle of liberty for the Irish by depriving Bradlaugh of his own.[1] T. P. O'Connor, a radical journalist, also defended Bradlaugh's right to his seat. Then there was Parnell himself, a Protestant, who kept silent during the early debates on Bradlaugh's admission. When he did at last speak, he said he could recall no time when 'he was less confident in the belief that the mass of the Irish people were behind him. . . . Catholic members for Ireland had felt very strongly on this question—very strongly indeed.'[2] C. C. O'Brien, in his study, provides a curious analysis of the reasons for Parnell's stand:

. . . members of the Parnellite faction tended to become attached, not so much to the liberal party as an institution, as to the person of Gladstone himself or, in several cases at this time, to the radical wing of the liberal party under Chamberlain and Dilke. The famous Bradlaugh case first revealed the extent of these sympathies. In the first division (24 May 1880) as to whether the 'notorious atheist' should be allowed to take his seat, 13 home rulers, including 7 Parnellites, voted in his favour, and it later became clear that 5 other Parnellites supported him. Such opinions, so remote from the views of the constituencies represented by these men, may not have been entirely due to the influence of English radicals, but they certainly revealed a mental atmosphere among certain Parnellites favourable at this time to a rapprochement with a section of Gladstone's party.[3]

Such an analysis, which sees Parnell's support of Bradlaugh as necessarily opposed to Parnell's inner convictions and rather as a deliberate attempt to buy sympathy from English radicals, is misleading for several reasons. One, it completely ignores the distinction between voting for a man's views and

[1] *Hansard*, ccliii (1880), 657.   [2] Ibid., col. (1880), 1305.
[3] O'Brien, *Parnell and his Party*, pp. 49–50.

supporting his right to hold them. The vote of 24 May 1880, which O'Brien cites, was not, after all, a vote for atheism; it was merely a vote in favour of having a select committee of the House of Commons explore Bradlaugh's legal right to take the Parliamentary Oath. Secondly, it makes Parnell's motives out to be too exclusively political. Although O'Brien's thesis that Parnell for a time deliberately cultivated (and even simulated) radicalism in order to win the support of revolutionary-minded Irishmen for an ultimately moderate course is on the whole convincing, it does not altogether suffice here.

It is difficult to discover Parnell's own religious views; like many things about that enigmatic leader, they remain in part a mystery. He was born a member of the Church of England and formally remained one to his death. For a while, however, he was attracted to the Plymouth Brethren, a quietist Nonconformist sect, and in 1880 he may well have been an agnostic. In 1885 he confided to his associate, T. P. O'Connor, that he had faith, 'that he had once lost it, but that it had come back again'.[1] Both O'Donnell and Parnell's associate, T. M. Healy, who first became an M.P. in 1881, attribute Parnell's intervention in the Bradlaugh case to the unfortunate influence of T. P. O'Connor.[2] O'Connor's own account differs considerably. He recalls that Parnell had received conflicting counsel and long hesitated as to his course.

But I remember well his coming down to the lower smoking-room one night, and declaring that he was disgusted with some of the bigoted sentiments he heard expressed, and that he felt he must speak. I agreed with his views of the Bradlaugh question, but I dreaded the consequence to his position as a leader if he expressed them, and asked him to pause; but he had made up his mind, and went up and made a speech on Mr. Bradlaugh's behalf.[3]

In that speech, Parnell observed that Bradlaugh's views were not his own—according to T. P. O'Connor, he was particularly revolted by Bradlaugh's ideas on birth control[4]—

[1] T. P. O'Connor, *Parnell*, pp. 170–1.
[2] O'Donnell, *Irish Parl. Party*, i. 464. Healy is cited as saying of O'Connor to Parnell, 'He is ruining you'. See Hamilton Fyfe, *T. P. O'Connor* (London, 1934), p. 102.
[3] O'Connor, *Parnell*, p. 91.   [4] Ibid., pp. 91–92.

but that Bradlaugh's views were irrelevant to the constitutional issue before the House. Parnell protested even more
strongly against Bradlaugh's imprisonment. 'I cannot believe',
he declared, 'that the Irish constituencies would desire their
Members to vote for the imprisonment of anybody.'[1] Arthur
Moore and the O'Donoghue at once publicly contradicted
Parnell, but Parnell and five other Home Rulers none the less
joined the otherwise solitary Labouchere in voting against
Bradlaugh's arrest. Parnell and four colleagues visited Bradlaugh that same afternoon in the office of the Sergeant-at-
Arms to tender their cordial sympathy.[2]

C. C. O'Brien's analysis overlooks another factor as well—
that for many of Parnell's followers, Bradlaugh was more than
a mere symbol of radicalism. He had long held a reputation as
an English friend of Irish causes, and many of them knew him
personally. Bradlaugh had helped draft a Fenian Declaration
of Independence for Ireland in 1867 and had spoken on
behalf of the 'Manchester Martyrs'; Justin McCarthy and the
O'Donoghue had been associated with Bradlaugh in a
Trafalgar Square demonstration that same year.[3] Even F. H.
O'Donnell had, in 1875, twice lectured in Bradlaugh's Hall
of Science under the pseudonym, 'A Catholic'.[4] Joseph
Biggar, Michael Davitt, and William O'Sullivan had participated with Bradlaugh at an English Land Law Reform
Conference earlier in 1880.[5] Parnell himself was, as was Bradlaugh, a Vice-President of the Democratic League of Great
Britain and Ireland and had had private meetings with Bradlaugh both in Glasgow and at the Hall of Science in London.[6]
M.P.s like O'Connor Power spoke publicly of Bradlaugh's
'friendship for Ireland'. T. P. O'Connor recalled that as
Bradlaugh 'had been a strong friend of Ireland in her darkest
days, he ought to be defended by Irishmen in his day of
need'.[7]

Though numerous Irish M.P.s were acquainted with Bradlaugh, this hardly made his name a household word in

---

[1] *Hansard*, ccliii (1880), 658.   [2] *Freeman's Journal*, 24 June 1880, p. 5.
[3] Bonner & Robertson, *Bradlaugh*, i, chap. xxv; Justin McCarthy, *Reminiscences* (London, 1899), ii. 176, 327.   [4] *N.R.*, 29 Aug. 1880, p. 186.
[5] Bonner & Robertson, *Bradlaugh*, ii. 35; *N.R.*, 8 Feb. 1880, pp. 84–85.
[6] *Tablet*, 7 May 1881, p. 737; *N.R.*, 19 Apr. 1885, p. 305.
[7] *Hansard*, ccliii (1880), 723; O'Connor, *Parnell*, p. 90.

Ireland. Objections to Parnell's course began to be voiced almost immediately in the Irish press, and T. P. O'Connor was denounced from the pulpit of one of the churches in his constituency for supporting Bradlaugh.[1] The *Freeman's Journal*, the leading Parnellite daily in Dublin, was placed, to be sure, in a considerable dilemma by Parnell's decision to support Bradlaugh's legal stand. In May 1880 it had denounced Bradlaugh as 'a blatant, brazen, howling Atheist', and the possibility that he might take the oath as 'a shocking and horrible thing', but the tone of its editorials changed markedly in June, and upon the defeat of Labouchere's motion to let Bradlaugh affirm, it commented mildly: 'With the wisdom of the attitude of the House we cannot quite agree.' 'Those who have carefully studied the history of popular assemblies', the *Freeman's Journal* philosophized, 'can scarcely doubt that Mr. Bradlaugh will fight his way into the House of Commons.'[2]

The journal was immediately reproved in a lengthy letter to the editor by a Catholic priest. He indignantly denied Parnell's contention that Bradlaugh's imprisonment was repugnant to the feelings of the Irish constituencies: 'Well, sir, a fouler slander was never uttered.'

The Irish [he went on] have in some instances followed Mr. Parnell against their priests; but he is greatly mistaken if he thinks that a temporary overthrow of clerical influence has shaken the deep foundations of the Christian faith that were laid in Ireland ages ago, and cemented with the blood of glorious martyrs.

Ah no. We may be hot-headed and impulsive, but we . . . have no sympathy with Atheism, blasphemy, and the fruits of a foul philosophy. We recognize no freedom of opinion there . . . .

For my part, I should rather see the foreign rule of England, bad as it is, replaced by the iron despotism of Russia, and Ireland turned into a waste like Siberia, than look for freedom through a political alliance with Bradlaugh and his 100,000 Atheists.[3]

This letter was reprinted in full in the *Tablet*, the leading Catholic weekly in England, and thus had the implied endorsement of Cardinal Manning. According to one biographer of of Parnell, Parnell's support for Bradlaugh was an act for

[1] *N.R.*, 13 June 1880, p. 408.
[2] *Freeman's Journal* (Dublin), 22 May 1880, p. 5; 25 June 1880, p. 4; 24 June 1880, p. 5.   [3] Ibid., 26 June 1880, p. 5.

which Cardinal Manning never forgave the Home-Rule leader.[1]

Parnell's failure to 'be guided by the instincts of Catholic Ireland'[2] had repercussions among Catholic circles in Ireland and England, and it stimulated similar controversy within the Home-Rule ranks at Westminster. The excitement of the Bradlaugh debate led to a fist fight between Philip Callan and T. P. O'Connor on 24 May, and the subsequent debate over Bradlaugh's arrest 'threatened to merge into a civil war among the Irish members'.[3]

The paradoxical result was that, on a number of divisions in 1880, the Parnellites sitting on the Opposition side were more inclined to favour the Liberal position than Shaw's contingent on the Ministerial benches. On Labouchere's resolution that Bradlaugh be permitted to affirm, 18 Parnellites voted in opposition and 9 in favour. Of Shaw's men, 13 opposed and only 1 voted for the resolution. Shaw, like Parnell a Protestant, abstained. Shortly before the vote on Gladstone's compromise resolution to permit Bradlaugh to affirm at his legal risk, a group of Home Rulers headed by Philip Callan attempted to convince a party caucus to pledge a united vote against the motion. Parnell's adherents, by a mere 9 to 8 margin, managed to defeat Callan's proposal and thus leave each Home Ruler free to vote as he saw fit.[4] The outcome was that on Gladstone's resolution, 15 of the 37 Irish Nationalists voting supported Gladstone, thereby making Home-Rule opposition to Bradlaugh relatively ineffective on this occasion.

The vigour of several of the Roman Catholic Home Rulers did not go unnoticed in the English press. *The Times*, for

---

[1] Joan Haslip, *Parnell* (London, 1936), p. 149. Though C. C. O'Brien, F. S. L. Lyons (*The Fall of Parnell, 1890–1891*) and others have argued convincingly that English Nonconformist opinion was more influential than the Irish Catholic hierarchy in bringing about Parnell's downfall after the divorce scandal, the antipathy of Manning and Pope Leo XIII remain undisputed. See, for example, Emmet Larkin, 'The Roman Catholic Hierarchy and the Fall of Parnell', *Victorian Studies*, iv, June 1961, p. 329.

[2] F. H. O'Donnell in a letter to *Freeman's Journal* reprinted in *Tablet*, 3 July 1880, p. 24.

[3] *Freeman's Journal* (Dublin), 25 May 1880, p. 5; Lucy, *Two Parliaments*, ii. 41.

[4] *Freeman's Journal* (Dublin), 2 July 1880, p. 5.

example, noted that while Liberals and even some Conservatives opposing Gladstone's resolution proposed remedial
legislation, 'the Roman Catholic Home Rule members stood
almost alone in declaring against any solution of the Question'.[1] For the moment they did not fully dominate their
party, since the newspaper-reading public saw Parnell as
a vocal champion of Bradlaugh's right to his Parliamentary
seat. Such domination was, however, soon to come.

During the autumn and winter of 1880–1 the 'Irish Question'
increased in intensity with a resumption of the 'land war'
and renewed reliance by Parnellite M.P.s upon the tactics of
Parliamentary obstruction. Gladstone attempted to meet the
problem with a new coercion act on the one hand and with
the complex Irish Land Act of 1881 on the other. After
Bradlaugh's brief tenure in Parliament that same autumn
and winter ended with an adverse legal decision, he was re-
elected in Northampton. Eleven Home Rulers favoured and
only four opposed Northcote's consequent successful motion
to exclude him. Neither Parnell nor T. P. O'Connor participated in the division. The *Freeman's Journal* was still able to
view the proceedings philosophically. 'No doubt when the
heated passions cool down, it will be seen that an Act of
Parliament alone can deal with a difficult and intricate
question' like the Bradlaugh case.[2] Yet in May 1881 Irish
members helped block any attempt by the Government to
introduce such legislation, and when three months later a
frustrated Bradlaugh attempted a one-man assault into the
chamber which barred him, the *Freeman's Journal* called
him a 'straw-stuffed Wilkes' whose 'charlatanism . . . has no
settled conviction', and described his assault on Parliament as
'the last resort of a collapsing demagogue at his wits' end
for further inflation'.[3] By this time, indeed, the attitude of
Irish Nationalist M.P.s, and in fact of Irish M.P.s generally,
had become overwhelmingly hostile, and so it was to remain
for the next five years.

By the time Bradlaugh attempted to take the oath again,
at the opening of the 1882 session of Parliament, the Irish

[1] *The Times*, 2 July 1880, p. 9.
[2] *Freeman's Journal* (Dublin), 28 Apr. 1881, p. 5.
[3] Ibid., 4 Aug. 1881, p. 4.

party had already decided 'that in the event of any member of the Government moving the previous question *in re* Bradlaugh, that we as a party vote against the motion'. The decision was greatly aided by a 39 to 1 margin against the man among the Home Rulers. Only Philip Nolan, who had resigned shortly before as Home-Rule Whip, dared break the unanimity. Of the 103 Irish M.P.s (including Conservatives and Liberals, as well as Home Rulers) 68 had voted against supporting Bradlaugh and but 3 in favour. 'It was evident', noted the *Freeman's Journal*, 'that the Irish vote had turned the scale.'[1] On the successful motion calling for Bradlaugh's expulsion after the self-swearing incident, the Irish Nationalist margin against Bradlaugh was 27 to 3, and at least one Irish M.P. subsequently went to Northampton to campaign personally against the heretic.[2] Although Bradlaugh was re-elected, the House of Commons, by a vote of 257 to 242, blocked his admission again. The Irish Nationalist margin was 25 to 5 against Bradlaugh, and this quite obviously determined the outcome.

The import of the Irish vote was duly noted by Conservatives as well as Liberals. Charles N. Newdegate, the veteran Tory who had clashed with Cardinal Manning during the 1870's over the conditions in Roman Catholic convents, rejoiced that resistance to Bradlaugh 'has formed a bond of union between myself and the Roman Catholic members of this House'. Henry Labouchere, Bradlaugh's loyal colleague, was equally outspoken, 'I think, from their point of view, Irish members never made a greater mistake . . . .'[3]

Parnell himself kept silent on the Bradlaugh case for several years and abstained on the vital divisions—an enforced abstention, no doubt, during his tenure in Kilmainham Jail—but by March 1883 he had veered definitely into the anti-Bradlaugh camp. It was the Affirmation Bill debate of that year which brought Irish protestations of unity against Bradlaugh and the legislative measure proposed by the Liberal Government to their highest pitch of intensity. Irish M.P.s opposed even the introduction of the bill, ordinarily a mere

---

[1] Ibid. (Dublin), 8 Feb. 1882, p. 5.
[2] *N.R.*, 19 Mar. 1882, p. 243.
[3] *Hansard*, cclxxviii (1883), 1738, 1464.

formality, and Irish speakers dominated the debate during the last week of April and the first days of May. 'All Ireland, from Cape Clear to the Giant's Causeway, is against it', declared James Carlile McCoan. 'If it were, therefore, the last vote I should ever give in the House, and if the fate of the Government were at stake, I would record it against this Bill.'[1] Tim Harrington agreed that 'upon this question there is more unanimity among Members representing Irish constituencies than upon any question which for a long time past has come before the House'.[2] The party had decided several weeks earlier to make the issue a party question and had resolved 'that the Irish Parliamentary Party act together as a party in strenuously opposing the government Affirmation Bill and that the whips be requested to act at once to issue a strong whip to all members of the Party requesting their immediate and constant attendance in their places in the House of Commons to resist determinedly the government proposals'.[3]

Richard O'Shaughnessy was one of three Irish M.P.s who disagreed; the O'Donoghue and Benjamin Whitworth were the others. 'If I had a vote in the borough of Northampton', declared O'Shaughnessy, 'I would travel 100 miles to give it against Mr. Bradlaugh . . . but that is not the question here.'[4] That was the question here, however, for a great majority of Irish members. The Affirmation Bill was defeated by the razor-thin margin of 292 to 289, but the Irish Home-Rule Party contributed 45 votes to the majority and only 3 to the minority. The margin for all Irish M.P.s was 69 to 3 against the bill. The intensity of the contest is revealed by the fact that Parnell made a personal appeal to the O'Gorman Mahon, a veteran Irish radical long friendly to Bradlaugh, to refrain in this instance. As for the inebriated Charles Joseph Fay, he had been prepared to stagger into the 'Aye' Lobby in the company of Lord Kensington, one of the Liberal Whips, when a fellow Irishman, Philip Callan, pounced upon him. Shouting 'You damned hound! You damned sneak!' Callan pulled a protesting Fay away from Kensington's arms and dragged him forcibly into the 'No' Lobby.[5] If the intention

[1] *Hansard*, cclxxviii (1883), 1479–80.   [2] Ibid., col. 1483.
[3] Mahon MSS., file 17, fol. 4.   [4] *Hansard*, cclxxviii (1883), 1780–1.
[5] *N.R.*, 13 May 1883, pp. 353–7; Wolff, *Rambling Recollections*, ii. 118.

of Fay's vote is thus suspect, then O'Shaughnessy's vote may be equally so. He had resigned from the Home-Rule League in 1882 and his application to Gladstone for a government job was pending at the time the division took place.[1]

According to Sir Winston Churchill the credit for the defeat of the Affirmation Bill was assigned almost solely to Lord Randolph Churchill.[2] Yet a survey of the contemporary press indicates that at least as much attention was paid to the Irish vote. The Northampton *Mercury*, the Edinburgh *Scotsman*, and the London *Daily News* all gave prominence to the role of the Irish M.P.s. It was 'obvious', observed the *Daily News*, 'that this "famous victory" has been won by means of the Irish vote . . . '.[3] Nor were the Irish reluctant to lay claim to the triumph. 'Bradlaugh Bowled Out by the Irish Vote', proclaimed *United Ireland*, the most radical of the nationalist weeklies.[4] T. P. O'Connor was even more enthusiastic: 'Nobody denies that it was the Irish vote which was the real, the influential, the potent factor in the whole struggle; that it was the Irish vote *alone* which had the balance of power between the two sides, and that it was the Irish vote which, by its solid union, gave the victory to the Conservatives.'[5] The statistics tend strongly to confirm that conclusion. The question that remains is: Why were the Irish so unitedly hostile to the aspirations of the Northampton M.P.? Was it antagonism toward Bradlaugh personally? Was the motive political and Bradlaugh merely a stick with which to beat a Liberal Government? Or was the motive in some sense ultimately religious?

Many Irish members during 1881, 1882, and 1883 defended their anti-Bradlaugh votes on the basis that Bradlaugh had favoured coercive measures against Ireland during his brief tenure in Parliament. T. P. O'Connor, addressing a London audience, denounced Bradlaugh as 'that arch-coercionist'.[6] Henry George, then Dublin correspondent of the New York *Irish World*, justified Irish opposition to Bradlaugh in similar

[1] G.P. (B.M.), 44546, fol. 209; *Tablet*, 4 May 1882, p. 326.
[2] Churchill, *Randolph Churchill*, i. 255.
[3] London *Daily News*, 5 May 1883.
[4] Cited by Humanitas, *Bradlaugh and the Irish Nation*, p. 10.
[5] T. P. O'Connor, *Gladstone's House of Commons*, p. 335.
[6] Cited by Humanitas, *Bradlaugh and the Irish Nation*, p. 12.

terms. 'When Bradlaugh was in the House [of Commons]', wrote the author of *Progress and Poverty*, 'he voted steadily for coercion, and had he taken his place this Session, it was certain that the Government would have had no stauncher supporter of its policy of imprisonment and terror.'[1]

Tim Healy sought in a pamphlet to give statistical backing to the accusation. Bradlaugh, reported Healy, had as M.P. voted against 'coercion' 37 times, for 'coercion' 78 times. Bradlaugh found this lumping together of all his votes in Parliament most misleading. Most of those 78 votes related not to legislative measures at all, Bradlaugh observed, but purely to procedural questions such as votes of adjournment. Even according to Healy's reckoning, moreover, only three English M.P.s had voted 'against coercion' more often than Bradlaugh.[2] Yet however often Bradlaugh might contradict this version of his brief Parliamentary career, the story was repeated; and after the Affirmation Bill vote one Irish member shouted 'That's Irish retaliation on Bradlaugh', referring, according to *United Ireland*, 'to the recreant conduct of the member for Northampton on the Coercion Bill'.[3] It would seem, nevertheless, that Bradlaugh's record on the Irish question was not the true motive for the Irish attitude but rather a rationalization which anti-clerical Irish M.P.s found especially convenient.

What of a collateral explanation for the progressive alienation between Bradlaugh and the Irish radical leaders— that they had become rivals in the English working-class and land-reform movements? Parnell's attitude toward co-operation with English radicals was always ambiguous. It had become obvious to him during the winter of 1880-1 that tactics of parliamentary obstruction would gain only infinitesimal support among English radicals. 'We fear', wrote the *Freeman's Journal*, 'that little help from this quarter can be expected during the session.'[4] 'While approving of many of their objects,' wrote Thomas Burt, a working-class M.P., about the Irish M.P.s, 'I have felt ever-increasing aversion to

---

[1] Cited in *N.R.*, 16 Apr. 1882, p. 309.

[2] T. M. Healy, *A Record of Coercion* (Dublin, 1882), cited in *N.R.*, 12 Feb. 1882, p. 108; 4 Oct. 1885, p. 219.   [3] *United Ireland*, 5 May 1883, p. 5.

[4] *Freeman's Journal* (Dublin), 15 Jan. 1881, p. 5.

their methods.'[1] The English worker was too proud of his Parliament to wish it destroyed.

Yet Irish Nationalists never quite gave up the hope of winning English working-class support. A party convention in January 1881 decided to hold meetings all over England to present the case against coercion. In March Parnell agreed to address such gatherings in order to explain the Irish policy of obstruction and explore the possibility of 'an alliance between the English and Irish democracies'.[2] In August Parnell and other Home-Rule leaders attended a Newcastle upon Tyne convention of a National Land League of Great Britain. During these years, Parnell and his associates maintained a friendly relationship with H. M. Hyndman and other socialists and with Helen Taylor, John Stuart Mill's stepdaughter.[3] Friendly relations were also maintained with Henry Labouchere and with John Morley, in whose election to Parliament in 1882 the Irish party took considerable interest.[4]

As early as the summer of 1881 Bradlaugh himself had been so alienated by Irish hostility that he no longer trusted the Irish as co-workers in any English organization devoted to land reform. All this makes relevant an interesting comment made by Annie Besant in 1883:

> The hatred of Mr. Parnell and his colleagues to Mr. Bradlaugh has a very simple root; he served Ireland before her service was a well paid one, and when danger, not gold, was reaped by it. He denounced outrages always, while Mr. Parnell and his colleagues declined to do so. During the past two years he has tried, and tried successfully, to prevent Mr. Parnell and his colleagues from seducing English workers into his League, and he has foiled the skilful attempts to form secret societies among English workers in the large towns. These are the reasons for the hatred shewn him by the men who disgrace Ireland in the House of Commons, and the few hotheaded Englishmen who then blamed him for his

---

[1] Thomas Burt, 'Working Men and the Situation', *Nineteenth Century*, April 1881, p. 612.

[2] *Freeman's Journal* (Dublin), 20 Jan. 1881, p. 5; 23 Mar. 1881, p. 5.

[3] Mahon MSS., file 10, fol. 13; G. D. H. Cole, *British Working Class Politics, 1832–1914* (London, 1941), p. 86.

[4] Hamilton Diary (B.M.), 48632, p. 137; *Freeman's Journal* (Dublin), 7 Feb. 1882, p. 5.

action will see now the horrors from the contamination of which
he saved them.[1]

Mrs. Besant could herself be rather 'hotheaded' when
defending her idols and she is not the most reliable of
witnesses, yet this comment and others indicate at least that,
if competition for English working-class support did not
initiate the rupture between the Irish party and Bradlaugh,
it may well have intensified it.

Perhaps the most commonly accepted reason for Parnellite
opposition to Bradlaugh is a purely political one, that Parnell's
supporters felt it in their own interest to oppose the prevailing Government on any and every occasion so long as it
failed to promote Home Rule and so long as it insisted upon
coercive measures against Irish unrest. 'To turn out the
Gladstone Government', wrote T. P. O'Connor in 1891, 'at
that time was the chief business of an Irish party and the best
thing for Ireland.'[2] Joseph Biggar's explanation for his anti-
Bradlaugh vote of February 1882 was strictly political:

> Our party are resolved to vote against the Government if they
> propose to admit Mr. Bradlaugh. If his admission had been pro-
> posed by Mr. Labouchere, the question would have been an open
> one, and part of our party would have supported him. The present
> Government treated us worse than any Tory Government could
> have done, and we are resolved to oppose it by every means in
> our power.[3]

Such a stand was not inconsistent with Parnell's own reputation for concentrating all his attention upon Irish interests.
Corroborating evidence for this hostility between the Parnellites and Gladstone's Ministry is not lacking. In a number of
by-elections in 1881 and 1882 the Irish influence was thrown
to the Conservative candidate, and in the municipal elections
of 1881 the Irish vote contributed significantly to Conservative gains.[4] 'Like all the members of my Party', recalled
T. P. O'Connor in his memoirs, 'I came for a while positively

---

[1] *N.R.*, 25 Feb. 1883, p. 115.
[2] T. P. O'Connor, *Parnell: A Memory*, p. 158.
[3] Cited in *N.R.*, 19 Feb. 1882, p. 136.
[4] (Copy) Brand to Sir George Grey, 4 Sept. 1881, Hampden MSS.; *Tablet*,
5 Nov. 1881, p. 719.

to detest Mr. Gladstone.'[1] The feeling was cordially recipro-
cated by many Liberals if not, to the same degree, by Gladstone himself.

Since evidence of hostility between Liberals and Irish
Nationalists can be supplemented with evidence of at least a
partial *rapprochement* between the Parnellites and Conservatives such as Lord Randolph Churchill, all this would then
be sufficient to explain why several Irish M.P.s, once the
Affirmation Bill defeat was announced, had shouted 'A Cheer
for Spencer'. Their meaning was sufficiently clear, concluded
the Edinburgh *Scotsman*. It was Lord Spencer's rule as
Viceroy in Ireland 'that had taken the Parnellites as a body
into the Lobby against the Bill of the Government'.[2]

There remains a final piece of evidence which indicates
that at least one adherent of Home Rule considered a strong
anti-Bradlaugh stand as a logical method of bringing that
objective closer to achievement. William Franklin Haston
set forth his line of reasoning in a private letter to the
O'Gorman Mahon in February 1882:

Do you remember my telling you a few weeks ago that the
Cabinet had discussed Home Rule, and were prepared to admit to
modifications of it in their Programme? From Mr. Gladstone's
Speech on last (Thursday) night you have the Principle conceded
although he quibbles as usual about Details. What a clever
electioneering agent he is! What a sop to Cerberus he threw! He
evidently thinks he can fill the Mouths of the Home Rulers with
this hope, stop them baying for the rest of the Session and make
them follow him docilely into the Division Lobby. The Bradlaugh
defeat brought Home Rule within the scope of 'practical politics'
but let Home Rulers beware—Agitation of a most violent and
revolutionary kind did not affect their purpose so fully as this one
defeat—Show Gladstone that he can be driven from office and he
will evolve anything they like from his 'inner consciousness'! . . .
their only chance is of opposing every measure he brings forward
and rendering themselves not alone dangerous but intolerant to
him.[3]

A picture of unrelieved antagonism between Home Rulers
and Gladstone according to which the Irish had but a single

[1] T. P. O'Connor, *Memoirs*, i. 171.
[2] Cited in *N.R.*, 13 May 1883, p. 359.
[3] Mahon MSS., file 11, fol. 2.

interest, to defeat the Liberal Ministry, would, however, be very wide of the mark. T. P. O'Connor does indeed record his recollection that during these years 'all communication between our Party and English colleagues in the House of Commons was cut off by absolute boycott',[1] but memory plays him false.

There was first of all no lack of volunteer emissaries—Henry Labouchere, Joseph Chamberlain, and the then unknown Mrs. O'Shea among them. Secondly, direct communications did not cease completely. Not only did twenty professed Home Rulers continue to receive the Liberal Whip as late as 1885,[2] but many men who did not receive the Whip, like the O'Gorman Mahon, retained their ties with the Liberal party. When a Post Office position fell vacant in County Clare in August 1881 the Government asked Mahon to make a nomination. Earlier that year his advice in a similar matter had not been heeded, and he protested vehemently. 'After having for upwards of sixty years given unswerving support both in and out of the House to the Liberal party' he deemed it unjust for his wishes to be ignored.[3]

Interestingly enough, this same attitude carried over into certain political questions. When the question of placing limits upon the length of debate stirred the House of Commons in 1882, Mahon—completely ignoring the fact that it was Irish obstruction which had made this a pressing issue—wrote dispassionately to Parnell in favour of a change of Parliamentary rules:

The Question of 'La Clôture' is before the House—My Knowledge of its beneficial working in Foreyn [*sic*] Senates disposes me to support the proposition. It will be carried despite the opposition of the Tory party—which naturally enough would & does aim at obtaining the support of the Home Rulers! but the Tory party is in irreconcilable antagonism to the idea of an Irish administration in any shape or form however as are also many of the Whigs, but from the Liberals guided by the pronouncements already uttered by Mr. Gladstone there is a gleam of hope . . . .[4]

Eventually the Home-Rulers did give at least half-hearted

[1] T. P. O'Connor, *Memoirs*, i. 226.   [2] G.P. (B.M.), 44631, fol. 117.
[3] Mahon MSS., file 10, fols. 13, 7.   [4] Ibid., file 11, fol. 2.

support to Gladstone on this issue, a decision that caused some Conservatives to speak of an 'unholy alliance'.[1]

The fact of the matter is that the Irish party was not as monolithic as it seemed during these years—the number who supported Parnell on all occasions varied from year to year— nor did the Liberal Government view the Irish party as an un- mixed evil. After Irish obstruction and Land League violence had reached a high point in 1881, there was a trend toward conciliation in 1882. After several months in Kilmainham Jail, Parnell was released in May 1882 on the understanding that if the Government would provide for some 100,000 Irish tenant farmers who owed large arrears in rent, he in turn would co-operate cordially for the future with the Liberal party in forwarding Liberal principles and measures of general reform'.[2] The so-called Kilmainham Treaty was im- mediately marred by the murder in Phoenix Park, Dublin, of Lord Frederick Cavendish, the newly named Chief Secretary for Ireland, and his Under-Secretary. Yet what may be termed 'the spirit of Kilmainham' continued to prevail to a degree. Immediately after the Phoenix Park murders, indeed, Parnell, who was not in any sense responsible for them, made to Gladstone the astonishing offer to resign his leadership of the Irish party should the Liberal Prime Minister deem it desirable.[3]

Gladstone turned down the offer and during the following two-and-a-half years the Irish Question subsided somewhat. In January 1883 Lord Granville privately wrote to Gladstone of Parnell's 'somewhat conciliatory course'.[4] Gladstone himself considered Irish support for Liberal candidates in English constituencies uncertain but worth cultivating;[5] and while Parnell remained to him a sphinx, he confided to his Private Secretary in 1883 that the Irish leader 'probably works for & with the law as far as he dare, & . . . possibly does not in his heart of hearts hate the Govt.'[6] Of the conduct of the Irish party, noted one of Gladstone's secretaries in

[1] Cited in Hamilton Diary (B.M.), 48633, p. 25.
[2] J. L. Garvin, *The Life of Joseph Chamberlain*, i (London, 1932), 369.
[3] G.P. (B.M.), 44269, fol. 42.
[4] Ibid. 44175, fol. 25.
[5] Ibid. 44546, fol. 47.
[6] Hamilton Diary (B.M.), 48634, p. 10.

March 1884, 'there has been little to complain lately'.[1] Nor was the Conservative press loath to contrast time and again Gladstone's almost 'effusive' treatment of co-operative Irish M.P.s with his hostility toward the Tories. In October 1883 the Conservative *Saturday Review* wrote disdainfully of 'vigorous co-operation' between the two groups.[2] A chart prepared for Gladstone listing the 'important divisions' on which the Parnellites had voted against the Government showed none in 1880 and 1881, only one in 1882, two each in 1883 (including the Affirmation Bill) and 1884, and five in 1885.[3] Our conclusion must be that since Irish M.P.s did so often disagree with one another and since the hostility of the Parnellites to the Government was hardly unvarying, neither political necessity nor tactics dictated unremitting Irish opposition to Bradlaugh's admission to Parliament.

The ultimate explanation for that opposition must therefore be sought in religious feeling. That such sentiments were strong among numerous Irish M.P.s had become apparent during the spring of 1880 and remained obvious thereafter. Frank Hugh O'Donnell solemnly assured the House of Commons that 'though he was a Catholic, he would sooner that Englishmen remained Protestants, that Catholicity made no inch of progress for another century . . . than that they enter the filthy abyss opened to them by the head of Her Majesty's Government'.[4] Comparable references to their religion were made by numerous Irish M.P.s during the Affirmation Bill debate. Observing that Catholics continued to be ineligible for a number of public positions, A. H. Bellingham went on to insist that 'nine out of every ten Catholics in the country would prefer that those disabilities should continue, and that there should be even backward legislation of a penal character, than that this Affirmation Bill should become law'.[5]

The sincerity of such attitudes may well be accepted, Although the relationship between the Home-Rule party and the Catholic hierarchy in Ireland, and even more the Catholic

---

[1] Hamilton Diary (B.M.), 48635, p. 136.
[2] *Saturday Review*, 27 May 1882, p. 651; 6 Oct. 1883, p. 419.
[3] J. L. Hammond, *Gladstone and the Irish Nation* (London, 1938), p. 313.
[4] *Hansard*, cclxvi (1882), 91. [5] Ibid. cclxxviii (1883), 1615.

hierarchy in England, was frequently an ambiguous one, there were close ties between numerous Irish M.P.s and the Church. Two M.P.s held the title of Private Chamberlain to the Pope. A public meeting of an organization such as the Westminster Diocesan Education Fund Committee would usually find a number of Irish M.P.s on the platform. Cardinal Manning continued to be a frequent visitor to the House of Commons gallery and lobby.[1] In August 1881 some forty Irish Nationalist M.P.s signed the following memorial to Cardinal Manning: 'We gladly avail ourselves of this opportunity of renewing for ourselves and for our country the expression of that profound reverence and affectionate regard which it has so often been to us a pleasure and a duty to testify to your Eminence, whose words of wise counsel and tender sympathy are always gratefully esteemed by the Irish people.'[2] Small wonder that Cardinal Manning could write complacently to Archbishop Croke of Dublin that same year: 'I think I can safely say that the Irish people were never more reasonably religious than they are today, and as a rule so thoroughly devoted to their clergy.'[3]

Does this imply that T. P. O'Connor, Joseph Biggar, O'Connor Power, John Barry, and other Irish M.P.s who had supported Bradlaugh in 1880—including Parnell himself—all underwent a religious conversion during the year that followed? Such a supposition is, to say the very least, unlikely. Parnell's relationship with the Catholic hierarchy in England remained a delicate one. He might dare offend the bishops in particular instances and even seek anti-clerical support, yet he always retained numerous clerical adherents and he was well satisfied to have a priest on the platform at every Land League meeting.[4] Parnell's overt defence of Bradlaugh, moreover, antedated both Mannings's public intervention in the case and the widely publicized petitions against the Affirmation Bill signed by every Catholic bishop in England and Ireland.

[1] Cf. *Tablet*, 18 June 1881, p. 972; Barry O'Brien, *Parnell* (London, 1899), ii. 8.

[2] Cited in the *Rock*, 12 Aug. 1881, p. 569.

[3] Cited in Shane Leslie, *Henry Edward Manning: His Life and Labours* (London, 1921), p. 385.

[4] O'Brien, *Parnell and his Party*, p. 54.

Parnell's relationship with the Church reached a low point in the spring of 1881 when he solicited the support of Parisian radicals like Victor Hugo and Clemenceau and went so far as to disparage the authority of the Pope.[1] One Irishman predicted at the time: 'I cannot foretell Parnell's future, but it strikes me he has enlisted new friends . . . whose adherence will bring ruin to his cause—else he must crush the Priests.'[2] But Parnell had no intention to 'crush the Priests'. Archbishop Croke, who saw Parnell as 'one of the greatest benefactors of the Irish people',[3] never broke with the man until the divorce case, and in the course of 1882 and 1883 the relationship improved so much that bishops and priests cooperated with the laity in collecting a testimonial fund on Parnell's behalf.[4] If Parnell was not the man to speak freely of his religious feelings, he appears to have been a realist about religion. Ultimately he could not afford to antagonize the Catholic Church outright on an issue on which it had taken so determined a stand as the Affirmation Bill, especially if the cause at stake did not seem worth the bother. There was involved, moreover, not only Parnell's relationship with the Catholic hierarchy but also his relationship with his own supporters. 'The silliest of all the ignorant legends that have gathered about Parnell's name', wrote his associate William O'Brien, 'is that of his scornful masterfulness in dealing with his own lieutenants.'[5] He had to take them into account. Parnell had convinced himself that the Irish cause dictated the staunchest opposition to Bradlaugh—he had no further hesitations and no apparent regrets. For as the most prominent of the biographers of Parnell has recognized, in his dealings with the English 'morality was the last thing he thought of . . .'.[6]

Most of the Parliamentary colleagues who had shared Parnell's pro-Bradlaugh stand in 1880 accepted his reversal of position, though some had subsequent misgivings. T. P. O'Connor, for example, devotes several pages of his

---

[1] *Saturday Review*, 5 Mar. 1881, p. 298.   [2] Mahon MSS., file 8, fol. 10.
[3] Cited in *Tablet*, 16 Apr. 1881, p. 616.
[4] Barry O'Brien, *Parnell*, ii. 23; St. John Ervine, *Parnell* (Harmondsworth, 1944), p. 162.
[5] William O'Brien, *The Parnell of Real Life* (London, 1926), p. 59.
[6] Barry O'Brien, *Parnell*, ii. 32.

memoirs to the early months of the Bradlaugh case—the time he was defending Bradlaugh's rights—while non-committally dismissing the subsequent five years as a 'long and very discreditable conflict'.[1] T. M. Healy, a frequent advocate of church interests throughout a volatile career, confided to a fellow passenger on an Atlantic crossing that his views on religion differed little from Bradlaugh's, but that since he represented 'a priest-ridden constituency' he was obliged to attack the representative of Northampton. When Bradlaugh reported the incident in his weekly journal, Healy denounced the report as 'a series of falsehoods'.[2] Healy appeared thereafter to take even greater relish in attacking Bradlaugh, yet how different was his tone when he looked back on one of the incidents of the case in his autobiography many years later. 'With the frame of a giant and the courage of a lion he [Bradlaugh] resisted. I thought his agony dreadful and felt that the police would not have handled any Irishman so ungently as that lone, friendless Englishman.'[3]

While *United Ireland* faithfully opposed the Affirmation Bill, the tone of its articles indicates a certain mock reserve. It described the bill as one of those measures 'on which you can always reckon upon patriots, dead as logs on other questions, to blaze up'. To be sure, the journal added cryptically, the bill was one 'on which all sorts of Irish members happen to agree'.[4]

At least one prominent Home Ruler did not agree, but even Michael Davitt was fully consious of clerical displeasure. A letter Davitt wrote in January, 1883, is enlightening :

. . . The Halifax meeting was—organized by—friends of—Mr. Bradlaugh ! ! ! !
I expect the calling of a Vatican Council after that, in order to pronounce on my conduct. The meeting was a success and a most interesting one, as numerous questions were put me by Englishmen—one being a reference to Irish M.P.s voting against Bradlaugh. I declared that *I* would have voted for him, had I been a M.P., inasmuch as he was fairly elected.[5]

---

[1] T. P. O'Connor, *Memoirs*, i. 44, 74.
[2] Cited in *N.R.*, 12 Mar. 1882, p. 209; *N.R.*, 2 Apr. 1882, p. 273.
[3] T. M. Healy, *Letters and Leaders of My Day* (New York, 1929), i. 167.
[4] *United Ireland*, 28 Apr. 1883, p. 5.
[5] The reference in the Davitt MSS. was kindly supplied by Professor T. W. Moody, Trinity College, Dublin.

All this demonstrates, not that Parnell was in any sense a tool of the Catholic hierarchy, but that he and all other Irish Nationalist M.P.s had to keep the hierarchy in mind in their calculations, so that if on some issues they offended the Church, they might redress the balance with occasional favours. The almost unanimous opposition to Bradlaugh after 1880 would appear to have been one such favour, especially since it could plausibly, if inappropriately, be defended on the basis of other motives as well, not least of party unity. The hierarchy, in any case, was properly appreciative:

But, after all [ran a *Tablet* editorial], it is the Irish members to whom the laurels are due, and English Catholics may well be gratefully mindful that it was Irish voices and Irish votes which chiefly prevented atheism from having a share in English law-giving. . . . In whatever else divided, in the face of aggressive atheism Ireland is true to herself, and her members are as one.[1]

The significance of the religious factor is confirmed by the actions of the Irish Liberals. An analysis of the Liberal vote indicates that on thirteen key roll calls 73 per cent. of English Liberals tended to favour Bradlaugh's admission, an attitude characteristic also of 71 per cent. of the Welsh Liberals and 64 per cent. of the Scottish Liberals, but of only 7 per cent. of the Irish Liberals. Characteristically, only one of fourteen Irish Liberals supported Gladstone on the Affirmation Bill—the others either abstained or opposed—and Robert Dyer Lyons, a Liberal M.P. from Dublin, was among the most vocal of Bradlaugh's opponents. Irish Home-Rule opposition, especially when thus abetted by the Irish Liberals, could and did hold the balance of power. Bradlaugh had never succeeded in establishing a permanent branch of the National Secular Society in Ireland, and observing the agitation against the Affirmation Bill on the part of Roman Catholic churches, Orange lodges, Protestant Episcopal dioceses, and Land League leaders, he wrote depairingly: 'The movement in Ireland against the Affirmation Bill at least shews that there is something on which Irishmen can unite.'[2]

---

[1] *Tablet*, 12 May 1883, p. 721.   [2] *N.R.*, 9 Apr. 1883, p. 225.

XX

'THE GRAVE ALONE...'

'I f I am not fit for my constituents', Bradlaugh had told the assembled House of Commons in February 1882, 'they shall dismiss me, but you never shall. The grave alone shall make me yield.' Now another sixteen months had passed. The much-vaunted Affirmation Bill had been taken up by the Gladstone Ministry and supported by the Prime Minister himself in one of his most eloquent speeches. Bradlaugh had at long last felt certain of victory, only to see the bill go down to defeat amidst the frenzied cheers of the Opposition. It was enough to dishearten even the most persistent of men, but Bradlaugh was not daunted.

The bill had been defeated during the early morning hours of 4 May—Ascension Day, as a number of religious journals were smugly to observe—and not many hours thereafter Speaker Brand found Charles Bradlaugh at his door with an announcement and a request. He was once more prepared to enter the House of Commons by taking the appropriate oath of allegiance, and, at the very least, he hoped to have the opportunity of addressing the House of Commons again. The Speaker, who only two days earlier had noted that 'the Bradlaugh cloud . . . hangs over the House like a pall', was not unsympathetic. Whatever perplexities the famous iconoclast had caused him in his official position, the Speaker was aware that Bradlaugh had always done his best to remain on civil terms with him.[1] 'Mr. Bradlaugh is in a humble frame of mind', wrote the Speaker to Gladstone. He was, however, most anxious to have another chance to speak before the House. If he were given that chance and dealt with fairly,

---

[1] Brand to Gladstone, 2 May 1883, G.P. (B.M.) 44195, fol. 158. Brand had written the following note to Bradlaugh earlier that year: 'I am sincerely obliged to you for your expression of respect towards myself and you may be assured that every step which I have taken from first to last with respect to your position has been dictated by a sense of duty to the House, & from no personal motive towards yourself.' Hampden MSS.

perhaps he would not prove too much of an irritant for the rest of the session.[1]

Shortly after the session began at 2 p.m. on 4 May Bradlaugh as often before advanced down the aisle to the Speaker's Table, only to be met by the now traditional motion on the part of Sir Stafford Northcote that he be not allowed to go through the form of the oath. Bradlaugh was, however, permitted to address the assembly from the bar, a point of vantage he now occupied for the fourth time and had made uniquely his own.

He began to speak in a low tone, explaining carefully why he had made no attempt to take his seat since his last election in March 1882. He had waited patiently in the hope of seeing the Affirmation Bill pass. He claimed as always, however, the right—indeed the duty—of doing whatever was necessary towards becoming a fully-fledged Member of Parliament. Speaking with 'a touch of pathos',[2] Bradlaugh sought to rebut some of the many personal attacks he had been forced to endure without chance of reply during the past two weeks of debate. He had never paraded his religious views in the House, he insisted, although 'Members have been industrious in reading all the things I have ever written, and some things I have never written'. At the very least, he suggested, let the House be 'logical'. On the one hand it refused him his seat, on the other hand it did not challenge his right to be elected M.P. Either let the House declare his seat vacant at once or else let it introduce a bill disqualifying him from the right to represent any constituency. He ended on a note of dignified appeal. Lord Randolph Churchill had stated, observed Bradlaugh, that both sides had gone too far to recede. Bradlaugh disagreed.

The House honours me too much in putting me on one side and itself on the other. The House being strong should be generous. The strong can recede; the generous can give. But constituencies have a right to more than generosity. They have a right to justice. The law gives me that seat; in the name of the law I ask for it. I regret that my personality overshadows the principles involved in this question. But I would ask those who

[1] Hampden Diary, entry for 4 May 1883, G.P. (B.M.), 44195, fol. 160.
[2] London *Daily Telegraph*, 5 May 1883, cited in *N.R.*, 13 May 1883, p. 358.

9. *Bradlaugh at the Bar of the House of Commons* (Walter Sickert)

10. Cardinal Manning and Charles Stewart Parnell

have touched my right, not knowing it; who have found for me vices which I do not remember in the memory of my life—I would ask them whether all can afford to cast the first stone—or whether, condemning me justly for my unworthiness, they will, as just Judges, vacate their own seats, having deprived my constituents of their right here to mine?[1]

The speech was regarded, even by opponents, as a praiseworthy example of rhetoric. The moderately sympathetic *Daily News* considered it 'admirable'; the highly sympathetic *Scotsman* felt certain it would have 'its place in history'. Even *United Ireland*, the Parnellite organ, conceded that the speech was marked by 'great ability' and 'considering the circumstances, by great moderation'.[2] Yet it remains dubious whether the oration changed a single vote. Labouchere countered Northcote's motion by moving 'the previous question', but after several hours of debate, his motion was defeated by a decisive margin, 271 to 165. The majority was made up of 212 Conservatives, 38 Home Rulers, and 21 Liberals. The minority was confined solely to Liberals. Refusing to heed the pleas of his advisers, Gladstone considered himself and his Cabinet bound to support Labouchere, thus falling victim to a 'further & more crushing defeat' than that of the night before.[3]

The Affirmation Bill and its aftermath remained in the news throughout the rest of May as the victors congratulated one another and as Liberal Party chieftains debated whether or not some other legislative measure might infuse new spirit into the demoralized supporters of the Government.[4] The ranks of the victors too were briefly upset, however, when Lord Randolph Churchill decided to clinch the victory already won by giving notice of a motion to add a paragraph to the Standing Orders of the House of Commons. Henceforth 'any person who has claimed to make a solemn affirmation in lieu of taking the said Oath, shall not be afterwards

[1] *Hansard*, cclxxviii (1883), 1844–51.
[2] *United Ireland*, 12 May 1883, p. 3; London *Daily News* and *Scotsman* cited in *N.R.*, 13 May 1883, pp. 356, 358.
[3] Hamilton Diary (B.M.), 48633, p. 190.
[4] Cf. Hamilton Diary (B.M.), 48633, p. 199; G.P. (B.M.), 44130, fol. 247; 44189, fol. 220.

permitted to take & subscribe the said Oath, except only by a Resolution of the House after due notice in that behalf'. Such a resolution, if passed, would bind not merely a single session of Parliament but all future Parliaments as well and would bar Bradlaugh from taking the oath at any time thereafter. Bradlaugh's colleague, Henry Labouchere, immediately gave notice of a substitute motion: 'That this House is not prepared to limit the present rights of Constituencies to be represented in future parliaments by persons who have been properly elected, and who are not disqualified from sitting and voting by the Law.'[1]

Northcote, whose relations with the insubordinate Lord Randolph were then even more strained than usual, was very much perturbed. What if Labouchere's substitute motion carried? Would this not wipe out the glory of the Affirmation Bill triumph? Since Churchill was unwilling to listen to him, Northcote pleaded with Salisbury to try to dissuade the party maverick. Salisbury replied politely that he doubted whether his own influence over Churchill was greater than Northcote's, but he did agree that 'it would be a great pity to spoil your victory by courting an unnecessary defeat'. Salisbury did nothing more, however, until Cardinal Manning also pleaded with him to restrain Churchill from reopening the Bradlaugh question in a form 'most disadvantageous to us, and most advantageous to Mr. Labouchere & his friends'. A number of Liberals and several Irish members who had opposed the Affirmation Bill had explained to Manning that they would vote in favour of Labouchere's amendment. Thus 'the work of the majority & all its influence in the country would be reversed'. Salisbury took due notice of Manning's fears, and working through his nephew Arthur Balfour he succeeded in prevailing upon Churchill to withdraw his motion.[2] Sir Henry Drummond Wolff and several other Tory stalwarts regretted that Churchill's motion should have been 'sacrificed to the

[1] See Churchill to Northcote, 15 May 1883, Iddesleigh MSS. (B.M.), 50021, fol. 86.
[2] See Northcote to Salisbury, 11 May 1883, Salisbury MSS.; Salisbury to Northcote, 13 May 1883, Iddesleigh MSS. (B.M.), 50020, fols. 57–59; Manning to Salisbury, 26 May 1883; Balfour to Salisbury, 28 May 1883, Salisbury MSS.; Shane Leslie, *Manning*, pp. 318–19.

jealousy of some of our mediocrities',[1] but Sir Stafford North-cote was vastly relieved. While touring the country later that year, he was time and again presented with addresses of con-gratulation for his 'noble stand' against the atheist. At Cardiff in November he called upon men of all religions to stand 'side by side and fight the great battle which has to be fought —the battle of Christianity and religion against Infidelity'.[2]

For Manning the Affirmation Bill triumph had long since turned sour. It was during the week prior to the decisive vote on the Affirmation Bill that the *Daily News* had published a one-line paragraph: 'We hear that Cardinal Newman has declined to join in any action against the Affirmation Bill.' The probable source of the paragraph was a hint to the editors by Malcolm MacColl, an Anglican clergyman who strongly favoured the Affirmation Bill and who, after an exchange of letters, had correctly concluded that Newman shared his views at least in part. Newman had first expressed his doubts two years earlier whether the Catholic Church ought even to take a stand on the issue: 'As far as I can see', he had written privately, 'Catholics cannot, to any good effect, bring out a really strong protest on the subject without being open to the retort, "Why, what right have you to speak? You would be nowhere but for the Act of 1829 in your favour, and now you grudge for others what you have got for yourselves."'[3] Yet Newman had cautioned MacColl not to publicize his doubts lest they dampen the genuine religious sentiments the anti-Affirmation Bill campaign had been arousing.

For Catholics the paragraph was, however, a minor bomb-shell, sufficient to deter at least one Irish M.P. from speaking against the bill 'from a Catholic point of view'.[4] There was consternation in Manning's office, and the Conservative *Morning Post* and the *Tablet* hastened to counteract the impression created. 'With reference to a statement which appeared in the *Daily News* we are authorised to state that his Eminence Cardinal Newman does not in any way approve of the Government Affirmation Bill.'[5]

[1] Wolff to Salisbury, 1 June 1883, Salisbury MSS.
[2] Cited in *N.R.*, 14 Oct. 1883, p. 248; 18 Nov. 1883, p. 330.
[3] (Draft) Newman to Father Lockhart, 25 Sept. 1881, Newman MSS.
[4] Henry Bellingham to Newman, 26 Apr. 1883, Newman MSS.
[5] *Tablet*, 5 May 1883, p. 686.

Since there is no evidence that Newman *had* authorized this second paragraph, he obviously disliked having it taken as his last word on the subject. And when, a few days after the Affirmation Bill had been defeated, a Protestant layman sought a clarification of Newman's views, the Cardinal did not merely oblige with a detailed reply but consented to its publication:

I cannot consider the Affirmation Bill involves a religious principle; for, as I had occasion to observe in print more than thirty years ago, what the political and social world means by the word 'God' is too often not the Christian God, the Jewish, or the Mahometan—not a Personal God, but an unknown God—as little what Christians mean by God as the Fate, Chance, or Anima Mundi of a Greek philosopher.

Hence it little concerns Religion whether Mr. Bradlaugh swears by no God with the Government, or swears by an Impersonal, or Material, or Abstract and Ideal Something or other, which is all that is secured to us by the Opposition . . . .

. . . Looking at the [Affirmation] Bill on its merits, I think nothing is lost to Religion by its passing, and nothing gained by its being rejected.[1]

When two weeks later the *Manchester Examiner* in a closely reasoned article surmised that if Newman had been an active politician rather than an octogenarian sage in semi-retirement his position would have been identical with Gladstone's, Newman wrote a letter of appreciation to its editor.[2]

Manning's feelings may well be imagined. It was not the first time he and Newman had clashed; but the *Tablet* was outraged. It looked upon Newman's views 'with a deep and lasting regret'. In his long retirement, maintained the *Tablet*, Newman had lost touch with the feeling of the nation and he had now poured cold water upon the revival of the religious spirit which the Affirmation Bill battle had evoked.[3] Yet the Newman papers make clear that a considerable number of Catholic clergy and laymen shared the Cardinal's views, notwithstanding the impression of monolithic unity which Manning had so carefully cultivated. One self-

---

[1] (Draft) Newman to F. W. Chesson, 8 May 1883, Newman MSS. Reprinted in *N.R.* of 21 May 1883, and elsewhere.

[2] *Manchester Examiner*, 21 May 1883. Clipping in Newman MSS.

[3] *Tablet*, 19 May 1883, p. 761.

described 'humble Catholic' even went so far as to charge the entire Catholic clergy as 'guilty of great injustice in joining the hue and cry after Mr. Bradlaugh'.[1] Newman hastened to assure the correspondent that he had no personal knowledge of Bradlaugh and had confined himself to general principles when giving his views on the matter.

After Newman's intervention, the anti-Bradlaugh crusade lost its savour for Manning. For Manning, though his gifts lay in the world of practical church politics rather than in literary eloquence, had always envied Newman's graceful style and his reputation for philosophical detachment. The predominant note in Manning's next pastoral letter to the clergy and laity of Westminster was one of gloom rather than triumph. 'You have lately asked of those who make our laws that none should legislate for us except those who believe there is a Divine lawgiver Whose law is supreme. But it seems as if we are being carried down a stream against which we cannot prevail, and from which there is no escape.' Although Manning later denied that his pastoral letter had been motivated by Newman's stand, it none the less ended his active participation in the anti-Bradlaugh crusade.[2]

Cardinal Manning's discomfiture was of no immediate advantage to Bradlaugh. The summer of 1883 could not but be a frustrating one for him. Almost all possible means of redress had already been tried. A campaign of petitions in favour of his cause had successfully raised over one hundred and fifty thousand signatures in 1881 and again in 1882 and 1883, but the religiously inspired anti-Affirmation Bill campaign of 1883 had altogether overwhelmed the efforts of his own supporters, and during the summer of 1883 Bradlaugh asked his petitioners to cease their work for the time being.[3] Bradlaugh might menace his Parliamentary opponents with defeat at the next general election—especially those 'sham Liberals' who had voted against him—but if it was indeed 'public feeling in the constituencies' which, according to The Times, had caused these Liberals to vote as they did then such threats of political revenge would have little effect.

[1] Joseph P. Devine to Newman, 23 May 1883, Newman MSS.
[2] Tablet, 26 May 1883, p. 832; Manning to Ullathorne, 17 May 1883, Manning MSS.   [3] N.R., 7 Sept. 1884, p. 161.

The fact that a general election was not in the immediate offing weakened them even further.[1] In the summer of 1881, when a similar feeling of frustration had gripped Bradlaugh's supporters, Annie Besant had proposed the issue of an ultimatum. Unless Bradlaugh were admitted within two-and-a-half months, all his followers would cease to consume alcoholic beverages and snuff in order to injure Tory brewers and publicans, and, indirectly, the tax income of the Government. When the Government promised to aid Bradlaugh during the session to come, the proposal was dropped, and because of Bradlaugh's own doubts as to its practicality it was not revived.[2]

There remained the possibility of revolution, but while Bradlaugh from time to time uttered remarks hinting at violence, he publicly condemned the possibility. An occasional supporter might suggest that the situation called for another Cromwell, or perhaps another Pride's Purge, but Bradlaugh dissented. 'To use physical force effectively and successfully', he replied to one offer of military assistance by members of volunteer regiments, 'means revolution. . . . No man should even contemplate revolution, unless he is reasonably certain that he can make and sustain a better government than the one he destroys.' Bradlaugh was faced with an impossible dilemma, and in an open letter to Northcote, he frankly confessed this: 'If I succeeded by physical force in overcoming the unlawful force you are weak enough now to rely on, I should still further, and perhaps irreparably, damage the reputation of that Parliament, respect to which I have always, long ere I was a member of it, sought to inculcate.'[3]

What possibilities remained? The most obvious was to appeal once again to public opinion and to hold a series of meetings throughout the kingdom climaxed by another Trafalgar Square demonstration in London. Observing how often he was misrepresented in the public press, Bradlaugh admitted that 'it makes me a little despair of convincing my

---

[1] *The Times* cited in *N.R.*, 2 Sept. 1883, p. 151. See also *N.R.*, 31 Dec. 1882, p. 483; 15 July 1883, p. 33.
[2] *N.R.*, 29 May 1881, p. 436; 21 Aug. 1881, p. 195.
[3] *N.R.*, 20 May 1883, p. 379; 22 July 1883, p. 57; 30 Sept. 1883, p. 210.

antagonists by any ordinary use of reason'. Yet he remained as certain as ever that 'it is only by constantly agitating public opinion that victory can be won'.[1] At the very least he could refute the *Daily Telegraph* when it referred to 'the absence of anything like wide-spread agitation on behalf of Mr. Brad-laugh's claim', the London *Standard* when it declared that 'Mr. Bradlaugh has proved a wet squib', and the *Saturday Review* when it dismissed Bradlaugh's supporters as 'a strag-gling and harmless little mob'.[2]

The new campaign was launched with a manifesto entitled: 'May the House of Commons Commit Treason? An Appeal to the People.' Bradlaugh's answer was a defiant 'yes'. In disregarding the votes lawfully given in a free con-stituency and his own unimpeached election returns, 'the House of Commons has been guilty of treason against the Constitution'. Like John Wilkes one hundred years earlier, he had been deprived of his rightful seat in Parliament and like John Wilkes he intended to make the House of Com-mons admit that his exclusion was 'subversive of the rights of the whole body of the electors of this kingdom'. It was the analogy of his case to that of Wilkes which Bradlaugh tended to stress much more often than any resemblance to the prob-lems of O'Connell or Rothschild. Admittedly he did not resemble Wilkes in every way. 'John Wilkes had private fortune, he had rich and titled friends. I have no fortune and my friends are amongst the poor.'[3]

Both his friends and his enemies regarded Bradlaugh as a man of the people. 'The people', to be sure, were envisaged in diverse ways. To one of the anonymous pamphleteers who attacked Bradlaugh 'the people' consisted of 'cobblers of acrid aspect, dogmatic tailors, restless clerks, and unspeak-able ragtag'. To another, they were 'the low grovelling class'. To the *Country Gentleman* they represented 'the great unwashed and rowdy element in the land'.[4] The Reverend

---

[1] *N.R.*, 16 Oct. 1881, p. 323; 29 June 1884, p. 505.

[2] Cited respectively in *N.R.*, 22 May 1881, p. 410; 16 July 1882, p. 36; and 2 Sept. 1883, p. 145.

[3] *N.R.*, 27 May 1883, p. 385; 8 May 1881, p. 369.

[4] Anonymous, *Otherwise: Or Quite Another Tack* (London, 1882 [?]), p. 13; Anonymous, *John Bull's Family Affairs* (London, 1882), p. 13; *Country Gentleman* cited in *N.R.*, 3 Sept. 1882, p. 170.

C. Williams, one of Bradlaugh's Anglican sympathizers, regarded Bradlaugh's exclusion as a grievance especially among the working classes, while John Morley's *Pall Mall Gazette* on one occasion depicted his exclusion as 'the proscription by an upper-class Assembly of a self-made man who is going to tell them some disagreeable truths'.[1] Bradlaugh obviously was very much a self-made man though not literally of working-class origin. He very much liked to be thought of, however, as 'a man of the people', and he certainly had greater claim to the title than had the vast majority of Members of Parliament.

Bradlaugh had his own special vision of 'the people'. Their clothes were not expected to be fashionable but clean. They were expected to assert their constitutional rights but to do so in a disciplined and well-behaved manner at public meetings. They were not expected to have a lengthy formal education but to be sufficiently self-educated to be able to understand the *National Reformer*. They were expected, in any case, to take advantage of whatever educational opportunities were offered to them, and nothing made Bradlaugh prouder than to have a government school inspector testify to 'the hearty co-operation of the burgesses and particularly the working classes of Northampton, in carrying into effect the provisions of the Education Act'.[2] 'The people' were expected to be individualists who had saved small sums weekly to buy their own houses, independent artisans who might organize together into societies and co-operatives but whose ultimate resource remained 'self-help' rather than private—or government—patronage. 'The people', moreover, were expected to adopt middle-class social customs just as Bradlaugh himself had done. Bradlaugh was conscious of class distinctions, but he believed that persons of every rank ought to be treated in identical fashion. If it was courteous to remove one's hat when speaking to a lady, then it was equally appropriate when addressing a maidservant. The one personal memory of Bradlaugh which Alderman Percy Adams of Northampton retains—he was ten at the time of

[1] C. Williams, *Reasons for the Affirmation Bill becoming Law* (London, 1883), p. 30; *Pall Mall Gazette* cited in *N.R.*, 12 Mar. 1882, p. 237.
[2] Cited in *N.R.*, 7 May 1882, p. 362.

Bradlaugh's death—is that the great iconoclast always lifted his hat when greeting his grandfather's maid, a custom observed by almost no one else.[1] 'The people' for Bradlaugh were a working class striving to adopt middle-class ideals and social customs, thus creating a classless society which preserved neither legal nor social privilege.

There were meetings in Northampton, in Leeds, in Stockton, in Carlisle, and in many other cities. By 11 June 1883 Bradlaugh was able to report on them to Gladstone: 'As the London press prefers to support the view that public feeling is against me in my parliamentary struggle I beg to report that since the rejection of the affirmation bill, I have addressed various meetings & that in all of these the decision has been either unanimously against my illegal exclusion from my seat or that the dissentients at most have been the very smallest minority.'

There were 2,000 people present at many of these meetings, 6,000 at others, and over 30,000 at one outdoor meeting in the north of England. 'These meetings', Bradlaugh went on, somewhat plaintively, 'are almost entirely ignored by the London press—I shall continue these meetings as long as my strength permits in all the great centres of population for I am sure that the manufactured majority of petition signatures does not represent the real feeling of the country.—My only excuse for intruding this on you is that my fight is a very difficult one in face of the organized misrepresentation I have to face.'[2]

The campaign came to an end with two gatherings in London. The first was in St. James's Hall in July, with Labouchere as chairman. Bradlaugh pledged again that the struggle would end only when he, a Member of Parliament, moved the expunging of the resolutions of exclusion just as John Wilkes had once done. There followed a Trafalgar Square meeting on 5 August, when London Working Men's clubs such as the Amalgamated Cab Drivers' Society, the Cobden Working Men's Club, the Amalgamated Boot and Shoe Makers' Society, and the Tower Hamlets Radical Club

---

[1] Conversation with Alderman Percy Adams in Northampton, 23 Feb. 1957. See also Besant, *An Autobiography*, pp. 138–9.

[2] G.P. (B.M.), 44111, fols. 134–5.

joined forces with similar groups attracted from Northampton and other parts of England. The provincial groups were aided by railways which offered cheap excursion rates to the capital and by hotelkeepers who advertised 'bed and breakfast 2s. 6d.' in the pages of the *National Reformer*. 'Experience', admitted *The Times*, 'has enabled the managers of these meetings to make their organisation all but perfect.' The Reverend Stewart Headlam presided. The band played the 'Marseillaise' and 'See, the Conquering Hero Comes!' Pictures of Bradlaugh and the Northampton tricolours waved in the breeze together with dozens of placards identifying the various organizations and asking for 'Liberty, Equality, Fraternity' or 'Bradlaugh and Constitutional Rights'. An appropriate resolution was moved on the platform in the centre of the vast assembly. The people roared their unanimous approval, and copies of the resolution were forthwith dispatched to Gladstone, Northcote, the Speaker of the House, and Queen Victoria.[1] Although such meetings produced no immediate rewards for Bradlaugh, they were at least repaid with a public testimonial from Gladstone himself. In the course of an address during August, the Prime Minister agreed that 'a great struggle had been initiated in the country. I am sorry to speak of a great struggle between an individual and the House of Commons; but it is a great and serious struggle, in which every man knows which Party is finally to be the winner ....'[2]

At the same time that this campaign of meetings was going on, Bradlaugh was off on still another tack. He formally announced to the Speaker and to Gladstone on 5 July 1883 that 'in accordance with the requirements of my constituents I beg respectfully to inform you that I shall in compliance with the law at an early date take my seat for the Borough of Northampton'.[3] The publication of this letter caused Northcote to move a new resolution asking the Sergeant-at-Arms to exclude Bradlaugh 'until he undertake not further to disturb the proceedings of the House'. The Conservatives issued an urgent whip, but Gladstone decided to abstain. The

[1] *N.R.*, 5 Aug. 1883, p. 83; 12 Aug. 1883, pp. 98–100.
[2] *Hansard*, cclxxiii (1883), 1529.
[3] G.P. (B.M.), 44111, fol. 137.

result was that the motion was approved 232 to 65, with only a few prominent Liberals such as Chamberlain and Dilke voting with the minority. Bradlaugh thereupon inquired from the Speaker whether taking the oath fell under the heading of 'disturbing the proceedings of the House'. The Speaker replied that in Bradlaugh's case it did, and that Sergeant-at-Arms Gossett had been given orders to keep him out. Bradlaugh thereupon reserved the right 'to offer every resistance in [his] power to this utterly unwarrantable use of force'. He wrote to Gossett directly to the same effect.[1]

Was Bradlaugh planning to storm the ramparts again? Did he have physical violence in mind after all? Bradlaugh spoke portentously on one occasion of 'the graver form which this struggle is likely to assume',[2] and the House of Commons police detail was reinforced. For several weeks there was an extra police guard at the inner door, and special police sentries patrolled the House of Commons lobbies. Innocently passing through the lobby on one occasion to consult some law books in the House of Commons Library, Bradlaugh found himself shadowed like another Guy Fawkes. Bradlaugh derived some amusement from this general concern. His case had at any rate not been forgotten completely. Bradlaugh's immediate purpose in all this had, to be sure, been a rather unmilitant one, to lay the groundwork for yet another legal case, this time against the Sergeant-at-Arms.[3] *Bradlaugh* v. *Gossett* is the title it was to assume in the law books, where it was to join a number of others whose import and significance it will next be our purpose to assay.

[1] Hampden MSS. Also *N.R.*, 15 July 1883, pp. 33–34; 22 July 1883, pp. 49–50.
[2] *N.R.*, 23 Sept. 1883, p. 195.
[3] *N.R.*, 5 Aug. 1883, p. 87; 12 Aug. 1883, p. 101; 19 Aug. 1883, p. 113.

XXI

CHARLES BRADLAUGH AND THE LAW

PERHAPS the most paradoxical aspect of Charles Bradlaugh's multi-faceted career is that this man, customarily honoured as popular leader or feared as disruptive demagogue, also had the mind of a lawyer. He cherished grand principles, yet he was at the same time intimately familiar with—indeed, he delighted in—the complexities and peculiarities of English law. And though the House of Commons remained the major arena of Bradlaugh's parliamentary struggle, there was another—the courts of law. It had been the law courts which Bradlaugh's enemies had employed in 1881 to deprive him of an active role in Parliament. It was the law courts which they used as well in scarcely veiled attempts to drive him into bankruptcy.[1] And it was the law courts which Bradlaugh used in turn in attempts to reverse the judgement of Parliament. It was the law courts also which he employed, one suspects, as a means of keeping his case in the public eye when other means seemed ill-advised, for the courtrooms of his day rivalled the music halls in providing public entertainment.[2] It was the law courts, not least of all, which enabled Bradlaugh to display that unusual degree of self-acquired skill which made him the outstanding amateur lawyer of late-nineteenth-century England. It may well be true, as G. W. Foote suggested long ago,[3] that only an expert lawyer could do full justice to this phase of Bradlaugh's career, but a comprehensive account of the Bradlaugh case requires at least a summary review of the relevant legal cases.

The case of *Clarke* v. *Bradlaugh*, recounted in Chapter X, had resulted in the decision by the Court of Appeal in March 1881 that Bradlaugh had been ineligible to enter the House

[1] Cf. London *Morning Advertiser*, cited in *N.R.*, 14 Aug. 1881, p. 170.
[2] *Times Literary Supplement*, 11 Dec. 1959, p. 720.
[3] G. W. Foote, *Reminiscences of Charles Bradlaugh* (London, 1891), p. 23.

of Commons by means of making an affirmation. Having been rebuffed on his interpretation of how the Oaths Act of 1866 had been amended by subsequent legislation giving the right to affirm to non-believers, Bradlaugh decided not to appeal from this particular decision to the final court of appeal, the House of Lords. The decision in *Clarke* v. *Bradlaugh* had thus deprived him of his seat in Parliament, but Bradlaugh was no means through with the case. Henry Clarke seemed eager, after all, to collect the £500 which came with conviction. According to the relevant Act of Parliament, moreover, Bradlaugh might be sued for £500 on account of each vote he had given in Parliament during 1880–1. This would have amounted to a grand total of £355,000. Bradlaugh hastened to see to it that Joannes Swaagman, one of the National Secular Society's Vice-Presidents, instituted a friendly suit to recover all this vast sum with the exception of the initial £1,000. Even if Clarke were to be successful in winning his £500, no other political enemy could take further financial advantage of him.[1]

Yet the loss of even £500, not to mention the accumulating legal costs, was one which Bradlaugh could ill afford. Was there some other way by which the penalty might be disallowed? Bradlaugh decided on a legal technicality. According to English law, a judicial act must be presumed to have been done at the earliest hour of the day. Under this presumption, argued Bradlaugh, the writ issued against him on 2 July 1880 must have been issued before his first vote in the House of Commons. It was thus invalid. Justice Denman, though congratulating Bradlaugh upon his legal skill, disallowed the argument. 'A legal fiction', he ruled, 'is for the purpose of doing justice, not for defeating it.'[2]

Bradlaugh thereupon tried another tack. He contended that Clarke's suit was invalid because the writ had not only theoretically but actually been issued before Bradlaugh had cast his first vote in Parliament. A jury trial was held to determine the facts. According to the plaintiff's case, Parliament assembled at 2 p.m. on 2 July 1880. As soon as

---

[1] *N.R.*, 15 Oct. 1882, p. 257. A third claimant had sued for the second £500, but the claim was never pressed.
[2] Cited in *N.R.*, 26 June 1881, p. 21.

Bradlaugh cast his first vote, Charles Newdegate, M.P., a friend of the plaintiff who had 'taken care that Mr. Clarke should not be without funds for the purpose of carrying on the litigation which was to determine the question', rushed out of the House and took a cab to his solicitor's office. The solicitor then sent a clerk to obtain the writ. Newdegate thereupon returned to the House of Commons, and when Bradlaugh emerged, Newdegate personally served him with the writ.

Newdegate's obvious involvement in a suit supposedly initiated by Henry Clarke, a one-time surveyor, gave Bradlaugh an opportunity to cross-examine this Parliamentary veteran. Newdegate had been a Member of Parliament since 1843. He had served as Lord Derby's Whip for eleven years at the time when a successful effort was being made to keep Jews out of Parliament. He had strongly opposed the liberalizing Parliamentary Oaths Act of 1866; and during the 1860's and 1870's he had consistently advocated a Parliamentary investigation into Catholic convents in England.[1] As soon as Bradlaugh appeared on the Parliamentary horizon, Newdegate had fastened upon him as his latest *bête noire*. As late as 1880, Newdegate, 'that most respectable representative of defeated causes and exploded fallacies',[2] was considered a possible Conservative candidate for the Speakership of the House.[3] His colleagues admittedly did not flock to hear a Newdegate oration, and when on one occasion in the midst of an anti-Bradlaugh philippic the House of Commons clock unaccountably stopped, there was widespread amusement. Commented *Funny Folks*, one of the rivals of *Punch*:

> *Strange* that the clock stopped during such a speech,
> Nay, whilst a member could such doctrines preach,
> Breathing the spirit of the stake and rack,
> The wonder is the clock did *not go back*![4]

It was not surprising that Bradlaugh should relish the opportunity to interrogate so consistent an enemy. Since the

[1] Childers to Granville, 23 Jan. 1881, Granville MSS. (P.R.O.), file 30/29 fol. 118; see also *N.R.*, 28 Jan. 1883, p. 51.
[2] Northampton *Mercury*, 26 June 1880, p. 5.
[3] *Truth*, 11 Mar. 1880, p. 326.
[4] *Funny Folks*, 18 Feb. 1882.

House of Commons had assembled at 2 p.m. that first day, since the first vote had not taken place until at least two hours later, and since the Writ Office had closed at 4 p.m., Bradlaugh hoped to show that the timetable outlined by the prosecution was impossible. Bradlaugh began his questioning of Newdegate by demonstrating that the latter's memory for details was extremely hazy. The next day the cross-examination resumed:

> Bradlaugh: Have you had any conversation with anyone about this case since you left the Court last night?
> Newdegate: Yes.
> B: With whom?
> N: Several members of the House.
> B: Will you kindly name them?
> N: I spoke to some of the officers.
> B: Name the members first. I will go step by step.
> N: Well upon my honour . . .
> B: You cannot remember?
> N: Oh, yes.
> B: Then, please remember. (After a long pause.) Why do you take so long, sir?
> N: I really forget the names. I wish to be accurate but members usually ask me . . .
> B: Name some members to whom you spoke about this case after quitting the Court.
> N: At this moment, upon my honour, I cannot remember, for I was asked in passing from the Court to the House . . . .[1]

And so it went on. When a clerk from the Writ Office testified that the writ had been obtained at 3.30 p.m., Bradlaugh's case seemed even stronger. The writ must have been issued before the first division in which Bradlaugh participated. Foote considered Bradlaugh's interrogation of Newdegate a 'flaying alive', and even Sir Hardinge Giffard, Clarke's attorney, conceded 'Mr. Newdegate does not, I think, throw much light on the matter'.[2] None the less, the jury eventually held against Bradlaugh. As one juror admitted to a casual bystander: 'No matter what the case was nor what the

---

[1] *N.R.*, 24 July 1881, pp. 101-2. The *National Reformer* reprinted the full stenographic reports of this as of all major legal cases in which Bradlaugh participated.

[2] Foote, *Bradlaugh*, p. 26; *N.R.*, 31 July 1881, p. 134.

evidence, I'd never find a verdict for such a man as Brad-laugh.'[1]

Bradlaugh was disappointed, but not for long. He asked for a new trial on the ground that 'the verdict was against the evidence', and he succeeded in coming up with new evidence as to the precise time of the disputed division. The pages of *Hansard* did not include exact times, but the news bulletin telegrams sent to the major London clubs by the Central Press news service had exact times stamped upon them, and they bore out Bradlaugh's contention that his first vote had been cast after 4 p.m. The Divisional Court granted Bradlaugh a new trial on this basis in December 1881, but the Court of Appeal reversed this decision three months later on a technicality.[2]

Bradlaugh had again been defeated, but he was still not through. For he challenged the *Clarke* v. *Bradlaugh* ruling on another point, a much more fundamental one. Even conceding that Bradlaugh had voted in Parliament without having taken the required oath, was it legal for Henry Clarke, 'a common informer', to sue Bradlaugh or ought the plaintiff to have been the Crown in the person of the Attorney-General? When the Court of Appeal ruled against Bradlaugh's contention that Clarke's suit had been invalid, he appealed to the highest court of all, the House of Lords. The case was heard in March 1883 by the Lord Chancellor and four other lords, the type of body before which Bradlaugh—surprisingly—was at his best. He was less successful before juries, but his skill in legal research and examination almost invariably impressed judges. When he addressed the bench, G. W. Foote observed, 'his whole manner was changed. He was polite, insinuating, and deferential. His attitude towards the judges was admirably calculated to conciliate their favour. I do no meant that *he* calculated. He had quite a superstitious veneration for judges and it never varied.'[3]

The Parliamentary Oaths Act of 1866 stated merely, Bradlaugh maintained, that if an M.P. votes without having taken

[1] Cited in *N.R.*, 7 Aug. 1881, p. 155.
[2] *N.R.*, 7 Aug. 1881, p. 150; 11 Dec. 1881, p. 453; 5 Mar. 1882, p. 179.
[3] Foote, *Bradlaugh*, p. 23.

the appropriate oath, 'he shall for every such offence be subject to a penalty of £500, to be recovered by action in one of
Her Majesty's Superior Courts at Westminster'. No mention is
made of a 'common informer'. Indeed the tendency to make
use of 'common informers' had been steadily diminishing in
English law, and precedent strongly suggested that such
a 'common informer' had no right to legal costs unless the
statute so specified.[1] The court's verdict was announced on
9 April 1883. The Parliamentary Oaths Act of 1866 had not
made it clear whether Parliament intended to give 'common
informers' the right to sue. The grounds for such a suit were
therefore insufficient, and Bradlaugh was upheld in his contention. Not only was he not liable to pay the £500 fine, but
it was Clarke who had to pay the costs of Bradlaugh's appeal.[2]
Bradlaugh was jubilant; his opponents in the House of
Commons were very much put out by the decision.[3] The
Manchester Guardian marvelled: 'Mr. Bradlaugh has achieved
a rare and probably unprecedented success as a layman conducting his own case before the English Courts.'[4]

Nor was this the end of the story. For in the process of
cross-examining Newdegate during the trial referred to
above, Bradlaugh had obtained Newdegate's admission that
he had indemnified Henry Clarke against any possible losses
the latter suffered in his suit against Bradlaugh. Did this not
make Newdegate guilty, thought Bradlaugh, of the crime of
maintenance? In due course Bradlaugh instituted a legal suit
against Newdegate under a still unrepealed statute dating
back to the fourteenth-century reign of King Richard II.
Newdegate was guilty, Bradlaugh charged, of 'maliciously
contriving and intending to injure and prejudice Mr. Bradlaugh and to vex, harass, and impoverish him, and subject
him to heavy expenses, [and of having] wrongfully entered
into a bond to Clarke to indemnify him all costs and
expenses . . .'.[5] The Divisional Court dismissed the charge
on the grounds that no 'case of oppression' had been made
out, but Bradlaugh as usual did not let this deter him, and

---

[1] *N.R.*, 11 Mar. 1883, pp. 161–73.
[2] *N.R.*, 15 Apr. 1883, pp. 242–5.
[3] Cf. Hampden Diary, entry for 11 Apr. 1883.
[4] Cited in *N.R.*, 22 Apr. 1883, p. 301.
[5] *N.R.*, 25 Sept. 1881, pp. 276–8; 10 Dec. 1882, p. 404.

by March 1883 the matter had reached the Queen's Bench before none other than Lord Coleridge, the Lord Chief Justice. For once Bradlaugh did not argue his own case, though he helped prepare it. Newdegate's lawyers, who included once again the eminent Sir Hardinge Giffard, M.P. and ex-Solicitor-General, contended that the charge was not maintainable since Clarke had won his original case. They argued, moreover, that Newdegate had a legitimate right to help determine 'a question of great public interest' and that eminent lawyers had called the law of maintenance obsolete. Newdegate had used Clarke as an intermediary under the mistaken impression that as a Member of Parliament he could not institute such a suit.

Bradlaugh's attorney retorted that according to legal authorities 'it is an offence for any kind of person, without interest in the subject matter of the action, to support and assist with money one of the parties to the suit, and this was equally an offence, whether the action in question was rightly or wrongly brought'. The question was no longer one of whether or not Bradlaugh should keep his seat in Parliament, but whether or not Clarke should collect the penalty; and Newdegate could hardly claim to have a legitimate interest in that penalty.[1]

Since Newdegate had already admitted indemnifying Clarke, ruled Justice Coleridge, the question at issue was not one of fact but one of law. The practice of maintenance was uncommon, conceded the Lord Chief Justice, but the law against it remained on the statute book, and it was obvious that Clarke would never have dreamed of suing Bradlaugh had it not been for Newdegate's support. Bradlaugh's entry into Parliament, Coleridge went on, was supposedly a question in which the cause of true religion was involved. 'And no one', he added wryly, 'not well acquainted with the history of human affairs can be aware of the strange obliquities of which men will be guilty in what they think the defence of what they think is the cause of religion.' Maintenance, moreover, was for Bradlaugh no mere technicality. Without Newdegate's aid, Clarke would not have sued, and yet if Clarke lost the case and pleaded bankruptcy, Bradlaugh

[1] N.R., 18 Mar. 1883, pp. 180–2; 25 Mar. 1883, pp. 194–6.

could not collect a penny. The law of maintenance might be ancient but it was upheld by Coke and Blackstone and had been held a legal offence as recently as 1873. Coleridge's judgement was therefore for Bradlaugh. 'I assume', he concluded, 'that Mr. Newdegate will pay the costs recoverable under the bond given to Mr. Clarke. For the residue of the costs and the expense which Mr. Bradlaugh has been put to as between attorney and client, and the various expenses he has had to bear—for all these Mr. Newdegate is responsible in damages. I think that Mr. Bradlaugh is entitled to an indemnity for every loss which Mr. Newdegate's maintenance has caused him . . . .'[1]

The results of this second legal triumph over Newdegate within a month were predictable. Bradlaugh was profoundly gratified. Lord Coleridge, the hostile comments of Lord Randolph Churchill and others notwithstanding, was well satisfied with his own ability in preventing religious prejudice from blinding him to the cause of justice.[2] *The Times* viewed the result with equanimity. After all, if one side took down 'a rusty blunderbuss', it could not with grace complain if the other side shot back 'with primitive javelins or arrows'.[3] The only unfortunate aspect of these two legal triumphs for Bradlaugh was that they came in the midst of the Parliamentary battle over the Affirmation Bill, thus goading his opponents to special fury.

Bradlaugh's legal victories, even if they had not gained him his seat in Parliament, were none the less injurious financially to Newdegate and consequently more troublesome to the Conservative party leadership than Bradlaugh was himself aware at the time. When the Anglican *Rock* observed in April 1883 that Newdegate ought not to be left to defray the legal costs himself, 'that is, if he will consent to receive any help',[4] it must have been ignorant of the fact that Charles Newdegate was devoting much of his time and energy to pleas for financial aid. A Newdegate Testimonial Fund had been begun as early as August 1881 to assist the

---

[1] *N.R.*, 29 Apr. 1883, pp. 323–5.
[2] E. H. Coleridge, *Life of Lord Coleridge*, ii. 289–91.
[3] Cited in *N.R.*, 13 May 1883, p. 364.
[4] The *Rock*, 27 Apr. 1883, p. 265.

veteran M.P. in the actions he had taken 'to vindicate the Christian character of Parliament . . .'.[1] This fund had succeeded in raising over £1,400 with the aid of four £100 contributions, including one by the Duke of Cumberland. By early 1883 this sum had long since been exhausted, and even before the second of the two legal setbacks, Newdegate was appealing to the Marquess of Salisbury for additional financial aid on the ground that his leadership in the resistance to attempts to invalidate the recognition of God by Parliament had revitalized true Conservative feeling.[2] A second fund drive for Newdegate raised £2,000 more, aided as it was by a £100 cheque from Salisbury himself, as well as by £20 from Northcote, and contributions from over thirty Tory M.P.s, numerous peers, and clergymen. By August 1883 Newdegate felt forced to remind Salisbury that even this second drive had fallen short by £1,300 of meeting the legal expenses he had incurred. 'I have never considered this a mere party contest; it is much more—but it has afforded the Conservative party their only permanent and effective success, since 1880. In fact, it has reunited the Conservative party with public opinion.'[3]

Lord Harlech, the Chairman of the Newdegate Testimonial Fund Committee, eventually undertook, presumably with Salisbury's blessing, to launch a third drive on behalf of Newdegate to make up the lacking £1,300. He did so, however, only on the understanding that Newdegate would not press an appeal from Lord Coleridge's decision in the maintenance case and would cease to sponsor two clerical journals, the *Churchman* and the *Guardian*, which had taken strong anti-Bradlaugh stands. Newdegate's lawyer strongly recommended that the offer be accepted, and Newdegate reluctantly agreed. Yet by May 1884 Newdegate felt impelled to make still another personal appeal to Salisbury. He had met the conditions specified by the heads of the party and yet the money had not all been forthcoming. He hoped that Salisbury had not been heeding 'certain busybodies with little knowledge of the facts [who] are spreading misrepre-

---

[1] Cited in *N.R.*, 28 Aug. 1881, p. 209.
[2] Newdegate to Salisbury, 5 Apr. 1883, Salisbury MSS.
[3] Newdegate to Salisbury, 22 Aug. 1883, Salisbury MSS.

sentations'.[1] It is fairly obvious that by the summer of 1884 Newdegate and his anti-Bradlaugh activities had become a nuisance to the Conservative party leadership. However genuine his motives, his skill was very much open to question. The Bradlaugh case may have proved a blessing to the Conservative party, but it was a mixed blessing.

As soon as one judicial decision had deprived Bradlaugh of his seat in the House of Commons, he began to play with the hope that another judicial decision would somehow restore that seat to him. Precedents were decidedly against him, as he well knew. Back in the fifteenth century, in *Thorpe's* case, the judges had declined to interfere in what was deemed a matter of Parliamentary privilege, and the decision had never been overruled:

A question arose upon Privilege, and the Lords entertaining some doubt, called upon the Judges to give their opinion, which they after deliberation declined to do stating, 'that they ought not to answer that question for it hath not been used aforetime that the Justices should in *anywise* determine the Privilege of the High Court of Parliament, for it is so high and so mighty in its nature that it may make law, and that that is law it may make no law; and the determination and knowledge of that Privilege belongeth to the Lords of the Parliament and not to the Justices'.[2]

The identical sentiments were voiced by the Attorney-General, Sir Henry James, in 1880: 'The House had that inherent power which every Court has, to maintain order within its walls, and to prevent its orders from being treated with contempt. There could therefore be no power of reviewing the proceedings of the House.'[3] In his first 'Appeal to the People' Bradlaugh apparently conceded the point. 'There is no remedy', he wrote, 'in the law courts against the House of Commons, if that House should do injustice.'[4] And yet Bradlaugh was on several occasions to assume the reverse, and both his attempt to enter Parliament by force in August 1881 and his self-administration of the oath in February 1882 were to be made focal points of lawsuits.

It was after the self-swearing episode and the subsequent

[1] Newdegate to Salisbury, 23 May 1884, and enclosures, Salisbury MSS.
[2] Cited in Great Britain, Parliamentary Papers, 1837, vol. xviii, 127.
[3] *Hansard*, ccliii (1880), 655–6.   [4] *N.R.*, 8 May 1881, p. 369.

expulsion that Alderman Gurney of Northampton instituted a suit against Bradlaugh for not having taken his seat in Parliament. Bradlaugh's legal reply was that he had, that his self-administered oath was valid. The suit fared badly in the courts. The House of Commons refused to take official notice of it, and the judges eventually dismissed it as collusive. Was not Alderman Gurney one of Bradlaugh's staunchest supporters? 'We do not sit here to give opinions and decide points, except when there is real controversy between the parties.' Bradlaugh replied that, since the House of Commons was not Parliament but only one of three parts of Parliament, it could not overrule the law by a mere resolution. The courts, moreover, had permitted a collusive action in the case of *Miller* v. *Salomons* in the 1850's for the purpose of testing a constitutional right. The case was none the less dismissed, and all Bradlaugh's efforts to appeal from the decision failed.[1]

Having been rebuffed in this instance, Bradlaugh decided after all to attempt to test the legality of the House of Commons' resolution under which he had been thrust out of Parliament on 3 August of the previous year. He therefore sued Assistant Sergeant-at-Arms Erskine for having forcibly removed him from a place in which he was legally entitled to be. The case did not come before Justice Field of the Queen's Bench Division until December 1882. Bradlaugh, who once again argued his own case, contended that Erskine's plea that he had been carrying out the orders of the House was insufficient if those orders were illegal. Bradlaugh conceded that the House might, once he was within its walls, arrest him or suspend him or expel him, 'but the House has no authority, I submit, to stop me from entering the House'.[2] Statute law commanded him to take his seat; indeed it was the right of the House—it had used it in Mary Tudor's day —to punish those M.P.s who refused to take their seats once duly elected. Bradlaugh rested his case primarily upon *Stockdale* v. *Hansard* (1837), in which Justice Holt had contended that 'the court is not precluded on the ground of

---

[1] *N.R.*, 21 May 1882, pp. 388–91; 2 Apr. 1882, pp. 282–3; 19 Nov. 1882, pp. 353, 357–9; 26 Nov. 1882, p. 369; James to Brand, 27 Mar. 1882, Hampden MSS.   [2] *N.R.*, 10 Dec. 1882, pp. 417–27.

Parliamentary privilege from considering whether the
authority of the House constitutes, in point of law, sufficient
justification of the act, nor from giving judgment in favour
of the plaintiff if it appears the justification is insufficient'.[1]

Sir Henry James, who defended Erskine, retorted that the
House of Commons alone decided upon the privileges of its
members. 'It is within the walls of Parliament, and by Parliament only, that the determination of what are its rights, and
what is its law, can be arrived at.' Though the claim of
Parliamentary privilege might not itself be legally sufficient,
no other court might overrule such a claim when it was
backed by an official order of the House.[2] Justice Field, not
surprisingly, held for the defendant. 'The House of Commons is a portion of the Highest Court of the realm', he
declared, and 'its one undoubted and clear privilege is that
no other Court has power to examine into the effect of the
authority of the House, or to question the form in which that
authority is exercised'.[3]

In the summer of 1883, as has been noted above, Bradlaugh initiated a similar action by suing the Sergeant-at-Arms
himself, R. A. Gossett, for preventing Bradlaugh from ful-
filling his Parliamentary duty. The only distinction between
this case and the case of *Bradlaugh* v. *Erskine* was that the
Speaker had in the meantime conceded that the mere attempt
to take the oath might under the House of Commons resolution be deemed a 'disturbance'. The Government refused
Bradlaugh's request to co-operate by having the case heard
by a special court.[4] The case was finally argued in December
1883 before Lord Coleridge and two other judges. Bradlaugh cannily cited in his own support the case of *Clarke* v.
Bradlaugh which had gone against him. In that instance the
plaintiff had charged Bradlaugh with not having taken the
appropriate oath of office. The fact that a resolution of the
House forbade him from so doing did not avail him as a defence against the charge. The court had thus, by implication,
decided that a resolution of the House could not contra-
vene statute law. Why ought it not to do the same now?

[1] Ibid., p. 420.   [2] *N.R.*, 24 Dec. 1882, pp. 468–79.
[3] *N.R.*, 21 Jan. 1883, p. 35.
[4] G.P. (B.M.), 44111, fol. 139; 44219, fol. 110.

The argument was clever but not convincing, and Bradlaugh was only too aware that no recent precedents specifically met his case. Yet he still felt strongly that a court ought to be able to examine whether a given order of the House lay within its own jurisdiction and whether one House might by resolution dispense with a Parliamentary statute such as that of King Richard II's reign: 'Every burgess who absents himself, or does not come to Parliament, is liable to fine and imprisonment.'

The court once more ruled against Bradlaugh. 'The plaintiff', Justice Coleridge conceded, 'argued his own case and argued it with abundant learning and ability', yet he had been unable to unearth a single decisive precedent for his suit. Bradlaugh was right in contending that a resolution of the House of Commons could not by itself change the law of the land. Yet if it were conceded that the House remained the absolute judge of its own privileges, then it obviously could in limited areas 'practically change or practically supersede the law'. While courts might on occasion be forced to consider the legality of Parliamentary resolutions, in this particular case the precedent against judicial review had to stand. Justice Coleridge added, almost regretfully: 'If injustice has been done, it is an injustice for which the courts of law afford no remedy.'[1]

In the midst of all these legal suits, many of them instituted by Bradlaugh himself, came still another case which seemingly bore no relation to Bradlaugh's Parliamentary struggle, though in reality it did. In the summer of 1882 Bradlaugh was charged by Sir Henry Tyler, with the approval of the Public Prosecutor, of being guilty of blasphemy. According to an act of William III which defined the crime of blasphemy, any person twice found guilty of blasphemy was ineligible to become a Member of Parliament. Sir Henry Tyler's motives were thus obvious enough.[2]

The case revolved not about Bradlaugh's own *National Reformer* but about items printed by the *Freethinker*, a weekly journal begun during the spring of 1881 by G. W. Foote

[1] *N.R.*, 16 Dec. 1883, pp. 385–99; 17 Feb. 1884, pp. 113–14.
[2] *N.R.*, 16 July 1882, pp. 37–39, 42; *St. Stephen's Review* cited in *N.R.*, 13 Jan. 1884, p. 17.

and William Ramsey, two of Bradlaugh's lieutenants in
the National Secular Society. Until December 1881 the
official publisher of the new project remained the Free-
thought Publishing Company, Bradlaugh's and Mrs.
Besant's own company; and until February 1882 the *Freethinker* continued to be advertised in the *National Reformer* as a publication of the Freethought Publishing Company. Bradlaugh
had no personal connexion with the publication at any time
—he never wrote for it or helped to edit it—but even after
February 1882 William Ramsey remained the manager of the
Freethought Publishing Company. By the winter of 1881
the *Freethinker*'s attacks upon religion had begun to increase
in vigour, and comic sketches ridiculing Bible stories and
basic Christian tenets were added. Bradlaugh and Mrs.
Besant began to disapprove—though not publicly—feeling
that the publication 'was lowering the tone of Freethought
advocacy and giving an unnecessary handle to its foes'.[1]

The major London newspapers deemed the prosecution
ill-advised, though journals such as the *Whitehall Review* and
the *Rock* were delighted. The only regret of the Catholic
Universe was that, once Bradlaugh was convicted, his sentence
would 'be a ridiculously light one, in comparison to what it
would be if England were a Christian country . . .'.[2]

Bradlaugh's legal dilemma was to clear himself without at
the same time creating greater difficulties for two men whose
tactics he might regard as mistaken but who were none the
less his friends and associates. His initial steps were all of
a technical nature. He sought various delays. He succeeded
in having the trial transferred from London's Criminal
Court, the Old Bailey, to the Queen's Bench Division. He
also forced the prosecution to define precisely the items
termed blasphemous—and in the process managed to have
several *Freethinker* issues bearing pre-1882 datelines dropped
from consideration.[3] Finally Bradlaugh sought to have himself tried separately rather than as a co-defendant with
Ramsey and Foote. The net result of all these steps—and

[1] Besant, *Autobiography*, p. 283. See also *N.R.*, 22 Apr. 1883, pp. 305–7.
[2] Cited in *N.R.*, 17 Sept. 1882, p. 195. *Daily News* and *The Times* cited in
N.R., 23 July 1882, pp. 78–79.
[3] Foote, *Bradlaugh*, p. 29; Bonner & Robertson, *Bradlaugh*, ii. 316–19.

others less successful—was that the trial eventually took place before Lord Chief Justice Coleridge and a jury in April 1883.

After a preliminary hearing Coleridge granted Bradlaugh's request that he be tried separately, although Sir Hardinge Giffard, once again Bradlaugh's legal opposite, contended that it was 'most urgent' that Bradlaugh be tried with the others. Giffard went on to attempt to show that while Bradlaugh might have severed his formal connexion with the *Freethinker* before the offending items had been published, the Freethought Publishing Company had continued to occupy the same premises and the *Freethinker*'s publisher had remained as manager of Bradlaugh's publishing concern. The *Freethinker*'s professed purpose of waging aggressive war against Christianity had been the same from the beginning, and the publication could not have come out without Bradlaugh's concurrence, even if Bradlaugh had derived no personal profit from it.[1]

Apparently the prosecution had done its best to uncover any such possible profit. One of its witnesses, the manager of the bank at which Bradlaugh kept his account, admitted that Giffard's assistant had inspected Bradlaugh's bank account under circumstances of most dubious legality. There was a murmur of surprise and indignation in the court, a feeling shared by Justice Coleridge himself. The revelation, especially since the bankbook inspection had obviously produced no evidence incriminating Bradlaugh, did the prosecution's case no good.[2] Bradlaugh was able to confine his own defence to an attempt to prove that he had had no personal connexion with the *Freethinker*, and since they no longer were co-defendants, he was able to have Ramsey and Foote corroborate the point. Annie Besant also appeared in the witness box to testify that as a result of her carelessness the *Freethinker* had continued to be advertised as a Freethought Publishing Company publication for two months after this connexion had been broken. In his summing up Bradlaugh observed that, despite all attempts to do so, Giffard had failed to prove that anyone but Ramsey was the

[1] *N.R.*, 15 Apr. 1883, pp. 257–69.
[2] Besant, *Autobiography*, p. 292.

publisher of the paper from December 1881 on. Admittedly Ramsey had continued to act as Bradlaugh's publishing manager, but he had the right to conduct a private business on the side and all accounts were kept separate. 'I shall ask you to find', Bradlaugh told the jury,

that this prosecution is one of the steps in a vindictive struggle, a vindictive fight, a vindictive attempt to oppress and to crush a political opponent. . . . It is an endeavor to make me technically liable for a publication with which I have nothing to do, and I will ask you to defeat it here. . . . I have no question here about defending my heresy, not because I am not ready to defend it when it is challenged in the right way, and if there be anything in it that the law can challenge. I have never gone back from anything I have ever said. I have never gone back from anything I have ever written. I have never gone back from anything I have ever done. And I ask you not to allow this Sir Henry Whatley Tyler, who dares not come here to-day, to use you as the assassin uses the dagger, to stab a man from behind whom he never dares to face.[1]

In his charge to the jury, Chief Justice Coleridge noted that there were two questions at issue: (1) were the passages in question blasphemous, and supposing them to be blasphemous, (2) was Bradlaugh guilty of publishing them? Merely to criticize Christianity, declared Coleridge, was not to commit blasphemy, 'because you may attack anything that is part and parcel of the law of the land in respectful terms without committing a crime or misdemeanor; otherwise no alteration in any part of the law of the land ever could be argued by anybody'. The proper criterion, since the blasphemy laws admittedly remained on the statute book, was a 'malicious and mischievous intention [and] a state of apathy or indifference to the interests of society'. But the more immediate question was that of Bradlaugh's complicity: 'There is so general a dislike and disapprobation', Coleridge went on, 'of many of the opinions and many of the acts of Mr. Bradlaugh, that we ought to examine ourselves with singular and anxious care, lest we come to a conclusion hostile to a person of whom we disapprove, upon evidence which would not satisfy us in the case of a person of whom we approve.'

[1] N.R., 22 Apr. 1883, pp. 281–4.

Bradlaugh had freely admitted that he shared a general sympathy with the views expressed by the *Freethinker*; the question at issue, hower, was not his moral guilt but his legal guilt: 'If he has not been proved to be responsible for this publication within the meaning of the [law], better—a thoussand times better—that he should be acquitted than that the faintest or slightest disturbance of justice or distortion of the law should be made for the sake of a cause, however good.' After deliberating for two hours, the jury returned a verdict of 'Not Guilty'.[1]

After Bradlaugh's acquittal Foote and Ramsey were tried separately for blasphemy. Foote sought to show in his defence that many things had been printed of a character similar to the *Freethinker* passages which had not been prosecuted for blasphemy. In what Gladstone was to call a 'luminous and most interesting Judgment'[2] Coleridge conceded this, but reminded Foote that so long as the blasphemy laws were unrepealed this kind of defence was insufficient. The jury disagreed on a verdict, and further prosecution was abandoned. In the meantime, however, the City of London had brought a separate indictment for blasphemy against the Christmas 1882 issue of the *Freethinker*, which featured a cartoon illustration of the biblical passage in which God 'shows his backsides' to Moses. The presiding judge, Justice North, asked that the law be strictly heeded. He defined blasphemy as denying the existence of God or scoffing at sacred subjects such as the Trinity or Holy Scriptures. All the references which Foote made to publications ranging from John Stuart Mill to the Salvation Army *War Cry* were deemed irrelevant by the judge. After the first jury had disagreed, a second found the two defendants guilty. Justice North thereupon sentenced Foote to a year in prison and Ramsey to nine months in prison. Making himself heard amidst the hisses of an audience of outraged fellow secularists Foote declared: 'My lord, I thank you; it is worthy of your creed.'[3]

Bradlaugh, even if not altogether sympathetic towards Foote's tactics, regarded Justice North's conduct of the trial

[1] *N.R.*, 22 Apr. 1883, pp. 312–14.   [2] G.P. (B.M.), 44546, fol. 124.
[3] *N.R.*, 6 May 1883, pp. 340–2; Bonner & Robertson, *Bradlaugh*, ii. 325–6.

and his charge to the jury as totally lacking in judicial impartiality, and for the only time in his life he addressed a public letter to a judge accusing him of unjudicial conduct. The verdict was cheered, to be sure, by a number of religious journals, but its wisdom was doubted by many others, and a memorial asking the Home Secretary to mitigate Foote's and Ramsey's sentences was signed by such men as T. H. Huxley, Herbert Spencer, Leslie Stephen, and Frederic Harrison. The National Secular Society aided the two men and their families with a Prisoners' Aid Fund, but attempts to have the sentences shortened proved unavailing. Foote did have the ultimate compensation of a hero's welcome upon his release from jail in February 1884.[1]

Thus far the law courts had not obtained Bradlaugh his Parliamentary seat, but neither had they been valueless. They had provided him with a number of highly satisfying victories and a widening popular recognition that Charles Bradlaugh was no mere street-corner demagogue. He was a highly skilled lawyer, one of the cleverest outside the profession. It may be true, as Sir Ivor Jennings has suggested,[2] that Bradlaugh was 'too good' a lawyer—that he had too much skill in clutching at legal straws and building upon antiquated precedents—and that he ought to have devoted his attention to grand principles instead. But the law for Bradlaugh remained one highly legitimate means towards an end he regarded as no more than just—the realization of the grand principle of constitutional representation and legal equality for all, and if the law had not attained that end for him it was not for want of trying.

1 N.R., 18 Mar. 1883, p. 177; 20 May 1883, p. 382; 2 Mar. 1884, pp. 146–7.
2 W. Ivor Jennings, 'Bradlaugh and the Law', Champion of Liberty, ed. J. P. Gilmour (London, 1933), p. 325.

XXII

BRADLAUGH AS
SECULARIST AND POLITICIAN

BRADLAUGH's Parliamentary struggle never absorbed all his energies, and during the 1880's he remained the foremost free-thought lecturer in England. If he was now a little more cautious in giving 'full swing to his passionate eloquence',[1] this hardly implied a recantation. Indeed, Bradlaugh's audiences during the early 1880's were, not surprisingly, larger than ever; and though he spoke often on political topics, he hardly forsook the cause of secularism. When, at a Sheffield meeting early in 1883, a member of the audience arose to castigate those who defended a man 'who said there was no God', Bradlaugh indignantly denied that he had ever made that statement. 'Perhaps Grace has touched him', suggested the Conservative *Saturday Review*; 'but whether he has made up his mind that the beauty of Mr. Gladstone's character is an argument for Theism, or that it is impossible to attack Lord Randolph Churchill's father's pension without making some little sacrifice, or that generally speaking Paris is worth a Mass, it is impossible to say.'[2] The fact of the matter was that Bradlaugh's definition of atheism remained as before considerably more subtle than his enemies would concede. Bradlaugh's great crime for many remained the same it had always been, to popularize free thought among the working classes:

When any persons write [observed Bradlaugh in 1884] pretending that scepticism is good for the educated, but that no attempt should be made to shake the religious faith of the working masses, you may fairly doubt either the soundness of their heresy, or their love for the people. The great bulk of the open accessions to free-thought, during the past twenty-five years, have been from

[1] Foote, *Bradlaugh*, p. 7.
[2] *Saturday Review*, 10 Feb. 1883, p. 172.

amongst the wage-earning classes. Usually those who affect contempt for the intelligence of the masses are persons without ability to win their affection.[1]

Bradlaugh's assessment is supported in numerous contemporary works by professing Christians.[2]

Bradlaugh, in any case, continued to conduct occasional oral and written debates with clergymen, including in December 1881 the eminent Dr. McCann, a lecturer for the Christian Evidence Society. In 1882 appeared a third and greatly revised edition of Bradlaugh's *Genesis: Its Authorship and Authenticity*. It was written upon the assumption that 'either the first eleven chapters of the Old Testament are true or the whole fabric of our national religion is false'. The appraisal by the *Westminster Review* illumines Bradlaugh's standing in the biblical scholarship of the times. The reviewer called it

an aggressive and inartistic work, but certainly one which exhibits considerable reading, a creditable amount of knowledge, some acquaintance with Hebrew, and a correct negative appreciation of the so-called Mosaic records . . . . In concluding his case, he omits no opportunity of embarrassing his opponents by exposing the inconsistencies, puerilities, and extravagances of the more orthodox among them, and contrasting them with the verdict of the more learned and liberal of their own creed.

If Bradlaugh's conclusions could no longer be gainsaid, then it could be observed that neither were they any longer novel—

> And thrice he routed all his foes
> And thrice he slew the slain . . . .

It could also be observed, the reviewer plaintively concluded, that Bradlaugh showed no 'reasonable sympathy with old forms of faith, with the traditions, often very beautiful, of an ever-learning, ever-unlearning humanity'.[3]

From September 1884 on, Bradlaugh began to publish occasional 'Doubts in Dialogue', sometimes clever and sometimes pedestrian short pieces purporting to be conversations

---

[1] *N.R.*, 28 Sept. 1884, p. 217.
[2] e.g. A. M. Fairbanks, *Christianity in the Nineteenth Century* (London, 1883), p. 32.   [3] *Westminster Review*, January 1883, p. 204.

between an atheist and a theist. The excerpts below are illustrative:

Theist: Your Atheism is mere negation.

Atheist: Not so, except as the affirmation of any truth negates the falsehood it contradicts.

T: Your Atheism leads men to vice.

A: First, that is rather abuse than argument, and if true, would scarcely demonstrate the existence of God. Are all Theists virtuous? . . .

T: Why should not an Atheist lie and steal and cheat, if he can do it without being found out?

A: Why should he? It is easier to tell the truth than to lie, especially if you cultivate the habit of truth-telling; stealing and cheating are practices of social misdoing which involve at least the possibility of being discovered. An Atheist cannot clear himself from rascality by repentance. He finds it much more comfortable and profitable to encourage habits of truthfulness and honesty in others by practising them himself.[1]

It is not surprising that Bradlaugh should devote himself frequently to rebutting the charge that atheism represented mere negation and that it led to vice, for he was in the midst of a continuous struggle to make clear that approval of birth control did not necessarily imply advocacy of 'free love' or opposition to marriage. Bradlaugh repeatedly explained that he regarded marriage as socially desirable. He saw it as a bond between two people who have 'equal rights and duties. . . . On the whole, the man is not inferior to the woman, . . . the woman is not inferior to the man, but in the speciality of each there is much that the other cannot do. . . . If they both be of opinion that their continued union would tend to misery, it would be better for them to separate than to live in strife and unhappiness.'[2] Bradlaugh admittedly favoured the possibility of divorce; as he once asked a clerical opponent: 'Do you think it more moral to irrevocably bind together in continued misery than to change the law and leave some hope?'[3]

Yet the charge that Bradlaugh was an advocate of sexual licence continued to be flung at him from pulpit, Parliament,

[1] N.R., 11 Jan. 1885, p. 21.   [2] N.R., 27 Nov. 1881, p. 427.
[3] N.R., 2 Nov. 1884, p. 289.

and periodical, and the reply never did catch up with the assertion. When the Bishop of Manchester on one occasion attributed to Bradlaugh views the very reverse of those he held, the latter wondered despairingly whether 'it is possible that I can misrepresent my antagonists as much as they misrepresent me and those who work with me'.[1] The reputation of *The Fruits of Philosophy* continued to hover unflatteringly over Bradlaugh. Six years after his death, indeed, when the Wilson Publishing Company of Chicago issued an edition of *Fruits of Philosophy: A Treatise of the Population Question* it attributed the authorship to Charles Bradlaugh and Mrs. Annie Besant and—perhaps appropriately—listed the book as part of Volume Four of Wilson's 'Library of Fiction'.

Bradlaugh continued to be elected year after year as President of the National Secular Society, and there is little doubt that his political notoriety gained him new free-thought adherents. An average of more than fifteen hundred new members was reported annually, and new branches were continually being opened. Even if these gains are balanced by unreported losses, it is fairly obvious that by 1883 the National Secular Society was larger and more flourishing than ever before in its history. According to the Committee on Infidelity of the Salisbury Diocesan Synod, 'there are few places of any considerable size in which it has not one or more branches or agents for the distribution of its publications . . .'.[2] In 1881 the Leicester branch opened a new Secular Hall built at a cost of £4,000. G. W. Foote and others who had broken with Bradlaugh over the advisability of taking on the legal defence, in 1876, of *The Fruits of Philosophy* rejoined him in 1880. There remained centrifugal forces within the society, but Bradlaugh skilfully held the society together. It was organization on a national scale, he maintained, which made possible a Benevolent Fund to aid needy members and a special lecturing fund to assist the poorer branches, as well as large-scale petitioning and legal aid.[3] And if, as Bradlaugh conceded in 1884, 'some think that

---

[1] *N.R.*, 16 Oct. 1881, p. 323.
[2] Cited in *N.R.*, 27 Apr. 1884, p. 278. See also *N.R.*, 4 June 1882, p. 419; 20 May 1883, p. 371; 8 June 1884, p. 387, for annual reports of additions in members and branches.
[3] *N.R.*, 7 May 1882, p. 362.

I wield the authority of this office hardly and harshly',[1] then it remained true that the great mass of his adherents were supremely loyal followers. Such devotion, at least, is reflected in the actions of the member who with his daughter travelled from a village in Nottinghamshire to the annual conference at Plymouth by means of tandem tricycle.[2]

Bradlaugh's National Secular Society obviously fulfilled many of the functions of a religious denomination. Bradlaugh addressing a huge Trafalgar Square assembly, observed the *Pall Mall Gazette*, 'bore a not remote resemblance to a friar preaching in the market-place to a vast and attentive congregation'.[3] And indeed Bradlaugh continued to perform such functions of a religious leader as naming children. 'It would save much trouble', he noted in 1882, 'if parents who wish their children named would clearly write beforehand, on half a sheet of notepaper, the names and address of the father and mother, the date of the child's birth, and the name to be given to the child, so that a proper certificate of the naming may be afterwards sent.'[4] Bradlaugh still gave out free legal advice concerning such matters as the right to affirm in the courts—'Persons claiming to affirm should do so quietly and respectfully'—and the right to withdraw children from compulsory religious education in board schools.[5] He advised his followers on their self-improvement—he recommended Macaulay's *Essays* for elocution and Hume's *History of England* for general education[6]—and frequently lectured them on their behaviour. They ought not to use sensational titles or coarse language in advertising lectures. Nor ought they to make financial commitments they could not keep or to elect youthful recruits to office. 'In a large voluntary society like the N.S.S. its rapid increase of members renders it, above all, needful that there shall be the severest strictness in its discipline.'[7] Bradlaugh encouraged the use of the regular panel of society

---

[1] *N.R.*, 8 June 1884, p. 389.   [2] *N.R.*, 1 June 1884, p. 377.
[3] Cited in *N.R.*, 25 Feb. 1883, p. 116.
[4] *N.R.*, 22 Oct. 1882, p. 282.
[5] *N.R.*, 5 Nov. 1882, p. 314; 30 Jan. 1881, p. 74.
[6] *N.R.*, 11 May 1884, p. 329.
[7] e.g. *N.R.*, 19 Nov. 1882, p. 362; 28 Oct. 1883, p. 282; 22 July 1883, p. 58.

lecturers, consisting—apart from certain veterans—of men who either held a university degree or had passed a special examination in literature, science, and theology. Bradlaugh's own lectures might be advertised with the letters 'M.P.' following his name only if they dealt with political topics. If the lectures were theological Bradlaugh's title was to be omitted.[1] If Charles Bradlaugh wished to hold his secular adherents to strict account in personal and public behaviour it was only because of his pride in them. 'I say that taken 100 per 100 to compare with the congregations of any church or chapel in similar rank of life, the Freethinkers are more sober, more pure, more honest, more industrious, more active in political reform, and more useful generally.'[2]

The two religious organizations which most exercised the National Secular Society during the 1880's were the Salvation Army, then in its infancy, and the Roman Catholic Church. To most free-thinkers the former movement seemed an unfortunate (yet surprisingly successful) return to primitive superstition. Bradlaugh characterized it as a 'mixture of enthusiasts, lunatics, and hypocrites who feel it their duty to worship with the accompaniment of vocal and instrumental noise, some hideous and never harmonious'.[3] This appraisal differs little from that of the more genteel clergy. Bradlaugh did not consider it a major threat to his own organization; he cautioned his followers repeatedly, however, against taking part in processions hostile to the movement or becoming involved in open-air fights with the Salvationists.[4]

The Roman Catholic Church seemed a more significant enemy, and the political activities of the Catholic bishop in Northampton and of Cardinal Manning nationally confirmed this danger for Bradlaugh. Most free-thinkers agreed with Catholics in regarding Protestantism as a half-way house between Rome and atheism; and an attack by a Catholic clergyman usually excited Bradlaugh more than one from a Protestant minister. As he told the annual conference of the National Secular Society in 1883, 'The fight between us and Rome must come one day. It may be far off; it may be

---

1 *N.R.*, 23 Sept. 2883, p. 199; 27 Aug. 1882, p. 154.
2 *N.R.*, 12 Oct. 1884, p. 244.   3 *N.R.*, 30 Apr. 1882, p. 345.
4 *N.R.*, 13 Aug. 1882, p. 121.

tomorrow—the fight between Rome and Rationalism, between the fullest assertion of the right of private judge ment and the most complete submission to authority'.[1]

Rome was the enemy, but not all means were justified in combating this enemy. In 1880 Bradlaugh had strained his ties with French colleagues by opposing some of the French laic laws and, more specifically, the expulsion of the Jesuits from France. 'I believe', declared Bradlaugh, 'the Roman Catholic Church to be the persistent and unvarying foe of all progress, social, political, and religious, but my weapons against this Church are limited to the weapons which I think fair and just against myself.' He tried to convince Gambetta that the expulsions were not merely impolitic but inconsistent with free-thought principles.[2] The political objects a free-thinker ought to strive for, thought Bradlaugh, were complete freedom of worship, with neither legal privilege nor legal penalty of any kind for believer or unbeliever. This meant the disestablishment of the Church of England, the repeal of all blasphemy laws, and the universal right to replace oaths with affirmations. Free-thinkers did not ask for the legal shackling of religion. 'If we cannot win with reason, I will not try to win with force.'[3]

In the meantime it was the legal fetters—actual and potential—upon free thought that Bradlaugh had to contend with. One of the most flourishing of the activities of the National Secular Society was its Hall of Science classes in chemistry, physiology, botany, mathematics, and other subjects, which had begun in the winter of 1879. Students in them took examinations given by the Science and Art Department of the Government, which in turn awarded financial grants to the school in accordance with the number of its students who passed the state examination. The Department at the time was directed by T. H. Huxley. Sir Henry Tyler, hoping to injure Bradlaugh in this indirect fashion, introduced resolutions in the House of Commons in 1881 and 1882 to the effect that 'This House is of opinion that the Hall of Science, by reason of its associations, is not a proper

[1] N.R., 20 May 1883, p. 378.
[2] N.R., 14 Nov. 1880, p. 353; 27 Jan. 1884, p. 49.
[3] N.R., 27 Jan. 1884, p. 49.

place, and Dr. E. B. Aveling and Mrs. Besant and members of the Bradlaugh family are not proper persons to be employed in the instruction of persons in connection with the Science and Art Department of Her Majesty's Government'.[1] He carefully refrained from bringing these motions to a vote, though A. J. Mundella, the Liberal minister accountable for the department, found occasion to observe that Bradlaugh's daughters were 'well qualified' to teach chemistry and botany. Mundella, in any case, could not see how persons could be refused the benefits of the Science and Art Department because of the religious opinions of their teachers.[2] For the time being the number of Hall of Science students taking state examinations kept growing (from 115 in 1880 to 214 in 1882).

The Hall of Science instructors were less successful when it came to continuing their own education. In 1877 Hypatia and Alice Bradlaugh had become the first women students at the City of London College,[3] but in 1883 shortly after Alice Bradlaugh and Mrs. Besant had enrolled in a botany class at University College, London, they were excluded on the grounds that 'there is some prejudice against you'. Bradlaugh appealed to Lord Kimberley, President of the Council of University College, but the Council confirmed the initial decision. T. H. Huxley, under whom Annie Besant had studied physiology, described her as 'a very hard-working student' and joined in a memorial asking a general meeting of the college to reconsider the decision. Such a meeting was held late in July of 1883, but it reaffirmed the earlier decision.[4]

The leadership and scope of the National Secular Society did not remain static during the 1880's. In 1884 John M. Robertson became a regular contributor to the *National Reformer*, and in 1885 George Bernard Shaw contributed a novel, in serial form, to Bradlaugh's and Mrs. Besant's monthly magazine, *Our Corner*. Since G. W. Foote was at the

[1] *N.R.*, 12 Feb. 1882, p. 104.
[2] *N.R.*, 3 Apr. 1882, p. 296; *Hansard*, cclxviii (1882), 543; cclxx (1882), 472, 1260-2.
[3] A. Bonner and C. B. Bonner, *Hypatia Bradlaugh Bonner*, p. 30.
[4] *N.R.*, 13 May 1883, pp. 361-2; 20 May 1883, pp. 380-1; 10 June 1883, p. 420; 29 July 1883, pp. 67-69.

same time editing the weekly *Freethinker* and the monthly *Progress*, free-thought periodical literature seemed to be flourishing. Moreover the National Secular Society leaders had become charter members of a newly formed International Federation of Freethinkers, which, like the National Secular Society, held annual conferences.

But if there were gains, there were losses as well. The major one was Edward B. Aveling, who had seemed in 1879 a notable acquisition. The son of an Irish Protestant clergyman, he was an able, attractive speaker with a firm grounding in science and a definite flair for popularization. His coming had been the immediate impetus behind the Hall of Science classes, and when he was dismissed from his lectureship in Comparative Anatomy at London Hospital, the generally reputed reason was his public identification with Bradlaugh.[1] When Aveling won election to the London School Board from Westminster in November of 1882 it seemed to be another victory for the cause of secularism. But by this time Bradlaugh had begun to have doubts about his associate. There were rumours in the air about Aveling's constant financial crises, about petty pilferings, and unrepaid loans. There were rumours also about a first wife who had left but not divorced him because of cruelty, and of intimacies with girl students and with stage-struck young ladies who assisted him in 'Readings Grave and Gay' in fashionable West End halls. Aveling may well have been attracted to free thought initially by the dynamic and personable Annie Besant, but by 1882 this flame was cooling, and socialism and Eleanor Marx, the daughter of Karl Marx, had apparently taken the place of free thought and Annie Besant in Aveling's affections.[2] As Mrs. Besant noted bitterly in 1884, 'he never touched Socialism in any way, or knew anything about it, until in 1882 he took to reading at the British Museum, and unfortunately there fell into the company of some of the Bohemian Socialists, male and female, who flourish there'.[3]

Aveling began to write for socialist publications and to attack Bradlaugh as a friend of landlords. In the summer of

[1] *N.R.*, 18 Dec. 1881, pp. 476–7.
[2] Williams, *The Passionate Pilgrim*, pp. 132–44.
[3] *N.R.*, 4 May 1884, p. 310.

1884 he resigned his post as a N.S.S. Vice-President and cut all ties with the free-thought movement. Soon after, he contracted a 'free Union' with Eleanor Marx, even though his legal wife was still alive. His accession to socialism appeared to many socialists to be a notable one—among other things, he and Eleanor Marx were the first to translate *Das Kapital* into English—but it soon became apparent that Aveling's nature had not changed. He continued to borrow shamelessly from friends and to carry on flirtations with women. He disappeared for a while in the 1890's, having sold all Eleanor Marx's possessions behind her back. When he returned he was legally married to a young actress, his first wife having finally died. The shock was too much for Eleanor Marx, who committed suicide, though publicly excusing Aveling. 'There are people who lack a certain moral sense just as others are deaf or shortsighted or are in other ways afflicted. And I began to realise the fact that one is as little justified in blaming them for the one sort of disorder than [*sic*] for the other. We must strive to cure them, and if no cure is possible, we must do our best.' Aveling himself died in 1899 while reading a book in an easy chair, only to be immortalized as Dubedat in Shaw's *The Doctor's Dilemma*.[1]

If Bradlaugh's interest in secularism did not wane during the years of his Parliamentary struggle, neither did his interest in a variety of political issues not directly related to his efforts to enter the House of Commons. For one thing Bradlaugh maintained a considerable interest in foreign policy. He was by inclination and background a 'Little Englander'. He had denounced Disraeli's purchase of the Suez Canal shares in 1875 and had participated in a number of 'anti-Jingo' demonstrations at the time of the 1878 war scare with Russia. Thus it was not surprising that in the summer of 1882 Bradlaugh should have opposed the Gladstone Government's intervention in Egypt, a consequence of an uprising against the inept Khedive by followers of Colonel Arabi, a contemporary Egyptian nationalist. When the British shelled Alexandria and occupied the major cities of Egypt, John Bright resigned in protest from the Liberal Cabinet.

[1] E. Bernstein, *My Years of Exile*, pp. 160-5.

Bradlaugh's sympathies lay with Bright. 'Does anyone know what we want in Egypt?' he asked, in a pronouncement with a curiously modern ring:

We did not try to put down Prim, or Serrano, or Castelar. Yet Spain owed us money as well as Egypt. It is all nonsense to talk of danger to the Suez Canal. Until we bombarded Alexandria there had never been even a menace against the free passage of the Canal. If we speak of the Christians killed in the Alexandria riots, urge that these riots justified interference, I ask have we interfered in Germany or Russia when the Jews were slaughtered and robbed wholesale?[1]

John Bright believed that 'thoughtful and Christian men' would 'condemn' British intervention in Egypt,[2] but the Archbishop of York felt otherwise. 'Through God's great goodness', he proclaimed, 'the struggle of a few hours has scattered the rebels, has made order and freedom possible in Egypt, has rescued that country from the impending loss of next year's crops, and has prevented its ruin.'[3] The actual fighting in Egypt came to an end within two months, and the National Secular Society proved to be one of the few organizations in London to exercise itself greatly over the matter. By October the issue was dead for the time being, though it had confirmed one matter for Annie Besant. 'The war Egypt proves that England is still a very Christian nation. A nation of Atheists would not have entered upon a war so wicked because so unjustifiable.'[4]

In 1884 war had come to the Sudan, and Bradlaugh protested against British intervention in that area against men 'whom it is the fashion just now to call rebels and traitors, though they only fight in and for their own land'.[5] The war in the Sudan led the following February to the débâcle at Khartoum and the death of General Gordon, a defeat highly damaging to the Gladstone Ministry. Bradlaugh, who had charged the Duke of Cambridge with great inefficiency in the organization and supplying of British troops in Egypt,

---

[1] N.R., 13 Aug. 1882, p. 114.
[2] The Public Letters of John Bright, p. 273.
[3] Cited in N.R., 24 Sept. 1882, p. 215.
[4] N.R., 8 Oct. 1882, p. 246. See also N.R., 17 Sept. 1882, p. 206.
[5] N.R., 23 Mar. 1884, p. 193.

had had grave doubts about the propriety of Gordon's advance. In the meantime Annie Besant contributed a number of articles to the *National Reformer* demonstrating that Gordon, *the* hero of the moment, while a man of undoubted physical courage, had clay feet.[1] At a peace demonstration at St. James's Hall, called at Bradlaugh's suggestion in April of 1885, Bradlaugh once again denounced those who urged that Britain's greatness rested upon imperial prestige.

It was said that if we left the Soudan, we should lose our prestige and tarnish our glory. But our prestige had not grown out of our wars, and our glory had not been made on the battlefield. . . . This country had grown by her factory chimneys, not by the cannon's mouth, not by her vessels of war, but by her productions which, sent to every part of the world, carried in ships bearing a peaceful flag, and not a fiery one, and these giving scope to the results of our artisan skill had extended our dominion and made our comfort possible. . . . War left to the vanquished the bitterness of despair and the hateful hope of revenge; and to the victor what did it bring? Debt, discredit, demoralisation, and brutalisation lasting through generations. It made false, sham glory, so that people put up monuments to men whose merit was that they had disfigured humanity and trampled it underfoot.[2]

While Bradlaugh did not think of himself as 'usually given to denying the value and importance of our Colonial possessions',[3] he had consistently opposed additional expansion and imperialistic excesses in various parts of Africa. His attitude towards Ireland reflected the same viewpoint and, his treatment by Irish Nationalist M.P.s notwithstanding, Bradlaugh steadfastly opposed new coercive legislation and remained in general sympathy with the Home-Rule programme.

There were political questions closer to home which also interested Bradlaugh, such as the drive to commute perpetual pensions. This, as noted in Chapter IX, had been Bradlaugh's pet project during his brief period of service in the House of Commons. Bradlaugh's subsequent exclusion

[1] *N.R.*, 22 Feb. 1885, pp. 177, 182; 26 Apr. 1885, pp. 326–7; 3 May 1885, 340–2.
[2] Cited in *N.R.*, 12 Apr. 1885, p. 293.
[3] *N.R.*, 10 Apr. 1881, p. 281.

halted his campaign to set up a Select Committee on the subject. In 1884 Bradlaugh discovered in the newspapers that Gladstone's Government had been quietly dealing with the matter and was commuting the pensions on a basis of slightly less than twenty-seven times their yearly value. Thus the £4,000 pension which went annually to the Duke of Marlborough was being brought to an end with the payment of £107,000 over a ten-year period. Bradlaugh protested against what he deemed an unduly high rate of compensation, especially in the case of the descendants of the Duke of Marlborough, whose pension had not been, in Bradlaugh's view, 'meritoriously acquired'.[1] Bradlaugh did receive the opportunity to consult the Chancellor of the Exchequer, H. C. E. Childers, and one of the Secretaries to the Treasury, Leonard Courtney, on the subject, but the important decisions had by that time been taken. Bradlaugh obviously felt slighted, though Gladstone, in a personal note, assured him that no discourtesy had been intended.[2] The reaction of the London press was that Bradlaugh's thunder had been stolen, and the Northampton *Mercury* bluntly observed that 'one reason for Mr. Bradlaugh's return to Parliament will be removed'.[3]

The one major domestic change brought about by the second Gladstone Ministry was the Reform Bill of 1884. Bradlaugh gave it his most vigorous assent, regretting only his inability to be in Parliament to vote for an amendment granting the suffrage to women as well. Curiously enough both Northcote and Gladstone had expressed themselves as, in principle, in favour of such a step, and Northcote was strongly urged by one suffragette that if the women of Northampton received the vote, Bradlaugh would forthwith be defeated.[4] Bradlaugh virtually conceded this, but argued none the less that women, some of whom had been granted the franchise in municipal elections in 1868 and in school-board elections in 1870, ought to have comparable rights on

[1] *N.R.*, 25 May 1884, p. 357.
[2] *N.R.*, 1 June 1884, p. 369; 15 June 1884, pp. 401–2; 29 June 1884, p. 497.
[3] *N.R.*, 1 June 1884, p. 374; Northampton *Mercury* cited in *N.R.*, 25 May 1884, p. 359.
[4] Iddesleigh MSS. (B.M.), 50041, fol. 230.

the national level.[1] Gladstone successfully opposed the suffrage amendment on the grounds that its adoption would defeat the Reform Bill in the House of Lords.[2]

As matters turned out, the House of Lords did reject the bill, on the ground that it was not accompanied by a satisfactory re-apportionment measure. The result was a flurry of agitation on behalf of either the abolition or the complete alteration of the House of Lords. Bradlaugh played an active role in this campaign, addressing another huge rally at St. James's Hall in August 1884 and becoming a charter member of a new organization working for an end to the upper chamber. '. . . the House of Lords is fortunate in its enemies', thought the *Saturday Review*. 'With Sir Wilfrid Lawson, Mr. Labouchere, and Mr. Bradlaugh shouting for abolition . . . the wicked Peers may perhaps pluck up a little heart.'[3] The dilemma in which the peers found themselves was, to be sure, a more fundamental one, that of being an increasingly obvious anachronism in an increasingly democratic society. The veteran Lord Shaftesbury had seen this clearly enough half a decade earlier, when he wrote: 'The Lords are now placed in a ridiculous position. If they show resistance, they are denounced as opposing the will of the country, and threatened with extinction; if they show none, they are declared to be of no value whatever in the working of the Constitution.'[4]

Bradlaugh himself, it soon turned out, regarded the replacement of the House of Lords by an elected Senate as preferable to complete abolition. The latter object could be attained at the moment only by revolution, and with memories of 1848 and 1871 still present, revolution could not be condoned for this purpose.[5] An attempt in the House of Commons by Labouchere to set such a change into motion proved abortive, and when in November, with the Queen's encouragement, Gladstone and Salisbury were able to agree upon a compromise solution by which the Franchise Reform Bill and a Re-apportionment Bill would both reach the House

[1] *N.R.*, 26 Aug. 1883, p. 140.
[2] Hamilton Diary (B.M.), 48636, p. 72.
[3] *Saturday Review*, 16 Aug. 1884, p. 209.
[4] Cited by A. Patchett Martin, *Life of Robert Lowe*, ii. 455.
[5] *N.R.*, 14 Sept. 1884, p. 177; 21 Sept. 1884, pp. 192–3.

of Lords, agitation on the subject died quickly. The Prime Minister, complained Annie Besant, 'has preferred a royal smile to the nation's love', and she called for a Radical in the Cabinet to 'repudiate this betrayal'. Bradlaugh himself was forced to concede a month later, however, that 'the tempest has been suddenly appeased'.[1]

The same sense of the possible which influenced Bradlaugh to advocate the alteration rather than the abolition of the House of Lords led him during the 1880's to subdue his advocacy of a republic for England. Bradlaugh's republican instincts remained very much at work in his analysis of waste in royal expenditure,[2] and in his professed sympathy with France and the United States—he was welcomed most cordially in Paris again in December 1883, and continued to receive numerous invitations from America—but obviously there were no immediate prospects in this area for the moment. Yet Bradlaugh's own concept of political democracy, which envisaged the Member of Parliament as the embodiment of public opinion within his constituency, impressed many Englishmen as equally extreme. M.P.s no longer enjoyed their former superiority over those who elect them, complained the London *Standard* in 1884. 'Few men have done more within a short time to vulgarize the position of a member than Mr. Bradlaugh, with his incessant talk about obeying the orders and seeking the permission of his constituents.'[3]

The day when Bradlaugh could be held up as the acme of dangerous radicalism was passing rapidly, however, for the precise years of Bradlaugh's Parliamentary struggle also mark the emergence of modern socialism in England. H. M. Hyndman's Democratic Federation (later Social Democratic Federation) dates from 1881, and William Morris's Socialist League and the Fabian Society were both founded in 1884. This development, though 'little noticed by the magnates of politics',[4] was observed quickly by Bradlaugh, immersed as he was in the world of London working-class movements.

---

[1] *N.R.*, 23 Nov. 1884, p. 341; 28 Dec. 1884, p. 449.
[2] e.g. *N.R.*, 7 May 1882, pp. 355–7.
[3] London *Standard*, 11 Mar. 1884, cited in *N.R.*, 16 Mar. 1884, p. 187.
[4] R. C. K. Ensor, *England, 1870–1914*, p. 100.

By 1884 Bradlaugh regarded himself and his organization as very much the rival of the new socialist groups, which treated him and his ideas with open disdain. Karl Marx himself had dismissed Bradlaugh as 'the huge self-idolator',[1] while Hyndman was equally contemptuous. As he put it in January 1884, 'Gladstone, Salisbury, Northcote, Hartington, Chamberlain, Bradlaugh, Churchill simply represent so many names by which so many among the workers are induced to neglect their own interests'.[2] In the winter of 1883–4 Bradlaugh delivered a series of lectures critical of socialism, a new interest which reached a climax on 18 April 1884, when Bradlaugh and Hyndman, before a capacity audience in St. James's Hall, debated the question: 'Will Socialism benefit the English People?'

Hyndman began by defining socialism as 'an endeavour to substitute for the anarchical struggle or fight for existence an organised co-operation for existence'. It was at once an historical theory and a political programme which would end contrasts between wealth and poverty as well as brutal class competition, repeated industrial crises, and onerously long working hours. 'We know right well', he declared, 'that three or four hours work a day is more than sufficient to cover comfort and luxury for every man.' All this could be accomplished by the collective ownership of land, capital, machinery, and credit.

Bradlaugh commenced his side of the argument by conceding the existence of many social evils in England. While Hyndman 'wants the state to remedy them,' Bradlaugh went on, 'I want the individuals to remedy them'. Hyndman's definition of socialism left out one thing, that it would require revolution to be carried out, for 'no Socialistic experiment has ever yet succeeded in the world'. Small groups had succeeded temporarily on the basis of devotion to a religious ideal or toward a particular leader, but even they distinguished their common property from that of the world around them. Socialism strictly defined meant simply the denial of individual private property and 'affirms that society organised as the State should own all wealth, direct all

---

[1] Cited by Williams, *The Passionate Pilgrim*, p. 139.
[2] *N.R.*, 3 Feb. 1884, p. 74.

labour, and compel the equal distribution of all produce'. Such a state would paralyse progress by constricting individual initiative, and it could be brought into being only by the forceful dispossession of all property-owners. And the majority of the English people *were* property owners in that they owned many things not necessary for bare existence.

I urge [continued Bradlaugh] that the only sufficient inducement to the general urging on of progress in society is by individual effort, spurred to action by the hope of private gain; it may be gain of money, it may be gain in other kind, it may be gain in the praise of fellows or sharing their general happiness; but whatever it is, it is the individual motive which prompts and spurs the individual to action.

How could there be freedom of opinion in a state-directed society? How could Hyndman himself lecture or print a newspaper in such a society? 'Will the state advance funds for the paper to advocate that you may make a revolution to overturn it?' The chief difficulty with Hyndman's ideas was that they were airy generalities which casually dismissed the actual problems confronting a society in which the state monopolizes everything.

'I must confess,' retorted Hyndman in rebuttal, 'when I entered this hall I did not expect that I had to explain all the details of bottle-washers, cooks, and cabmen in the remote future.' Hyndman disclaimed any originality in his vision of socialism, whose roots went back to Owen and which had been scientifically demonstrated by Karl Marx. Bradlaugh spoke of the danger of revolution, but was not this revolution already under way? Was not the life of the skilled worker less and less secure? Socialists, Bradlaugh had argued, promoted the use of force. 'Is there no force used to-day at all? Has he not himself been the victim of force?' Progress was the result of higher aims than personal selfishness. 'My opponent says all individuality will be crushed. I say individuality is crushed to-day.'

Bradlaugh countered by renewing his dissection both of Hyndman's premises and his conclusions. It was all very well for socialists to write that 'gunpowder helped to sweep away feudalism with all its beauty and all its chivalry, when new forms arose from the decay of the old. Now far stronger explosives are arrayed against capitalism.' Such an analysis certainly did not fit the England of the 1880's, a land in which more and more workers were property-owners, a land in which voluntary building societies, friendly societies, co-operative societies, and savings banks had improved life and not worsened it. 'It is no use flinging about vague figures and big words.' Hyndman dismissed all too easily the problems a socialist state would have to face. 'But are these details not worth dealing with? Why do you jeer at the bottle-washer? Surely the bottle-washer is as good as the prince.' Of course contemporary England was not a utopia. 'I have always claimed that the rich take too much; but it is not true that they take all.' Many factory owners had come to realize that when they treated their workers better, both groups profited. Bradlaugh's own programme was one of social reform, of combination and co-operation for particular purposes, but not of socialism. Socialism would mean revolution and revolution would mean destruction.

> I speak for the people [he concluded] who are ready to suffer much if they may redeem some, who know that the errors of yesterday cannot be sponged away in a moment to-day, and who would try slowly, gradually to mould, to modify, to build, and who declare that those who preach international Socialism, and talk vaguely about explosives, are playing into the hands of our enemies, and giving our enemies an excuse to coerce us.[1]

Radicals outnumbered the socialists in the audience, which was hostile to Hyndman from the start. In any case, observed the *Pall Mall Gazette*, 'against so practised a gladiator Mr. Hyndman had little chance . . .'.[2] Yet the Bradlaugh–Hyndman debate served to give the Social Democratic Federation and its leader more publicity than they had ever received before.[3]

The battle lines were now drawn. As the *Sozial-Demokrat*, a German paper, put it, the St. James's Hall meeting had made one thing clear, that Bradlaugh, 'the bourgeois Malthusian

---

[1] *N.R.*, 27 Apr. 1884, pp. 289–97.
[2] Cited in *N.R.*, 27 Apr. 1884, p. 302.
[3] Cf. Cole, *British Working Class Politics, 1832–1914*, p. 89; Maccoby, *British Radicalism, 1853–1886*, p. 334.

and Atheistic Pope . . . has at last openly declared himself as against the English working classes. . . . As everywhere, so also in England, the Freethought movement only serves to turn away the workers from their true object, class war.'[1] Under the cover of social reform, snorted Hyndman later that summer, Bradlaugh, Cardinal Manning, and the Prince of Wales sat 'huddled together'. Bradlaugh, in turn, took considerable satisfaction in puncturing the socialist tendency to declaim in terms of absolutes. When Hyndman urged the immediate 'nationalisation of the land' Bradlaugh retorted that he was delaying practical measures of land reform. When Hyndman warned that 'a bloodier revolution is coming than the French one', Bradlaugh answered: 'Murder is never useful; dynamite and outrage are always harmful.' When socialists described the English government as an 'absolute despotism' Bradlaugh became wholly scornful. 'There are many faults and mischiefs in England, but if "absolute despotism" is an accurate term of description for the British Government at home, then new adjectives and adverbs of extremeness are required to properly describe, say, the Government of Russia.'[2]

Perhaps Bradlaugh became too involved with the extravagance of socialist propaganda and therefore missed its sparks of genuine idealism. Perhaps he became too resentful of the personal abuse which many socialists heaped upon him to view their ideas in perspective. Yet a profession of socialism by Stewart Headlam no more ended Bradlaugh's friendship with him than had his theological convictions, nor did it prevent a cordial relationship between Bradlaugh and George Bernard Shaw. His opposition to socialism brought out in Bradlaugh—and, for the moment, even more in Annie Besant—signs of an intolerant nationalism which saw the advocates of socialism as primarily German Jews, 'wild refugees, alien to the national life, careless of the national welfare, and ignorant of the national traditions'.[3] His opposition to socialism may also have pushed Bradlaugh into a too

---

[1] Cited in *N.R.*, 11 May 1884, p. 324.
[2] Cited in *N.R.*, 10 Aug. 1884, p. 108; *N.R.*, 14 Oct. 1883, p. 252; 17 Feb. 1884, p. 106; 13 Jan. 1884, p. 27; 28 Dec. 1884, p. 462.
[3] *N.R.*, 11 May 1884, p. 324. The words are Annie Besant's.

doctrinaire hostility toward measures of social reform which he might otherwise have come to favour. None the less, the very critical analysis which socialist doctrines were forced to undergo in Britain at the hands of professed working-class leaders such as Bradlaugh did much to mould the ultimate development of socialist thought in Britain. As for Bradlaugh—at whom the epithet of 'socialist' had so often been flung—he found himself for the first time the hero of journals which had never looked favourably upon him before. The *St. James's Gazette*, Queen Victoria's favourite newspaper, which had steadfastly opposed his admission to Parliament, considered his reply to Hyndman 'a remarkably effective demonstration of certain of the truths which cannot be too often urged against the well-meaning but mischievous enthusiasts who preach Socialism on public platforms'.[1]

Socialism as a rival force was, in any case, to play a continuing role in Bradlaugh's life from then on, and Bradlaugh's convictions on the subject were to influence, however coincidentally from Bradlaugh's own point of view, the ultimate outcome of his Parliamentary struggle.

[1] Cited in *N.R.*, 27 Apr. 1884, p. 276.

XXIII

THE TURNING OF THE TIDE

However Bradlaugh's time may have been diverted with questions of foreign policy, the problems of a national free-thought organization, and threats of socialism, it was the Parliamentary struggle that remained uppermost in his mind. And as a new session of Parliament approached early in 1884, Bradlaugh prepared to take new steps to keep his case alive. It may well be that by this time he had abandoned all hopes of ever sitting in the current Parliament,[1] but a new general election was not in the immediate offing, and for the sake of his Northampton constituents and his own future prospects he could not afford to drop out of sight.[2]

In a new manifesto Bradlaugh declared it to be his duty to present himself again as a lawful member of Parliament. He had uncovered a useful antiquarian titbit, that one Sir John Northcote had protested to Cromwell's Parliament in 1658 that legislation was incomplete so long as any properly chosen member was kept from his place by brute force. Might not the present Sir Stafford Northcote profit from the advice of his distant ancestor? The odds were against him, Bradlaugh conceded, but not completely: 'The Tories are against me; Cardinal Manning is against me; the Jesuits are against me; the Papal brigade is against me; the State church parsons are against me; the pensioned families are against me. But they know that despite all this I am not alone; I have the heart of the people with me'.[3]

Some 50,000 copies of the manifesto were distributed within a month; but what else was Bradlaugh to do? If he attempted to take the oath, Northcote would as usual move that he be not allowed to go through the form, and Northcote

---

[1] Cf. Hampden Diary, entry for 8 Feb. 1884.
[2] For references to occasional difficulties in keeping Bradlaugh's political organization in Northampton satisfied, see Thomas Adams MSS., *passim.*
[3] *N.R.*, 6 Jan. 1884, pp. 1–2.

would as usual be upheld. The chances for a new Affirmation Bill were nil. The legal hopes had all proved vain—all but one. What if he administered the oath to himself once again, and his right to do so were then tested in the law courts, not by a private citizen—this had been dismissed as collusive in 1882—but by the Crown in the person of the Attorney-General? The plan was privately broached to Gladstone, and he agreed. It was, after all, in line with the latter's oft-expressed preference to have Bradlaugh test his right to take the oath in the law courts as he had once tested his right to affirm. The Cabinet concurred.[1]

The Opposition, to be sure, was not informed of the plan, though an urgent whip had as usual been sent to all Tories. The House of Commons was packed on the night of 11 February 1884, and wherever there was room to sit, squat, or stand, members huddled together. The interest aroused by Bradlaugh's case, concluded a veteran observer of Parliament, 'was in no way abated'.[2] Suddenly Bradlaugh appeared on the scene, and flanked by two fellow M.P.s, Henry Labouchere and Thomas Burt, he advanced down the aisle to the Speaker's Table. Northcote rose to make his customary motion, but by this time Bradlaugh was reciting the words of the oath. He kissed the New Testament, signed the declaration, left it on the table, and, bowing gravely to the startled Speaker, withdrew once again to the bar.[3]

Amidst the uproar, Sir Stafford Northcote finally obtained the opportunity to move 'that Mr. Bradlaugh be not permitted to go through the form of repeating the words of the oath'. The motion seemed, to say the least, anti-climactic, since Bradlaugh had obviously just gone through that very form and presumably had no intention of doing so a second time. In the ensuing debate Gladstone explained that the law officers of the Crown would challenge the legality of the steps Bradlaugh had just taken. Labouchere assured the House that Bradlaugh had now legally taken the oath. Conceding, by implication, that Bradlaugh had once called part of the oath a meaningless form, Labouchere went further:

---

[1] Cabinet Minutes of 10 Feb. 1884, G.P. (B.M.), 44645, fol. 30.
[2] McCarthy, *England under Gladstone, 1880–1884*, p. 330.
[3] Lucy, *Two Parliaments*, ii. 373–4.

'I confess that, for my part, I do regard these words of the oath as an utterly unmeaning form—utterly and absolutely an unmeaning form. To me they are just the same superstitious incantation as the trash of any Mumbo-Jumbo among African savages.'[1] Labouchere's words, more extreme than any expression Bradlaugh had used in the course of his Parliamentary battle, roused a storm of angry 'Oh's' and 'Ah's' on the Opposition benches, but no one rose to challenge Labouchere's right to his seat. Lord Randolph Churchill and Tim Healy, a vociferous Irish M.P., were more concerned with preventing Bradlaugh from exercising his Parliamentary vote. Apparently fearful that the courts might after all uphold Bradlaugh's claims, the Opposition strove to find a way to prevent him from casting a vote. The Speaker declared himself powerless to stop Bradlaugh from voting without prior instructions, and when the division on Northcote's motion took place, Bradlaugh entered the 'Noes' Lobby.

Northcote's motion was carried, none the less, 280 to 168. The majority was made up of 218 Conservatives, 42 Home-Rulers, and 20 Liberals. The minority consisted solely of Liberals. Before these results had been officially announced, Tim Healy moved that Bradlaugh's vote be expunged from the records in order that 'no basis should be given for a mock action in the courts of law'. Sir Henry James observed reasonably enough that in the very act of officially disallowing Bradlaugh's vote, the House of Commons would admit that he had voted. Healy persisted with his motion, however. It was carried, 258 to 161. Bradlaugh again joined the 'Noes', thus voting a second time. When Northcote thereupon moved that Bradlaugh be excluded 'from the precints of the House until he shall engage not further to disturb the proceedings of the House', Labouchere promised on Bradlaugh's behalf that Northampton's junior M.P. would not attempt to take his seat again until the legal question had been settled, but Northcote and the Conservatives insisted on a division. It went against Bradlaugh, 228 to 120, though the latter had the limited satisfaction of thereby taking part in one last Parliamentary division before the

[1] *Hansard*, cclxxxiv (1884), 455.

doors of the House of Commons were once again shut against him.[1]

The groundwork for a new legal case having been laid, Bradlaugh forthwith resigned his seat in Parliament in order to seek a new vote of confidence from his Northampton constituents. Technically, to be sure, it was illegal to resign from the House of Commons, and while Bradlaugh's right to his seat had been successfully challenged, the legality of his election had not. A member could resign only by being appointed to the office of Steward of the Chiltern Hundreds, one of several offices of ancient origin the actual duties of which were non-existent but required the holder to relinquish his Parliamentary seat. Bradlaugh's appointment was, as usual, made automatically upon Bradlaugh's request by the Chancellor of the Exchequer. In this particular instance Lord Randolph Churchill and the Tory press were strongly critical of the action of the Government in thus affording Bradlaugh a new opportunity for electoral success.[2] Their protests went unheeded, however, and Bradlaugh found himself immediately embroiled in a vigorous political campaign.

Bradlaugh capitalized upon the manner in which he had been relieved of his Parliamentary duties, and in one election address he declared:

Friends, when I stood in 1868, a good, earnest man asked me a question which I then thought very foolish. He asked me whether I would ever take office under the Crown. And I remember telling him I didn't think I should ever have the chance; yet it is as an official under the Crown that I stand before you this evening . . . as Steward and Bailiff of the Three Hundreds of Chiltern. So that if to-night you detect any difference in the kind of things I say to you, you must remember that I am speaking with the responsibilities of office upon me.[3]

Bradlaugh saw the possibility of another election victory as a fitting response to the latest action of the House of Commons, and his campaign was by no means conducted in a predominantly humorous vein. Bradlaugh's key theme

[1] Lucy, *Two Parliaments*, ii. 374.
[2] *Hansard*, cclxxxiv (1884), 659–65; 'The Bradlaugh Muddle', *Saturday Review*, 16 Feb. 1884, p. 200.   [3] *N.R.*, 24 Feb. 1884, p. 129.

was that the voters should repudiate men like Lord Randolph Churchill who had reviled the Northampton electorate. It was bad enough, declared Bradlaugh, that such men should sit in Parliament, 'but it becomes monstrously foul when a nominee, who lives on the shoemakers of Northampton's earnings, who calls them "scum", should claim the right to negate their choice'.[1] The Northampton *Mercury*, the Moderate Liberal paper which even in the course of four years had developed little respect for Bradlaugh, conceded that for many voters this was the decisive issue, that both he and the borough of Northampton had been victims of injustice.[2]

The Opposition put on a spirited campaign. Dramatic touches were provided by one Dr. Buszard, who characterized Bradlaugh as one 'who sighed for a revolution after the manner of the French Revolution of 1789, with its hecatombs of victims and its torrents of blood'. H. C. Richards, who ran as Conservative candidate against Bradlaugh for the first time (though he had been campaigning for many months), did his best to subordinate politics to religion, and he appealed to all Liberals to support 'the higher claims of our common Christianity'.[3] By 1884, this type of appeal was hardly novel in Northampton, and the election results bore this out: Bradlaugh 4,032, Richards 3,664. Bradlaugh's majority, which had been 695 in 1880, 132 in 1881, and 108 in 1882, was now once again a respectable 368 votes. Any hopes which the Conservatives—or certain Liberals—might ever have had of settling the case by defeating Bradlaugh in Northampton had obviously been dashed for good. Several hundred new voters had been registered in the borough since the previous election, and among them Bradlaugh supporters clearly outnumbered opponents.[4] 'The offence of a constituency where some scores or hundreds of voters take glasses of beer or five-pound notes', asserted the *Saturday Review*, 'is, in any philosophical estimate, venial as compared with the offence of a constituency which obstinately returns a person like Mr. Bradlaugh.'[5] There is a note of despair discernible in

[1] *N.R.*, 17 Feb. 1884, p. 117.
[2] Northampton *Mercury*, 16 Feb. 1884, p. 5.
[3] *N.R.*, 17 Feb. 1884, p. 106; 24 Feb. 1884, p. 131.
[4] *N.R.*, 3 Sept. 1882, p. 161.
[5] *Saturday Review*, 16 Feb. 1884, p. 199.

this complaint, and several other periodicals were led to wonder whether it was not the House of Commons rather than the constituency which was at fault.

As soon as the election results were in, Bradlaugh gave private assurances to Gladstone and to Speaker Brand—who conveyed them to Northcote—that he would not present himself in the House of Commons again until the legality of his oath had judicially been settled.[1] Northcote none the less introduced a new resolution asking that Bradlaugh be excluded from the precincts of the House of Commons. The decision struck the Speaker as unfair and Edward Hamilton deemed it 'rather sharp practice' toward Bradlaugh. '. . . the feeling that he is being bullied is on the increase.'[2] Despite his inclination to believe that Northcote had once again been 'over-ruled by the most fiery spirits at the Carlton [the Conservative party club]' Bradlaugh wrote another devastating public letter to Sir Stafford: 'Yours is a mean and spiteful act, Sir, unworthy of an English gentleman. . . . You have allied yourself at Westminster with men whom you denounced in Ireland as "traitors and disloyal", in order that, with their help, you might insult an English constituency. . . . For shame, Sir Stafford Northcote! . . . You wear knightly orders. You should be above a knave's spitefulness.'[3]

Northcote's reply was a calm, almost apologetic, defence of his course in the House of Commons, and when in late March 1884 Bradlaugh requested the House's permission to make use of the Commons Library, Northcote observed 'nothing could be more reasonable than the request that Mr. Bradlaugh makes in that letter . . .'. When Tim Healy objected to the question being dealt with at that time, the Deputy Speaker observed 'questions involving the privileges of a Member of Parliament have . . . precedence over all other Business'.[4] For some purposes Bradlaugh was apparently a Member of Parliament after all. When a special session

[1] G.P. (B.M.), 44111, fol. 143; 44315, fol. 146; Northcote to Brand, 21 Feb. 1884, Hampden MSS.

[2] Hampden Diary, entry for 21 Feb. 1884; Hamilton Diary (B.M.), 48635, p. 106.

[3] Cited in N.R., 9 Mar. 1884, p. 161.

[4] Hansard, cclxxxvi (1884), 1137–8.

of Parliament convened later that year, Northcote quietly chose not to renew the restrictive resolution, so that Bradlaugh regained the right to enter that portion of the Commons chamber outside the bar.[1]

In the meantime, the Crown—in the person of Sir Henry James—had sued Bradlaugh for £1,500 in the Queen's Bench Division for having three times voted in Parliament without first properly taking the oath. The Government employment of Sir Hardinge Giffard ensured that the suit was to be anything but a collusive one. While faced with the awe-inspiring prospect of tilting legal lances with the leading advocates of both major parties, Bradlaugh did have the satisfaction of knowing that the trial was to take place 'at bar' before three judges and a special jury in the court of the Lord Chief Justice. This procedure, used only when 'the case is of great difficulty and importance', had been last employed in the Tichborne case, a *cause célèbre* of the previous decade.[2]

The trial began on 13 June 1884, and the Attorney-General led off by observing that the questions in dispute were less issues of fact than issues of inference and of law. According to the Oaths Act of 1866, each Member of Parliament had to take an oath of allegiance which included the words 'I swear . . . . So help me God.' This had to be done while the House was in session and the Speaker in the chair. Standing orders provided that the taking of the oath must not interrupt other debate or business. Turning to Bradlaugh's particular case, the Attorney-General sought to prove that these conditions had not been fulfilled. Bradlaugh had admittedly read the words of the oath and kissed the New Testament, but the Speaker had been crying 'Order, order' at the time—meaning that other business lay before the House—and the Clerk of the House had not administered the oath as he customarily did.

The second question, 'one of course of greater substance and importance', was whether Bradlaugh was 'a person who can make an oath within the meaning of the words of the legislature'. Bradlaugh, in requesting the right of affirmation

<hr>

[1] *N.R.*, 2 Nov. 1884, p. 291.
[2] *N.R.*, 16 Mar. 1884, pp. 180–1; 6 Apr. 1884, p. 232; 13 Apr. 1884, p. 241; 1 June 1884, p. 376.

as a legal witness and in his letter of 20 May 1880 had indicated that an oath had no binding effect upon his conscience. Bradlaugh had declared, Sir Henry James conceded, that a promise would be binding upon him. Yet the statute called for an oath rather than for a promise.

Bradlaugh had the opportunity to cross-examine the witnesses produced by Sir Henry James, and in questioning Sir Erskine May, the Clerk of the House, Bradlaugh obtained the concession that the manner in which the oath was ordinarily administered was a matter of custom rather than one of standing orders or of law. Sir Erskine May further admitted that the Speaker might have been sitting for a time while the self-administration of the oath was going on.

In order to document his proposition that Bradlaugh as an atheist could not technically take an oath, the Attorney-General introduced into the record the entire transcript of the evidence heard by the second Select Committee in 1880. Bradlaugh retorted that the evidence produced by the Attorney-General was insufficient to prove that Bradlaugh held no belief in a Supreme Being four years later on 11 February 1884. No evidence as to his state of mind on that last occasion had been submitted.[1]

On 16 June Bradlaugh personally began the case for the defence. He referred to previous decisions in which the judges had held that the words 'So help me God' were not an 'essential' portion of the oath, and he went on to cite his own frequent assurances that the essential portion of the oath would be fully binding upon him. One of the three judges, Baron Huddleston, interrupted these proceedings to muse out loud: 'What was passing through my mind was this, that the whole of the matter that has been agitated in the House of Commons, and that is agitating us to-day, would be set at rest in a moment in one word, by saying, "I do believe in a Supreme Being who has the power to reward and punish."'

This was, to be sure, the one concession Bradlaugh could never make. Bradlaugh did not enter the box in his own defence during the trial. He went on at great length, however, to try to show that while the self-administration of the oath

[1] *N.R.*, 17 June 1884, pp. 417–20, 427; 19 June 1884, pp. 433–9.

might have been irregular it had in no sense been illegal. The Speaker had said nothing at the time about having been defied.

Bradlaugh then came to grips with the issue of the oath. Let them assume, he suggested, that he was a defendant in a case of perjury. If in such a case he were to argue in his defence that four years earlier, on another occasion, a judge had decided that an oath was not binding upon his conscience, would the judge in the perjury case accept the proposition that since the oath-taking had been a sham he therefore was innocent of perjury? No judge would even consider so astounding a proposition. In this hypothetical case, as in the actual case at issue, to take an oath meant precisely that, to take an oath. Lord Coleridge interrupted to comment that in the hypothetical case Bradlaugh had outlined, his going through the form of the oath would have been quite sufficient to subject him to legal penalties. That was precisely his point, agreed Bradlaugh. 'Because I say the law recognizes no distinction between going through the solemn form and the reality. There has no such distinction ever been drawn in the history of jurisprudence.'[1]

In his summing up Bradlaugh reiterated the argument that the Crown was introducing legal novelties. According to the Parliamentary Oaths Act of 1866, he insisted, there were but two classes of persons, those who affirmed and those who took the oath. In order to win a verdict in this trial, the Crown had in effect to create a third class, those who could take neither oath nor affirmation, a class the courts had not hitherto recognized.

In his own summing up the Attorney-General paid a personal compliment to Bradlaugh, who 'has utilised the time at his disposal with great ability, and with relevancy . . .'. Yet the fact that the House of Commons had itself been dissatisfied with Bradlaugh's oath could hardly be overlooked by the judges. The ultimate question was: Did Bradlaugh believe in a Supreme Being? That he had had no such belief four years before had already been demonstrated. That he had such a belief at the present time might have been indicated by Bradlaugh's stepping into the witness box rather

[1] *N.R.*, 19 June 1884, pp. 446–8; 20 June 1884, pp. 449–58.

than his relying on the negative inference of lapse of time. Admittedly, Bradlaugh had time and again stated that he would be bound upon his honour and conscience. 'Gentlemen,' proceeded Sir Henry James, 'all I can say is that from what I have seen of Mr. Bradlaugh's conduct elsewhere, and the way in which he has fulfilled his promises in every respect, I have no reason to doubt that any promise he gave would be binding upon his honour and conscience. . . . But it is not enough that the promise should be binding upon his honour and conscience. . . . The law has asked for an oath.'[1]

The interpretation of the law was for the judges, declared the Chief Justice in his charge to the jury, but questions of fact were for the jury to decide. After three hours, the jury returned with its replies to the questions posed:

1. Was the Speaker sitting or standing while the oath was being administered? He was sitting.

2. What was his purpose? To prepare notes to address to the defendant.

3. Was it for the purpose of allowing the defendant to take the oath? No.

4. Did the defendant believe in a Supreme Being? We unanimously agree that the defendant had upon the 11th February 1884 no belief in a Supreme Being.

5. Was an oath binding upon his conscience? It was not binding upon his conscience as an oath.

6. Had the House of Commons full cognisance of these matters? Yes.

7. Did the defendant take the oath according to the practice of Parliament? Not according to the full practice of Parliament.

8. Did the defendant take and subscribe the oath? Not as an oath.

The judges consequently found for the Crown.[2]

The Press reaction was predictable. The Conservative *Morning Post* and *Standard* saw the struggle as ended for good. The Liberal papers reflected upon the injustice which had been done to Bradlaugh. *The Times* observed that 'the trial will probably satisfy no one that the sanction of an oath is necessary to make members of Parliament faithful to their obligation of allegiance'. As for Bradlaugh himself, he

[1] *N.R.*, 24 June 1884, pp. 463–80; 1 July 1884, pp. 1–3.
[2] *N.R.*, 6 July 1884, pp. 26–28.

conceded nothing. He would appeal. 'I have never yet been beaten in any of my big legal struggles', he declared defiantly.[1]

When Bradlaugh, in December 1884, asked for a new trial on the basis that the verdict was against the evidence, his request was refused. Bradlaugh then took the case to a Court of Appeal made up of the Master of the Rolls and Lord Justices Cotton and Lindley. All the old arguments were rehashed. 'I say, my lords,' declared Bradlaugh, 'there has never been a case in the whole of English history in which, after an oath has been completely taken, there has been held to be any jurisdiction to set that oath aside and say it has not been taken.'[2] The Attorney-General contended that the suit ought to be considered a criminal suit and that therefore no right of appeal existed. The Court upheld Bradlaugh's contention that it was a civil suit and that he did have the right of appeal, but on the main issue Bradlaugh lost again. The lower court was upheld. The relevant Oaths Act, the judges proclaimed, did indeed have the effect of excluding from Parliament all persons 'who, like the defendant, cannot lawfully make a declaration and who cannot take the oath; and to render them liable to penalties if they do sit and vote'. Bradlaugh immediately expressed the desire to appeal from the decision to the final court of appeal, the House of Lords, but the very fact that he delayed eleven months before doing so demonstrates that he was by this time aware of the hopelessness of his legal position.[3]

One of the ironies of the long-drawn-out agitation over Bradlaugh's admission to Parliament is that, at the very time when his legal position had never looked darker, the tide of public antipathy had begun slowly to recede from the height it had reached at the time of the struggle over the Affirmation Bill. 'I suppose the country has not been so deeply stirred by anything within the last five years as it was stirred by that proposal', recalled Sir Michael Hicks-Beach, the new Conservative leader in the House of Commons, in 1885.[4] By that time the matter no longer loomed quite so large.

[1] Cited in *N.R.*, 6 July 1884, p. 17; 13 July 1884, p. 38.
[2] *N.R.*, 21 Dec. 1884, pp. 436–45.
[3] *N.R.*, 1 Feb. 1885, pp. 67, 81–110; 4 Feb. 1885, 113–28; 7 Feb. 1885, pp. 129–42; 10 Jan. 1886, p. 17.
[4] *Hansard*, ccxcviii (1885), 1675.

Not that the change was a sudden one. Although for the *Saturday Review* Bradlaugh had already by the autumn of 1884 become one of many 'forgotten things',[1] this was hardly true for all Conservatives. Tory speakers still made occasional references to Bradlaugh as 'an apostle of the most hideous forms of immorality' or merely as a 'disgusting reptile'.[2] And Lord Randolph Churchill continued consistently to use the issue as a stick with which to beat the Gladstone Ministry. The unfortunate state of the country, declared Lord Randolph in January 1884, was the result of 'the policy of statesmen who for party purposes are ready to deride morality and paralyse law; who, to gain a few votes either in Parliament or in a borough, ally themselves equally with the atheist or with the rebel'.[3] A man who could refer to Gladstone as 'the Moloch of Midlothian' and as 'an evil and moonstruck minister' would hardly hesitate to dismiss Bradlaugh as a 'seditious blasphemer'. He did, admittedly, feel compelled on one occasion to explain that in referring to Bradlaugh's supporters as 'mob, scum, and dregs' he was not indicating the vast mass of English working men but merely those 'who are always ready to place themselves at the disposal of any politician, whether he be Mr. Chamberlain or Mr. Bradlaugh, whose one and only object is to subvert altogether the peace of the country and to destroy the foundations on which law and order repose'.[4] It was a curious fact, remarked Gladstone to Edward Hamilton in 1884, that 'real vulgar abuse' invariably 'emanated from scions of the highest aristocracy'.[5]

Sir Henry Drummond Wolff and Cardinal Manning in a more roundabout fashion continued to make occasional references to the Bradlaugh case as well. Others saw divine retribution in the water shortage which afflicted Northampton during the summer of 1883. An organization calling itself the Daily Prayer Union recommended the following: 'We bless Thee for outstretching Thy hand from heaven to prevent

---

[1] Cited in *N.R.*, 19 Oct. 1884.
[2] Cited in *N.R.*, 23 Mar. 1884, p. 194; 14 Dec. 1884, p. 385.
[3] Lord Randolph Churchill, *Speeches of the Right Honourable Lord Randolph Churchill, 1880–1888*, collected by Louis J. Jennings (London, 1889), ii. 56.
[4] Cited by G. W. Foote, *Lord Randolph Churchill, The Woodstock Bantam* (London, 1885), p. 5, and in *N.R.*, 26 Oct. 1884, p. 273.
[5] Hamilton Diary (B.M.), 48635, p. 75.

professed atheism having a place in our Parliament.' Reports from Turkey that Noah's Ark had been discovered on Mount Ararat caused one religionist to ponder: 'If the Ark has come down, what about Bradlaugh and such as he? It would be the greatest blow that infidelity and atheism could receive from any quarter.'[1]

In the meantime, the Affirmation Bill struggle had improved relations between Conservatives and Irish M.P.s in the House of Commons. Irish members tended to forget that in 1880 Lord Randolph Churchill had denounced them as a 'gang of political desperadoes alien in race and religion', and at least one Irish M.P. spoke of an actual 'alliance between Catholicism and Conservatism'.[2] The Irish Nationalists remained consistently in the anti-Bradlaugh camp, though Tim Healy threatened playfully on one occasion that the Irish might reverse course, if only to teach Sir Stafford Northcote the lesson that he could not continue to play the role of successful champion of Christianity without their aid. Yet the threat was not carried out, and although the Bradlaugh case was made an open question for Home-Rule members in 1884, the party remained steadfastly hostile.[3] Healy and Parnell both participated in the Bradlaugh case debates of 1884 and 1885. Their attitude helped to cement the Irish-Conservative *entente* which toppled the Gladstone Ministry in June 1885, and greatly influenced the results of the general election five months later.

It was in the Liberal ranks that a subtle shift became most noticeable. To some extent it is attributable to the widespread circulation of Gladstone's Affirmation Bill speech during 1883 and 1884. W. M. Rathbone of Liverpool, a Liberal M.P. representing a Welsh constituency, had the speech reprinted at his own expense and, with Gladstone's approval, sent a copy to every clergyman in the Church of England, every minister of the Scottish Church, and every Nonconformist minister in the British Isles. An accompanying letter read as follows:

Your perusal of the enclosed is requested in the interests of

[1] *N.R.*, 9 Sept. 1883, p. 168; 23 Dec. 1883, p. 422; 26 Aug. 1883, p. 134.
[2] Cited in *Tablet*, 27 Nov. 1880, p. 675; *Hansard*, cclxxx (1883), 807.
[3] Cited in *N.R.*, 10 Feb. 1884; Newcastle *Daily Chronicle*, 12 Feb. 1884. (Clipping in Cowen MSS., file B 329.)

Religion, which, in our opinion, is imperilled by the recent action of the House of Commons [the defeat of the Affirmation Bill]. That action has seriously advanced the popularity of Mr. Bradlaugh among a very active section of the working classes previously opposed to Atheism. It has enormously increased the popularity and sale of his works. It has, we fear, by causing him to be regarded as the Champion of Popular Rights, converted many working men from a position of neutrality towards Religion into its active opponents; and it is calculated to promote the creation in this country of that class of bitter, proselytising Atheistic Communism which is already so dangerous to law and order in Continental countries, but has hitherto been rare in our own.[1]

The results were not dramatic, but from then on Gladstone found himself frequently acknowledging 'with pleasure' pledges by Anglican clergymen and others to support a future Affirmation Bill.[2] Lord Aberdeen, shortly before being appointed Lord High Commissioner to the General Assembly of the Church of Scotland, had also given wide publicity to a circular deploring the rejection of the Affirmation Bill. When the question of the propriety of this action was raised in the House of Commons, Gladstone commented sardonically that 'however wrong Lord Aberdeen might be in thinking a speech delivered by me worthy of perusal, it is not an offence of which the House could well take notice'.[3]

Liberals came to be more nearly unanimous in condemning the actions of the House of Commons towards Bradlaugh. In any party meeting in which the question was raised, noted William Woodall, M.P., in March 1884, 'there was a strong party-feeling on the side of justice as against the side of the House...'.[4] Nor was Bradlaugh denied all personal sympathy. Bradlaugh's behaviour 'would entitle him to give many of his opponents lessons in good taste and good manners', declared one Liberal candidate. Although one recent biographer of Gladstone has concluded that the Prime Minister 'thought as badly of the man as he did of his opinions'[5] he fails to

[1] Cited in G.P. (B.M.), 44481, fol. 38; see also G.P. (B.M.), 44480, fols. 309–10. [2] Cf. G.P. (B.M.), 44485, fols. 263, 264.

[3] *Hansard*, cclxxix (1883), 1332.

[4] Cited in *N.R.*, 9 Mar. 1884, p. 163.

[5] Magnus, *Gladstone*, p. 278.

document the judgement. Though Gladstone's hostility towards Bradlaugh's religious views can hardly be in dispute, and though Gladstone discouraged private meetings with the Northampton M.P., so 'that there should be no room for misrepresentation as to what may pass between us',[1] it seems clear that he had some appreciation of Bradlaugh's courage, perseverance, and sense of duty. He even denied the contention of one correspondent that atheists lacked a conscience. 'I cannot hold that proposition', wrote Gladstone, 'in the face of such facts as [George Jacob] Holyoake, such as at one time John S. Mill.... God may have been pleased to impress upon our nature enough of himself to imply the rudimentary obligation & faculty which may suffice for some natures, though not for the common man.'[2] Gladstone's daughter Mary and son Herbert, with whom he frequently discussed the case, came increasingly to voice sympathy for Bradlaugh personally. Had not Bradlaugh repeatedly declared that the oath and affirmation were 'absolutely binding' upon him, Herbert Gladstone impatiently reminded one critical correspondent. 'Why in the name of justice . . . do you refuse to believe what he says?' In 1883 Herbert Gladstone publicly avowed his hope that Northampton would continue to return Bradlaugh at every future election.[3]

Equally gratifying to Bradlaugh was increasing support from Radical Birmingham. Francis Schnadhorst, the leader of the Liberal caucus in the city, served as chairman at a giant rally addressed by Bradlaugh early in 1885. 'Be sure of it,' he told the crowd, 'that as soon as the 2,000,000 of new voters exercise their rights under the Seats Bill [the Reform Act of 1884 and the accompanying Redistribution Act], no power left in the House of Commons will be able to resist the recognition of Mr. Bradlaugh's position and the constitutional principle for which he contended.'[4] Joseph Chamberlain became increasingly outspoken in his support, and once the

---

[1] (Copy) Gladstone to Bradlaugh, 21 June 1881, G.P. (B.M.), 44544, fol. 183.　　　[2] (Copy) G.P. (B.M.), 44544, fol. 180.
[3] Viscount Gladstone MSS. (B.M.), 46049 [comments on letters by Whitaker, 1882]; Sir Charles Mallet, *Herbert Gladstone: A Memoir* (London, 1932), p. 107; *Mrs. Mary (Gladstone) Drew: Her Diary and Letters*, ed. Lucy Masterman (London, 1930), p. 238 and *passim*.
[4] *N.R.*, 1 Mar. 1885, p. 195.

Gladstone Ministry had resigned and he felt himself no longer constrained by Cabinet responsibilities, he supplemented verbal praise with a cheque for twenty guineas to help defray Bradlaugh's legal expenses.[1] By 1885 Bradlaugh could with justice declare: 'Now, at any rate, there are rifts in the clouds.'[2]

A somewhat greater display of courage on the part of Liberal politicians may have been a partial reflection of the more numerous, and less often qualified, pledges of support which Bradlaugh was receiving from Nonconformist ministers and others. For Stewart Headlam and his Guild of St. Matthew this represented no change, though Headlam could still create a minor sensation in 1884 by speaking in an offhand manner of 'my friend, Mr. Bradlaugh'. His *Church Reformer* noted that 'the comfortable, well-to-do middle-class people . . . are now taking up Mr. Bradlaugh . . . '.[3] The *Primitive Methodist* was equally outspoken, and by the summer of that year the *Jewish World* had to come to the conclusion that 'thanks to the virulent persecution of his antagonists, the aversion with which he was originally regarded, rightly or wrongly, by various sections of the religionists, is rapidly being transformed on all sides into sympathy with him as a suffering and patient martyr in a great constitutional cause'.[4]

A comparable subtle shift of attitude is discernible in the daily press. Bradlaugh had always had a number of provincial papers very much in his corner, papers such as the Edinburgh *Scotsman*, the South Wales *Daily News*, the Liverpool *Mercury*, the Birmingham *Daily Mail*, and the *Manchester Guardian*. The London papers had been less consistent. While the *Daily News*, the *Chronicle*, and *Pall Mall Gazette* all supported Bradlaugh's admission, both the *Daily News*, regarded as the country's leading Liberal paper, and the *Pall Mall Gazette*, under John Morley's editorship the country's leading Radical paper, had often been so caustic about Bradlaugh personally that he spoke of them as false friends. What especially distressed him was the failure—a deliberate one in his view—of

---

[1] *N.R.*, 8 Feb. 1885, p. 145. Chamberlain's letter is quoted in *N.R.*, 2 Aug. 1885, p. 76.   [2] *N.R.*, 8 Feb. 1885, p. 146.
[3] Cited in *N.R.*, 17 Feb. 1884, p. 104; 25 May 1884, pp. 353–4.
[4] Cited in *N.R.*, 20 Jan. 1884, pp. 38, 55.

the London press to report, fully or at all, the numerous meetings he addressed. The *Morning Post*, the *St. James's Gazette*, and the *Morning Advertiser*, the leading Conservative papers in the city, were consistently hostile. In the middle of the political spectrum stood the *Telegraph*, Liberal with strong Conservative leanings, the *Standard*, Conservative with strong Liberal leanings, and *The Times*. The chief proprietor of *The Times* was John Walter, a Whiggishly inclined Liberal M.P., and Gladstone was often unhappy with its editorial policy. On one occasion he privately termed it 'the most blackguard paper',[1] but Bradlaugh considered it generally fair, partly because it provided the most complete reports of the legal cases in which he was involved. Then, too, it had treated the Bradlaugh case from the first as a grave constitutional question for which Bradlaugh's exclusion was no adequate solution. Once Northampton had returned Bradlaugh for a fourth time in February 1884 the stand of *The Times* became even less equivocal: 'The results of the election at Northampton must strengthen the conviction that the policy pursued in the House of Commons toward Mr. Bradlaugh has been a tissue of mistakes.'[2]

This trend of opinion increasingly coincided with what had been the general theme of newspaper opinion abroad. For the Bradlaugh case was widely reported on the Continent— 'Every incident relating to the Oaths Bill and Mr. Bradlaugh is reported at Rome and Florence and throughout the cities of Italy by telegram in all the chief newspapers', reported one tourist in the spring of 1881[3]—and newspaper opinion, especially in the anti-clerical French and Italian press, was generally sympathetic to Bradlaugh. Thus the Paris *Journal des Débats* saw 'all this show of orthodoxy [as] only tyranny or hypocrisy'. On the morrow of the Affirmation Bill defeat, the same journal declared: 'It is freedom of conscience rather than the Government which has sustained a rebuff . . . .'[4] The case was also widely reported throughout the British Empire. The Toronto *Bystander* of Canada carried a stinging

[1] Hamilton Diary, entry for 7 July 1883 (B.M.), 48634, p. 19.
[2] *The Times*, 20 Feb. 1884, p. 10.
[3] *N.R.*, 26 June 1881, p. 12.
[4] Cited in *N.R.*, 22 May 1881, p. 424, and in G.P. (B.M.), 44481, fol. 60.

condemnation by Goldwin Smith of the attacks on Brad-laugh.[1] Contemporary New Zealand furnished Bradlaugh with an even greater satisfaction, for not only did the legislature there enact an Affirmation Bill in 1885, but Robert Stout, one-time editor of that colony's *Freethought Review*, was chosen Prime Minister.[2]

In the United States, newspaper opinion was also largely favourable to Bradlaugh's case, though sympathetic newspaper editorials were tinged with anti-British sentiments. 'It is a pitiable spectacle,' opined the Chicago *Morning News*, 'that of the British House of Commons, in the last quarter of the nineteenth century, ejecting and injuring a member because of his religious views.' The Omaha *Daily Republican* concurred. 'Let England talk of Catholic intolerance, of monarchical despotism; let her boast of free institutions, of liberty of conscience—but let her no longer boast that she is the enlightened apostle of progress. The world points at her with scorn and mocking.'[3] The Chicago *Herald* considered the case 'astonishing' and throwing 'much light on English conservatism and English prejudices'. Things were different in the United States, exulted the *Chicago Tribune*. Americans chose their politicians like their architects, on the basis of their abilities rather than on the basis of their theological opinions. Perhaps fifty members of the Congress of 1880, estimated the *Tribune*, held opinions very similar to those of Bradlaugh.[4] Occasional American papers might be critical of Bradlaugh's character or belief, but there appeared to be a general consensus that, as the New York *Sun* put it, the House of Commons had placed itself on record 'as the most bigoted assembly that exists in any part of the civilized world'. 'Of course there cannot be any controversy upon this question', agreed the *New York Times*. 'The merits are all with Bradlaugh.'[5] 'If you were a citizen of the United States', wrote Dr. E. B. Foote of New York to Bradlaugh,

I think no greater interest could be manifested than is among the Liberals of this country for your success in your efforts to

[1] Cited in *N.R.*, 22 May 1881, p. 411.
[2] *N.R.*, 3 Jan. 1886, p. 1; 12 Oct. 1884, p. 248.
[3] Cited in *N.R.*, 4 Sept. 1881, p. 237; 11 Sept. 1881, p. 247.
[4] Cited in *N.R.*, 5 Aug. 1883, p. 87; 1 Aug. 1880, p. 119.
[5] Cited in *N.R.*, 21 May 1883, p. 391; 2 Sept. 1883, p. 151.

secure the seat to which you have been honorably elected by the electors of Northampton on three occasions. I am inclined to think that the name of Charles Bradlaugh is as familiar to most people in the United States as that of any member of the United States Senate or of Congress.[1]

A £5 contribution to Bradlaugh's Constitutional Rights Fund accompanied the letter.

[1] Cited in *N.R.*, 11 Oct. 1885, p. 235.

XXIV

THE TRIUMPH OF PERSEVERANCE

DURING the spring of 1885 Bradlaugh staked his immediate hopes upon a new Affirmation Bill introduced by Charles Henry Hopwood, the Liberal M.P. whose vote on the Select Committee in 1880 against Bradlaugh's right to affirm had proved so damaging. Bradlaugh encouraged a new petition campaign, while the *Church Times* urged churchmen to bestir themselves in opposition to the bill.[1] The petition campaign on neither side rivalled the intense efforts of 1881, 1882, or 1883, but Bradlaugh did succeed in amassing over 77,000 signatures by June.[2] Although a Conservative, Percy Windham—one of the two Conservatives who had briefly supported Bradlaugh's case in 1880—co-sponsored the measure, there was never any great likelihood of its passage. It was an easy matter in the Parliament of the 1880's to block a private member's bill from coming to a vote, and Gladstone showed no inclination to renew the battle in a dying Parliament.[3]

The disintegration of the second Gladstone Ministry had been a possibility as early as 1883; the diary of one of Gladstone's secretaries is filled with reflections on the likelihood of the Prime Minister's resignation. The Reform Bill of 1884 had temporarily revived the popularity of the Liberal party in the country; the Irish had given it their support and the Conservative leadership found it difficult flatly to oppose the measure. The year 1885 had begun, however, with the failure of a relief expedition to the Sudan to reach General Gordon in time, a development generally attributed to Cabinet bungling. Never had the Ministry been less popular, and not the least of its critics was the Queen. 'She will never be happy', Gladstone had confided three years before, 'till she has hounded me out of office.'[4] The Liberal Cabinet succeeded

---

[1] Cited in *N.R.*, 22 Feb. 1885, p. 179.
[2] *Report of the Select Committee on Parliamentary Petitions*, 1885.
[3] *N.R.*, 22 Feb. 1885, p. 179; 8 Mar. 1885, p. 215; 20 Mar. 1885, p. 257.
[4] Hamilton Diary (B.M.), 48632, p. 88.

in surviving a few months longer, but after Chamberlain's scheme for local government in Ireland had once again revealed a deep cleavage within the Government, Gladstone may have welcomed the Parliamentary defeat on the budget, which came on 8 June 1885, as a result of Irish opposition and Liberal abstentions. Gladstone resigned the next day. No immediate general election was possible because the Franchise Reform Act and the accompanying bill to redistribute seats required several months more for the drawing of district boundaries and registration of new voters. The Conservative party agreed to form a government for the time being, even though the Liberals retained a small overall majority in the House of Commons. Lord Salisbury became the caretaker Prime Minister.

Had such an event occurred several years earlier, the choice might well have been Sir Stafford Northcote. But in the course of five years the supposed party leader in the House of Commons had too often proved to be the follower of the fiery Lord Randolph Churchill, whose opportunistic efforts had revived Conservative spirits. In 1883 he had helped to sponsor the Primrose League, 'a new political society which should embrace all classes and all creeds except atheists and enemies of the British nation',[1] and his election, in 1884, as chairman of the National Union of Conservative Associations, had transformed the party leadership into a Salisbury–Northcote–Churchill triumvirate. That same year Churchill and Salisbury had joined forces, a development generally welcomed by party members, though regretted by John Gorst, one of Churchill's 'Fourth Party' associates, as a sell-out of 'Tory democracy'. But no reconciliation could come with Northcote, a man who had wishfully imagined Churchill breaking with the Conservative party in order to join the Radical wing of the Liberals[2] and a man for whom Churchill had no respect whatsoever. And so when the Conservative Government took office, Northcote was 'kicked upstairs' and created Lord Iddesleigh. Though he

    [1] Winston S. Churchill, *Life of Lord Randolph Churchill*, i. 257.
    [2] Northcote to Salisbury, 3 June 1884, Salisbury MSS; Harold E. Gorst, *The Fourth Party*, pp. 302 ff. Churchill did consider the possibility briefly early in 1884. Dilke MSS. (B.M.), 43938, fols. 143, 144.

received the title of First Lord of the Treasury, that title was not on this occasion identical with that of Prime Minister. 'I have always thought that the operation might have been performed with rather more consideration', observed the new Lord Iddesleigh a few months later.[1] Lord Randolph Churchill became the new Secretary of State for India and Sir Hardinge Giffard (as Lord Halsbury) the new Lord Chancellor. It was hardly reassuring to Bradlaugh to see two such consistent enemies receive such obvious promotions. The leadership of the Commons, to be sure, was entrusted to Sir Michael Hicks-Beach, a Conservative M.P. who had played no active role in the Bradlaugh case.

Bradlaugh had no desire, however, to let the new government forget his existence, especially since its creation had extinguished his slim hopes in the success of Hopwood's Affirmation Bill. He therefore presented himself once again to take the oath on 6 July 1885. Sir Michael Hicks-Beach interrupted with the motion Northcote had customarily made. Since the courts had declared Bradlaugh incapable of taking an oath, declared Sir Michael, his swearing would constitute an 'illegal mockery'. The Bradlaugh case was admittedly 'a question of vast importance to the country', but it might well be relegated to the constituencies and to the House of Commons soon to be elected. Charles Henry Hopwood submitted an amendment putting the House on record as favouring legislation permitting the substitution of affirmations for oaths. Gladstone, although surprised by Bradlaugh's decision to revive the question in the outgoing Parliament and advised by Sir Henry James that he had no obligation to advise the House on the issue,[2] spoke warmly in support of Hopwood's amendment. 'A grievous wrong' had been done to Northampton, declared Gladstone in what the *Freeman's Journal* termed 'the strongest and most earnest plea which has yet been submitted in favour of the rejected elected of Northampton'.[3]

Although the Liberal Federation of Birmingham and the National Reform Union urged all Liberals to be present,

[1] Iddesleigh to Hicks-Beach, 30 Jan. 1886, St. Aldwyn MSS. file PCC, fol. 77.	[2] G.P. (B.M.), 44219, fol. 185.
[3] *Freeman's Journal* (Dublin), 7 July 1885, p. 4.

Gladstone made no attempt to have the issue treated in the Commons as a party question. It was otherwise with the Conservatives, who issued an urgent ministerial whip, and with the Parnellites, nine of whom cut short a stay in Ireland to return to Westminster in time to vote against Bradlaugh.[1] The result was a vote of 263 to 219 against Hopwood's amendment, 'an agreeable surprise to the Government', according to the Conservative *Morning Post*.[2] Voting for the Hopwood amendment were 1 Conservative, 4 Home Rulers (three of whom had earlier broken with Parnell), and 214 Liberals. Voting against it were 218 Conservatives, 35 Parnellites, and 10 Liberals.

The reactions were predictable. The *Non-Conformist* castigated the 'weak-kneed' Liberals who, by deserting Gladstone, had promoted Bradlaugh to martyrdom. The Roman Catholic *Universe* was 'heartily sick of Mr. Bradlaugh; we do not like the man's face, his manner, or his opinions. He is a nuisance. We wish someone would induce him to emigrate.'[3] As for Queen Victoria, she thought that Sir Michael Hicks-Beach had acted 'with great prudence and firmness in his new and difficult position'.[4]

Even while Parliament was still in session, the forthcoming general election had become the chief focus of public interest. The election of 1885 was in several respects a peculiar one. In contrast to other British elections, the campaign went on for several months. Unlike 1874 or 1880 there were no major issues which clearly differentiated the two parties. Though Gladstone defined the difference in an aphorism—'The principle of Liberalism is trust in the people, qualified by prudence; the principle of Conservatism is mistrust of the people, qualified by fear'[5]—aphorisms may sometimes serve as substitutes for issues.

The election was so soon to be overshadowed by the Home Rule controversy that it is forgotten that the Irish question, while it affected the election of 1885, was then more the

[1] *Freeman's Journal* (Dublin), 6 July 1885, p. 5.
[2] Cited in *N.R.*, 12 July 1885, p. 21.
[3] Cited in *N.R.*, 19 July 1885, pp. 43, 42.
[4] St. Aldwyn MSS., file PCC, fol. 73.
[5] *Why I am a Liberal*, ed. Andrew Reid (London, 1885), cited in *N.R.*, 29 Nov. 1885, p. 339.

source of internal party division than a solid plank in either party's platform. Gladstone's own election manifesto spoke of land law reform and of changes in the House of Lords. Chamberlain's 'Unauthorised Programme' struck fear in the hearts of Anglican clergymen and Roman Catholics alike. Indeed the spectre of disestablishment and of secular education caused Manning to re-enter the political arena with new fervour. *How Shall Catholics Vote at the Coming Parliamentary Election?* was the title he gave to a widely distributed pamphlet. A Catholic's first duty, he observed, was 'to sustain, to confirm, to uphold, and to perfect, everything of Christian truth, and of natural morality still subsisting in the English people'. All threats to the Crown and the House of Lords must be resisted, since these were original Catholic institutions. 'In this sense every Catholic must be conservative.' Catholics might be Liberals as well, but hardly advocates of the false liberalism which had promoted the Education Act of 1870.[1] Manning 'has certainly detached more Catholics from the Liberal party than any other individual', Lord Granville had commented privately to Chamberlain a few months before, and this election manifesto was hardly likely to reverse the process.[2]

Only a minority of Liberal M.P.s would have agreed that either disestablishment or changes in the education law were the key issue of the day, though they often found themselves on the defensive on both issues. 'The only thing that I see', announced Lord Salisbury in October 1885, 'is a wave of infidelity which is sweeping over the land.' To this Gladstone 'bows his head submissively'.[3] Paradoxically, Gladstone was at that very moment interrupting his election activities with a thoroughly orthodox discourse on 'The Dawn of Creation and of Worship' in the *Nineteenth Century*.

For other Conservatives the key issue remained a closely related aspect of the religious question, the Bradlaugh case. All the failures of the second Gladstone ministry, declared Colonel Milne-Holme, a Conservative M.P., stemmed from

---

[1] Henry Edward Manning, *How Shall Catholics Vote at the Coming Parliamentary Election?* (London, 1885), *passim*.

[2] Granville MSS., file PRO/29, fol. 117.

[3] Cited in *N.R.*, 25 Oct. 1885, p. 260.

its acknowledging of 'the principle of Atheism in the House of Commons'. There were two big issues for Colonel Hill, the Conservative candidate for Bristol South: 'The first was Christianity *versus* Atheism . . . and the other was the Queen and Constitution *versus* Republicanism.'[1]

New ammunition to Conservative speakers was provided by a Baptist minister, the Reverend J. T. Almy, who in *Almighty God or Bradlaugh?* concluded that to admit Bradlaugh into the House of Commons would be 'to bring down the British Constitution from the mountain top of Christianity, where it was placed by Alfred the Great, and where by the grace of God it has been kept ever since . . .'. The pamphlet was liberally sprinkled with quotations from Bradlaugh's writings in regard to God, Christianity, and the Bible. To admit Bradlaugh, Almy argued, would constitute not progress but retrogression. He conceded that anti-Bradlaugh agitation helped to publicize the iconoclast's doctrines; but 'if everyone had always acted upon this principle evil had never been denounced'. It might be true, as another clergyman had argued, that it was inconsistent for Christians to oppose Bradlaugh's entry into Parliament, since God loads the Infidel with blessings. Yet even God, thought Mr. Almy, 'draws the line somewhere'. Every M.P. who favoured an affirmation bill ought to be opposed.[2]

Bradlaugh's chief efforts during the autumn of 1885 were directed toward raising the constitutional issue in every individual conflict, and his followers supported him loyally. This meant the wide distribution of a number of Bradlaugh's pamphlets as well as a pamphlet written by one of his associates, William Platt Ball, under the pseudonym of Humanitas. *Charles Bradlaugh, M.P., and the Irish Nation* was designed to counter Irish opposition. Few candidates found it possible therefore to avoid taking a stand on the issue, and by November Bradlaugh was able to announce with pride that 'an enormous change has taken place in the public opinion of England, Wales, and Scotland on this question, especially during the last two years'. Of 350 Liberal candidates who had addressed constituencies, only 3 opposed Bradlaugh or

[1] Cited in *N.R.*, 25 Oct. 1885, p. 258; 13 Sept. 1885, p. 161.
[2] Almy, *Almighty God or Bradlaugh?* (London, 1885), pp. 3, 18, 20, 21.

an affirmation bill publicly;[1] 195 were formally pledged to enact an affirmation bill. What was even more comforting was the fact that many Liberal candidates upheld Bradlaugh's cause with apparent enthusiasm. Leonard Courtney detected in English towns and cities 'a great and increasing wave of anger at the treatment Mr. Bradlaugh is receiving . . . '. Fred Inderwick saw the case as a blot upon England's international reputation for civil and religious freedom. William Woodall recalled hearing Bradlaugh plead his case alone at the bar of the House of Commons: 'It was a very impressive sight and it recalled to my mind the saying of Madame Roland as she was being led to the guillotine: "O liberty, O liberty, what crimes have been committed in thy name!" I could not but feel: "O religion, O religion, what wrongs have been done in thy name!" '[2]

What was even more encouraging for Bradlaugh was that a few Conservatives also were coming out in favour of an affirmation bill, though some of them qualified their generalized support by opposing any bill whose chief purpose would be to gratify 'the vanity of Mr. Bradlaugh'.[3] The majority of Conservative candidates remained steadfast in opposition, if only because—in A. J. Balfour's words—his admission would 'mistakenly or not . . . shock the most respectable feelings of the country'.[4] Yet if certain Liberals were still taunted with the cry of 'atheist', then many a Conservative meeting was interrupted with 'three cheers for Bradlaugh'. The Bradlaugh case was an issue in the election of 1885, and if it was not the key issue, then it was as widely discussed and as clear-cut a party issue as any other.

Bradlaugh had an election campaign of his own on his hands. In April 1885 he published his 'Radical Programme', which asked that

as in the United States of America the Illinois log-splitter and the Massachusetts shoemaker [William Wilson, Vice-President during Grant's second term] rose to be chief magistrate and deputy-chief magistrate of the great Transatlantic Republic, so in this country

[1] N.R., 8 Nov. 1885, p. 294; Maccoby, English Radicalism, 1853–1886, p. 319.
[2] Cited in N.R., 11 Oct. 1885, p. 226; 16 Aug. 1885, p. 97; 11 Oct. 1885, p. 225. [3] N.R., 23 Aug. 1885, p. 113.
[4] Cited in N.R., 25 Oct. 1885, p. 258.

the poorest and lowest-born, if with honor, vigor, earnestness, perseverance, and intelligence enough for the struggle, may find no law-created artificial barrier to hinder his rising or filling the place he is fit for.[1]

In practice this meant the reapportionment of taxation, an end to the monopoly of high office by a few families, and the separation of Church and State. It meant payment for Members of Parliament and indeed the payment of election expenses generally. Yet Bradlaugh's Radicalism implied also an overall reduction in national expenditure and an avoidance of 'the tendency to look to Government to provide food and work for the people'.[2]

For a number of years Bradlaugh had played with the idea of running in more than one constituency in the coming general election in order to dramatize his role as champion of constituency rights. This type of multi-constituency candidacy was rare in the 1880's, though Charles Stewart Parnell had been elected for three seats in 1880, two of which he necessarily had then to resign. When early in 1885 members of the National Secular Society in East Finsbury encouraged Bradlaugh to become a candidate there, he readily accepted. East Finsbury was a constituency in the London area newly created by the Reapportionment Act of that year; there was therefore no sitting member. It was, moreover, the area in which Bradlaugh's Hall of Science was located, and he knew it well. It had the symbolic value of being part of Middlesex County, which John Wilkes had represented in Parliament, and a victory there would demonstrate Bradlaugh's ability to secure the electoral support of others besides the 'poor cobblers' of Northampton.

In April the Liberal and Radical Association of East Finsbury, whose secretary, the Reverend F. Summers, was a Nonconformist clergyman, endorsed Bradlaugh's candidacy. A London school-board inspector, Marchant Williams, decided, however, to seek the nomination as well. Williams refused, moreover, to abide by any sort of arbitration— either by mass meeting or by Liberal party leadership— as to whether he or Bradlaugh was to represent the party

[1] *N.R.*, 26 Apr. 1885, p. 321.
[2] *N.R.*, 3 May 1885, p. 337; 10 May 1885, p. 353.

in the borough. The two men were essentially agreed on political issues, but Williams contended—with some effectiveness apparently—that a protest candidacy was merely a tribute to Bradlaugh's 'personal vanity'. Bradlaugh would in any case win in Northampton, and even if Bradlaugh won East Finsbury as well, the result would have to be a second election (for which Bradlaugh's supporters had chosen one James Rowlands as candidate). The split in the Liberal ranks made the success of the Conservative candidate, James Bigwood, all the more likely, and on 13 October 1885 Bradlaugh decided to withdraw from the race, to the great surprise and disappointment of his London supporters. Williams was now forced to agree to an arbitration of his claims as opposed to those of Rowlands. The party's decision was awarded to Rowlands—a matter which afforded Bradlaugh some satisfaction—though Williams, in withdrawing his own candidacy, described the decision as 'infamous'. Possibly as a result of the abstention of Williams's supporters, the Conservative candidate won the seat at the general election. Rowlands was, however, to be successful in the district in the elections of 1886 and 1892.[1]

Once the decision had been taken to give up the East Finsbury candidacy, Bradlaugh was once again able to concentrate upon Northampton. 'The opposition there', Labouchere had said, 'does not amount to much, but the electors like to see the candidates hanging around at election times.'[2] Bradlaugh could not view the matter quite so lightly, but not even he was particularly worried about his prospects. Now that the Northampton *Mercury* was solidly in his favour, the Liberal party of the borough was as united as it had ever been. Indeed the Conservatives conceded one of the two seats—Northampton was one of the relatively few two-member districts which remained after the Reapportionment Act of 1885—by nominating only one candidate to oppose

---

[1] This paragraph is based upon a series of brief articles in the *National Reformer* of which the following are the most important: 1 Feb. 1885, p. 65; 8 Mar. 1885, p. 213; 24 May 1885, pp. 389–90; 14 June 1885, p. 434; 21 June 1885, pp. 449–50; 27 Sept. 1885, p. 199; 4 Oct. 1885, pp. 214–15, 219; 25 Oct. 1885, pp. 257–62; 6 Dec. 1885, p. 359; 13 Dec. 1885, p. 371; G. D. H. Cole, *British Working Class Politics, 1832–1914*, p. 266.

[2] Viscount Gladstone MSS. (B.M.), 46015, fol. 53.

Bradlaugh and Labouchere, the same H. C. Richards who had unsuccessfully contested Bradlaugh's re-election in 1884. Richards put on a businesslike but not truly intense campaign, and Bradlaugh found matters going so tranquilly that one of his associates wondered 'whether he felt quite at home in this his seventh contested election for the borough'. A few days before polling, the Conservatives did launch a last-minute house-by-house distribution of Almy's pamphlet as well as a display of placards announcing that a vote for Bradlaugh would be a wasted vote. Finally on election morning, hundreds of Northampton voters received letters posted in London and signed 'East Finsbury', urging them to vote for Labouchere but not for Bradlaugh. The final results were, however, decisive enough: Labouchere, 4,845; Bradlaugh, 4,315; Richards, 3,890.[1]

The General Election of 1885 had not been fought over clear-cut issues, and its outcome was equally indecisive: 335 Liberals, 249 Conservatives, 86 Irish Nationalists. The election results were evidently a personal victory for Charles Stewart Parnell, who now controlled all but 17 of Ireland's 103 constituencies, rather than the 30 to 40 seats which his loyal supporters had occupied during the previous five years. The results indicated that while the Liberals could not govern without Irish support, the Conservatives could not govern even with it. For the election of 1885 was in a peculiar sense a triumph for Gladstone as well. It was nothing comparable to the repudiation which had ended his first ministry in 1874. The second Gladstone Ministry may have been marked by much internal party discord, several setbacks abroad, and few dramatic triumphs at home, and yet in 1885 the Liberal party demonstrated in England, Scotland, and Wales, at least, the same overall dominance it had shown in 1880. This is partly attributable to the fact that the numerous losses to the Conservatives in the major cities of England and the virtual wiping out of the Liberal party in Ireland were counterbalanced by gains in the counties, where the newly enfranchised rural electorate demonstrated its gratitude to the Liberal party. The Liberal totals in England might have

[1] *N.R.*, 22 Nov. 1885, p. 325; 29 Nov. 1885, pp. 340, 341, 346; 6 Dec. 1885, p. 353.

been still higher had it not been for Parnell's last-minute pro-Tory manifesto. The Irish and Conservatives had, admittedly, been on good terms throughout 1885. Salisbury's Government had ended the Crimes Act, had passed a tenant land purchase act, and was at least considering the prospect of extending greater local self-government to Ireland. Irish objectives in July 1885 are candidly revealed by the London correspondent of the *Freeman's Journal*:

> The members of the Irish Party generally are of opinion that the question [of Home Rule] had much better be dealt with by a Tory than a Liberal Administration, for whatever settlement the Tories would bring in would be certainly broadened and improved by the Liberals as it passed through the House of Commons, and would be more easily passed by the House of Lords. This is one of the reasons which have induced Irish leaders, for the present at least, to give as many seats as they can to the Tories of England and Scotland.[1]

That policy remained, however, an unofficial one until two days before the first poll in November. Then Parnell issued a manifesto—a document drafted by T. P. O'Connor—urging Irish voters in England to vote for the Conservatives instead of the Liberals—'the men who coerced Ireland, deluged Egypt with blood, menace religious liberty in the school, the freedom of speech in Parliament, and promise to the country generally a repetition of the crimes and follies of the last Liberal Administration.'[2]

The Parnell Manifesto cost the Liberal party some thirty seats according to the estimate of a recent student of the subject.[3] The Conservative *Saturday Review*, always suspicious of the flirtation between Conservatives and the Irish party, might protest that it was 'either childish or dishonest' to attempt to account for the Conservative gains by citing 'the Irish thunderstorm',[4] but few historians concur. Yet how desperately Parnell needed those thirty seats six months later

---

[1] *Freeman's Journal* (Dublin), 6 July 1885, p. 5.

[2] Cited by T. P. O'Connor, *Memoirs*, ii. 8, 9.

[3] Robert Rhodes James, 'Charles Stewart Parnell', *History Today*, January 1957, p. 16; R. C. K. Ensor, *England, 1870–1914*, suggests 25 to 40 (p. 95).

[4] *Saturday Review*, 5 Dec. 1885, p. 729.

when Gladstone's Home Rule Bill was defeated by that precise margin!

For Bradlaugh the election results brought more cheer than gloom. The results in Ireland did not surprise him, and, with one exception, the attempts of hostile Irish M.P.s to secure English constituencies had failed. Although Conservatives like Lord Randolph Churchill and the former Hardinge Giffard were now Cabinet officers, it was consoling to see Charles Newdegate retired and Henry Drummond Wolff defeated. And though friendly Liberals such as Charles Henry Hopwood had been beaten, it was satisfying to see many a 'weak-kneed Liberal' out of Parliament as well. Robert Dyer Lyons no longer represented Dublin. Samuel Morley in Bristol, Charles Norwood in Hull, and William Torrens in Finsbury had decided not to seek re-election. Hubert Jerningham, the Roman Catholic who had repudiated his election-time promise to support an affirmation bill, had not been supported for re-election, and his efforts to become the Liberal nominee at Blackpool were likewise thwarted.[1] The number of Roman Catholics in Parliament had increased (there were now seventy-nine from Ireland, three from England, and one from Scotland), but so had the number of working-class members and Scottish crofters. Bradlaugh's old friend Joseph Arch, the farm union leader, had finally achieved his ambition of being elected M.P.[2] The new Parliament seemed more promising than the old, and for the moment Bradlaugh could afford to turn from politics in order to contribute articles to the *National Reformer* on 'The Christian Religion'.[3]

Yet the future was not wholly promising. The election was barely over before the Manchester *Evening News* printed a most disturbing paragraph by its London correspondent: 'It is the avowed intention of the Conservatives to attempt to re-enact the resolution of the last Parliament excluding Mr. Bradlaugh from the House, and, inasmuch as they will be supported by the Parnellites—acting under the influence of the Irish Roman Catholics—they will very likely carry the

[1] *N.R.*, 25 Oct. 1885, p. 257; 29 Nov. 1885, p. 337; 6 Dec. 1885, p. 362.
[2] *N.R.*, 20 Dec. 1885, p. 386; 27 Dec. 1885, p. 405.
[3] *N.R.*, 13 Dec. 1885, p. 370.

day.'[1] The Irish–Conservative coalition might indeed go so far, the correspondent continued, as to pass a resolution awarding the second Northampton seat to the defeated Richards. Two weeks later the same paper reported the chilling news that the Clock Tower rooms were once again being prepared for use as a prison.[2]

For the time being, Bradlaugh kept his own counsel. He may indeed have felt uncertain of the proper course. His colleague, Labouchere, had argued confidently in 1881 that in a new Parliament 'it is not pretended by his most virulent opponent in the House of Commons that he would not be at perfect liberty to take the oath'.[3] But Lord Randolph Churchill had branded this point of view as utterly erroneous, since every succeeding Speaker would be bound to follow the ruling of Speaker Brand[4]—and at the moment Churchill was in office and Labouchere was not. Numerous journals, moreover, were citing the Court of Appeal decision earlier that year as proof that Bradlaugh was intrinsically incapable of taking the oath. Bradlaugh decided thereupon to explore another possibility, and on 18 December 1885 he inquired of Sir Michael Hicks-Beach whether in the event of Mr. Serjeant Simon's introducing an affirmation bill—the Liberal M.P. had agreed to replace the recently defeated Charles Henry Hopwood as sponsor—the Conservative Government would be willing to 'give an early day for taking a division on its second reading'.

Hicks-Beach consulted both Salisbury and Lord Randolph Churchill before replying. Salisbury suggested that the Conservative Government make no promises of any kind, even at the risk of having Bradlaugh take the oath. If Bradlaugh did take the oath, suggested Salisbury, Bradlaugh could always be prosecuted. The subject would then occupy the law courts rather than the House of Commons, a prospect which Salisbury regarded as the preferable one, thereby displaying a point of view curiously akin to Gladstone's.[5]

[1] Cited in N.R , 13 Dec. 1885, p. 371.
[2] Cited in N.R., 27 Dec. 1885, p. 401.
[3] Morning Post, 14 Dec. 1881, clipping in G.P. (B.M.), 44111, fol. 113.
[4] Hansard, cclxxviii (1883), 1444.
[5] Bradlaugh to Hicks-Beach, 18 Dec. 1885, St. Aldwyn MSS., file PCC,

Hicks-Beach therefore sent Bradlaugh a carefully worded non-committal reply; the Government could make no promises as to the order of business during the coming session.

Churchill was dubious about this decision. It might be best, he agreed, to deal with Bradlaugh in the law courts, 'but in this matter the party will lead the Gov[ernment], and will insist upon a row, & if we hold back we may have a new fourth party springing into existence'. If Bradlaugh actually succeeded in taking the oath in the usual manner, the law courts might not entertain any suit against him, and 'a very large number of our supporters in the country would be much shocked by our apparent want of principle & pluck'. Would it not be shrewder to explore the possibility of promising Bradlaugh a debate on an affirmation bill on the condition that he not attempt to take the oath?[1] Churchill proceeded to confer privately with Labouchere, and by 11 January 1886 Hicks-Beach had also expressed his willingness to make a confidential agreement promising Bradlaugh the opportunity of an affirmation bill debate in return for abstention from the oath. After all, Churchill privately assured Hicks-Beach, even if the subject were debated in Parliament, 'I have little doubt of successful opposition to the Affirmation Bill.'[2]

Bradlaugh must have been strongly tempted to accept the offer. 'I have always sought to obtain the passing of an Affirmation Bill,' he had written two weeks earlier, 'and am still ready to bear much personal inconvenience, if by so doing I can secure the earlier enactment of such a measure.'[3] By 11 January 1886 however, he was less willing to make such an arrangement, because rumours had been circulating that Sir Michael Hicks-Beach had been carrying on a correspondence with the Speaker over the Bradlaugh case, and that the Speaker might not permit objections to be made to Brad-

fol. 58; (Copy) Hicks-Beach to Churchill, 21 Dec. 1885, St. Aldwyn MSS., file FCC, fol. 10.

[1] Churchill to Hicks-Beach, 24 Dec. 1885, St. Aldwyn MSS., file PCC, fol. 82.

[2] Churchill to Hicks-Beach, 10 Jan. 1886, St. Aldwyn MSS., file PCC, fol. 82; (Copy) Hicks-Beach to Churchill, 11 Jan. 1886, St. Aldwyn MSS., file PCC, fol. 82.   [3] N.R., 27 Dec. 1885, p. 401.

laugh's taking the oath if he came up to the Table in the usual manner.[1] The Speaker had indeed been in consultation, not only with Hicks-Beach, but with Sir Henry James, the ex-Attorney-General. James had written him a detailed memorandum 'urging him to refuse to allow any interference with Bradlaugh's taking of the oath'. Gladstone, who had been similarly concerned, was relieved to hear James's assurance that the responsibility was that of the Speaker, who might be expected to deal 'firmly and constitutionally with it'. Gladstone was pleased to note 'the risk of further embroilment rather less than I had feared it might be . . .'.[2]

The Speaker's decision would obviously be significant, as it had been in 1880 and 1881; but the Speaker in 1886 was no longer Henry Brand, who had retired in 1884, but Sir Arthur Wellesley Peel, the youngest son of the Prime Minister. Peel had not indeed been the first choice of the Cabinet at the time. Sir Farrer Herschell, the Solicitor-General, and George Joachim Goschen, Gladstone's one-time First Lord of the Admiralty, had both seemed preferable, but Herschell declined the honour and Goschen was too near-sighted.[3] So Peel became the choice of the Cabinet and was elected by Parliament. He had been a loyal Liberal M.P. for twenty years but had participated so seldom in House of Commons debates that many M.P.s could scarcely recall hearing him speak at all. His inaugural speech impressed the House all the more; Peel held the promise of becoming a firm and able presiding officer.[4] At least one M.P., Charles Newdegate, expressed fears at the time that a change of Speaker might affect the Bradlaugh case,[5] while Northcote was needlessly fearful that Bradlaugh might use the election of a new Speaker as a time to sneak into Parliament.[6]

By the time the new Parliament assembled on 13 January

---

[1] Peel had indeed given precisely that decision to Hicks-Beach, a development the latter deemed 'not satisfactory'. Peel to Hicks-Beach, 22 Dec. 1885, St. Aldwyn MSS., file PCC, fol. 58; Hicks-Beach to Salisbury, 24 Dec. 1885, Salisbury MSS.

[2] James to Gladstone, 29 Dec. 1885, G.P. (B.M.), 44219, fols. 196–9; Lord Askwith, *Lord James of Hereford*, pp. 149–52.

[3] G.P. (B.M.) (Cabinet Minutes), 44644, fol. 115; 44195, fols. 166, 167.

[4] McCarthy, *England under Gladstone, 1880–1884*, pp. 333–4.

[5] Hampden MSS.

[6] Northcote to Giffard, 31 Dec. 1883. Halsbury MSS.

1886 Bradlaugh had made up his mind to take the oath like any other member. Rumours of all kinds still filled the newspapers, however. Sir R. E. Webster, the Conservative Attorney-General, announced that the party would 'be true to the position it had taken in the past'. A Cabinet meeting in Hicks-Beach's house decided to issue a four-line whip asking all Conservative M.P.s to be on hand the first day to oppose Bradlaugh. The *Standard* spoke of new lawsuits. The *Freeman's Journal* considered 'the end of the Bradlaugh difficulty' to be 'as far off as ever . . .'.[1]

The House of Commons was crowded, much more so than it had been on 29 April 1880. The first step was to re-elect Peel as Speaker—the only formal action that could according to custom precede the swearing-in ceremonies. As soon as Speaker Peel had himself taken the oath, he announced that he had received a letter from Hicks-Beach tracing the lengthy background of the Bradlaugh case and asking the Speaker to prevent Bradlaugh from taking the oath before the House had opportunity to vote upon his admission, 'a proceeding which I believe, if fully constituted, it would decline to sanction'.[2]

Amid breathless excitement, the Speaker pronounced his ruling. He recalled that at no time during the previous Parliament had his predecessor, in dealing with Bradlaugh, taken independent authority upon himself. He had merely followed the instructions of the House. They were now, however, assembled in a new Parliament. 'I know nothing of the Resolutions of the past. They have lapsed; they are void; they are of no effect in reference to this case.' It was, moreover, not merely the right but the duty, the legal obligation, of all members to take the required oath. 'I have no authority,' insisted Peel, 'I have no right, original or delegated, to interfere between an honourable Member and his taking of the Oath. . . . It is not for me, I respectfully say, it is not for the House, to enter into any inquisition as to what may be the opinions of a Member when he comes to the Table to take the Oath.'[3]

---

[1] Cited in *N.R.*, 17 Jan. 1886, pp. 33–34; 10 Jan. 1886, p. 18; *Freeman's Journal* (Dublin), 13 Jan. 1886, p. 6.
[2] *Hansard*, cccii (1886), 21.   [3] Ibid., cols. 21–24.

Sir Michael Hicks-Beach tried to object, but the Speaker ruled him out of order since he had himself not yet taken the oath and might not therefore take part in debate. Many Liberals cheered, while the Conservative M.P.s, most of them ready and eager to march into the Lobby on an anti-Bradlaugh resolution, reacted with dismay. The rumour spread that an anti-Bradlaugh resolution would be introduced as soon as the first forty members had taken the oath and a quorum had been constituted. Ordinarily, members were called alphabetically in accordance with the name of their constituency, but this procedure rapidly broke down, as nearly four hundred members pushed and shoved, striving to make their membership in the House complete. Bradlaugh was in their midst. The Clerk and the Assistant Clerk administered the oath to a score of members at a time, but so great was the crush that it took Bradlaugh over an hour to complete the procedure of reading the oath, kissing the New Testament, inscribing his name on the roll, and shaking hands with the Speaker. No hostile resolution had been presented, and all of a sudden it was all over. 'And so there came this curious end in absolute quietness to all the fierce conflicts of so many years.'[1]

There were still the post-mortems, of course. The Liberal press was well satisfied; *The Times* and the *Telegraph* urged the Conservative Government to do nothing further in the matter. The *Morning Post* and the *Saturday Review* were highly indignant, and the *Tablet*, which regarded the new House as 'less favourable to the claims of Mr. Bradlaugh than the last', urged the Government to take legal action.[2] On 26 January Hicks-Beach was asked by a Conservative M.P. whether the Government contemplated any immediate steps to prevent Bradlaugh from sitting and voting. The Chancellor of the Exchequer replied that the Government would await a final ruling of the House of Lords in the still pending legal suit.[3] Hicks-Beach, the able but unimpassioned leader of the Commons who had carefully steered clear of the Northcote–

---

[1] Sir Richard Temple, *Letters and Character Sketches from the House of Commons* (London, 1912), p. 3; *Punch*, 23 Jan. 1886, p. 46; *The Times*, 14 Jan. 1886, p. 8; T. P. O'Connor, *Memoirs*, ii. 24.

[2] *Tablet*, 16 Jan. 1886, p. 81.   [3] *Hansard*, cccii (1886), 419.

Churchill conflict of the previous Parliament, did not seem to have his heart in the matter. 'I think that my own feeling was', he wrote a few years later, 'that so far as Parliament was concerned the matter had best come to an end.'[1] The Conservative *Standard* was led to wonder plaintively 'whether the pertinacity of a single individual shall be allowed to gain a victory over the law of the land'.[2]

The subject soon thereafter left the province of the Conservative Cabinet altogether. Late in January it was defeated in Parliament, and the Gladstone–Parnell 'Home Rule' Ministry took over. Gladstone obviously had no desire to take further legal steps,[3] and when a Conservative Government returned to office after another election later that year, it too seemed uninterested in prolonging the controversy. Edwin de Lisle, a Tory M.P. and, incidentally a Roman Catholic, explained the decision in this manner: 'The Tories took up the principle of supporting the oath, and having fought for that principle they were content to leave to the Almighty to punish those who took the oath wantonly or unreverently.'[4] It would have solved a great many problems —personal as well as constitutional—had the Bradlaugh case been left in the hands of the Deity from the start.

[1] St. Aldwyn MSS., file PCC, fol. 82.
[2] Cited in *N.R.*, 24 Jan. 1886, p. 49.
[3] So announced his Attorney-General on 11 Mar. 1886. *Hansard* ccciii (1886), 442.
[4] Cited in *N.R.*, 22 Aug. 1886, p. 116.

XXV

THE RIGHT TO AFFIRM

BRADLAUGH's entry into Parliament had settled his personal problem but had left open the question of principle. Indeed for Bradlaugh himself there still loomed a decision in the House of Lords. The lower court and the Court of Appeal had both ruled—in part on the basis that an atheist could not swear—that Bradlaugh had not truly taken the oath on the occasion of his self-swearing in 1884, and in the spring of 1886 the suit was still pending. Now that the original objective of that legal suit had been attained by other means, Bradlaugh was anxious to drop it. The unfavourable decision which was in prospect would, at worst, cause him to forfeit his seat, and, at best, prove embarrassing. He therefore appealed to Gladstone for a *stet processus*. The new Lord Chancellor, Lord Herschell (the former Sir Farrer Herschell), advised Gladstone that for reasons of legal consistency such a request could not be granted. Gladstone acceded to the Lord Chancellor's arguments, though sympathetic to Bradlaugh's point of view. '. . . The unhappy man', wrote the Prime Minister, 'has been persecuted with immense hypocrisy, & has suffered heavily in defence of a public principle undeniably sound tho' in some of its consequences disagreeable.'[1]

The relief which a sympathetic Liberal ministry felt compelled, on the basis of principle, to refuse, was granted a few months later by a Conservative ministry in which Lord Randolph Churchill served as leader of the House of Commons. Churchill's motives are obscure, except that he had obviously convinced himself by the autumn of 1886 that the Bradlaugh case was dead and ought therefore to be buried without further ado. This manifestly opportunistic turnabout was not sufficient to placate Bradlaugh after six years of harassment, and in the course of that year and the next

[1] G.P. (B.M.), 44548, fol. 104.

Bradlaugh found a number of opportunities to embarrass the noble lord, even if only in so petty a manner as opposing an appropriation to make minor repairs at Marlborough House.[1] In an open letter to Churchill, Bradlaugh had occasion to refer to 'old English gentlemen' as constituting 'a class to which I, as well as yourself, am a stranger—I from birth, and you from habit'.[2] When the Conservative Government committed an Irish priest for using threatening language toward magistrates, Bradlaugh observed that Churchill himself had declared only three years earlier that the Crown could procure decisions favourable to Bradlaugh from certain judges. Was this not a comparable affront to the integrity of the judiciary, asked Bradlaugh? Churchill denied the charge, but Bradlaugh returned to the fray armed with the appropriate quotations, and in the ensuing debate, noted a neutral observer, 'Randolph seems to have got badly mauled'.[3] Thereafter Bradlaugh and Churchill, who had in the meantime dramatically descended to the role of mere back-bencher, reached a *modus vivendi*.

The last significant legal suit had thus been disposed of—though Bradlaugh had to pay the costs—but it was not to be the last lawsuit of his career. When in 1888 one Charles R. MacKay published a *Life of Charles Bradlaugh, M.P.*, Bradlaugh charged him with libel and won his case. The court judged the book to be not legally saleable, and Bradlaugh's daughter and grandson have successfully used their legal powers to see to it that no English library lists the volume in its catalogue.[4]

Bradlaugh continued to work for the passage of a bill which would legalize the option of affirmation for anyone who wished to make use of it. Serjeant Simon had introduced such a bill in 1886, but it had not come to a vote. Bradlaugh himself introduced a similar bill in 1887, and succeeded in gaining the support of the Conservative Solicitor-General, Sir Edward Clarke, and, ironically, that of Lord Randolph Churchill, who suggested that an affirmation bill would at

---

[1] Bonner & Robertson, *Bradlaugh*, ii. 363, 371; Temple, *Letters*, p. 239.
[2] Cited by Bonner & Robertson, *Bradlaugh*, ii. 372.
[3] Wilfrid S. Blunt, *The Land War in Ireland: Excerpts from Diaries* (London, 1912), p. 253.   [4] Bonner & Robertson, *Bradlaugh*, ii. 397-9.

least secure that 'the Parliamentary oath in future will in all probability only be taken by those who believe in and revere its effective solemnity'.[1] Moreover a Conservative M.P., J. R. Kelly, agreed to co-sponsor the measure. The result was that when Bradlaugh's bill came up for debate, the Conservative Government decided not to make a party issue of the matter. Close to one hundred Conservative back-benchers succeeded, however, in staging an all-night filibuster against the bill, and Bradlaugh agreed to withdraw it for the time being.[2]

The bill was reintroduced the following year with the tacit consent of the Government. Not that all opposition had disappeared. The Protestant Alliance urged petitions against the bill, and Cardinal Manning and fourteen other Catholic bishops declared solemnly that 'to efface the recognition of God in our public legislature is an act which will surely bring evil consequences'.[3] In the House of Commons, Edwin de Lisle, once dubbed 'the member for Catholic England',[4] spoke warmly against the bill. The ensuing petition campaign was but a pale shadow, however, of the vast drive of 1883. The feeling was widespread that since the oath had obviously not served as a deterrent to atheist M.P.s, its sacredness might be better safeguarded by permitting than by denying the universal right to affirm. Eventually even the Archbishop of Canterbury conceded that the bill contained 'nothing contrary to the articles of the Church or the ethics of religion'.[5] Nor ought the significance of the favourable attitude of Liberal Unionists to be overlooked.

Bradlaugh, who had been carefully preparing the groundwork, moved the second reading of the bill in March 1888, in what even the Catholic *Tablet* conceded to have been 'a very moderate speech'.[6] It was no longer a party question, contended Bradlaugh, 'and I trust that it may be dealt with and settled now without a particle of bitterness, or even of recollection'. The debate was temperate, for the most part, although one Conservative was certain that the bill 'would

---

[1] Cited ibid. ii. 378.
[2] Temple, *Letters*, pp. 345–7; *N.R.*, 15 Jan. 1888, p. 39.
[3] *N.R.*, 1 Apr. 1888, p. 221; *Tablet*, 21 Apr. 1888, p. 638.
[4] *Freeman's Journal* (Dublin), 5 Feb. 1891, p. 5.
[5] Cited in *N.R.*, 9 Dec. 1888, p. 380.   [6] *Tablet*, 17 Mar. 1888, p. 424.

strike a fatal blow, not only at the character of the British people, but the stability and endurance of the British Empire'. He appealed to the Irish members, but they 'now sat silent and acquiescent'.[1] On 15 March 1888, after Bradlaugh had successfully ended debate by invoking closure, the bill passed by a vote of 250 to 150. It was supported by 140 Liberals, 45 Liberal Unionists, 30 Home Rulers, and 35 Conservatives. It was opposed by 148 Conservatives, 1 Liberal Unionist, and 1 Home-Ruler. The result was a great triumph for Northampton's junior member. 'All moderate men will hail such a settlement', declared *The Times*. 'A triumph of common sense', announced the *Daily Telegraph*. 'While our sentiment is against the Bill,' sighed the *Standard*, 'we are afraid that all experience is for it.'[2]

The bill still had to be piloted through the committee stage, at which time amendments might be added. Ironically this step proved troublesome for Bradlaugh. In order to obtain the degree of Government co-operation he deemed necessary for final passage, Bradlaugh had consented to introduce an amendment providing that any person claiming to affirm had first to object to the oath on the basis 'either that he has no religious belief, or that the taking of an oath is contrary to his religious belief'. Bradlaugh duly introduced such an amendment in committee only to find some of his fellow Liberals up in arms. John Morley, George Otto Trevelyan, and others objected that the bill was being emasculated and that a new and needless inquiry into religious beliefs was being begun. The amendment was adopted, however, 172 to 166, and when the *Daily News* termed the bill now 'worse than useless', Bradlaugh took strong exception. For the first time, he insisted, men without religious belief would be allowed to affirm in Parliament, as Justices of the Peace, as solicitors and barristers, and in Scotland—which had not been affected by the acts of 1869 and 1870—as witnesses and jurors.[3] Bradlaugh felt disheartened:

Some folk, especially of our own party, are very unreasonable, and write as though it were in my power to compel the House of

---

[1] *Hansard*, cccxxiii (1888), 1185, 1201; *The Times*, 15 Mar. 1888, p. 9.
[2] Cited in the *Rock*, 16 Mar. 1888, p. 3.
[3] *N.R.*, 15 July 1888, p. 37; 22 July 1888, p. 55.

11. "August 3rd 1881–March 14th 1888" (*St. Stephen's Review*, 24 March 1888)

12. Bradlaugh's grandson and great-great-grandson stand at the statue of Charles Bradlaugh in Northampton (1966)

Commons, and also the House of Lords, to accept any form of words I please. Those who say that no bill at all is better than an enabling bill which does not meet all their views, are exceedingly reckless, and only serve the enemy.[1]

Surely half a loaf was better than no bread.

Having survived its committee stage, the bill survived a third reading as well, by a vote of 147 to 60. The Irish Nationalists, in contrast to 1883, took almost no part in the debate, and the majority abstained. A significant number—including Parnell, T. P. O'Connor, and the O'Gorman Mahon, for all of whom 1888 constituted a second reversal—voted in favour of the bill. Bradlaugh, it must be recalled, had supported the Home Rule Bill of 1886 so eloquently that one of the Irish members approached him in the lobby on one occasion to say: 'Mr. Bradlaugh, you have been the best Christian of us all.'[2]

When in November 1888 the House of Lords took up the bill, the second reading was moved by Earl Spencer and supported by, among others, Lord Chief Justice Coleridge. The Lord Chancellor, the one-time Sir Hardinge Giffard, was opposed, but the bill was in due course accepted without further amendment, and on 24 December 1888 became the law of the land.[3] Its provisions read as follows:

1. Every person upon objecting to being sworn, and stating, as the ground of such objection, either that he has no religious belief, or that the taking of an oath is contrary to his religious belief, shall be permitted to make his solemn affirmation instead of taking an oath in all places and for all purposes where any [oath is or shall] be required by law, which affirmation shall be of the same force and effect as if he had taken the oath . . . .

2. Every such affirmation shall be as follows: 'I, A. B., do solemnly, sincerely, and truly declare and affirm' and then proceed with the words of the oath prescribed by law, omitting any words of imprecation or calling to witness.

3. Where an oath has been duly administered and taken, the fact that the person to whom the same was administered had, at the

[1] *N.R.*, 15 Apr. 1888, p. 241.
[2] Cited by Bonner & Robertson, *Bradlaugh*, ii. 196.
[3] *N.R.*, 25 Nov. 1888, p. 347.

time of taking such oath, no religious belief, shall not for any purpose affect the validity of such oath.[1]

And so victory had been won for principle as well. Not that the Affirmation Bill was to be Bradlaugh's only claim to attention in Parliament. He proved to be an exceptionally assiduous private member. He was responsible for the setting up of a Government Bureau of Labour Statistics and for a Truck Act which forbade employers to pay wages in the form of produce or scrip redeemable only in company stores. He campaigned successfully for a Royal Commission to examine the injurious market tolls charged by numerous town councils. As a member of a Parliamentary Select Committee he investigated corruption in the Corporation of London and he served as one of Queen Victoria's 'trusty and well-beloved' counsellors on a Royal Commission on Vaccination. He was one of the earliest English supporters of the Indian National Congress, whose fourth annual meeting he addressed in 1889, and his interest in the affairs of Britain's largest colony won him the sobriquet 'The Member for India'. In the lobbies of the House of Commons Bradlaugh was before long spoken of as a possible future Liberal Cabinet minister.[2]

Yet Bradlaugh's triumphs were tinged with tragedy. There were setbacks in Parliament, where he failed in his attempts to repeal the two-century-old blasphemy laws; they remain part of British law to this day, a dead letter for most purposes but a source of irritation for free-thinkers. Most of Bradlaugh's disappointments, however, came outside Parliament. The greatest by far was the defection of Annie Besant. For ten years she and Bradlaugh had been of one mind—if not of one temperament—and their joint editorship of the *National Reformer* had proved an unusually harmonious relationship.

---

[1] The act, 51 & 52 Vict. c. 46, may be found in *Statutes at Large* (3rd rev. ed., London, 1950), xi. 464–5. Although Bradlaugh from time to time paid lip service to the ideal of abolishing all oaths, it is noteworthy that he did not regard oaths as valueless. When a Parliamentary committee of which he was a member heard startling testimony, Bradlaugh interrupted the proceedings to move that all subsequent witnesses be put under oath. Cf. Sir Herbert Maxwell, *Life of William Henry Smith, M.P.*, ii. 39 f.

[2] Bonner & Robertson, *Bradlaugh*, ii, *passim*; Annie Besant to Moncure Conway, 28 Dec. 1886, Conway MSS.

Then in 1885 Mrs. Besant had begun to drift toward socialism. Re-reading the Bradlaugh–Hyndman debate 'away from
the magic of Mr. Bradlaugh's commanding eloquence and
personal magnetism', she began to think more highly of the
arguments for socialism, regretting only that by their bitter
denunciations of Bradlaugh's magnanimity the socialists had
created such a wide gulf.[1] By the end of the year she had
joined the Fabian Society.

Her decision was a blow to Bradlaugh, but he uttered no
word of criticism in public, and she remained co-editor for
another two years, leaving the paper with a divided editorial
policy. Bradlaugh gave her and her new colleagues legal
assistance when their right to hold socialist meetings in
Trafalgar Square was disputed, and on one occasion Bradlaugh addressed a Fabian conference. In October 1887 Mrs.
Besant resigned as co-editor, aware of their deepening differences on public policy and of the fact that she was now more
hindrance than help to Bradlaugh in his Parliamentary career.
Though she remained a member of the National Secular
Society and an occasional contributor to the *National
Reformer*, Bradlaugh missed her greatly. He felt an even
deeper blow two years later when she announced her conversion to theosophy.[2] Paradoxically, Mrs. Besant had first
come into contact with Colonel Olcott and Madame Blavat-
sky in 1882 when the two leaders of this new religious movement, then in Madras, India, had publicly expressed their
sympathy with Bradlaugh in his Parliamentary struggle and
had subsequently contributed to the *Freethinker* defence
fund. At that time Annie Besant had observed that 'there is
a radical difference between the mysticism of Theosophy and
the scientific materialism of Secularism',[3] but by 1889 she
obviously felt otherwise. In 1890 Annie Besant resigned
from the National Secular Society.

Nor was this Bradlaugh's only loss, for in December 1888
his elder daughter, Alice Bradlaugh, died of typhoid fever at
the age of thirty-two. Her death necessitated the closing of
the Hall of Science school after ten years during which its

[1] Besant, *Autobiography*, p. 302.
[2] Besant, *Autobiography*, pp. 319–20, 344, and *passim*; Williams, *The
Passionate Pilgrim*, p. 165.   [3] *N.R.*, 12 June 1882, p. 453.

students had consistently compiled excellent scores in the competitive examinations held by the Department of Science and Art. In the meantime, the circulation of the *National Reformer* had also begun to decline, partly because many hundreds of miners in Durham and Northumberland had turned elsewhere for political inspiration. Under the editorial and typographical ministrations of John M. Robertson, a future Member of Parliament and historian of note, and of Hypatia Bradlaugh Bonner, Bradlaugh's younger daughter, its standards remained high. In the early 1890's it added young Ernest Newman to its staff as music critic.[1] Its professed policy was as always 'Republican, Atheistic, and Malthusian', and Bradlaugh, who also contributed an article, 'Humanity's Gain from Unbelief', to the *North American Review* in 1889, took a renewed interest in theological themes.

Not the least of Bradlaugh's difficulties was the spectre of debt. He had never had a private source of income, and there was no pay for Members of Parliament. The more conscientiously he devoted himself to his legislative duties, the more difficult it became to make ends meet. Every week-end had to be devoted to lectures, and there seemed to be no time for the fishing trips to Scotland he loved. Yet the sums outstanding grew no less. Hearing of Bradlaugh's dilemma, W. T. Stead, then editor of the *Pall Mall Gazette*, launched a nation-wide subscription drive in 1888 which in conjunction with other drives raised close to £2,500 in a month. Bradlaugh was both grateful and embarrassed. But his financial burdens had been greatly eased for the time being.[2]

In October 1889 Bradlaugh, who looked like a powerful athlete but whose medical history included a number of serious illnesses, was struck down by Bright's disease, a kidney ailment which brought him close to death. He began to recover during his voyage to India and by January 1890 he spoke of himself as 'marvellously better'. But the feeling was delusive.[3] 'He recovered,' wrote his colleague, Henry Labouchere, 'but he came out of it a broken man. He would not, however, admit this, and he struggled on in the House

---

[1] A. Bonner and C. B. Bonner, *Hypatia Bradlaugh Bonner*, pp. 34–35, 64.
[2] Bonner & Robertson, *Bradlaugh*, ii. 400–1.
[3] Ibid., pp. 408–10.

of Commons, at public meetings and at his desk. . . .'[1] In February 1890 he regretfully gave up the presidency of the National Secular Society.

There was one final aim upon which Bradlaugh had long set his heart, to expunge from the Journals of the House of Commons the original resolution of 23 June 1880, the first to declare that 'Mr. Bradlaugh be not permitted to take the Oath or to make the Affirmation'. There was an historical precedent for Bradlaugh's action. In May 1782 the House of Commons had decided by a vote of 115 to 47 that the resolution of 1769 declaring John Wilkes incapable of being elected to Parliament ought to be expunged, since it was 'subversive of the Rights of the Whole Body of Electors of this Kingdom'.[2] His own exclusion ought similarly to be expunged, Bradlaugh believed, and every year a motion to this effect stood in his name. In January 1891 he was fortunate enough to be given a date for its consideration, but he had once again fallen gravely ill. He was cheered by the news that Dr. I. A. Hunter, a fellow Liberal, had undertaken to present the resolution on his behalf and that Gladstone had promised to speak in its favour. 'We shan't carry it this time,' Bradlaugh told his daughter, 'but if we only get a good vote I shall be satisfied.'[3]

By the time Dr. Hunter had the opportunity of presenting the resolution, Bradlaugh's illness was the principal topic of conversation in all the London political clubs, and prayers for his recovery were being said in many London churches. Gladstone spoke powerfully on behalf of the resolution but the initial inclination of the Government was to oppose a motion which called into question the integrity of Conservative Members of Parliament of barely a decade before. W. H. Smith, the leader of the Commons, while conceding that Bradlaugh 'has been undoubtedly a valuable addition to this House', made it clear that the Government would not yield. The issue appeared settled when Sir Stafford Northcote, the son of the earlier Sir Stafford, made a personal appeal

---

[1] Cited by Thorold, *Life of Labouchere*, p. 161.

[2] Cited by Betty Kemp, 'The Stewardship of the Chiltern Hundreds', *Essays Presented to Sir Lewis Namier*, ed. Richard Pares and A. J. P. Taylor (London, 1956), p. 212.   [3] Northampton *Daily Reporter*, 5 Feb. 1891.

to Smith, observing that a considerable number of Conservative back-benchers intended to vote for the motion. Smith gave way, and when Hunter agreed to amend the resolution to omit the words 'subversive of the Rights of the Whole Body of Electors of this Kingdom', the resolution expunging Bradlaugh's original exclusion from Parliament was declared passed unanimously.[1] The Clerk of the House solemnly drew a red line across the resolution in the copy of the journal kept in the Commons Library and respectfully requested the librarians of the British Museum, Oxford, Cambridge, Dublin, and Edinburgh to do the same.[2] 'There is no example on record', observed *The Times* the next day, 'of such a remarkable reversal of the deliberate judgment of the Legislature within so brief a period.'[3] A jubilant Dr. Hunter telegraphed the news to Bradlaugh's bedside, but the latter was in a coma and too ill to understand. He never fully regained consciousness and died two days later on the morning of 30 January 1891.

The funeral took place at Brookwood Cemetery four days later. The approaches to Waterloo Station were crowded for an hour as five thousand mourners rode out to the scene of the burial. Bradlaugh's relatives were present. So were his steadfast National Secular Society and Northampton associates. Sixteen Members of Parliament were there, including Labouchere and John Morley. Gladstone sent a wreath. Stewart Headlam was present as were at least five other clergymen. The Women's Franchise League was represented by Mrs. Emmeline Pankhurst. India was represented by, among many others, a young law student named Mohandas Gandhi. In accordance with Bradlaugh's express wishes, there was no formal ceremony of any kind. Not a single word was spoken, and in complete silence—except for a gentle English rain—Charles Bradlaugh's coffin was lowered into the grave.[4]

[1] *Hansard*, cccil (1891), 1158–76; Sir Richard Temple, *Life in Parliament* (London, 1893), p. 296; Bonner & Robertson, *Bradlaugh*, ii. 418–20.

[2] Sir Thomas Erskine May, *A Treatise on the Law, Privileges, Proceedings, and Usage of Parliament*, 11th ed., ed. by T. Lonsdale Webster and William Edward Grey (London, 1906), pp. 203–4.

[3] *The Times*, 28 Jan. 1891, p. 9.

[4] Northampton *Daily Reporter*, 4 Feb. 1891; Williams, *Passionate Pilgrim*, p. 201.

XXVI

THE SUMMING UP

BRADLAUGH and his Parliamentary struggle now lie more than three-quarters of a century in the past. The particulars of that struggle have been related in considerable detail, and it may be worth while to summarize briefly the most significant aspects of the case.

In one sense, the conflict was the outgrowth of a series of fortuitous coincidences. Had Sir Henry James advised Bradlaugh in April 1880 that his claim to affirm was untenable, Bradlaugh might have taken the oath immediately. Had not Charles Henry Hopwood decided that Bradlaugh was ineligible to affirm—he was the only Liberal member on the first Select Committee of that year to do so and he subsequently publicly regretted his stand—Bradlaugh might have affirmed. Had Speaker Brand ruled in 1880—as his successor was to do in 1886—that he was powerless to prevent a Member of Parliament who wished to take an oath from doing so, Bradlaugh might have become a member of the House of Commons in May 1880. It is apparent that on several occasions during the spring of that year, Bradlaugh might have taken his seat without further ado. Indeed, he did take that seat in July 1880, only—at the initiative of a certain Conservative M.P., Charles N. Newdegate—to have a judicial decision deprive him of that privilege nine months later, a decision afterwards in part to be reversed. But the facts are, of course, that the Attorney-General advised as he did, that Hopwood voted as he did, that the Speaker ruled as he did, that Newdegate saw fit to initiate the legal suit, and that such hypothetical speculations are consequently of little historical value. A similar pattern of coincidence may be found to lie at the root of the Dreyfus affair and many another *cause célèbre*.

The Bradlaugh case was, however, not simply an accident. It was a constitutional issue, which raised a number of very subtle questions of legal interpretation as well as the over-riding question of the precise relationship between Parliament and the ordinary law courts. Bradlaugh's legal claim to affirm was a reasonable one, which might well have been upheld. His subsequent appeals to the courts merely demonstrated anew that English law does not subscribe to the doctrine of 'judicial review'. The affair provided novelties in plenty: an atheist publicly drawing attention to his disbelief in oaths on the very day he proposes to take one; Members of Parliament permitted to interrupt a colleague in the process of oath-taking. But to define the Bradlaugh case as a question of constitutional interpretation would be comparable to describing the question of civil rights in the twentieth-century United States as no more than a series of judicial interpretations of the Fourteenth Amendment.

The Bradlaugh case aroused men's passions. It was more than a temporary stumbling-block along that direct path toward greater religious and political liberty which historians have charted through nineteenth-century England. The primary motive such historians ascribe to Bradlaugh's opponents is 'politics'. And surely there was politics enough. For a party so disastrously defeated as the Conservatives had been in 1880 the temptation to tie to so devout a Prime Minister as Gladstone the albatross of 'atheism' was too tempting a possibility to be long resisted. But the Conservatives were a minority. The Speaker's rulings could have been over-ridden, if the Liberal party had not added its own quota of opposition votes—and, even more, of abstentions—to every Bradlaugh division. Politics, as such, fails equally to explain altogether the attitude of the Irish Nationalists.

Lord Randolph Churchill and the other anti-Bradlaugh leaders raised a storm that was greater than they had expected because it revealed a strong substratum of popular feelings. It is easier to sense this feeling than to define its precise nature. The Bradlaugh case will be cited, wrote the *Scotsman* in 1881, 'by the historians of a comparatively near future, as an almost incredible illustration of the confusion of ideas which existed in England, in the ninth decade of the century, as to the real meaning of the principle of toleration and religious equality'.[1]

[1] Cited in *N.R.*, 3 July 1881, p. 36.

Perhaps the case signifies that Members of Parliament were more tolerant, or more religiously indifferent, than their constituents. For the revulsion against Bradlaugh was real enough. It was a mixture compounded of a dread of 'atheism' —a word hardly more respectable today than it was then— of revolution, and of immorality. The Bradlaugh case has been interpreted as a class struggle, but it was not so simple, unless one were to sum up Bradlaugh's major crime as lack of respectability, that of being a man of the people who openly and clearly challenged the conventions of his day. Some of Bradlaugh's opponents may have been hypocritical, but not all.

Certainly it is clear that many a clergyman came, for the moment, to look upon the Bradlaugh case as a last stand of religion against the assaults of higher criticism, cultural relativism, and biological evolution. The Roman Catholic Church provided a driving force to this movement which belied its numbers. Cardinal Manning may well have recognized a joint religious attack upon Bradlaugh's respectability as a means whereby his adopted church might raise its own claims to full acceptance in nineteenth-century England. If so, this suggests that he was able to capitalize upon that same substratum of popular emotion. While the reaction of the Irish Nationalist M.P.s was, as has been indicated in an earlier chapter, more complex than a simple reflection of religious feelings, the unanimity of feelings which Parnellites here came to share with non-Parnellite 'Home-Rulers' and with the small residuum of Irish Liberals was not accidental. Ironically enough, in the very process of resisting Bradlaugh, one-time opponents of equal rights for Catholics and Jews reconciled themselves to changes that had long since taken place.

To recognize the reality of the popular, if not universal, feeling of revulsion is to realize the depth of the Liberal party's dilemma. For a party which had practically adopted the one major implication of political democracy—that the wishes of constituents ought to be respected—it was most embarrassing to be on the side of the minority. It is only appropriate then to pay tribute to Gladstone's courage, to his self-discipline, indeed, in upholding the rights of a man who appeared superficially at least utterly opposed to many of his underlying convictions. Yet it has been shown earlier that Gladstone, too, was somewhat slow in recognizing in Bradlaugh a question of principle which deserved the out-pouring of eloquence it finally received in the Affirmation Bill debate of 1883. If it be just to praise Gladstone's courage and sense of duty, might it not be equally relevant to question his political shrewdness? Had Gladstone exerted the neces-sary discipline, had Gladstone made Bradlaugh's admission a party question, as he appeared to do once in 1880, might not the dust have settled more quickly, might not the action have been accepted as a *fait accompli* and not remained an open wound? It is possible to suggest this, though in fairness to Gladstone it must be conceded that it reflects the wisdom of hindsight and ignores the real danger of a Liberal revolt. To make the Bradlaugh case a question of confidence might conceivably have necessitated an election fought by Glad-stone on most unfavourable terms.

Perhaps the surprising thing is that so many Liberals did repeatedly, on the basis of principle, vote for Bradlaugh's admission. In this stand the Liberal party was upheld by one great weapon, which proved to be both a weakness and a strength, the doctrine of progress. Underlying the day-by-day ups and downs was an implicit confidence that ulti-mately the Liberal party was on the side of progress and that progress ultimately dictated Bradlaugh's admission. This was not merely probable. To Liberal spokesmen it was 'certain', it was 'as sure as there's a sun in the heavens', it was 'as sure as night follows day'.[1] This pervasive conviction was shared even by some members of the Opposition. Yet the profession of progress could also become a substitute for practical action. Since in the long run Bradlaugh would undoubtedly win, both he and the Liberal party could afford to be patient. In the long run, Bradlaugh may well have felt, we are all dead.

The question may legitimately be raised, why, if opposition to Bradlaugh was indeed founded upon a strong popular emotion rather than upon politics in a narrower sense,

[1] London *Daily Chronicle*, 22 May 1880; Alfred Milnes, cited in *N.R.*, 29 Nov. 1885, p. 638; Hamilton Diary (B.M.), 48633, p. 199

did this opposition collapse so quickly after Speaker Peel had permitted Bradlaugh to take the oath in 1886? The answer can be found in many things. The general election of 1885 had demonstrated that the more virulent feelings against Bradlaugh had already begun to subside. The political reversals of the following year help to account for it. Before pressure could be brought on any Conservative Government to initiate new legal action, it had been replaced by Gladstone's Third Ministry, which obviously had no intention of taking further action. And by the time Salisbury's second ministry assumed office that summer, the Home Rule issue had come completely to dominate the ideological horizon. Parliamentary passions over Irish Home Rule reached a pitch of intensity comparable only, according to contemporaries, to the debates over the Reform Bill of 1832.[1]

Even the most religiously minded of the Irish Nationalists cared more for Home Rule than for the renewal of a conflict which had ended without forcing them to vote against their theological convictions. The Affirmation Bill debate of 1888 revealed that, although many Conservatives remained consistent, other members of the party had long had doubts as to the desirability of continuing the Bradlaugh spectacle. As for the almost absurd reversal of Lord Randolph Churchill, it was consistent with his character. He had been guided by expediency alone, and the case had been for him no more than a *jeu d'esprit*. While Churchill may deserve credit as a rallying point for Conservatives in the 1880's, he behaved often enough like an overgrown schoolboy. 'I have no longer any energy or ideas & am no more good except to create disturbance', he told Hicks-Beach in 1885.[2] But had he ever been good for anything more? It is not surprising that Bradlaugh had more respect for the principles, narrow as they might be, of a Newdegate, than for the political acrobatics of a Churchill. 'Good copy' the latter certainly was, but one wonders whether the London *Standard* was not right when

[1] Cf. Morley, *Gladstone*, iii. 321 ff.; J. L. Hammond and M. R. D. Foot, *Gladstone and Liberalism* (London, 1952), p. 181.

[2] St. Aldwyn MSS., file PCC, fol. 30. Parliament 'had never been guided by any other principle than expediency', he declared in 1883. See *N.R.*, 27 May 1883, p. 385.

it wrote in 1885 : 'The truth is, that Lord Randolph Churchill is a much over-rated man . . . .'[1]

Changes in the ideological climate obviously help also to explain the readiness with which Bradlaugh came to be accepted. In 1880 Bradlaugh could still be depicted as being politically on the far left. By 1888 this was obviously much less true. Bradlaugh had remained consistent, but the rest of the world had not. Joseph Chamberlain had popularized much of Bradlaugh's programme, and he had come to be an ally of the Conservatives. Socialism had become a small but vibrant force in English life, and at least some of the men who, as Professor Brinton has argued,[2] ought long before to have seen Bradlaugh as their unwitting ally rather than as their enemy came at last to recognize him as such. 'During the interval', grudgingly conceded the *Saturday Review* in 1891, 'Parliament has made acquaintance with persons infinitely less tolerable than he ever was.'[3] Bradlaugh had explained often enough that he was not a socialist, but only when men saw him, as fully fledged Member of Parliament, vote against proposals such as a government-sponsored eight-hour day for miners did they take him at his word.

Finally, it may be observed that shifts in popular feeling cannot always be explained on the basis of reason alone. To say that a particular public mood has passed is not to say that it never existed. If every age is an age of transition, then in the realm of ideology in Britain the 1880's were obviously more such an age than the 1870's or the 1890's.

The Bradlaugh case had numerous effects in its day. It divided the Liberal party and weakened Gladstone's Second Ministry. It furnished the opportunity for Lord Randolph Churchill and his 'Fourth Party' rebellion. It helped solidify a temporary Conservative–Irish understanding. Parnell's role in the early stages of the case may well have strengthened the distrust of the Catholic hierarchy in England and Ireland sufficiently to speed his downfall in 1890. One might therefore come to the paradoxical conclusion that the Bradlaugh

[1] Cited in *N.R.*, 9 Aug. 1885, p. 87.
[2] Crane Brinton, *English Political Thought in the Nineteenth Century*, pp. 251–2.
[3] *Saturday Review*, 31 Jan. 1891, p. 119.

case helped to divide all three political parties of the day. Yet the conflict had a positive result as well. It established for all time the principle that neither by his religion nor by his lack of religion might a man be disqualified from serving in Parliament or in many a humbler office. By means of his speech on the Affirmation Bill of 1883, perhaps the greatest of all his orations, Gladstone placed the majority of the Liberal party squarely behind the doctrine of complete toleration of the most diverse of political and religious opinions.

What of the long-range influence of Bradlaugh and the Bradlaugh case? He has by no means been forgotten, though his influence has proved a curiously diffuse one. Although Bradlaugh's *National Reformer* collapsed two years after his death, his grandson is the president of the World Union of Freethinkers, and his own National Secular Society still exists. It is in many ways a relic of the Victorian past. None of Bradlaugh's successors as president of the society, G. W. Foote, Chapman Cohen, Frank Ridley, and David Tribe. whatever their abilities, have shared the breadth of Bradlaugh's interests. In any case the enemy they now face is not Bible-worship but religious apathy. Bradlaugh's Liberal party is today also in some ways a relic of the past, though like many another Victorian institution it may yet revive. Had he lived, he doubtless would have remained a Liberal to the last, as did his surviving daughter until her death in 1935.

And yet both Conservatives and Labourites have claimed Bradlaugh as their own. When the centenary of his birth sparked a major Bradlaugh revival in 1933, both Harold Laski in the *Daily Herald* and Harvey James in the *Daily Mail* could eulogize Bradlaugh, the first as an exponent of freedom, the second as an opponent of socialism.[1] In Northampton, where his marble figure looms in characteristic platform posture over Abington Square, two men keep Bradlaugh's memory alive. Alderman Percy Adams, grandson of Bradlaugh's election agent and Conservative ex-mayor, remembers him as a representative of individualism and minimizes his atheism. Alderman Walter Lewis, a one-time Welsh miner who worked his way up through Labour party

[1] *Literary Guide*, December 1933.

ranks to the position of mayor, finds Bradlaugh an inspiration for all who seek to defy class distinctions. Similarly the *New Statesman*, England's leading left-wing weekly, re-dedicated itself in 1957 to maintain not only its independent socialist outlook but to carry on 'the great tradition of of British radicalism, which includes Tom Paine as well as Bentham, Robert Owen as well as John Stuart Mill, Bradlaugh and Webb as well as Massingham. The core of that tradition . . . is that it contributes more happiness, more welfare, more of the reality of human freedom.'[1]

Curiously few of the issues with which Bradlaugh became identified in the nineteenth century have become outdated in the twentieth. A successful struggle for membership in the House of Commons similar to Bradlaugh's own has been carried on in recent years by Anthony Wedgwood Benn, 'the reluctant peer'. The question of self-government for India and the perennial issue of freedom of the press were to remain equally relevant, as is the question which caused him the greatest ignominy, birth control, surely one of the key issues of our times. Bradlaugh's ideas on this subject as well as many of his criticisms of religious fundamentalism have become commonplaces in most Protestant denominations. Even the narrower question of the right of affirmation as a badge of respect has not become completely outdated. At present approximately 6·5 per cent. of members entering the House of Commons choose to affirm rather than to take the oath,[2] and if this number includes Quakers and others with religious scruples, it obviously comprises also those who prefer the form on grounds of unbelief. Certainly the latter was true in 1906 of John Morley, the first man elevated to the House of Lords to insist upon affirmation, and in 1958 of Barbara Wootton, one of the first two ladies to be admitted to that august assembly.[3]

Finally what of Bradlaugh himself? It ought to be clear by now that this most un-Victorian Victorian was himself very much a representative of Victorianism at its best. This

[1] Kingsley Martin, 'The N.S. and the Nation', *New Statesman*, 6 July 1957, p. 5.

[2] Letter from Charles Pannell, M.P., 1 Apr. 1958.

[3] *Manchester Guardian Weekly*, 23 Oct. 1958, p. 3.

stormy petrel of the 1870's and 1880's, who gloried in his iconoclasticism in religion, in politics, and in social life, had the highest respect for tradition. His interest in England's history might descend into antiquarianism, but he showed the greatest deference to law; and the material pride and joy of his life, his library of seven thousand volumes, included some 250 law-books.[1] For Parliament, whatever temporary disillusionments he might suffer at its hands, he had a positive reverence. What distinguished him as Victorian is in part his individualism. For Bradlaugh was truly 'inner directed' and, though like all great orators he had the gift of catching quickly the spirit of an audience, he had the courage to take the unpopular stand as well. If he was caught occasionally in the dilemma which faces all leaders who advocate democracy —that the voice of the people will dispute their own—his nature, though sometimes petty over minor irritants, could show the largest measure of charity as well, as is demonstrated in his relationship with the Irish Nationalists. What finally distinguished Bradlaugh was his burning sincerity, which made its impress upon so many who came in contact with him, and the force of character, which as much as anything else brought about his latter-day reconciliation with many of his erstwhile opponents. 'A distinguished man and admirable Member of this House', was Gladstone's final verdict.[2] Bradlaugh was in typical Victorian fashion able to reconcile ultimate principles with practical compromises. This was his attitude in the 1860's—'Seek justice; but refuse no point which may be conceded'—and this was his attitude in the 1880's as well. 'All progressive legislation in this country is necessarily compromise. It is not possible to legislate on hard and fast lines of principle alone . . . but no compromise is final.'[3]

Perhaps such an assessment of Bradlaugh is merely another sign that 'we live in an age of rebunking, when it has become fashionable once more to take the Victorians almost as solemnly as they took themselves'.[4] But if the past may at

---

[1] *Catalogue of the Library of the late Charles Bradlaugh* (London, 1891).
[2] *Hansard*, cccil (1891), 1751.
[3] Cited by Bonner & Robertson, *Bradlaugh*, i. 223; ii. 188.
[4] Anonymous reviewer, *The Times Literary Supplement*, 6 May 1960, p. 291.

times be viewed with irony, ought it also to be viewed with derision? In an age of mass movements and ultimate weapons and total wars, the story of one persevering individual may seem lacking in significance—especially when his most obvious gift lay in that historically ephemeral art of oratory rather than in the written word. But such an appraisal may be a judgement upon our age rather than upon his. For the liberal heritage of unfettered freedom of expression, of personal courage and independence, and of peaceful political change within the framework of tradition is not irrelevant to our times.

XXVII

POSTSCRIPT:
THE BRADLAUGH CASE REVISITED

TWENTY years have passed since the revised draft for the initial publication of *The Bradlaugh Case* was completed. The decision of the University of Missouri Press to reprint the book and to issue for the first time a paperback edition has also provided me with the opportunity, in this chapter, to take another look at the subject. One of the great "growth industries" of Anglo-American publishing during the past two decades has been books and articles on the social and political history of Victorian Britain. Two articles have sought to rebut specific interpretations put forward in this book. Other works have broadened our understanding both of the lives of the major participants and of the institutions with which they were associated. Some of these works deal directly with Bradlaugh and his causes; others involve antagonists like Lord Randolph Churchill, Charles Stewart Parnell, and Charles Newdigate Newdegate. Yet others reassess the entire late-Victorian political and religious scene. This postscript chapter may also enable me to blunt a handful of barbs that were tossed at the book on its first appearance, along with bouquets, in British newspapers and periodicals as well as in scholarly journals on both sides of the Atlantic. My purpose is to deal in largely topical fashion with the following themes, themes that have either evoked controversy or inspired additional scholarly research:

1) Bradlaugh's career before 1880;
2) The Victorian secularist movement;
3) The birth control controversy;
4) The role of Lord Randolph Churchill;
5) The role of the Irish Nationalists;
6) The significance of religion and respectability;
7) Bradlaugh's years as Member of Parliament.

In 1971 David Tribe published the first fully documented twentieth-century biography of Bradlaugh,[1] and a number of scholars have

---

[1] David Tribe, *President Charles Bradlaugh, M.P.* (London and Hamden, Conn., 1971). Until then, according to A. O. J. Cockshut, Bradlaugh's reputation rested on "that most terrible ordeal of all, . . . to have one's life written by a devoted daughter." *The Unbelievers* (London, 1964), p. 86.

added to our understanding of the Victorian freethought movement. F. B. Smith summed up the Victorian secularist ethos in "The Atheist Mission, 1840–1900,"[2] and in a lengthy chapter in *The London Heretics, 1870–1914*, "The Secularists," Warren Sylvester Smith provided pointed pen-portraits of Holyoake, Bradlaugh, Besant, and Aveling.[3] By far the most comprehensive work on the movement, however, has been contributed by Edward Royle in *Victorian Infidels: The Origins of the British Secularist Movement, 1791–1866*[4] and in *Radicals, Secularists, and Republicans: Popular Freethought in Britain, 1866–1915*.[5] In these volumes Royle has, in methodical and largely topical fashion, examined the movement's leaders, followers, organizations, publications, finances, and concerns. The story is pushed forward into the twentieth century in more cursory fashion in David Tribe's *100 Years of Freethought* (London, 1967), and those members of the movement on which sufficient biographical information existed have been subjected to at times revealing prosopographical examination in Susan Budd's *Varieties of Unbelief: Atheists and Agnostics in English Society, 1850–1960*.[6] Her book also includes some acute observations on Bradlaugh's style of leadership and on the paradoxical manner in which he embodied "The Model Protestant."[7] In the meantime John Saville had collected twenty-seven of Bradlaugh's writings over three decades—including *The Impeachment of the House of Brunswick*. They were published in London and New York in 1970 in a single volume as *A Selection of the Political Pamphlets of Charles Bradlaugh*.

The books by Tribe and Royle were inspired, at least in part, by the revelation, after the death of Bradlaugh's only grandson in 1966, that a far larger collection of Bradlaugh papers had survived than I had been given reason to believe twenty years ago. Those papers were presented to the National Secular Society in 1967 by Bradlaugh's great-

---

[2] In Robert Robson, ed., *Ideas and Institutions of Victorian Britain* (London, 1967), pp. 205–35.

[3] London, 1967.

[4] Manchester and Totowa, N.J., 1974.

[5] Manchester and Totowa, N.J., 1980. Dr. Royle has also edited *The Infidel Tradition from Paine to Bradlaugh* (London, 1976). Lee E. Grugel has provided a brief modern biography, *George Jacob Holyoake: A Study in the Evolution of a Victorian Radical* (Philadelphia, 1976).

[6] London, 1977.

[7] Budd, *Varieties of Unbelief*, pp. 42–44. Also worth noting are a number of unpublished Ph.D. dissertations: Walter D. Nelson, "British Rational Secularism: Unbelief from Bradlaugh to the Mid-Twentieth Century" (history, University of Washington, 1963); Charles Krantz, "The British Secularist Movement: A Study in Militant Dissent" (history, University of Rochester, 1964); Joseph Anthony Ilardo, "The Bradlaugh Case: A Study of Parliamentary Debates Concerning the Affirmation-Oath Controversy, 1880–1891" (speech, University of Illinois at Urbana-Champaign, 1969).

grandson; they were carefully calendared in 1975 by Edward Royle; and they are (for the most part) now housed in London's Bishopsgate Institute and Library. A small collection of letters—many of them referred to in Hypatia Bradlaugh Bonner's biography of her father—was acquired by Oxford's Bodleian Library in 1964. Although the items in the Bishopsgate Institute collection—more than three thousand in all—are most plentiful for the 1880s (and for the activities of Bradlaugh's daughter after her father's death), they do illuminate significant aspects of Bradlaugh's earlier legal affairs and of his relations with his daughters and with some of his associates. They also provide hundreds of otherwise inaccessible newspaper clippings.

There was a high degree of consistency to both Bradlaugh's theological views and his political radicalism, but Tribe and Royle agree that it may be more fruitful to see Bradlaugh's career as a series of brief chapters focused on particular themes. In the early 1860s, for example, it is clear that, although Bradlaugh had been compelled to give up his hope of becoming an articled solicitor, he had become temporarily a prosperous businessman. He was at once a company promoter and secretary, an agent for several provincial insurance companies, and a loan broker for a number of Italian cities.[8] His family lived in a suburban villa, he employed two full-time maids, and he confined his speechmaking, both antireligious and political, to weekends. Yet, as Tribe observes, "Bradlaugh's nose for talent was infinitely greater than his nose for character. He preferred to take people on trust." Several of his associates in company promotion fell victim to the panic of 1866, when the great discount house of Overend and Gurney collapsed and scores of smaller banks and credit companies folowed suit. Bradlaugh did not go bankrupt either in that year or in 1870 when he wound up altogether his career as financier. Yet, as he himself was to concede, "I have great faculties for making money; and great faculties for losing it."[9] He avoided the disgrace of bankruptcy only by giving up his suburban villa, selling the furniture, persuading his creditors to give him extra time, and curtailing sharply his own expenses. Henceforth he would concentrate his energies on the *National Reformer*—by 1869 he was publicly identifying himself as "journalist"—on the National Secular Society, and on the causes that constituted mid-Victorian political radicalism.

Those causes included Ireland; but as two historians have noted recently,[10] his daughter's description of Bradlaugh's involvement with

[8] Tribe, *Bradlaugh*, p. 87.
[9] Ibid., p. 64; cited in ibid., p. 116.
[10] Nigel H. Sinnott, "Charles Bradlaugh and Ireland," *Journal of the Cork Historical and Archaeological Society* 77 (1972): 1–24; Fergus D'Arcy, "Charles Bradlaugh and the Irish Question: A Study in the Nature and Limits of British Radicalism, 1853–

the Fenians in 1867 (upon which I drew on pages 17 and 207) is contradictory. There is no question that Bradlaugh found it easier than did most Victorians to discern analogies between continental nationalism like that of Italy and Poland (with which a majority of Britons sympathized) and that of Ireland. Nor does there appear to be any question that two of the Fenian leaders, Thomas J. Kelly and Gustave Paul Cluseret, the proclaimers of the Irish Republic, had consulted Bradlaugh, or that the latter strongly approved of their call for "equal rights," "absolute liberty of conscience, and the complete Separation of Church and State." However much Bradlaugh might condemn the Irish land system and British misgovernment of Ireland, at that time he nevertheless found the notion of an Irish Republic fanciful, that of a Fenian revolution an invitation to vain and unnecessary bloodshed, and that of the complete separation of Ireland from the rest of the United Kingdom both unworkable and undesirable. Only a few years later, in 1872, did Bradlaugh begin to espouse a "Home Rule" solution (foreshadowing Gladstone's) under which the Irish people would have the opportunity "to legislate for themselves—just as the state of New York, and the state of Massachusetts" did.[11] As D'Arcy justly observes,[12] projectors of a violent insurrection like Kelly and Cuseret were scarcely interested in seeking mere "legal advice" from Bradlaugh. Presumably they sought practical assistance from London-based radicals, of whom Bradlaugh was one. The fact that the British Home Office, whose agents had infiltrated the Fenian movement and who at that time kept Bradlaugh's house under surveillance, failed to arrest Bradlaugh suggests that they could find no proof that he had ever counseled revolution. Bradlaugh's involvement in the 1867 revolt, Sinnott appropriately concludes, "was somewhat complex," but that complexity is unlikely ever to be made simple.

By 1870 Bradlaugh had become persuaded that the transformation of his native land into a republic *was* a realizable ambition, and the details of Bradlaugh's involvement with the English republican movement have recently been reappraised by Fergus D'Arcy.[13] Tribe notes in his biography that Bradlaugh at no time felt personal animosity toward Queen Victoria, but that, inspired by the Franco-

---

91," in Art Cosgrove and Donal McCartney, eds., *Studies in Irish History Presented to R. Dudley Edwards* (Dublin, 1979), pp. 228–56.

[11] See Sinnott, "Bradlaugh and Ireland," pp. 11–14.

[12] D'Arcy, "Bradlaugh and the Irish Question," pp. 234–35. See also Tribe, *Bradlaugh*, pp. 98–99.

[13] Fergus D'Arcy, "Charles Bradlaugh and the English Republican Movement, 1868–1878," *Historical Journal* 25 (June 1982): 367–83. See also an unpublished Ph.D. dissertation, Michael Pearson Smith, "Republicanism in Victorian Britain," (history, McMaster University, 1979).

Prussian War and by the creation of the Third French Republic, he came anew to see the monarchy as the pivot of a constitution that preserved a powerful state church and a body of privileged peers who symbolized and exemplified heredity rather than merit. Moreover, Bradlaugh insisted, the monarchy since Victoria's accession had cost the people of Britain seventy-five times as much money as the presidency had cost the people of the United States.[14] He became president of a London republican club, and he competed successfully with Karl Marx's abortive First International for leadership of a nationwide republican organization. For several months he toured the country lecturing on the subject to large audiences. Yet Tribe seems to take rather more seriously than the evidence warrants the possibility of Bradlaugh becoming president of a British republic in 1871 or 1872.[15] It was not British papers but American ones like the *New York World* that hailed him as "the coming Cromwell" and the *New York Herald* that speculated in 1872 that a rejection of the pending Alabama Treaty would lead to an Anglo-American war and "open the gates of Windsor Castle to Mr. Bradlaugh and his Republicans."[16]

Bradlaugh was so absorbed with republican agitation during 1871, 1872, and 1873, that, as Edward Royle has noted,[17] the National Secular Society practically dissolved during those years as a functional organization. Yet it remains one of Bradlaugh's chief claims to fame to have temporarily fashioned a significant organization out of a tradition of freethought that, as Royle confirms, can be traced back to Thomas Paine in the 1790s and Richard Carlile in the 1820s. Mid- and late-Victorian freethinkers also drew upon the anticlerical attitudes and the ethical teachings of Robert Owen though not upon his socialism. "No socialist myself," Bradlaugh was to write in 1877, "I cannot but concede that the movement [founded by Owen] had enormous value, if only as a protest against that terrible and inhuman competitive struggle, in which the strong were rewarded for their strength, and no mercy was shown to the weakest."[18]

It was the Owenites who first established Halls of Science as centers of both adult education and of nonalcoholic sociability, and it was George Jacob Holyoake who provided the connecting link between the Owenites of the 1840s and the secular movement of the late-Victorian era. It was Holyoake too who in 1851 coined the word *secu-*

[14] Tribe, *Bradlaugh*, p. 118.
[15] Ibid., pp. 128–29.
[16] *World* cited in Royle, *Radicals*, p. 201; *Herald* of 5 April 1872 cited in *Public Opinion*, 20 April 1872, p. 492.
[17] Royle, *Radicals*, p. 20.
[18] Charles Bradlaugh, *Five Dead Men Whom I Knew When Living* (London, 1877), p. 4.

larism as a "constructive" alternative to the mere disbelief implied for most people by *infidelity* or *atheism*. Holyoake was a conscientious worker and a skillful and often witty journalist, but he failed to evolve into either a dynamic speaker or a successful organizer. He "never moved on from being the pilot to being the captain of the ship."[19] To his own discomfiture he therefore found himself displaced by Charles Bradlaugh in the course of the late 1850s and early 1860s. Bradlaugh was an imposing man who developed into a forceful orator as well as trenchant writer, and Bradlaugh *did* possess organizational talents. He took over Holyoake's word, *secularism* (though unlike Holyoake he insisted that *secularism* implied *atheism*, at least *atheism* as defined by Bradlaugh), and during the 1860s he created a national organization that truly was national.

By the mid-1870s, the National Secular Society had come to incorporate almost a hundred local branches, a majority in London and in Lancashire, Yorkshire, Northumberland, and Durham. The system of dues that Bradlaugh originated (a smaller fee for those who enrolled through a branch than for those who enrolled directly in London), the hundreds of lectures he gave each year, and the *National Reformer* that he edited (with a weekly paid circulation by then of six thousand copies) held the movement together.[20] Both Bradlaugh's army background and his legal training help to account for his success. The price to be paid was a personal domination of the movement that troubled and at times alienated those secularist leaders who had been left by the wayside. "Why does a democrat like Mr. Bradlaugh," wondered George William Foote, "compare the party of which he is a member to a regiment of drilled machines, without will or purpose except to obey the word of command? I am not a soldier, but a citizen."[21] George Jacob Holyoake could wound even more deeply. Noting that in *The Freethinker's Textbook* Bradlaugh and Annie Besant had proclaimed "God=X," Holyoake anonymously proposed a revised version of the national anthem for use in the Bradlaugh republic. These are the first two stanzas:

> "X" save our graceless Chief,
> Reward his unbelief,
> "X" save our B.
> O'er Church victorious
> And throne, once glorious
> Now sole Lord over us—
> Xtol our B!

[19] Royle, *Radicals*, p. 4.
[20] Ibid., pp. 6–7.
[21] Cited in ibid., p. 12.

SCIENCE, our "X"! Arise!
Xplode B's enemies
    And squash them small!
Confound their politicks!
Frustrate their knavish tricks,
Ah "X"! those heretics
    Xtinguish all![22]

The problem of leadership may be endemic in successful popular movements, and if, in the context of the Victorian world writ large, secularism never constituted a mass movement, in the context of the century-old British freethought tradition, Bradlaugh's society did.

In a not unfriendly critique of the original edition, Brian Harrison suggested among other things that, in describing Bradlaugh, I had failed to give "sufficient emphasis to his speech and appearance: the man *looked* vulgar." Harrison went on to recall that Sir Alfred Pease had described Bradlaugh as "a great massive man, with a large peculiar face and an upper lip like a saddle-flap," who dropped his *h*'s in Cockney fashion.[23] The review evoked a spirited defense of his grandfather by Charles Bradlaugh Bonner, who dismissed accounts such as Pease's as "mean smears." The historian, Harrison justly responded, is faced with conflicting evidence as to how Bradlaugh spoke.[24] Critics did indeed assert that his oratorical manner, with "ill-constructed sentences . . . indifferently delivered," was "painfully repulsive" with *h*'s dropped and final *g*'s (in words ending in *-ing*) often left out altogether.[25] Yet such a picture accords poorly with Bradlaugh's appeal as a platform orator or in the House of Commons. If his style was at times loud and theatrical, it was also generally effective. If of a more rugged type than Gladstone's or Bright's, his manner caused the *Bolton Weekly Journal* to write, "He is an able speaker with a pleasing and cultivated enunciation."[26] Gladstone's son Herbert, who knew Bradlaugh well during the 1880s, recalled in 1925 that he did "remember occasions when in the excitement of a speech [Bradlaugh]

[22] Ion, *Blasts from Bradlaugh's Own Trumpet* (London, 1882), p. 28.

[23] *New Society*, 23 September 1965, p. 33.

[24] Ibid., 21 October 1965, pp. 29–30.

[25] *A Night with Bradlaugh By One Who Has Spent It* (London, 1882), p. 4.

[26] Issue of 22 February 1890; clipping in Bradlaugh MSS (Bishopsgate), #1728. See also Royle, *Radicals*, p. 91. In a book I had failed to note twenty years ago, David Anderson's *"Scenes" in the Commons* (London, 1884), Anderson provides this initial impression: "When seen with his long arms and heavy hands drooping or swinging by his sides, there is nothing dignified about him. . . . The cold eyes glisten with the hardness of polished steel. . . . When passive, the mask indicates force, scrutiny, and aggressiveness. When he smiles, the expression of his face is not altogether unamiable." Yet, Anderson goes on, his oratorical reputation was warranted. "His voice, if not uniformly melodious, is always resonant, his enunciation distinct, and his matter pithy and to the purpose" (pp. 64–65).

did drop an h but he did not do so in the general habit of speaking and it was not a marked peculiarity either of his conversation or his speeches."[27] Harrison is also right to suggest that cartoonists capitalized upon his drawn-down upper lip, and yet one wonders whether Bradlaugh's voice or appearance barred him from acceptability nearly so much as did some of his ideas and their implications. Many Britons did indeed assume these to be vulgar.

A revealing appraisal of Bradlaugh's personality was "delineated" in 1864 by "Professor" L. N. Fowler, a phrenologist; it was still sold to secularists in 1880. The reading of "bumps on the head" is usually recalled as a form of Victorian quackery, but nineteenth-century rationalists were as likely to be drawn to phrenology, that "science of the mind," as twentieth-century rationalists have been to schools of psychoanalysis—and practicing phrenologists often proved to be sensitive observers.[28] Fowler told Bradlaugh: "You are inclined, to put too much powder in your gun and fire as though you had large game every time. Your brain is over large, and your worldly energies are a little inferior. You have scarcely enough vitality, even with prudence, to live to an old age." The leading features of Bradlaugh's mind, according to Fowler, included originality, force, executive ability, indignation, and determination. "You have almost excessive Benevolence," Fowler observed, but such qualities were balanced by "large Combativeness and Self-Esteem." "You have not much Veneration" but "a fair degree of Spirituality." "You are more proud than vain" and possess a love of children "but not much passionate love." "You are much attached to home and place." Bradlaugh also possessed an active sense of the ridiculous and good powers of observation and synthesis but little cunning: "You are quite transparent in your thought and feelings." He was also versatile enough to become a successful teacher, lawyer, speaker, or statesman. "Take life as quietly, steadily, and uniformly as possible," Fowler advised, "and you may, by careful usages, reach a good old age."[29] The assessment may have been shrewd, but the advice was not taken.

But where did Bradlaugh fit within the context of both late-Victorian thought in general and the religious spectrum in particular? Since "Herbert Spencer, T. H. Huxley, Leslie Stephen and Frederick Harrison figure in the narrative only as signatories to petitions," Peter Fraser contended in his review in *History*, "the nature of the crisis of the 1880s of which the Bradlaugh Case formed a part is entirely misconceived. It was not just a 'religious' struggle but the first popular

---

[27] Viscount Gladstone MSS, British Library Add. MSS 46085, fol. 189. Cf. Tribe, *Bradlaugh*, 58.

[28] See Budd, *Varieties of Unbelief*, p. 24.

[29] Bradlaugh MSS (Bishopsgate), #741(A).

encounter between religion and scientific materialism," and of the latter creed Bradlaugh was "ignorant."[30] Fraser was right to suggest that I touched upon, rather than surveyed in detail, the mental world of those whom A. O. J. Cockshut has dubbed *The Unbelievers*. Whatever their individual peculiarities, John Stuart Mill, Arthur Clough, George Eliot, Mathew Arnold, Herbert Spencer, Thomas Henry Huxley, and Samuel Butler shared a disbelief in the truth of orthodox Christianity while remaining deeply concerned with problems of religion and morality. Back in the 1850s such agnostics felt "isolated in a society, where the religion they rejected, the morality they reverenced, and the respectability they so conspicuously embodied were generally held to be inseparable." They could not then be expected to foresee, Cockshut contends, how quickly their earnest and even pious manner would win them the respect and even the silent acquiescence of many of their educated compatriots.[31]

One may readily discern more than a touch of elitism in Fraser's undocumented assumption that merely because Bradlaugh was self-educated and often addressed unsophisticated audiences he could neither speak nor understand the language of Huxley or John Morley or Leslie Stephen or that of other members of the Victorian intellectual aristocracy. Fraser may never have sampled the *National Reformer*, many of whose articles on philosophy, economics, and science might as readily have graced the pages of the *Nineteenth Century* or the *Fortnightly Review*. Edward Royle has recently been led to marvel anew at how many hours of enlightenment the devoted reader was able to derive from his twopence. "It is hard to escape the conclusion," however, Royle goes on, "that the contents cannot have been easy to read. There was much earnest, intellectual matter, but little of humour and no concession to the sort of person who seems to have thrived on the vulgarities of the outdoor lectures."[32] Bradlaugh's original definition of atheism had been based on G. H. Lewes's exposition of Spinoza in the 1850s.[33] Bradlaugh and his colleagues were au courant with biblical higher criticism in Britain and on the continent as well as with writings of Darwinists like Huxley and Germany's Ludwig Buechner and Ernst Haeckl. It may in any case be a mistake for historians to postulate a single readily identifiable intellectual crisis in the 1880s or in any other decade. Such crises would seem to afflict no more than

[30] June 1966, p. 245.
[31] See A. O. J. Cockshut, *The Unbelievers: English Agnostic Thought 1840–1890* (London, 1964), p. 48. Cf. chapter 3, "Doubt," of vol. 2 of Owen Chadwick's magisterial *The Victorian Church*, 2 vols. (Oxford, 1966, 1970).
[32] Royle, *Radicals*, pp. 158–59.
[33] *National Reformer* of 9 November 1890, cited in Bradlaugh MSS (Bishopsgate), # 1962.

a portion of a society at any given time. Abstruse philosophical spec-
ulators coexisted with biblical fundamentalists in the 1880s as they
had a hundred years earlier and were to do a hundred years later, and
the apparently solid scientific materialism of one generation was all
too likely to be undermined by the relativistic uncertainty principle
of the next.

It is true that men like Huxley and Stephen did not seek Bradlaugh
out publicly, but surely it was the guilt by association with the dis-
reputable that was responsible and not the absence of a common
language or of analogous opinions. John Stuart Mill's experience had
proved that they had cause for concern. Yet Professor Robert Flint of
the University of Edinburgh did not treat Bradlaugh's views with
condescension (see p. 12) any more than did John Stuart Blackie,
Professor of Latin at the same institution and for many years "the
most prominent feature of the patriotic and literary life of Edinburgh."[34] "Nothing would give me greater pleasure," Blackie wrote
to Bradlaugh in 1880, "than to see you in Parliament. It would be
splendid to see you smashing some of the small men, and bowling
down even the giants like nine pins!"[35]

The irony remains that just as the ideas of Bradlaugh, Besant,
Aveling, Holyoake, and others were, if rarely original, then very
much part of the pattern of Victorian unbelief, so their movement as a
movement was far more immediately related to the world of Nonconformist religious life. Like the Nonconformist denominations, Royle
notes,[36] the branches of the National Secular Society were at once
"chapels" and "missions." They were chapels in the sense that they
served as social centers as well as institutions where "sermons" were
heard and important personal and public events ceremonially noted.
They also served as missions looking for new converts. Virtually all
secular society leaders and many society members—most of them,
according to the *Weekly Despatch* of 1879, independently minded
members of that same "small clerkly class" into which Bradlaugh had
been born—had themselves undergone an experience of conversion.[37]
Brought up within the Church of England or of an often fundamentalist Nonconformist sect, they had seen the light and now sought to
spread the word. The fact that each side was firmly convinced of its
ability to persuade the other helps to account for the willingness of
secularist lecturers and Christian preachers to debate one another so
readily during the 1860s and 1870s. The Christian Evidence Society

[34] *Dictionary of National Biography*, Supplementary Volume, p. 206.
[35] Bradlaugh MSS (Bodleian Library), fol. 141.
[36] Royle, *Radicals*, p. 120.
[37] Ibid., p. 109; Budd, *Varieties of Unbelief*, pp. 96–101; *Weekly Despatch* clipping in Bradlaugh MSS (Bishopsgate), #566.

(to which Bradlaugh's brother William belonged) and the National Secular Society were symbiotically related. Each throve on the attacks of the other. Each quoted the Bible for its own ends. Both were enemies of indifference. Both were fearful of apathy. And when biblical fundamentalism faded in early twentieth-century Britain so did the organized secularist movement.

The links between the British freethought movement and the advocacy of birth control dated to Richard Carlile's *Every Woman's Book* (1826). To the discomfiture of Holyoake and others, Bradlaugh reestablished the link early in his career with his pamphlet *Jesus, Shelley, and Malthus* (1861). Bradlaugh, it seems clear, saw the need to limit the size of families primarily in individual terms rather than in those of national or world demography. Too many children meant "overcrowded homes, high infant mortality, women old before their time, precautionary late marriages, and prostitution." [38] Only by a policy of family limitation would the lower classes ever truly escape poverty. Although Tribe goes on to suggest that Bradlaugh was not so much a sexual puritan as his daughter believed, he concedes that Bradlaugh was primarily concerned with the practice of contraception by married couples. [39] The astonishing furor that such teaching aroused among many Victorians can be explained only by the conviction on the part of critics that such teaching would not cement but destroy the marriage bond by promoting premarital indulgence, by encouraging adultery, and by endorsing prostitution. George Drysdale's *Elements of Social Science; or Physical, Sexual and Natural Religion*—first published anonymously in 1854—did provide such critics with considerable warrant. Indeed, this "Bible of the Brothel" denounced marriage as "one of the chief instruments in the degradation of women" and preached "free love." It went on to encourage every man and woman "to exercise fully [their] sexual organs." According to Drysdale, "chastity [and] sexual abstinence cause more real disease and misery in one year . . . than sexual excesses in a century." [40]

Bradlaugh could never fully escape the onus of having advertised and even commended Drysdale's work. The event that totally identified him with the cause of "Neo-Malthusianism" was, however, the

[38] Tribe, *Bradlaugh*, p. 74.

[39] Ibid., p. 70.

[40] Cited in ibid., pp. 50–51. For one of Bradlaugh's most virulent opponents, the Baptist preacher Henry Varley (see p. 97), the retention of their seed by men was, on the contrary, the first rule of good health. "It is a well-known fact," wrote Varley, "that any man who desires to excel and retain his excellence as an accurate shot, an oarsman, a pedestrian, a pugilist, a first-rate cricketer, a successful student, artist, or literary man must abstain from self-pollution and fornication." Even married men must limit sexual activity lest "they unwisely give their strength to the wife." *Lecture to Men* (London, 1883), p. 11.

Fruits of Philosophy trial of 1877. As the head of the flourishing secularist movement and as an aspiring candidate for Parliament, Bradlaugh had little incentive in 1877 to become the focus of a cause célèbre likely to divide his movement and undermine his political prospects. He came to see the case, it is true, more as an issue of freedom of the press than of promoting the teaching of contraception. The case separated him from Charles Watts, the man who for fifteen years had been his closest secularist associate. Watts concluded that the controversial pamphlet was not good enough to go to jail for; Watts's wife, Kate—the "first lady" of secularism until Annie Besant's arrival—concluded that Bradlaugh was unduly eager to make a martyr of her husband. Bradlaugh, on the contrary, decided that Watts had let down the cause of freethought by capitulating to the authorities and pleading guilty to the charge of having published an obscene book. It was then that Bradlaugh and Annie Besant decided to reprint the controversial volume on their own and to win the case, thus demonstrating that they were right and that secularist leaders like Watts, Foote, and Holyoake were wrong.[41] There is no question that Mrs. Besant, that well-bred, youthful, and courageous dynamo of passionate indignation, provided the impetus to urge on her idol and collaborator to challenge the public prosecutor.[42]

In the short run the case clearly disrupted the National Secular Society, and some of the founders of the rival British Secular Union and *Secular Review* were never to be reconciled to Bradlaugh's leadership, but the bulk of the membership remained loyal to their president. Once Bradlaugh and Besant had been arrested, their treatment of Watts was largely forgotten, and their courage in fighting (successfully) for the cause of freedom of publication was rewarded by larger lecture audiences and an increase in N.S.S. membership. Yet there was a price to be paid: Annie Besant lost the custody of her daughter, and Charles Bradlaugh acquired an albatross that would help to keep him out of Parliament for five years.[43]

The precise relationship between the Bradlaugh-Besant trial of 1877 and the dramatic decline in the British birthrate and the size of the average family from the 1870s to the 1930s remains in dispute. Norman Himes assumed a close correlation,[44] while Marie Stopes, the most influential proponent of family limitation in post–World War I

---

[41] Royle, *Radicals*, pp. 39, 96–97; Arthur Calder Marshall, *Lewd, Blasphemous, and Obscene* (London, 1972), p. 175.

[42] The story has recently been retold in Roger Manvell, *The Trial of Annie Besant and Charles Bradlaugh* (London and New York, 1976) and in S. Chandasekhar, *"A Dirty Filthy Book"* (Berkeley, 1981). The latter volume reprints Knowlton's and Annie Besant's pamphlets.

[43] Royle, *Radicals*, pp. 15, 17–20.

[44] See Peter Fryer, *The Birth Controllers* (London, 1965) pp. 111) 36.

Britain, argued that the trial had impeded progress by confounding contraception with atheism and obscenity.[45] What does seem clear is that perhaps a million pamphlets outlining possible methods of birth control were sold during the decade and a half after the trial. Annie Besant's *Law of Population* (1877) recommended a vaginal sponge, though she also mentioned condoms, syringing with a solution of sulphate of zinc or of alum, and coitus interruptus.[46]

As scholars like J. A. Banks have insisted,[47] at least as significant as method was motive. Upper- and middle-class "pioneer" families found such motive in the felt need to spend more of their income in educating their sons for posts in the civil service and the professions as well as maintaining their standard of living during the late-Victorian Great Depression. They thereby manifested a spirit of prudence while succeeding in all other respects in observing the dictates of conventional religious behavior. At a time when children had ceased to become economic assets by age seven but were instead prevented from working in factories and compelled to go to school, working-class families also found increasing cause to limit the size of their families.[48] What was truly decisive, argues Banks, was neither secularist propaganda by the Malthusian League nor organized Victorian feminism, which largely ignored the subject of birth control, but a gradually changing framework of attitudes in which most groups in society became "future-oriented."[49] Despite Banks's strictures, scholars like Patricia Branca[50] and Angus McLaren[51] have continued to advance the thesis that women were more involved in the birth control initiative than were men. The historical evidence for the subject may be a shade more plentiful than earlier scholars had assumed, yet it remains at once allusive and elusive. Is it indeed necessary to assume that, except in particular families, this was a matter on which the wishes and interests of husband and wife were necessarily at odds? The *Fruits of Philosophy* trial and the publicity it generated may well have served as both a catalyst and as a demographic milestone.[52]

---

[45] Royle, *Radicals*, pp. 256, 275.

[46] Fryer, *The Birth Controllers*, pp. 183–84. See also Angus McLaren, *Birth Control in Nineteenth Century England* (London, 1978).

[47] In *Prosperity and Parenthood: A Study of Family Planning Among the Victorian Middle Class* (London, 1954), with Olive Banks in *Feminism and Family Planning in Victorian England* (Liverpool, 1964), and most recently in the discursive but well-annotated *Victorian Values: Secularism and the Size of Families* (London, 1981).

[48] See especially *Victorian Values*, chap. 9.

[49] See ibid., chap. 6.

[50] *Silent Sisterhood: Middle Class Women in the Victorian Home* (London, 1975).

[51] *Birth Control in Nineteenth Century England*.

[52] So argues Chandasekhar for one. Richard Allen Soloway, *Birth Control and the Population Question in England, 1877–1930* (Chapel Hill, N.C., 1982) dates the onset of informed discussion from the time of the trial.

Neither critics of the original edition of *The Bradlaugh Case* nor newly opened papers have thrown significant additional light upon the events that precipitated the case: Bradlaugh's initial claim to affirm; the decision to appoint a select committee, a committee that by a single vote denied that claim; Bradlaugh's decision to take the oath and his controversial letter to *The Times*; the move to appoint a second committee; the resolution in the House of Commons to bar Bradlaugh from taking the oath; Bradlaugh's first speech before the bar and his temporary imprisonment; Gladstone's successful compromise resolution permitting Bradlaugh to swear but making that claim subject to judicial review. Speaker Brand may indeed have opened Pandora's box by failing to rule on the matter independently, but the fact remains that no major political figure at the time considered a select committee as anything other than the proper parliamentary response to Bradlaugh's request. There were numerous precedents for such a course, and Gladstone himself had criticized Disraeli's government in 1875 when John Mitchel, a convicted felon, had been chosen by an Irish constituency and then barred from his seat. Then Gladstone had insisted on "the prudence of enquiry." [53]

Since the book was first published, more light has been shed upon the careers of two of Bradlaugh's most effective opponents in the summer of 1880, Edward Gibson, whose confidence and precise reasoning "helped materially to win the battle" against Labouchere's resolution asking for Bradlaugh's admission, and Charles Newdigate Newdegate, whose initiative compelled the courts to review the legality of Bradlaugh's admission. [54] These books do not alter our understanding of Gibson's and Newdegate's roles and motives. A subject that has aroused much more controversy is the involvement of Lord Randolph Churchill.

In "The Fourth Party and the Conservative Opposition to Bradlaugh," [55] R. E. Quinault has argued that I had uncritically accepted the "Liberal explanation" for the virulence of the opposition to Bradlaugh, an explanation that, he admits, had also largely been accepted by Lord Randolph's son Winston and by John Gorst's son Harold. [56] Although I had called attention to the fact that many late Victorians came to look upon the Bradlaugh case as "a last stand of religion" against its enemies (p. 325), I had noted that Lord Randolph Churchill "had been guided by expediency alone, and [that] the case had been

[53] A. Tilney Bassett, ed., *Gladstone to His Wife* (London, 1936), p. 214.
[54] In A. B. Cooke and A. P. W. Malcolmson, eds., *The Ashbourne Papers, 1869–1913* (Belfast, 1974) and in Walter L. Arnstein, *Protestant versus Catholic in Mid-Victorian England: Mr. Newdegate and the Nuns* (Columbia, Mo., 1982).
[55] *English Historical Review* 91 (April 1976): 315–40.
[56] Ibid., p. 317.

for him no more than a *jeu d'esprit*" (p. 327). Quinault takes issue with this assessment on several grounds, and in the process he corrects my account on two points of detail.[57] He appears oblivious, however, to the fact that most of the evidence he has assembled supports my assessment. He criticizes me for having failed to consult the Churchill, Gorst, and Wolff papers, while at the same time conceding that he too has been unable to locate any Gorst or Wolff papers and that the Churchill papers—which were not made available to scholars until 1968[58]—contain only two letters "on the Bradlaugh question during the life of the Fourth Party."[59] He is therefore compelled to rely upon the testimony of F. H. O'Donnell, the eccentric Irish M.P. who is described by Churchill's most recent biographer as "unbalanced and contumacious."[60] Quinault seems unaware that when lobby correspondent Henry W. Lucy described Churchill's colleagues Wolff and Gorst as "the two champions of religion" he was being subtly ironic.

Quinault also chides me for suggesting that Lord Randolph's notorious quarrel with the Prince of Wales—which led to Churchill's "exile" in Ireland until 1880—"adds irony to Lord Randolph's defence of the royal family against Bradlaugh" (p. 45n). Quinault objects that "on the contrary, it gave Randolph a powerful inducement to oppose Bradlaugh as a way of restoring his credit with the Prince of Wales."[61] Indeed it did, but surely Churchill's behavior suggests opportunism rather more strongly than perfervid royalism. Queen Victoria understandably was not impressed. In 1881 (see p. 45n) she had suspected Churchill as the "person of rank" who had anonymously threatened her life. In 1885, when Churchill was Secretary of State for India, "he fulminated against . . . the malignant influence of the Queen," and after he had resigned from the Salisbury ministry in 1886, Queen Victoria confided to anyone who would listen that "she would do 'all I can to prevent such a catastrophe' as his return to the government."[62] That Churchill also objected to Bradlaugh because of the latter's wish to end the hereditary Marlborough pension would again seem to constitute a triumph of expediency over principle.

The oddest contention Quinault makes on behalf of the profundity

---

[57] On p. 331 he notes that a letter I attributed to Wolff should have been attributed to Balfour. On p. 328 he is, of course, quite right in observing that Marlborough House was the home of the Prince of Wales and had no connection with the dukes of Marlborough in the 1880s. (See my p. 314.)

[58] Then they were deposited at Churchill College, Cambridge, by Sir Winston Churchill's grandson, Winston Churchill.

[59] Quinault, "The Fourth Party," p. 316.

[60] Roy Foster, *Lord Randolph Churchill: A Political Life* (Oxford, 1981), p. 66.

[61] Quinault, "The Fourth Party," p. 326.

[62] Foster, *Lord Randolph Churchill*, pp. 199, 341–42.

of Churchill's religious convictions is that "Churchill was quick to realize that on the Bradlaugh issue the Irish Nationalists might prove invaluable allies for the Tories."[63] Indeed, he did. He was fully prepared to cooperate with Roman Catholic M.P.s throughout the duration of the second Gladstone ministry; from time to time he even spoke of the inevitability and hinted at the desirability of Irish Home Rule.[64] And in the summer of 1885 he encouraged the Irish Tory entente that ultimately motivated Parnell to urge his supporters in England and Scotland to vote Conservative in the general election of that year.

The following year, after Gladstone had introduced his Home Rule bill and the Irish Nationalist M.P.s had allied themselves with the Liberal party, Churchill toured Ulster, arousing Protestant Ulstermen to fight against the very M.P.s with whom he had been on close terms during the previous five years. Quinault cites Churchill's opposition to the "desertion of our Protestant co-religionists" as "evidence that Randolph was more personally concerned with religion than has generally been assumed."[65] Most observers then and since have considered this volte-face the rankest form of opportunism. As Churchill's most recent biographer has noted, much of what Churchill said in Belfast and in his public letters in 1886 contradicted his earlier pronouncements on Ireland. Gladstone considered Churchill's conduct even worse. As he confided to his secretary, "No man in a responsible position had ever done a wickeder act than was committed by Randolph Churchill when he advocated a breach of the law in Ulster."[66] Within a few years, Churchill and Gladstone were to encounter one another at occasional dinner parties, and the Liberal prime minister was willing enough to pay tribute to Churchill's "nimblemindedness." He continued to suspect, however, that the Conservative M.P. had "not a single grain of conviction in him."[67]

Most of Quinault's arguments on behalf of the depths of Churchill's religious feelings turn out to involve either his colleague Henry Drummond Wolff or Churchill's father. Of course, Churchill, as can-

[63] Quinault, "The Fourth Party," p. 333.

[64] See Foster, *Lord Randolph Churchill*, p. 86. In "Lord Randolph Churchill and Home Rule," *Irish Historical Studies* 36 (September 1979): 377–402, Quinault insists that Churchill was always an "enlightened" unionist and never flirted with Home Rule. Quinault discounts all evidence other than Churchill's public statements.

[65] Quinault, "The Fourth Party," p. 322.

[66] Foster, *Lord Randolph Churchill*, p. 257. Hamilton diary cited in ibid., p. 267. The portions of the diary of Gladstone's secretary up to 1885 have been published in Dudley W. R. Bahlman, ed., *The Diary of Sir Edward Walter Hamilton*, 2 vols. (Oxford, 1972).

[67] Cited in Foster, *Lord Randolph Churchill*, p. 375.

didate and as M. P., espoused the continued union of church and state
and the importance of a church role in education. As Foster observes,
to do less "would have been politically curious, not to say suicidal."[68]
Yet the same man was in no fashion an ardent churchgoer, and he once
confided to his wife that he thought "all religious differences sense-
less. . . . Don't say anything about this."[69] Churchill may well have
derived satisfaction from the workmen in a large printing firm who
thanked him for resisting "the onslaughts against the Constitution of
this great Empire" by "your successful opposition to the admission of
Atheists to a Christian House of Commons."[70] Analogously, Churchill was fully prepared to agree with a clerical correspondent about
the dangers of ritualism in the Church of England, but he was equally
aware that the passage of the Public Worship Act of 1874 had failed to
aid his party politically. Churchill therefore promised to do all in his
power to maintain the Protestant character of the established church
"pure and undefiled . . . consistently with what may appear to be the
general interests of the Tory party."[71]

If the Bradlaugh case had in no sense constituted a *jeu d'esprit* for
Churchill and his Fourth Party colleagues, would Gorst have written
to him in September 1880, "Could we not meet like the three Swiss
conspirators at a desolate spot like Didcot?"[72] Would Churchill—on
the occasion of the self-swearing incident described on p. 131—have
publicly suggested that Bradlaugh was kissing *The Fruits of Philosophy*
rather than the Bible?[73] If Churchill had truly seen his opposition to
Bradlaugh as a matter of fundamental philosophical principle, would
he have associated quite so readily and so often with Charles Dilke,
Joseph Chamberlain, and Henry Labouchere? As Foster notes, the latter was "part of Churchill's Bohemian life, centred on Brighton,
Paris, and backstage at Henry Irving's theatre."[74]

There is a final, remarkably rapid, volte-face that Quinault plays
down. As the Churchill papers reveal, as late as December 1885, after
the general election, Churchill hoped to keep the minority Conservative government in power—by attempting to bring about a party
trial of strength not on the subject of Irish Home Rule or on the issue
on which it did fall, Jesse Collings's "three acres and a cow" amendment, but on the issue of the parliamentary oath. By focusing on that
issue, Churchill suggested, the Conservatives might continue to at-

[68] Ibid., p. 66.
[69] Cited in ibid., p. 66.
[70] Lord Randolph Churchill MSS (Churchill College), # 268.
[71] Ibid., # 274.
[72] Ibid., # 7.
[73] Anderson, *"Scenes" in the Commons*, p. 129.
[74] Foster, *Lord Randolph Churchill*, p. 225. See also pp. 29, 224, 261.

tract enough Irish and Liberal allies to stay in power. The alternative was "the triumph of Mr. Bradlaugh . . . a shaking blow to the Tory Gov. & party."[75] The opportunity Churchill sought could not be realized: Bradlaugh *was* allowed to take the oath; the Salisbury government did fall. Later in the year, after the "Home Rule" election of July 1886, Salisbury returned as prime minister, with Churchill as temporary Chancellor of the Exchequer and leader of the House of Commons. Not long thereafter Churchill voted in favor of a Bradlaugh-sponsored Affirmation Bill, a replica of the very measure that he had denounced in 1883 as "a declaration of war against Christianity" and a "State recognition of Atheism" (see pp. 197–98). Churchill explained the turnabout on the basis that Bradlaugh's admission was now a fait accompli and that the passage of the measure would prevent the future desecration of the oath. A vote for affirmation in 1880, 1881, or 1883 would presumably also have avoided such desecration, but then such a measure would have been a "Bradlaugh Relief Bill." As Quinault insists, "This was a fine but real distinction."[76] Possibly so, yet it is difficult to understand how Gorst's votes against Bradlaugh's measure can be hailed as a tribute to their religious consistency while Churchill's vote in favor of the same measure can be cited as evidence of the strength of the latter's religious convictions.[77] As the North Lambeth Constitutional Club vainly reminded Churchill in 1887, "We did not work to get the Tory party into power, in order that they might toady Bradlaugh and stoop down to black his shoes."[78] If Bradlaugh's admission was a fait accompli from 1886 on, it was at least in part because Churchill—at Labouchere's request—supported a *stet processus* of the legal appeals still pending. By September 1886, Churchill had also "infuriated old guard Tories by promising Bradlaugh a committee on perpetual pensions," and by 1888—after Churchill's resignation from the cabinet—he had become in Parliament "an embarrassingly frequent ally" of his onetime *bête noire*.[79]

[75] Churchill MSS, # 1126 (Memorandum of December 1885).

[76] Quinault, "The Fourth Party," p. 334.

[77] Ibid., pp. 323, 330.

[78] Churchill MSS, # 2486.

[79] Foster, *Lord Randolph Churchill*, pp. 275, 362. In "The Fourth Party" Quinault does postulate some suggestive links between the anti-Bradlaugh campaign and the foundation of the Primrose League (pp. 333–38). In a subsequent article, "Lord Randolph Churchill and Tory Democracy, 1880–1885," *Historical Journal* 22 (1979): 141–65, Quinault argues persuasively that during those years "Churchill's tory democracy consisted of new means rather than new ends" (p. 163). Quinault repeatedly insists, however, on an absence of personal ambition and a degree of political consistency on the part of Churchill that largely ignores the "manic-depressive" tendencies in his personality and that fails to take account of the observations of Churchill's contemporaries.

To argue that Quinault's case is weak is not to deny that Lord Randolph Churchill's meteoric rise to political power during the 1880s (and his subsequent fall) remains one of the most fascinating episodes of late-Victorian political history. At a time when speeches outside Parliament were still avoided by most politicians and disapproved of by others, Churchill became the first Conservative to make himself at home among mass audiences. As the *Pall Mall Gazette* noted in 1883, he conveyed sympathy, he spoke in a vibrant manner, and he "artfully fosters the idea that every man's hand is against him, . . . and that he has nothing to trust to but the people's favour."[80] He was the first Briton both "to utilize and even in a sense to create the locomotive of publicity in an age which was just beginning to invent it." His speeches came to be fully reported in the press. He combined a notable talent for spotting a winning issue with a lighthearted approach to political consistency. Thus when in 1885 the independent Liberal paper the *Pall Mall Gazette* surveyed its readers as to who was the "Greatest English Statesman," Churchill was ranked eighth. In the "Greatest English Humbug" survey of the same year, he came in fourth.[81]

Although my assessment of Churchill's role has provoked historical controversy, my conclusions about the role of the Irish Nationalist party—as detailed in Chapter 19—have evoked little.[82] What has happened during the past two decades, however, is that several aspects of the relationship between Bradlaugh and Ireland, and between the Irish Nationalists and the British Radicals, have been explored far more fully. The article by Nigel H. Sinnott, referred to earlier in this chapter, readily accepts Bradlaugh, that "careful advocate of rationalism and constitutional meliorism, with the indignation of the romantic revolutionary peeping through," as one of a handful of late-Victorian Englishmen who truly understood Ireland and selflessly championed Irish causes.[83] Fergus D'Arcy is less sympathetic. He makes the legitimate point that Bradlaugh's views on Ireland did not remain constant, that in the late 1860s his reform program focused largely on Church disestablishment and changes in the land laws and that only from 1872 on did he advocate Irish Home Rule as part of a federal system for the British Isles. Only in the later 1880s did he

---

[80] Cited in Foster, *Lord Randolph Churchill*, p. 149. See also p. 95.

[81] Ibid., pp. 381, 174–75. Even "Greater Humbugs" were the Tichborne Claimant, Oscar Wilde, and General William Booth of the Salvation Army.

[82] The anonymous reviewer in the *Times Literary Supplement* of 11 November 1965 found much of the volume "extremely useful and splendidly executed," but he was less happy with my treatment of the Irish Nationalists. His reservations appear to rest, however, on a misreading of the relevant chapter.

[83] Sinnott, "Bradlaugh and Ireland," pp. 21–22.

develop a degree of sympathy for the frustrations that had caused Irish M.P.s to embark upon a policy of parliamentary obstruction.[84] D'Arcy readily concedes that, from 1886 to 1891, "Bradlaugh's record in the House of Commons was outstanding. No British M.P. entertained opinions on the Irish question in advance of his . . . despite the treatment accorded to him by most of the Irish Nationalist Members, in the years of his exile from the House."[85] Yet, D'Arcy insists, Bradlaugh was never as radical as were a few fellow Englishmen, none of them M.P.s, such as Richard Congreve, who in 1867 had advocated a completely independent Ireland.[86] Since Bradlaugh never did envisage Ireland as a completely independent nation, by so rigorous a standard he must necessarily be found wanting. What D'Arcy appears to forget, however, is that Parnell and most of his parliamentary followers would also have failed to meet such a test.

The wider question of how late-Victorian Radicals met the challenge of Ireland is explored most fully by Thomas William Heyck in *The Dimensions of British Radicalism: The Case of Ireland, 1874–95.*[87] Among other things, Heyck devotes an entire chapter to the dilemma the Radical wing of the Liberal party faced between 1880 and 1882 when Gladstone's government felt compelled to apply force as well as land reform to Ireland. Heyck calls attention to Bradlaugh as one of a handful of "maverick" Radicals who defied Gladstone on the 1881 coercion bill. He portrays the M.P. for Northampton five years later as one of the "extreme Radicals" who did most to promote the cause of Irish Home Rule within England.[88]

The peculiarities of the relationship between the Irish Nationalist Party and the Gladstone government, a subject on which I touched in Chapter 19, have been both amplified and clarified in Alan O'Day's *The English Face of Irish Nationalism: Parnellite Involvement in British Politics, 1880–86.*[89] In a series of thoughtful topical chapters, O'Day confirms that most members of Parnell's Irish party, their professions notwithstanding, did indeed retain a high degree of interest in matters not directly related to Ireland; half of them, after all, had either been born in England or had been educated there, or had lived and worked there for the greater part of their lives. They often saw themselves as representing not only Ireland but also those Irish (and their descendants) who had immigrated to England and Scotland during the previous half century.[90] O'Day also notes that the success of the

[84] D'Arcy, "Bradlaugh and the Irish Question," pp. 244–46, 253.
[85] Ibid., p. 255.
[86] Ibid., pp. 239–40.
[87] Urbana, Illinois, 1974.
[88] Heyck, *Dimensions of British Radicalism*, pp. 65, 183.
[89] Dublin, 1977.
[90] See especially chapters 2 and 7.

party derived in part from the work its youthful and vigorous representatives did for their constituents back home. For that reason they could not afford to alienate the Liberal government altogether, and the pattern from 1882 until early 1885 was one of the Liberal ministers often consulting Irish Nationalist M.P.s on matters of both patronage and legislation while becoming relatively inured to public abuse from those same M.P.s.[91] (As Lord Randolph Churchill once remarked, Irish M.P.s should be given wide latitude in explaining and even withdrawing statements they had made, since they "often used language to which they did not attach the same importance as their audience."[92])

By 1882, Gladstone had given up hope on the non-Parnellite Home Rulers as an effective alternate political force. By then the Roman Catholic Church had done the same, and in 1882 the Parnellites made their peace with that church, "and no more parading of religious independence on the part of the party marred the relationship." The party became "the parliamentary mouthpiece for Catholic interests."[93] Yet, on subjects unrelated to Bradlaugh or to denominational education, O'Day confirms that most Irish Nationalists continued to gravitate naturally to the Radical wing of the Liberal party. They shared a common interest in land reform, in franchise extension, in curbing imperial expansion, and in much else, and they had often appeared on the same public platforms.[94] When Bradlaugh was first elected to Parliament, a majority of those fellow M.P.s with whom he was already personally acquainted were indeed Irish Nationalists. It is not surprising then that, when asking a favor of Bradlaugh in June 1880, Parnell wrote in an apologetic tone: "I would not of course be entitled to ask you . . . esp. considering the recent action of the Irish members."[95] Nor is it surprising that many Irish members should for some years publicly justify their opposition not on religious grounds but on grounds of Bradlaugh's supposed record as a coercionist. When in 1882 Bradlaugh protested against Henry George conveying such an impression of his brief parliamentary record to George's American readers, the latter responded with genuine surprise: "I had heard from

[91] O'Day, *The English Face of Irish Nationalism*, pp. 76–77. Dr. O'Day has kindly called my attention to an error (on my p. 215). When John Morley stood for Parliament in 1883, Newcastle's Irish voters were urged to vote Tory. See F. W. Hirst, *Early Life & Letters of John Morley* (London, 1927), 2:162–63.

[92] Cited in Foster, *Lord Randolph Churchill*, p. 103. Foster goes on to note that the same comment could as readily have been applied to Churchill himself.

[93] O'Day, *The English Face of Irish Nationalism*, pp. 35, 85. According to Emmet Larkin, "Parnell was astutely courting the more conservative of the clergy." See "Church, State and Nation in Modern Ireland," *American Historical Review* 80 (December 1975): 1265.

[94] O'Day, *The English Face of Irish Nationalism*, p. 92.

[95] Bradlaugh MSS (Bishopsgate), unnumbered.

so many Englishmen as well as Irishmen that you supported coercion while in the House that I regarded it as a well known fact. I will, however, look further into the matter, and in the meantime will include your note in my next letter to the *Irish World*."[96] That Bradlaugh felt aggrieved by the manner in which Irish M.P.s had treated him is understandable; that, once seated in 1886, he so readily let bygones be bygones remains remarkable.

At about the same time that R. E. Quinault was arguing that I had unduly stressed the motive of political expediency in accounting for the opposition to Bradlaugh, Joe Rich upheld the opposite point of view, that I was giving undue emphasis to religious feeling. "My contention is," writes Rich, "that 'religious principle,' insofar as it would entail a conscientious determination either completely to prevent unbelievers from gaining admission to parliament or, more simply, to disqualify them from swearing a sacred oath, played a very small, indeed an insignificant role in the parliamentary opposition to Bradlaugh's claims."[97] What did play such a role, Rich goes on, was detestation of Bradlaugh as a person, fear of him as a threat to the Victorian social order and to the Victorian sense of propriety, and the expectation of political gain.

I have no quarrel with much of Rich's article, which, while generally employing different quotations, recapitulates the conclusions I advanced in Chapter 6, "Bradlaugh As Villain." Bradlaugh clearly outraged Victorian canons of respectability, and his ideas—especially as caricatured by his opponents—evoked a widespread sense of revulsion. Rich also writes of "Bradlaugh's unnecessary proclamation of unbelief" and of the fact that "the most notorious atheist was perfectly free to take the oath provided he had not officially informed the House of his unbelief."[98] Here Rich is on more slippery ground, inasmuch as Bradlaugh *never* professed his religious beliefs within the House of Commons. What he had done initially was to seek to *affirm* rather than to *swear*, and this desire could readily have been interpreted as a courtesy to fellow members rather than as an affront. As explained in Chapters 4 and 5, Bradlaugh's unbelief may indeed have been implied in that claim to affirm (which a select committee denied him by a single vote). It was not, however, shouted from the parliamentary rooftops.

Having myself called attention to the political calculation implicit

<hr>

[96] Bradlaugh MSS (Bodleian Library), fol. 162 (letter of Henry George to Bradlaugh, 11 April 1882).

[97] Joe Rich, "The Bradlaugh Case: Religion, Respectability, and Politics," *The Australian Journal of Politics and History* 21 (August 1975): 38.

[98] Ibid., pp. 41, 46.

in the actions of numerous Conservatives and Irish Nationalists, I have no quarrel with that portion of Rich's article. His argument is partially undermined, however, by a failure to suggest any plausible political reason for the opposition or abstention of a significant number of Liberals—and yet, had they not existed, the Conservatives and the Irish could not have barred Bradlaugh from the House of Commons for more than five years. Rich's definition of *religious principle* is, moreover, curiously narrow. He observes that during the 1880–1885 Parliament no law or resolution was passed that would permanently have barred unbelievers from gaining access. Who has argued to the contrary? Most late Victorians were not trained theologians, and even M.P.s forgot—until a Gladstone or a Newman reminded them—that the oath they were defending implied not a "Christian Parliament" but a bare test of theism. How much more likely their constituents were to overlook such a distinction! As I wrote on p. 324, Bradlaugh's parliamentary opponents "raised a storm that was greater than they expected because it revealed a strong substratum of popular feelings. It is easier to sense this feeling than to define its precise nature." Whether one dubs it respectability or religion ultimately matters little because a majority of late Victorians would have defined belief in God and attendance at religious services as a major (perhaps indispensable) prerequisite of respectability. And even otherwise respectable workingmen who stayed away from Sunday services rarely desired to be described as atheists. As I noted on p. 183, when the proreligious forces organized, their ability to obtain petition signatures far outdistanced Bradlaugh's most considerable talents as popular organizer. Oddly enough, Rich concedes the point without being aware that it undermines much of his argument. Thus he writes: "Opinion in the Irish constituencies, upon which" the Irish Nationalist M.P.s "depended for their seats, was, it seems, fiercely opposed to Bradlaugh."[99] As for the errant Liberals, "The fact is that the Liberals were constantly being reminded that in many of their constituencies 'it does a man great harm to be . . . regarded as an ally of Mr. Bradlaugh'; like the Irish, they 'dare not run the risk of their votes being misconstrued.'"[100]

The evidence for such a public mood is so widespread that its existence was scarcely challenged at the time by Bradlaugh or by Gladstone or any other Liberal supporter. As Leslie Stephen wrote in the *Fortnightly Review*, the "honest, stupid part of the church-going public feels that it has been insulted and is simply anxious to revenge

---

[99] Ibid., p. 49.
[100] *Spectator*, 11 February 1882; *The Times* (London), 13 June 1880. Both cited in Rich, "The Bradlaugh Case," pp. 50–51.

itself upon the insulter." [101] Atheism was the bar, according to Bradlaugh's Scottish sympathizer, Professor John Stuart Blackie. It "arrays against you in the field of public life," he told Bradlaugh, "not only the champions of local orthodoxy, and their troops of servile followers but the common sense of 999 out of every 1000 men in the country." [102] It was that spirit that caused Samuel Morley to offer to resign his parliamentary seat in 1881 if his Liberal constituents insisted upon his supporting Bradlaugh's admission. They did not. It was that spirit that caused the London *Standard* to remind Gladstone (with partial accuracy), "Mr. Bradlaugh is not less obnoxious to the Nonconformists than he is to Anglicans or Catholics." It was that same spirit that caused one Bradlaugh opponent to celebrate the failure of the 1883 Affirmation Bill with these words: "Since the defeat of the Spanish Armada in 1588, no defeat has brought so much Honour to England." [103]

Both Royden Harrison and Joe Rich have argued that the Bradlaugh case ought to a greater degree be viewed as an issue of social class. [104] It is true enough that Bradlaugh and his supporters were often denounced (misleadingly) as "the lowest and worst of the working classes" made up of "low-browed, coarse, and uneducated men." [105] It is equally true that when Bradlaugh supporters organized outdoor demonstrations to "vindicate the people's rights to the free and unrestricted choice of their representatives"—as in Halifax in 1883— "the great and the rich were conspicuous by their absence." [106] Yet the fact remains that the issue of Bradlaugh's admission sorely divided the upper and middle classes of British society, that the canons of respectability cut across all social classes, and that the party that "repeatedly claimed to be *the* defenders of British working-class interests" [107] in the 1880–1885 Parliament, the Parnellites, repeatedly voted against him. Historians who seek ammunition to support the thesis that all significant nineteenth-century developments resulted from clearly defined social-class rivalry must look elsewhere.

Scholarship since the early 1960s has shed less additional light on Bradlaugh's parliamentary supporters than on his opponents. The published diaries of William Ewart Gladstone have not yet reached the 1880s, and recent biographies like E. J. Feuchtwanger's *Glad-*

[101] In the issue of 1 August 1881, p. 178, cited in Rich, "The Bradlaugh Case," pp. 41–42.
[102] Bradlaugh MSS (Bodleian Library), fol. 143.
[103] Clippings in Bradlaugh MSS (Bishopsgate), #722, #949, #1040.
[104] *New Society*, 23 September 1965, p. 33; Rich, "The Bradlaugh Case," p. 42.
[105] Cited in Rich, "The Bradlaugh Case," p. 42.
[106] *Halifax Courier*, 16 June 1883; clipping in Bradlaugh MSS (Bishopsgate), #1046.
[107] O'Day, *The English Face of Irish Nationalism*, p. 87.

stone (London and New York, 1975) accept the essentials of the interpretation of the prime minister's approach set forth here. Peter Stansky goes so far, indeed, as to base one of ten chapters in *Gladstone: A Progress in Politics* [108] on the Affirmation Bill speech and Chapter 15 of this book. In "Cardinal Newman and the Affirmation Bill," [109] J. Derek Holmes has amplified my account (on pp. 229–31) and has placed it within the broader context of Newman's life as a theologian. In the original edition I failed to pay sufficient heed to two religious leaders who did strongly support Bradlaugh's admission on avowedly Christian grounds. R. W. Dale, the well-known Congregationalist minister from Birmingham, both spoke and wrote on Bradlaugh's behalf. "Every public act of injustice done in the name of religion," he declared, "every private wrong, enormously aggravates the difficulty of that task to which the ministers of the Christian faith are committed." [110] Another such sympathizer was Joseph Lester Lynne, who after a tempestuous religious career within the Church of England as "the Moody of the Upper Classes," succeeded as Father Ignatius in founding his own monastic community in rural Wales. Father Ignatius had successfully debated Bradlaugh in the Hall of Science during the 1870s, and in 1880 he offered Bradlaugh his support: "People make no fuss about Dean Stanley being Dean of Westminster and receiving thousands of pounds a year to preach the Gospel, which he believes no more than you do. You are a manly, honest, truthful person." [111]

The parliamentary struggle, as Edward Royle has made clear, had a paradoxical effect on Bradlaugh's National Secular Society. On the one hand, Bradlaugh's energies were increasingly concentrated on that struggle; of fifteen talks he gave in the course of a single week in May 1881, only one dealt specifically with religion. On the other hand, the movement by then had nine other approved lecturers touring the country, and in London the Halls of Science classes in mathematics and the natural sciences were training several hundred students a year. The total membership of the society reached its all-time high in 1883–1884 with 120 branches and approximately four thousand active, paid-up members. [112] Beyond these, there existed a penumbra of as many as one hundred thousand more casual sympathizers prepared to attend occasional lectures and participate in protest demonstra-

---

[108] New York and London, 1979.
[109] *Historical Magazine of the Protestant Episcopal Church* 36 (March 1967): 87–97.
[110] R. W. Dale, *The Bradlaugh Question* (London, 1882), p. 8.
[111] Bradlaugh MSS (Bodleian Library), fol. 151. According to Baroness de Bertouch's *Life of Father Ignatius* (London, 1904), Bradlaugh once declared: "Father Ignatius is the only man whose influence I fear for my followers" (p. 477).
[112] Royle, *Radicals*, pp. 133–36, 151.

tions. For many of the latter, however, Bradlaugh's appeal lay less in his antireligious views than in his role as radical politician, as "tribune of the people," and as a victim of bigotry and injustice. Whereas Bradlaugh "had previously been only one leader among many, now he was indisputably *the* leader." [113]

Those same years brought costs as well as consolations to Bradlaugh. The return to the N.S.S. of George William Foote in 1881 and the founding of his *Freethinker* gave the society an aggressively irreverent weekly journal to supplement the more ponderous (and increasingly political) *National Reformer*. The trial and imprisonment of Foote and his associates for blasphemy (see pp. 250–55) added three new martyrs to the movement's pantheon and may well have attracted additional support. Yet the intention of Foote's prosecutors had been less to imprison him than to implicate Bradlaugh and ultimately disqualify the latter for Parliament altogether as a bankrupt and a convict. They failed, but only at the cost of much time and money to Bradlaugh. [114] Even more troublesome by 1883 and 1884 was Dr. Edward Aveling, the scientist who a few years earlier had loomed as the most promising of new secularist leaders. Not that Bradlaugh ever found fault with Aveling's knowledge of science or his ability to teach or to popularize it. What did disturb him increasingly were rumors of Aveling's philanderings—it also turned out that he had a wife from whom he had never been divorced—and the incredible manner in which he borrowed sums of money from every secularist who sympathized with his ever-persuasive hard luck stories. By 1884 Aveling's total debts amounted to almost £500, perhaps £30,000 (or $45,000) in terms of purchasing power one hundred years later.

At first Bradlaugh hesitated to expel him from the movement. As he confided to his daughter Hypatia, "It would be open to the enemy to say he quarreled with Holyoake, with Foote, with C[harles] Watts, and now with Aveling." [115] After Aveling had revealed his "free love" marriage to Karl Marx's daughter Eleanor, however, Bradlaugh quietly but swiftly drummed Aveling out of the movement and compelled him legally to acknowledge responsibility for almost three hundred pounds he owed the Freethought Publishing Company. The Bradlaugh papers reveal a lengthy correspondence over the repayments, which—at the rate of a pound or less a week—Aveling made reluctantly and erratically over the next four years under threat of legal judgment. In the course of those years it was Britain's fledgling socialists who became the new victims of both Aveling's philanderings and his perennial borrowings. When the correspondence in the

[113] Ibid., p. 29.
[114] Ibid., pp. 32, 34, 159, 272–73.
[115] Bradlaugh MSS (Bishopsgate), # 1036.

Bradlaugh MSS peters out in 1888, much of Aveling's debt to Bradlaugh remained unpaid.[116]

By then Annie Besant had followed Aveling down the socialist path, and so had a number of the workingmen who had been attracted more by Bradlaugh's radicalism than by his secularism. As Royle has noted,[117] it was secularist lecture halls that gave many of Britain's socialist pioneers of the 1880s a first hearing. Yet for Bradlaugh and his successor as N.S.S. president, G. W. Foote, it was Christianity rather than capitalism that remained the prime enemy of human progress. Secularists indeed came to look upon a man like Keir Hardie as an archapostate: that the son of Glasgow secularists should convert to both socialism and Christianity was seen as the ultimate insult. However small in total membership the late-Victorian socialist societies were by Bradlaugh's death (and however unlikely they were to stage a revolution), their very existence demonstrated that the secularists had lost their place on the extreme left wing of the political spectrum. In the later 1880s, and even more under Foote in the 1890s, the National Secular Society declined steadily in numbers. As an organization it has survived into the 1980s, however, and *The Freethinker* (as a monthly) has, unlike the *National Reformer*, persisted as well. For the most part, though, like the Church of England and the Nonconformist chapels, organized secularism fell victim to unorganized indifference—as well as to socialism and hedonism. As George Bernard Shaw quipped in 1908, "Bible-smashing is tedious to people who have smashed their Bibles."[118]

The now available Bradlaugh papers confirm how extraordinarily assiduous a Member of Parliament Charles Bradlaugh became during the five years that were left to him after his admission in January 1886. "No official member of the Treasury bench attended more regularly than he did," marveled the *Glasgow Herald* in 1891.[119] Bradlaugh regarded himself as one of perhaps five or six working-class representatives in the House of Commons in the later 1880s, but unlike the socialists he foresaw the coming struggle between laborers and their employers as beneficial to both "if they are conducted mutually, usefully, thoughtfully" and without "the notion that either has the right or duty to destroy the other." He found absurd the belief in a millenium brought into being by "wild proclamations" or revolution. "We cannot feed millions of human beings by a decree that they shall have loaves!"[120] While upholding the right of public meeting,

[116] Ibid., #582, #1156, #1209,#1219, #1335, and passim. See also Tribe, *Bradlaugh*, pp. 227–30.
[117] Royle, *Radicals*, pp. 232–33, 238, 240–41.
[118] Cited in ibid., p. 329.
[119] Clipping in Bradlaugh MSS (Bishopsgate), #1241(A).
[120] Ibid., #1241(A), #1402.

Bradlaugh deplored the manner in which irresponsible socialist agita
tors had provoked the police in 1887 in order to produce "Bloody
Sunday." One man lay dead; 130 were injured.[121]

During those years, D'Arcy notes,[122] Bradlaugh turned himself
into the single most assiduous English defender of Irish interests just
as he became at the same time the M.P. most concerned with Indian
interests. As the chairman of the Sixth Annual Indian Congress declared in 1890 in Calcutta, "God has, I believe, in his good time prepared Mr. Bradlaugh to write and work for India."[123] He chaired the
select committee on Friendly Societies (1888), served on numerous
others, worked for the creation of labor exchanges, and failed completely only in his campaign to repeal the blasphemy laws. They were
not to be repealed until 1969.[124] He attended the annual dinner of the
Royal Society; he wrote for journals like the *Contemporary Review*; by
combing late medieval and early seventeenth-century parliamentary
journals, Bradlaugh even produced a two-part article for the April
and June 1893 issues of the *Universal Review* entitled "The Romance
of the House of Commons."[125] Bradlaugh became so caught up in that
romance himself that he neglected his other interests and, lacking a
regular source of income, fell increasingly into debt. Only on Satur-
days and Sundays could he still earn money from lectures. Although a
public subscription raised almost twenty-five hundred pounds on
Bradlaugh's behalf in 1888, by the time of his death he was in debt once
more.[126] Yet among the thousands of mourners who flocked to Brookwood Cemetery on 3 February 1891, in three special trains from Waterloo Station, there were many who felt persuaded that it was they who
were in Bradlaugh's debt and that they were laying to rest one of the
most remarkable men of the Victorian era. The books and articles and
dissertations that have appeared in the course of the past two decades
suggest that many of the causes with which Bradlaugh was associated
remain pertinent, that the controversies still smolder, and that the
personality continues to fascinate. When in 1983 John Canning
edited a book entitled *100 Great Nineteenth-Century Lives*[127] the inclusion of Charles Bradlaugh came as no surprise.

Champaign, Illinois
September 1983

[121] Royle, *Radicals*, p. 286; letter from Gladstone in Bradlaugh MSS (Bishopsgate), # 1439.
[122] D'Arcy, "Bradlaugh and the Irish Question," p. 254.
[123] Bradlaugh MSS (Bishopsgate), # 1780, p. 61.
[124] Ibid., # 1674, # 1264; Royle, *Radicals*, p. 274.
[125] 3:317–34; 4:92–113.
[126] Royle, *Radicals*, p. 184; Bradlaugh MSS (Bishopsgate), # 1392.
[127] London, 1983.

BIBLIOGRAPHY

MANUSCRIPT COLLECTIONS

Adams, Thomas, MSS. Northampton Central Public Library. Adams was Bradlaugh's election agent in Northampton.

Balfour, A. J., MSS. British Museum.

Beaconsfield, Earl of, MSS. Hughenden Manor, High Wycombe. Through courtesy of Mr. R. Romilly Fedden.

Bright, John, MSS. British Museum.

Chamberlain, Joseph, MSS. Library of the University of Birmingham.

Conway, Moncure Daniel, MSS. Library of Columbia University.

Cowen, Joseph, MSS. Newcastle upon Tyne City Library.

Deputies of the Protestant Dissenters, MSS. Minute Books for 1870–90. Guildhall Library, London.

Dilke, Sir Charles W., MSS. British Museum.

Drew, Mary (Gladstone), MSS. British Museum.

Gladstone, Viscount (Herbert), MSS. British Museum.

Gladstone, William Ewart, MSS. British Museum. Cabinet Minutes used with permission of the Cabinet office.

Granville, Earl of, MSS. Public Record Office. Granville was Secretary of State for Foreign Affairs during Gladstone's Second Ministry.

Hambleden MSS. Available through National Register of Archives. The papers of W. H. Smith, M.P., a Conservative leader during the 1880's.

Hamilton MSS. British Museum. The private diary of Sir Edward Walter Hamilton, one of Gladstone's private secretaries during his Second Ministry.

Hampden MSS. In private custody. The private diary and papers of Sir Henry Brand, 1st Viscount Hampden, Speaker of the House during the early 1880's. Through courtesy of the Hon. Thomas Brand.

Halsbury, Earl of, MSS. In private custody. The papers of Sir Hardinge Giffard, Conservative M.P., through courtesy of the present Earl of Halsbury.

Harrington, Timothy, MSS. National Library of Ireland, Dublin. The papers of an Irish Nationalist M.P.

Iddesleigh MSS. British Museum. The papers of Sir Stafford Northcote, Conservative leader of the House of Commons.

Kilbracken, Lord, MSS. British Museum. The papers of Arthur Godley, private secretary to Gladstone.

Mahon, The O'Gorman, MSS. University of Chicago. The papers of an Irish Nationalist M.P.

Manning, Henry Edward (Cardinal), MSS. St. Mary of the Angels, London. Through courtesy of the Oblates of St. Charles and the Rev. A. Chapeau.

Mundella, A. J., MSS. Library of the University of Sheffield. The papers of a member of Gladstone's Second Ministry.

Newdegate, Charles N., MSS. Warwick County Record Office. Through courtesy of Captain Humphrey Fitzroy-Newdegate.

Newman, John Henry (Cardinal), MSS. The Oratory, Birmingham. Through courtesy of Father C. Stephen Dessain.

Ponsonby, Sir Henry, MSS. British Museum. The papers of Queen Victoria's private secretary.

Salisbury, Marquess of, MSS. Christ Church College Library, Oxford Through courtesy of the present Marquess of Salisbury.

St. Aldwyn, Earl of, MSS. In private custody. The papers of Sir Michael Hicks-Beach, Conservative leader during the 1880's. Through courtesy of the present Earl of St. Aldwyn.

PUBLIC DOCUMENTS

Great Britain, *Hansard's Parliamentary Debates* (3rd series). 1880–6, 1888, 1891.

Great Britain, *Parliamentary Papers*:
'Report from the [First] Select Committee on the Parliamentary Oath', 1880, volume xii.
'Report from the [Second] Select Committee on the Parliamentary Oath (Mr. Bradlaugh)', 1880, volume xii.
'*Clarke* v. *Bradlaugh*', 1881, volume lxxvi.
'Parliamentary Oaths in Foreign Countries', 1882, volume lii.
'Bradlaugh and the Suit of Gurney', 1882, volume liv.
'Bill to Amend the Law Relating to Parliamentary Oaths', 1883, volume viii.
'Law Reports of the Queen's Bench Division', 1883, volume xi.
'Bill to Amend the Law as to Oaths', 1884–5, volume iii.
'Bill to Amend the Law as to Oaths', 1888, volume v.

Great Britain, *Report of the Select Committee on Parliamentary Petitions*, 1880–5.

Great Britain, *Statutes of the Realm*. 3rd ed. revised. London, 1950.

A SELECT LIST OF BOOKS AND PAMPHLETS

ALMY, J. T. *Almighty God or Bradlaugh?* 3rd ed., London, 1885.

ANONYMOUS. *John Bull's Family Affairs*. London, 1882.

ANONYMOUS. *Otherwise: or Quite Another Tack*. London, 1882 [?].

ASKWITH, LORD G. R. *Lord James of Hereford*. London, 1930.

BAILY, JOHN (ed.). *The Diary of Lady Frederick Cavendish*. Vol. ii. London, 1927.

BALFOUR, ARTHUR JAMES. *Chapters of Autobiography*. Edited by Mrs. Edgar Dugdale. London, 1930.

BASSETT, A. TILNEY (ed.). *Gladstone to his Wife*. London, 1936.

BENSON, ARTHUR CHRISTOPHER. *The Life of Edward White Benson, sometime Archbishop of Canterbury*. London, 1900.

BERNSTEIN, EDUARD. *My Years of Exile: Reminiscences of a Socialist.* Translated by Bernard Miall. London, 1921.

BESANT, ANNIE. *Autobiographical Sketches.* London, 1885.

—— *An Autobiography.* London, 1893.

BETTANY, F. G. *Stewart Headlam: A Biography.* London, 1926.

BLUNT, WILFRID S. *The Land War in Ireland: Excerpts from Diaries.* London, 1912.

BONNER, ARTHUR, and BONNER, CHARLES BRADLAUGH. *Hypatia Bradlaugh Bonner: The Story of her Life.* London, 1942.

BONNER, HYPATIA BRADLAUGH. *Charles Bradlaugh: A Record of his Life and Work, with an Account of his Parliamentary Struggle, Politics and Teaching, by John M. Robertson.* 2 vols. London, 1895.

BRADLAUGH, CHARLES. *A Cardinal's Broken Oath.* London, 1882.

—— *The Impeachment of the House of Brunswick.* 8th ed., London, 1881.

BRIGHT, JOHN. *The Public Letters of the Right Hon. John Bright, M.P.* Edited by H. J. Leach. London, 1885.

BRINTON, CRANE. *English Political Thought in the Nineteenth Century.* 2nd ed., London, 1949.

BRYCE, JAMES. *Studies in Contemporary Biography.* London, 1903.

BUCKLE, G. E. (ed.). *The Letters of Queen Victoria.* Second series. Vol. iii. London, 1928.

Catalogue of the Library of the Late Charles Bradlaugh. London, 1891.

A CATHOLIC FREETHINKER. *Mr. Bradlaugh the Model Protestant.* 2nd ed., London, 1883.

CHAMBERLAIN, JOSEPH. *A Political Memoir, 1880–1892.* Edited by C. H. D. Howard. London, 1953.

THE CHURCH DEFENCE INSTITUTION. *The Church Defence Handy Volume.* London, 1885.

CHURCHILL, LORD RANDOLPH. *Speeches of the Right Honourable Lord Randolph Churchill, M.P., 1880–1888.* Collected by Louis J. Jennings. 2 vols. London, 1889.

CHURCHILL, WINSTON S. *Life of Lord Randolph Churchill.* 2 vols. London, 1906.

COHEN, CHAPMAN. *Bradlaugh and Ingersoll: A Centenary Appreciation of Two Great Reformers.* London, 1933.

COLE, G. D. H. *British Working-Class Politics, 1832–1914.* London, 1941.

COLERIDGE, ERNEST HARTLEY. *Life & Correspondence of John Duke, Lord Coleridge.* Vol. ii. London, 1904.

CONWAY, MONCURE DANIEL. *Autobiography.* Vol. ii. London, 1904.

—— *Lessons for the Day.* London, 1907.

CORNWALLIS-WEST, MRS. GEORGE. *The Reminiscences of Lady Randolph Churchill.* London, 1908.

DAVIES, REV. CHARLES MAURICE. *Heterodox London.* 2 vols. London, 1874.

Dictionary of National Biography.

Dod's Parliamentary Companion, Forty-Eighth Year. 2nd ed., London, 1880. Also, editions of 1881–6, 1888.

ELLIOTT-BINNS, L. E. *Religion in the Victorian Era*. 2nd ed., Greenwich, Conn., 1946.
ENSOR, R. C. K. *England, 1870–1914*. Oxford, 1936.
EYCK, ERICH. *Gladstone*. Translated by Bernard Miall. London, 1938.
FOOTE, G. W. *Randolph Churchill: The Woodstock Bantam*. London, 1885.
—— *Reminiscences of Charles Bradlaugh*. London, 1891.
FYFE, HAMILTON. *T. P. O'Connor*. London, 1934.
GARVIN, J. L. *The Life of Joseph Chamberlain*. Vol. i: *Chamberlain and Democracy, 1836 1885*. London, 1932.
GASQUOINE, T. *In Memoriam: Charles Bradlaugh, A Sermon*. Northampton, 1891.
GILMOUR, J. P. (ed.). *Champion of Liberty: Charles Bradlaugh*. London, 1933.
GLADSTONE, VISCOUNT (HERBERT). *After Thirty Years*. London, 1928.
GORST, HAROLD E. *The Fourth Party*. London, 1906.
GOWER, LORD RONALD. *My Reminiscences*. Vol. ii. London, 1883.
GRETTON, R. H. *A Modern History of the English People, 1880–1922*. London, 1930.
GUEDALLA, PHILIP. *The Queen and Mr. Gladstone*. Vol. ii. London, 1933.
GWYNN, STEPHEN, and TUCKWELL, GERTRUDE M. *The Life of the Rt. Hon. Sir Charles W. Dilke*. 2 vols. London, 1917.
HAMILTON, LORD GEORGE. *Parliamentary Reminiscences and Reflections, 1868–1906*. Vol. i. London, 1916.
HAMMOND, J. L. *Gladstone and the Irish Nation*. London, 1938.
HANHAM, H. J. *Elections and Party Management: Politics in the Age of Gladstone and Disraeli*. London, 1959.
HARDIE, FRANK. *The Political Influence of Queen Victoria, 1861–1901*. Oxford, 1935.
HARRINGTON, G. F. *Northampton Election Difficulty*. London, 1881.
HARRISON, FREDERIC. *Autobiographical Memoirs*. 2 vols. London, 1911.
HASLIP, JOAN. *Parnell, A Biography*. London, 1936.
HEADINGLY, ADOLPHE S. *The Biography of Charles Bradlaugh*. London, 1880.
HEADLAM, STEWART. *Charles Bradlaugh, An Appreciation*. London, 1907.
—— *The Sure Foundation: An Address given before the Guild of St. Matthew, at the Annual Meeting, 1883*. London, 1883.
HEALY, T. M. *Letters and Leaders of My Day*. 2 vols. New York, 1929.
HIMES, NORMAN E. *Medical History of Contraception*. London, 1936.
HOLYOAKE, GEORGE JACOB. *Life of Bradlaugh*. London, 1891.
—— *Sixty Years of an Agitator's Life*. London, 1906.
HUMANITAS [WILLIAM PLATT BALL]. *Charles Bradlaugh, M.P. and the Irish Nation*. London, 1885.
HUTTON, ARTHUR WOLLASTON. *Cardinal Manning*. London, 1892.
JACKSON, T. A. *Trials of British Freedom*. Revised ed., London, 1945.
JAMES, ROBERT RHODES. *Lord Randolph Churchill*. London, 1959.
JENKINS, ROY. *Sir Charles Dilke: A Victorian Tragedy*. London, 1958.
KILBRACKEN, LORD. *Reminiscences*. London, 1931.

LANG, ANDREW. *Life, Letters, and Diaries of Sir Stafford Northcote.* Vol. ii. Edinburgh and London, 1890.
LESLIE, SHANE. *Henry Edward Manning: His Life and Labours.* London, 1921.
LUCY, HENRY W. *A Diary of the Salisbury Parliament, 1886–1892.* London, 1892.
—— *A Diary of Two Parliaments.* Vol. ii. London, 1886.
—— (ed.). *The Speeches of Lord Randolph Churchill.* London, 1885.
MACCOBY, S. *English Radicalism, 1853–1886.* London, 1938.
MACDONAGH, MICHAEL. *Parliament: Its Romance, Its Comedy, Its Pathos.* London, 1902.
MACKAY, CHARLES R. *Life of Charles Bradlaugh, M.P.* London, 1888.
MAGNUS, PHILIP. *Gladstone.* London, 1954.
MALLET, SIR Charles. *Herbert Gladstone: A Memoir.* London, 1932.
MANNING, HENRY EDWARD. *How Shall Catholics Vote at the Coming Parliamentary Election?* London, 1885.
—— *Miscellaneous Works.* Vol. iii. London, 1888.
MASTERMAN, LUCY (ed.). *Mrs. Mary (Gladstone) Drew: Her Diaries and Letters.* London, 1930.
MAWER, W. *The Latest Constitutional Struggle: A Register of Events.* London, 1883.
MAXWELL, SIR HERBERT. *Life and Times of the Right Honourable William Henry Smith, M.P.* Vol. ii. Edinburgh, 1893.
MAY, SIR THOMAS ERSKINE. *The Constitutional History of England since the Accession of George the Third.* Edited and continued to 1911 by Francis Holland. Vol. iii: *1860–1911.* London, 1912.
MCCANN, REV. DR., and BRADLAUGH, CHARLES. *Secularism: Unphilosophical, Immoral, and Anti-Social. Verbatim Report of a Three Nights' Debate.* London, 1882.
MCCARTHY, JUSTIN. *England under Gladstone, 1880–1884.* London, 1884.
—— *Reminiscences.* 2 vols. London, 1899.
MCGEE, JOHN EDWIN. *A History of the British Secular Movement.* Girard, Kansas, 1948.
MILL, JOHN STUART, *Autobiography.* New York, 1924. (First published in 1873.)
MORLEY, JOHN. *Life of William Ewart Gladstone.* 3 vols. London, 1903.
NETHERCOT, ARTHUR H. *The First Five Lives of Annie Besant.* Chicago, 1960.
NORTHAMPTON TOWN AND COUNTY BENEFIT BUILDING SOCIETY. *A Century of Service.* Northampton, 1948.
O'BRIEN, CONOR CRUISE. *Parnell and his Party, 1880–1890.* Oxford, 1957.
O'BRIEN, R. BARRY. *The Life of Charles Stewart Parnell.* 2 vols. 2nd ed., London, 1899.
O'CONNOR, T. P. *Charles Stewart Parnell: A Memory.* London, 1891.
—— *Gladstone's House of Commons.* London, 1885.
—— *Memoirs of An Old Parliamentarian.* 2 vols. London, 1929.

O'DONNELL, F. HUGH. *A History of the Irish Parliamentary Party.* 2 vols. London, 1910.

OXFORD AND ASQUITH, EARL OF. *Fifty Years of Parliament.* Vol. i. London, 1926.

PAUL, HERBERT (ed.). *Letters of Lord Acton to Mary Gladstone.* London, 1904.

PELLING, HENRY. *The Origins of the Labour Party, 1880–1900.* London, 1954.

POLLOCK, FREDERICK. *Essays in Jurisprudence and Ethics.* London, 1882.

PURCELL, EDMUND SHERIDAN. *Life of Cardinal Manning: Archbishop of Westminster.* Vol. ii. London, 1895.

RAMM, AGATHA (ed.). *The Political Correspondence of Mr. Gladstone and Lord Granville, 1876–1886.* 2 vols. Oxford, 1962.

ROBERTSON, J. M. *The Life of Charles Bradlaugh.* London, 1921.

SNELL, LORD. *Men, Movements, and Myself.* London, 1936.

TEMPLE, SIR RICHARD. *Letters and Character Sketches from the House of Commons.* London, 1912.

—— *Life in Parliament [1886–1892].* London, 1893.

THOROLD, ALGAR LABOUCHERE. *The Life of Henry Labouchere.* London, 1913.

TORRENS, W. MCCULLAGH. *Twenty Years of Parliament.* London, 1893.

TREVELYAN, GEORGE MACAULAY. *The Life of John Bright.* New ed., London, 1925.

VARLEY, HENRY. *An Address to the Electors in the Borough of Northampton.* London, 1881.

WALLING, R. A. J. (ed.). *The Diaries of John Bright.* New York, 1931.

WARD, WILFRID. *The Life of John Henry, Cardinal Newman.* Vol. ii. London, 1912.

WEST, ALGERNON. *Recollections, 1832–1886.* Vol. ii. London, 1899.

WHARTON, CHARLES H. M. *Mr. Bradlaugh and the Oath.* Manchester, 1882.

WILLIAMS, REV. C. *Reasons for the Affirmation Bill becoming Law (though involving Bradlaugh Sitting).* London, 1883.

WILLIAMS, GERTRUDE M. *The Passionate Pilgrim: A Life of Annie Besant.* London, 1932.

WOLFF, HENRY DRUMMOND. *Rambling Recollections.* 2 vols. London, 1908.

ZETLAND, THE MARQUIS OF (ed.). *The Letters of Disraeli to Lady Bradford and Lady Chesterfield.* 2 vols. London, 1929.

ARTICLES AND PERIODICALS

Church Quarterly Review. 1880–6.

Edinburgh Review. 1880–6.

England. 1880–1.

ENSOR, R. C. K. 'Centenary of Bradlaugh', *Spectator*, cli (29 Sept. 1933), 408.

Freeman's Journal (Dublin). 1880–6, 1888, 1891.

HADLEY, W. W. 'Bradlaugh and Labouchere: An Episode in Constitutional History', *Northamptonshire Past and Present*, ii, no. 6 (1959), 273–82.

National Reformer. 1880–6, 1888, 1891.

Nineteenth Century. 1880–6, 1888, 1891.

Northampton *Mercury*. 1880–6, 1891.

Punch. 1880–6, 1888, 1891.

The *Rock* (London). 1880–6, 1888.

Saturday Review. 1880–6, 1888, 1891.

Scrapbook of newspaper clippings about the Bradlaugh case kindly lent by Alderman Percy Adams of Northampton.

Scrapbook of newspaper and periodical clippings kindly lent by Frederick W. Garley of London.

Tablet (London). 1880–6, 1888, 1891.

The Times. 1880–6, 1888, 1891.

Truth. 1880–1.

United Ireland. 1881–6.

Westminster Review. 1880–6.

Whitehall Review. 1880–1.

OTHER SOURCES

Personal interview with Alderman Percy Adams of Northampton, grandson of Bradlaugh's election agent, February 1957.

Personal interview with Mrs. A. Ball, octogenarian resident of Northampton, June 1957.

Personal interviews with Mr. Charles Bradlaugh Bonner, grandson of Bradlaugh, 1956–7, 1962.

Personal interview with Victor A. Hatley, Chief Reference Librarian, Northampton Central Public Library, February 1957.

Personal interview with Conor Cruise O'Brien, author of *Parnell and his Party, 1880–1890*, in Dublin, March 1957.

Letter from Charles Pannell, M.P., 1 April 1958.

Northampton Central Public Library collection of election campaign clippings relating to all nine election campaigns in which Bradlaugh participated.

INDEX